Photo by H. Walter Barnett

GENERAL SIR EDMUND HENRY HYNMAN ALLENBY, G.C.B., G.C.M.G.,
COMMANDER IN CHIEF OF THE EGYPTIAN EXPEDITIONARY FORCE
FROM JUNE 1917.

A BRIEF RECORD OF

THE ADVANCE OF THE EGYPTIAN EXPEDITIONARY FORCE

UNDER THE COMMAND OF

GENERAL SIR EDMUND H. H. ALLENBY, G.C.B., G.C.M.G.

JULY 1917 TO OCTOBER 1918.

Compiled from Official Sources.

SECOND EDITION.

(THE FIRST EDITION WAS PUBLISHED BY "THE PALESTINE NEWS.")

LONDON:
PUBLISHED BY HIS MAJESTY'S STATIONERY OFFICE.

To be purchased through any Bookseller or directly from
H.M. STATIONERY OFFICE at the following addresses:
IMPERIAL HOUSE, KINGSWAY, LONDON, W.C. 2, and
28 ABINGDON STREET, LONDON, S.W. 1;
37 PETER STREET, MANCHESTER;
1 ST. ANDREW'S CRESCENT, CARDIFF;
23 FORTH STREET, EDINBURGH;
or from E. PONSONBY, LTD., 116 GRAFTON STREET, DUBLIN.

1919.

Price 6/- Net

GLOSSARY.

Descriptive terms which occur with place names, and the abbreviations used :—

Abu = Father
Ain = Spring.
Beit = House.
Birket = Pool.
Bir = Well.
Deir = Monastery.
Ed, El, Er, Es, Ez = The definite article "the".
Jebel = Mountain
Jisr = Bridge.
Kefr = Village.
Khan = Inn.
Khurbet (abbreviation Kh.) = Ruin.
Makhadet = Ford.
Nahr = River.
Neby = A Prophet.
Ras = Head, cape, top.
Sheikh (abbreviation Sh.) = Chief, elder, saint.
Tel = Mound (especially one covering ruins).
Wadi = A watercourse (normally dry).

PREFACE.

This Record of the recent activities of the Egyptian Expeditionary Force to the East of the Suez Canal has been prepared in order that members of that Force may be able to take home with them an acceptable account of the great advance in which they played a part. Advantage has been taken of many official documents which are available and of the experience of officers still at General Headquarters in charge of the Departments with the work of which they were familiar during the operations. Thus it has been possible to compile the Record while the events which it details are fresh in the memory.

Thanks are due to the following officers for their kindness in supplying accounts of the work of their respective departments, or information concerning the same :—

    Major-Gen. H. B. H. WRIGHT, C.B., C.M.G., R.E. (Royal Engineers).
    Brig.-Gen. P. A. BAINBRIDGE, C.B., C.M.G., R.A.O.C. (Ordnance Services).
    Brig.-Gen. E. R. C. BUTLER, C.B., C.M.G., R.A.V.C. (Veterinary Services).
    Brig.-Gen. JELLICOE, D.S.O., R.A.S.C., and Lieut.-Col. H. J. HIGGS, A.M. (Egyptian Labour Corps).
    Brig.-Gen. Sir G. B. MACAULEY, K.C.M.G., C.B., and Lieut.-Col. W. G. TYRRELL, D.S.O., R.E. (Railways).
    Col. P. WARREN, C.M.G., R.E., and Lieut.-Col. F. H. KEMPE, M C. (Postal Services).
    Col. C. H. WHITTINGHAM, C.M.G., D.S.O. (Camel and Donkey Transport).
    Lieut.-Col. D. MCLEOD, D.S.O., M.C. (Palestine Lines of Communication).
    Lieut.-Col. H. C. B. WEMYSS, D.S.O., M.C., R.E (Signals).
    Lieut.-Col. G. E. BADCOCK, D.S.O., R.A.S.C., and Lieut.-Col. J. H. MORRIS, D.S.O., R.A.S.C. (R.A.S.C. Personnel and Mechanical Transport).
    Major A. W. DOBBIN, R.A. (Anti-Aircraft Section).
    Major W. J. MAULE, D.S.O. (Survey).
    Major G. F. BIRD, M.C., R.A.M.C. (Medical Services).
    Major R. C. HADDON (Camel and Donkey Transport).
    Major R. M. DIX, R.A.S.C. (Navy and Army Canteen Board).
    Capt. J. Mc G. GLEN, M.C., R.A.F. (Royal Air Force).

Thanks are also due to the following officers for their collaboration and advice in the preparation of the text which accompanies the Maps and of the various chronological summaries :—

    Major-Gen. Sir V. B. FANE, K.C.I.E., C.B.
    Major-Gen. Sir L. J. BOLS, K.C.B., K.C.M.G., D.S.O.
    Major-Gen. Sir J. S. M. SHEA, K.C.M.G., C.B., D.S.O.
    Major-Gen. Sir E. W. C. CHAYTOR, K.C.M.G., C.B., A.D.C.
    Brig.-Gen. HAMELIN, French Detachment.
    Brig.-Gen. S. M. EDWARDES, C.B., C.M.G., D.S.O.
    Brig.-Gen. C. F. WATSON, C.B., C.M.G.
    Brig.-Gen. G. de L. RYRIE, C.B., C.M.G., D.S.O
    Brig.-Gen. L. C. WILSON, C.M.G.
    Lieut.-Col. Cav. G. PESENTI, Italian Detachment.
    Lieut.-Col. W. E. DAVIES, C.M.G.
    Lieut.-Col. R. H. OSBORNE, D.S.O., M.C.
    Lieut.-Col. H. E. MACFARLANE, D.S.O., M.C.
    Lieut.-Col. A. H. C. KEARSEY, D.S.O.
    Lieut.-Col. G. K. M. MASON, D.S.O.
    Lieut.-Col. A. O'B. FFRENCH-BLAKE.
    The late Major D. H. ACWORTH, M.C.
    Major G. H. BELL, M.C.
    Major R. C. HADDON.
    Capt. R. H. ANDREW, M.C.
    Capt. F. L. SEYMOUR-JONES, M.C.
    Capt. A. W. MANNING, M.C.
    Capt. A. KINROSS, R.A.S.C.
    Capt. G. I. C. MARCHANT, R.A.
    Capt. J. ARMSTRONG.
    Capt. S. E. L. BADDELEY.
    Capt. E. G. HOLLEBONE.
    Lieut. N. EAST.
    Lieut. R. E. HEATHCOCK.

PREFACE.

Great assistance in the work of editing and of preparing the Record for the press has been given by Capt. L. M. GOTCH and Lieut. W. R. KAY. The former compiled the maps which form so important and interesting a feature of the Record, and acted in conjunction with "The Palestine News" and the Egyptian Government departments concerned in producing the Record.

The Director-General of the Survey of Egypt, Mr. E. M. DOWSON, C.B.E., and the Acting Controller of Printing for the Government of Egypt, Mr. W. H. CROSTHWAITE, O.B.E., undertook the reproduction of the maps and the printing; and the following officials of the Survey of Egypt were actively concerned in the production of the maps :—

- Mr. J. H. W. ROWNTREE.
- Mr. H. C. ALLEN, Superintendent of the Printing Office.
- Mr. G. DOUGLAS, M.B.E., Superintendent of the Photo Process Office.
- Mr. W. LOGAN, Superintendent of the Geographical Drawing Office.
- Mr. G. AITKEN, of the Geographical Drawing Office.

Mr. G. B. NEWTON, Technical Assistant to the Controller of Printing, acting as Official in charge of the Military Printing Section at the Government Press, was responsible for the printing of the letterpress, and gave much valuable advice.

Lieut. P. S. TAYLOR, Deputy Director of "The Palestine News" was responsible for the work in connection with the distribution of the Record.

Without the generous assistance and advice of these officers and officials, this Record of the Advance of the Egyptian Expeditionary Force under General ALLENBY could have been neither compiled nor published; and it is hoped that it will fill the gap so far as the history of the campaign in Palestine and Syria is concerned until the appearance of the Official History of the War.

H. PIRIE-GORDON, Lieut.-Colonel,
Military Editor.

The Palestine News,
   G.H.Q., E.E.F.
      February, 1919.

CONTENTS.

PORTRAIT OF GENERAL SIR E. H. H. ALLENBY, G.C.B., G.C.M.G. ... FRONTISPIECE.

	PAGE.
PREFACE ...	iii
GENERAL ALLENBY'S DESPATCHES :—	
(i) DECEMBER 16, 1917	1
(ii) SEPTEMBER 18, 1918	11
(iii) OCTOBER 31, 1918	25

Order of Battle of the Egyptian Expeditionary Force with which are included the names of General Officers and a brief record of service of the major formations :—

GENERAL HEADQUARTERS	37
GENERAL HEADQUARTERS TROOPS	38
EASTERN FORCE	39
DESERT COLUMN	39
*DESERT MOUNTED CORPS	39
*XXTH ARMY CORPS	41
*XXIST ARMY CORPS	42
*CHAYTOR'S FORCE	44
*FRENCH DETACHMENT	45
*ITALIAN DETACHMENT	46
*4TH CAVALRY DIVISION	46
*5TH CAVALRY DIVISION	49
*AUSTRALIAN MOUNTED DIVISION	51
*AUSTRALIAN AND NEW ZEALAND MOUNTED DIVISION	54
*3RD (LAHORE) DIVISION	56
*7TH (INDIAN) DIVISION	57
*10TH DIVISION	59
*52ND DIVISION	61
*53RD DIVISION	63
*54TH DIVISION	65
*60TH DIVISION	66
*74TH DIVISION	68
*75TH DIVISION	70
BRIGADES (NON-DIVISIONAL) :—	
*IMPERIAL CAMEL CORPS BRIGADE	72
*20TH INDIAN INFANTRY BRIGADE	73
*49TH INDIAN INFANTRY BRIGADE	73
PALESTINE LINES OF COMMUNICATIONS	73
LINES OF COMMUNICATION UNITS	75
FORCE IN EGYPT	77
ALEXANDRIA DISTRICT	78
DELTA AND WESTERN FORCE	79
MEDICAL SERVICES	79

Brief Records of the work of various branches of the Army : —

THE ANTI-AIRCRAFT SECTIONS	82
THE ROYAL ENGINEERS :—	
(1) WATER SUPPLY	83
(2) SIGNAL SERVICE	86
(3) SURVEY COMPANY	88
(4) MILITARY RAILWAYS	90
(5) ARMY POSTAL SERVICES	93
ROYAL ARMY SERVICE CORPS :—	
(1) ESTABLISHMENT AND SUPPLIES	94
(2) MECHANICAL TRANSPORT	95
(3) CAMEL AND DONKEY TRANSPORT	98
ORDNANCE WORK IN THE PALESTINE AND SYRIAN CAMPAIGNS	100
THE WORK OF THE MEDICAL SERVICES	104
ROYAL ARMY VETERINARY CORPS	106
LABOUR IN THE EGYPTIAN EXPEDITIONARY FORCE	107
NAVY AND ARMY CANTEEN BOARD	111
BRIEF RECORD OF THE WORK OF THE ROYAL AIR FORCE	112

An asterisk denotes where a brief Record of Service is included.

CONTENTS—continued.

Descriptive Text facing Plate.	Title of Plate.	Plate.
Explanatory Note to the Maps illustrating operations Lines of Communications, Oct., 1917	Reference to Conventional Signs	1
Lines of Communications, Oct., 1917, continued... ...	Lines of Communications, Oct., 1917	2
Operations from Oct. 28–Nov. 13, 1917	Advance through Palestine	3–14
Operations from Nov. 14–Dec. 8, 1917	Advance into Judæa...	15–26
Operations on Dec. 9 and 10, 1917	Occupation of Jerusalem	27
Operations from Dec. 11–31, 1917	Advance into Mount Ephraim and Sharon	28–30
Operations from Dec. 11–31, 1917	Area occupied as the result of operations from Oct. 28–Dec. 31, 1917.	31
	Development of Water Supply prior to operations Nov. 1–Dec. 31.	Inset 31
Operations from Feb. 18–21, 1918	Capture of Jericho	32 & 33
Operations from March 21–April 2, 1918	Amman Raid	34–36
Operations from April 29–May 1, 1918	Es Salt Raid	37 & 38
The Water Supply of Jerusalem and the XXth Corps Area.	Area occupied as the result of operations from Dec. 31, 1917–Sept. 18, 1918.	39
	Development of Water Supply XXth Corps front ...	Inset 39
The September Advance	British dispositions as shown by enemy Intelligence Service.	40
Operations from Sept. 18–20, 1918	Advance into Samaria	41–43
Operations from Sept. 18–20, 1918, continued	Area occupied as the result of operations from Sept. 18–20, 1918.	44
	Egyptian Labour Corps Oct. 28, 1917–Sept. 17, 1918...	Inset 44
Operations on Sept. 21–22, 1918	Advance through Samaria and into Galilee	45 & 46
Operations from Sept. 23–27, 1918	Advance through Gilead and Galilee	47 & 48
Sherifian co-operation in September	Area occupied as the result of operations from Sept. 21–27.	49
	Locations of Anti-Aircraft Section, Sept., 1918	Inset 49
Operations from Sept. 28–30	Capture of Damascus	50
Operations on Oct. 1 and story of the Arab Movement	Capture of Damascus	51
Story of the Arab Movement, continued	Area occupied as the result of operations from Sept. 28–Oct. 1.	52
	Egyptian Labour Corps, Sept. 18 onwards	Inset 52
From the Fall of Damascus to the Armistice	Advance through Northern Syria	53
Lines of Communications, 1918	Lines of Communications, Oct., 1918	54
The Military Administration of the Territory released from the Turks.	Military Administration of the Territory occupied by the Egyptian Expeditionary Force.	55
A Summary of the Terms of the Turkish Armistice (as published) which came into force on Oct. 31, 1918.	Turkish Empire, Oct. 31, 1918, showing conditions of Armistice and disposition of Turkish troops.	56

THE ADVANCE OF THE EGYPTIAN EXPEDITIONARY FORCE.

The following Despatches, sent by GENERAL SIR EDMUND H. H. ALLENBY, G.C.B., G.C.M.G., to the SECRETARY OF STATE FOR WAR, are republished from *The London Gazette*.

> General Headquarters,
> Egyptian Expeditionary Force,
> *December 16, 1917.*

MY LORD—

I have the honour to submit a report on the operations of the Force serving in Egypt and Palestine since June 28, 1917, the date on which I assumed command.

1. When I took over the command of the Egyptian Expeditionary Force at the end of June, 1917, I had received instructions to report on the conditions in which offensive operations against the Turkish Army on the Palestine front might be undertaken in the autumn or winter of 1917.

After visiting the front and consulting with the Commander of the Eastern Force,* I submitted my appreciation and proposals in a telegram dispatched in the second week of July.

2. The main features of the situation on the Palestine front were then as follows:—

The Turkish Army in Southern Palestine held a strong position extending from the sea at Gaza, roughly along the main Gaza–Beersheba Road to Beersheba. Gaza had been made into a strong modern fortress, heavily entrenched and wired, offering every facility for protracted defence. The remainder of the enemy's line consisted of a series of strong localities, viz.: the Sihan group of works, the Atawineh group, the Baha group, the Abu Hareira–Arab el Teeaha trench system, and, finally, the works covering Beersheba. These groups of works were generally from 1,500 to 2,000 yards apart, except that the distance from the Hareira group to Beersheba was about four and a half miles.

The enemy's force was on a wide front, the distance from Gaza to Beersheba being about thirty miles; but his lateral communications were good, and any threatened point of the line could be very quickly reinforced. (*See* PLATE 3.)

My force was extended on a front of twenty-two miles, from the sea, opposite Gaza, to Gamli.

Owing to lack of water I was unable, without preparations which would require some considerable time, to approach within striking distance of the enemy, except in the small sector near the sea coast opposite Gaza.

3. My proposals received the approval of the War Cabinet, and preparations were undertaken to enable the plan I had formed to be put into execution.

I had decided to strike the main blow against the left flank of the main Turkish position, Hareira and Sheria. The capture of Beersheba was a necessary preliminary to this operation, in order to secure the water supplies at that place and to give room for the deployment of the attacking force on the high ground to the north and north-west of Beersheba, from which direction I intended to attack the Hareira–Sheria line.

This front of attack was chosen for the following reasons. The enemy's works in this sector were less formidable than elsewhere, and they were easier of approach than other parts of the enemy's defences. When Beersheba was in our hands we should have an open flank against which to operate, and I could make full use of our superiority in mounted troops; and a success here offered prospects of pursuing our advantage and forcing the enemy to abandon the rest of his fortified positions, which no other line of attack would afford.

It was important, in order to keep the enemy in doubt up to the last moment as to the real point of attack, that an attack should also be made on the enemy's right at Gaza in conjunction with the main operations. One of my Commanders was therefore ordered to prepare a scheme for operations against Gaza on as large a scale as the force at his disposal would permit. I also asked the Senior Naval Officer, Egypt, Rear-Admiral T. Jackson, C.B., M.V.O., to afford me naval co-operation by bombarding the Gaza defences and the enemy's railway stations and depôts north of Gaza. Rear-Admiral Jackson afforded me cordial assistance, and during the period of preparation Naval Officers worked in the closest co-operation with my staff at General Headquarters and the staff of the G.O.C. troops operating in that region.

---
* Major-General (temporary Lieut.-General) Sir Philip Chetwode, Bt., K.C.M.G., C.B., D.S.O.

4. The difficulties to be overcome in the operations against Beersheba and the Sheria–Hareira line were considerable, and careful preparations and training were necessary. The chief difficulties were those of water and transport, and arrangements had to be made to ensure that the troops could be kept supplied with water while operating at considerable distances from their original water base for a period which might amount to a week or more; for, though it was known that an ample supply of water existed at Beersheba, it was uncertain how quickly it could be developed or to what extent the enemy would have damaged the wells before we succeeded in occupying the town. Except at Beersheba, no large supply of water would be found till Sheria and Hareira had been captured.

The transport problem was no less difficult; there were no good roads south of the line Gaza–Beersheba, and no reliance could therefore be placed on the use of motor transport. Owing to the steep banks of many of the wadis which intersected the area of operations, the routes passable by wheeled transport were limited, and the going was heavy and difficult in many places. Practically the whole of the transport available in the force, including 30,000 pack camels, had to be allotted to one portion of the eastern force to enable it to be kept supplied with food, water, and ammunition at a distance of fifteen to twenty-one miles in advance of railhead. Arrangements were also made for railhead to be pushed forward as rapidly as possible towards Karm, and for a line to be laid from Gamli towards Beersheba for the transport of ammunition.

A railway line was also laid from Deir el Belah to the Wadi Ghuzze, close behind the sector held by another portion of the eastern force.

Considerable strain was thrown on the military railway from Kantara to the front during the period of preparation. In addition to the normal requirements of the force, a number of siege and heavy batteries, besides other artillery and units, had to be moved to the front, and large depôts of supplies, ammunition and other stores accumulated at the various railheads. Preparations had also to be made and the necessary material accumulated to push forward the lines from Deir el Belah and Shellal.

5. During the period from July to Oct. the enemy's force on the Palestine front had been increased. It was evident, from the arrival of these reinforcements and the construction of railway extensions from El Tine, on the Ramleh–Beersheba railway, to Deir Sineid and Beit Hanun, north of Gaza, and from Deir Sineid to Huj, and from reports of the transport of large supplies of ammunition and other stores to the Palestine front, that the enemy was determined to make every effort to maintain his position on the Gaza–Beersheba line. He had considerably strengthened his defences on this line, and the strong localities mentioned in paragraph 2 had, by the end of Oct., been joined up to form a practically continuous line from the sea to a point south of Sheria, except for a gap between Ali Muntar and the Sihan Group. The defensive works round Beersheba remained a detached system, but had been improved and extended.

6. The date of the attack on Beersheba, which was to commence the operations, was fixed as Oct. 31. Work had been begun on the railway from Shellal towards Karm, and on the line from Gamli to El Buggar. The development of water at Esani, Khalasa, and Asluj proceeded satisfactorily. These last two places were to be the starting point for the mounted force detailed to make a wide flanking movement and attack Beersheba from the east and north-east.

On the morning of **Oct. 27** the Turks made a strong reconnaissance towards Karm from the direction of Kauwukah, two regiments of cavalry and two or three thousand infantry, with guns, being employed. They attacked a line of outposts near El Girheir, held by some Yeomanry, covering railway construction. One small post was rushed and cut up, but not before inflicting heavy loss on the enemy; another post, though surrounded, held out all day, and also caused the enemy heavy loss. The gallant resistance made by the Yeomanry enabled the 53rd (Welsh) Division to come up in time, and on their advance the Turks withdrew.

The bombardment of the Gaza defences commenced on Oct. 27, and on Oct. 30 warships of the Royal Navy assisted by a French battleship, began co-operating in this bombardment.

Capture of Beersheba, Oct. 31.

7. On the evening of **Oct. 30** the portion of the eastern force, which was to make the attack on Beersheba, was concentrated in positions of readiness for the night march to its positions of deployment.

8. The night march to the positions of deployment was successfully carried out, all units reaching their appointed positions up to time.

The plan was to attack the hostile works between the Khalasa road and the Wadi Saba with two divisions, masking the works north of the Wadi Saba with the Imperial Camel Corps and some infantry, while a portion of the 53rd (Welsh) Division further north covered the left of the corps. The right of the attack was covered by a cavalry regiment. Further east, mounted troops took up a line opposite the southern defences of Beersheba.

As a preliminary to the main attack, in order to enable field guns to be brought within effective range for wire-cutting, the enemy's advanced works at 1,070 were to be taken. This was successfully accomplished at 8.45 a.m., after a short preliminary bombardment, by London troops, with small loss, ninety prisoners being taken. The cutting of the wire on the main line then proceeded satisfactorily, though pauses had to be made to allow the dust to clear; and the final assault was ordered for 12.15 p.m. It was successful all along the front attacked, and by about 1 p.m. the whole of the works between the Khalasa road and the Wadi Saba were in our hands.

Some delay occurred in ascertaining whether the enemy still occupied the works north of the road; it was decided, as they were still held by small parties, to attack them from the south. After a preliminary bombardment the works were occupied with little opposition by about 7.30 p.m.

The casualties were light, considering the strength of the works attacked; a large proportion occurred during the advance towards the positions previous to the assault, the hostile guns being very accurate and very difficult to locate.

Meanwhile, the mounted troops, after a night march, for part of the force of twenty-five and for the remainder of thirty-five miles, arrived early in the morning of the 31st about Khasim Zanna, in the hills some five miles east of Beersheba. From the hills the advance into Beersheba from the east and north-east lies over an open and almost flat plain, commanded by the rising ground north of the town and flanked by an under feature in the Wadi Saba called Tel el Saba.

A force was sent north to secure Bir es Sakaty, on the Hebron road, and protect the right flank; this force met with some opposition, and was engaged with hostile cavalry at Bir es Sakaty and to the north during the day. Tel el Saba was found strongly held by the enemy, and was not captured till late in the afternoon.

Meanwhile, attempts to advance in small parties across the plain towards the town made slow progress. In the evening, however, a mounted attack by Australian Light Horse, who rode straight at the town from the east, proved completely successful. They galloped over two deep trenches held by the enemy just outside the town, and entered the town at about 7 p.m., capturing numerous prisoners.

The Turks at Beersheba were undoubtedly taken completely by surprise, a surprise from which the dash of London troops and Yeomanry, finely supported by their artillery, never gave them time to recover. The charge of the Australian Light Horse completed their defeat.

A very strong position was thus taken with slight loss, and the Turkish detachment at Beersheba almost completely put out of action. About 2,000 prisoners and thirteen guns were taken, and some 500 Turkish corpses were buried on the battlefield. This success laid open the left flank of the main Turkish position for a decisive blow. (*See* PLATE 5.)

The Attack on Gaza.

9. The actual date of the attack at Gaza had been left open till the result of the attack at Beersheba was known, as it was intended that the former attack, which was designed to draw hostile reserves towards the Gaza sector, should take place twenty-four to forty-eight hours previous to the attack on the Sheria position. After the complete success of the Beersheba operations, and as the early reports indicated that an ample supply of water would be available at that place, it was hoped that it would be possible to attack Sheria by Nov. 3 or 4. The attack on Gaza was accordingly ordered to take place on the morning of Nov. 2. Later reports showed that the water situation was less favourable than had been hoped, but it was decided not to postpone the attack.

The objectives of this attack were the hostile works from Umbrella Hill (2,000 yards south-west of the town) to Sheikh Hasan, on the sea (about 2,500 yards north-west of the town). The front of the attack was about 6,000 yards, and Sheikh Hasan, the furthest objective, was over 3,000 yards from our front line. The ground over which the attack took place consisted of sand dunes, rising in places up to 150 feet in height. This sand is very deep and heavy going. The enemy's defences consisted of several lines of strongly built trenches and redoubts.

As Umbrella Hill flanked the advance against the Turkish works further west, it was decided to capture it by a preliminary operation, to take place four hours previous to the main attack. It was accordingly attacked, and captured at 11 p.m. on **Nov. 1** by a portion of the 52nd (Lowland) Division. This attack drew a heavy bombardment on Umbrella Hill itself and our front lines, which lasted for two hours, but ceased in time to allow the main attack, which was timed for 3 a.m., to form up without interference.

It had been decided to make the attack before daylight owing to the distance to be covered between our front trenches and the enemy's position.

The attack was successful in reaching all objectives, except for a section of trench on the left and some of the final objectives in the centre. Four hundred and fifty prisoners were taken and many Turks killed. The enemy also suffered heavily from the preliminary bombardment, and subsequent reports from prisoners stated that one of the divisions holding the Gaza sector was withdrawn after losing thirty-three per cent of its effectives, one of the divisions in general reserve being drawn into the Gaza sector to replace it. The attack thus succeeded in its primary object, which was to prevent any units being drawn from the Gaza defences to meet the threat to the Turkish left flank, and to draw into Gaza as large a proportion as possible of the available Turkish reserves. Further, the capture of Sheikh Hasan and the south-western defences constituted a very distinct threat to the whole of the Gaza position, which could be developed on any sign of a withdrawal on the part of the enemy. (*See* PLATE 7.)

Our losses, though considerable, were not in any way disproportionate to the results obtained.

Advance from Beersheba.

10. Meanwhile on our right flank the water and transport difficulties were found to be greater than anticipated, and the preparations for the second phase of the attack were somewhat delayed in consequence.

On the early morning of Nov. 1 the 53rd (Welsh) Division, with the Imperial Camel Corps on its right, had moved out into the hills north of Beersheba, with the object of securing the flank of the attack on Sheria. Mounted troops were also sent north along the Hebron Road to secure Dhaheriyeh if possible, as it was hoped that a good supply of water would be found in this area, and that a motor road which the Turks were reported to have constructed from Dhaheriyeh to Sheria could be secured for our use.

The 53rd (Welsh) Division, after a long march, took up a position from Towal Abu Jerwal (six miles north of Beersheba) to Muweileh (four miles north-east of Abu Irgeig). Irish troops occupied Abu Irgeig the same day.

On **Nov. 3** we advanced north on Ain Kohleh and Tel Khuweilfeh, near which place the mounted troops had engaged considerable enemy forces on the previous day. This advance was strongly opposed, but was pushed on through difficult hill country to within a short distance of Ain Kohleh and Khuweilfeh. At these places the enemy was found holding a strong position with considerable and increasing forces. He was obviously determined not only to bar any further progress in this direction, but, if possible, to drive our flankguard back on Beersheba. During the 4th and 5th he made several determined attacks on the mounted troops. These attacks were repulsed.

By the evening of **Nov. 5** the 19th Turkish Division, the remains of the 27th and certain units of the 16th Division had been identified in the fighting round Tel el Khuweilfeh, and it was also fairly clear that the greater part of the hostile cavalry, supported apparently by some infantry ("depôt" troops) from Hebron, were engaged between Khuweilfeh and the Hebron Road.

Enemy's Counter-Stroke Defeated.

The action of the enemy in thus employing the whole of his available reserves in an immediate counter-stroke so far to the east was apparently a bold effort to induce me to make essential alterations in my offensive plan, thereby gaining time and disorganizing my arrangements. The country north of Beersheba was exceedingly rough and hilly, and very little water was to be found there. Had the enemy succeeded in drawing considerable forces against him in that area the result might easily have been an indecisive fight (for the terrain was very suitable to his methods of defence) and my own main striking force would probably have been made too weak effectively to break the enemy's centre in the neighbourhood of Sheria Hareira. This might have resulted in our gaining Beersheba, but failing to do more—in which case Beersheba would only have been an incubus of a most inconvenient kind. However, the enemy's action was not allowed to make any essential modification to the original plan, which it had been decided to carry out at dawn on Nov. 6.

By the evening of Nov. 5, all preparations had been made to attack the Kauwukah and Rushdi systems and to make every effort to reach Sheria before nightfall.

The mounted troops were to be prepared in the event of a success by the main force to collect, as they were somewhat widely scattered owing to water difficulties, and push north in pursuit of the enemy. Tel el Khuweilfeh was to be attacked at dawn on the 6th, and the troops were to endeavour to reach the line Tel el Khuweilfeh–Rijm el Dhib.

Assault on Kauwukah and Rushdi.

11. At dawn on the **6th** the attacking force had taken up positions of readiness to the S.E. of the Kauwukah system of trenches. The attack was to be commenced by an assault on the group of works forming the extreme left of the enemy's defensive system, followed by an advance due west up the railway, capturing the line of detached works which lay east of the railway. During this attack London and

Irish troops were to advance towards the Kauwukah system, bringing forward their guns to within wire-cutting range. They were to assault the south-eastern face of the Kauwukah system as soon as the bombardment had proved effective, and thence take the remainder of the system in enfilade.

The attack progressed rapidly, the Yeomanry storming the works on the enemy's extreme left with great dash; and soon after noon the London and Irish troops commenced their attack. It was completely successful in capturing all its objectives, and the whole of the Rushdi system in addition. Sheria Station was also captured before dark. The Yeomanry reached the line of the *Wadi Sheria to Wadi Union*; and the troops on the left were close to Hareira Redoubts, which was still occupied by the enemy. This attack was a fine performance, the troops advancing eight or nine miles during the day and capturing a series of very strong works covering a front of about seven miles, the greater part of which had been held and strengthened by the enemy for over six months. Some 600 prisoners were taken and some guns and machine guns captured. Our casualties were comparatively slight. The greatest opposition was encountered by the Yeomanry in the early morning, the works covering the left of the enemy's line being strong and stubbornly defended.

During the afternoon, as soon as it was seen that the attack had succeeded, mounted troops were ordered to take up the pursuit and to occupy Huj and Jemmamah.

The 53rd (Welsh) Division had again had very severe fighting on the 6th. Their attack at dawn on Tel el Khuweilfeh was successful, and, though they were driven off a hill by a counter-attack, they retook it and captured another hill, which much improved their position. The Turkish losses in this area were very heavy indeed, and the stubborn fighting of the 53rd (Welsh) Division, Imperial Camel Corps, and part of the mounted troops during Nov. 2 to 6 drew in and exhausted the Turkish reserves and paved the way for the success of the attack on Sheria. The 53rd (Welsh) Division took several hundred prisoners and some guns during this fighting. (*See* PLATE 8.)

The Fall of Gaza, Nov. 7.

12. The bombardment of Gaza had meanwhile continued, and another attack was ordered to take place on the night of the 6th–7th.

The objectives were, on the right, Outpost Hill and Middlesex Hill (to be attacked at 11.30 p.m. on the 6th), and on the left the line Belah Trench–Turtle Hill (to be attacked at dawn on the 7th).

During the 6th a certain amount of movement on the roads north of Gaza was observed by our airmen and fired on by our heavy artillery, but nothing indicating a general retirement from Gaza.

The attack on Outpost Hill and Middlesex Hill met with little opposition, and as soon, after they had been taken, as patrols could be pushed forward, the enemy was found to be gone. East Anglian troops on the left also found at dawn that the enemy had retired during the night, and early in the morning the main force occupied the northern and eastern defences of Gaza. Rearguards were still occupying Beit Hanun and the Atawineh and Tank systems, from whence Turkish artillery continued to fire on Gaza and Ali Muntar till dusk.

As soon as it was seen that the Turks had evacuated Gaza a part of the force pushed along the coast to the mouth of the Wadi Hesi, so as to turn the Wadi Hesi line and prevent the enemy making any stand there. Cavalry had already pushed on round the north of Gaza, and became engaged with an enemy rearguard at Beit Hanun, which maintained its position till nightfall. The force advancing along the coast reached the Wadi Hesi by evening, and succeeded in establishing itself on the north bank in the face of considerable opposition, a Turkish rearguard making several determined counter-attacks.

On our extreme right the situation remained practically unchanged during the 7th; the enemy made no further attempt to counter-attack, but maintained his positions opposite our right flank guard.

In the centre the Hareira Tepe Redoubt was captured at dawn; some prisoners and guns were taken. The London troops, after a severe engagement at Tel el Sheria, which they captured by a bayonet charge at 4 a.m., on the 7th, subsequently repulsing several counter-attacks, pushed forward their line about a mile to the the north of Tel el Sheria; the mounted troops on the right moved towards Jemmamah and Huj, but met with considerable opposition from hostile rearguards. (*See* PLATE 9.)

Charge of the Yeomanry at Huj, Nov. 8.

13. During the **8th** the advance was continued, and interest was chiefly centred in an attempt to cut off, if possible, the Turkish rearguard which had held the Tank and Atawineh systems. The enemy had, however, retreated during the night 7th–8th, and though considerable captures of prisoners, guns, ammunition, and other stores were made during the day, chiefly in the vicinity of Huj, no large formed body of the enemy was cut off. The Turkish rearguards fought stubbornly and offered considerable opposition. Near Huj a fine charge by some squadrons of the Worcester and Warwick Yeomanry captured twelve guns, and broke the resistance of a hostile rearguard. It soon became obvious from the

reports of the Royal Flying Corps, who throughout the 7th and 8th attacked the retreating columns with bombs and machine-gun fire, and from other evidence, that the enemy was retiring in considerable disorganization, and could offer no very serious resistance if pressed with determination. (*See* PLATE 10.)

Instructions were accordingly issued on the morning of the 9th to the mounted troops, directing them on the line El Tine–Beit Duras, with orders to press the enemy relentlessly. They were to be supported by a portion of the force, which was ordered to push forward to Julis and Mejdel.

The enemy opposite our right flank guard had commenced to retreat towards Hebron on the morning of the 8th. He was pursued for a short distance by the Yeomanry, and some prisoners and camels were captured, but the Yeomanry were then recalled to rejoin the main body of the mounted troops for the more important task of the pursuit of the enemy's main body.

By the 9th, therefore, operations had reached the stage of a direct pursuit by as many troops as could be supplied so far in front of railhead. The problem, in fact, became one of supply rather than manœuvre. The question of water and forage was a very difficult one. Even where water was found in sufficient quantities, it was usually in wells and not on the surface, and consequently if the machinery for working the wells was damaged, or a sufficient supply of troughs was not available, the process of watering a large quantity of animals was slow and difficult.

Increased Turkish Resistance.

14. On the evening of **Nov. 9** there were indications that the enemy was organizing a counter-attack towards Arak el Menshiye by all available units of the force which had retired towards Hebron, with the object of taking pressure off the main force, which was retiring along the coastal plain. It was obvious that the Hebron force, which was believed to be short of transport and ammunition, to have lost heavily and to be in a generally disorganized state, could make no effective diversion, and that this threat could practically be disregarded. Other information showed the seriousness of the enemy's losses and the disorganization of his forces. (*See* PLATE 11.)

Orders were accordingly issued to press the pursuit and to reach the Junction Station as early as possible, thus cutting off the Jerusalem Army, while the Imperial Camel Corps was ordered to move to the neighbourhood of Tel el Nejile, where it would be on the flank of any counter-stroke from the hills.

Operations on the **10th** and **11th** showed a stiffening of the enemy's resistance on the general line of the Wadi Sukereir, with centre about El Kustineh; the Hebron group, after an ineffective demonstration in the direction of Arak el Menshiye on the 10th retired north-east and prolonged the enemy's line towards Beit Jibrin. Royal Flying Corps reports indicated the total hostile forces opposed to us on this line at about 15,000; and this increased resistance, coupled with the capture of prisoners from almost every unit of the Turkish force, tended to show that we were no longer opposed to rearguards, but that all the remainder of the Turkish Army which could be induced to fight was making a last effort to arrest our pursuit south of the important Junction Station.

In these circumstances our progress on the 10th and 11th was slow; the troops suffered considerably from thirst (a hot, exhausting wind blew during these two days), and our supply difficulties were great; but by the evening of the 11th favourable positions had been reached for a combined attack. (*See* PLATES 12 & 13.)

The **12th** was spent in preparations for the attack, which was ordered to be begun early on the morning of the 13th, on the enemy's position covering Junction Station. Our forces were now operating at a distance of some thirty-five miles in advance of their railhead, and the bringing up and distribution of supplies and ammunition formed a difficult problem. The routes north of the Wadi Hesi were found to be hard and good going, though there were some difficult wadi crossings, but the main road through Gaza and as far as Beit Hanun was sandy and difficult. The supply of water in the area of operations, though good and plentiful in most of the villages, lies mainly in wells 100 feet or more below the surface, and in these circumstances a rapid supply and distribution was almost impossible. Great credit is due to all concerned that these difficulties were overcome and that it was found possible not only to supply the troops already in the line, but to bring up two heavy batteries to support the attack.

15. The situation on the morning of **Nov. 13** was that the enemy had strung out his force (amounting probably to no more than 20,000 rifles in all) on a front of twenty miles, from El Kubeibeh on the north to about Beit Jibrin to the south. The right half of his line ran roughly parallel to and only about five miles in front of the Ramleh–Junction Station railway, his main line of supply from the north, and his right flank was already almost turned. This position had been dictated to him by the rapidity of our movement along the coast, and the determination with which his rearguards on this flank had been pressed.

The advanced guard of the 52nd (Lowland) Division had forced its way almost to Burkah on the 11th, on which day also some mounted troops pushed across the Nahr Sukereir at Jisr Esdud, where they held a bridge-head. During the 12th the Yeomanry pushed north up the left bank of the Nahr Sukereir, and eventually seized Tel el Murreh on the right bank near the mouth.

The hostile commander may have hoped to exercise some moral effect on our plans by the presence of the southern portion of his forces on the flank of our advance ; if so, he was mistaken. The Australian mounted troops, extended over a wide front, not only secured this flank but pressed forward on the 12th towards Balin, Berkusie, and Tel es Safi. Their advanced troops were counter-attacked and driven back a short distance, but the enemy made no effort to press further forward. Arrangements were then made to attack on the 13th.

The country over which the attack took place is open and rolling, dotted with small villages surrounded by mud walls with plantations of trees outside the walls. The most prominent feature is the line of heights on which are the villages of Katrah and El Mughar, standing out above the low flat ground which separates them from the rising ground to the west, on which stands the village of Beshshit, about 2,000 yards distant. This Katrah-El Mughar line forms a very strong position, and it was here that the enemy made his most determined resistance against the turning movement directed against his right flank. The capture of this position by the 52nd (Lowland) Division, assisted by a most dashing charge of mounted troops, who galloped across the plain under heavy fire and turned the enemy's position from the north, was a fine feat of arms. Some 1,100 prisoners, three guns, and many machine guns were taken here. After this the enemy resistance weakened, and by the evening his forces were retiring east and north. (*See* PLATE 14.)

Capture of Junction Station, Nov. 14.

The infantry, who were sent forward about dusk to occupy Junction Station, met with some resistance and halted for the night, not much more than a mile west of the station. Early next morning (**Nov. 14**) they occupied the station.

The enemy's army had now been broken into two separate parts, which retired north and east respectively, and were reported to consist of small scattered groups rather than formed bodies of any size.

In fifteen days our force had advanced sixty miles on its right and about forty on its left. It had driven a Turkish Army of nine infantry divisions and one cavalry division out of a position in which it had been entrenched for six months, and had pursued it, giving battle whenever it attempted to stand, and inflicting on it losses amounting probably to nearly two-thirds of the enemy's original effectives. Over 9,000 prisoners, about eighty guns, more than 100 machine guns, and very large quantities of ammunition and other stores had been captured. (*See* PLATE 15.)

16. After the capture of Junction Station on the morning of the 14th, our troops secured a position covering the station, while the Australian mounted troops reached Kezaze that same evening.

The mounted troops pressed on towards Ramleh and Ludd. On the right Naaneh was attacked and captured in the morning, while on the left the New Zealand Mounted Rifles had a smart engagement at Ayun Kara (Rishon le Zion, six miles south of Jaffa). Here the Turks made a determined counter-attack and got to within fifteen yards of our line. A bayonet attack drove them back with heavy loss.

Flanking the advance along the railway to Ramleh and covering the main road from Ramleh to Jerusalem, a ridge stands up prominently out of the low foot hills surrounding it. This is the site of the ancient Gezer, near which the village of Abu Shusheh now stands. A hostile rearguard had established itself on this feature. It was captured on the morning of the 15th in a brilliant attack by mounted troops, who galloped up the ridge from the south. A gun and 360 prisoners were taken in this affair.

By the evening of the **15th** the mounted troops had occupied Ramleh and Ludd, and had pushed patrols to within a short distance of Jaffa. At Ludd 300 prisoners were taken, and five destroyed aeroplanes and a quantity of abandoned war material were found at Ramleh and Ludd.

Occupation of Jaffa, Nov. 16.

Jaffa was occupied without opposition on the evening of the 16th.

17. The situation was now as follows :—

The enemy's army, cut in two by our capture of Junction Station, had retired partly east into the mountains towards Jerusalem and partly north along the plain. The nearest line on which these two portions could re-unite was the line Tul Keram-Nablus. Reports from the Royal Flying Corps indicated that it was the probable intention of the enemy to evacuate Jerusalem and withdraw to reorganize on this line. (*See* PLATE 16.)

On our side the mounted troops had been marching and fighting continuously since Oct. 31, and had advanced a distance of seventy-five miles, measured in a straight line from Asluj to Jaffa. The troops, after their heavy fighting at Gaza, had advanced in nine days a distance of about forty miles, with two severe engagements and continual advanced guard fighting. The 52nd (Lowland) Division had covered sixty-nine miles in this period.

The railway was being pushed forward as rapidly as possible, and every opportunity was taken of landing stores at points along the coast. The landing of stores was dependent on a continuance of favourable weather, and might at any moment be stopped for several days together.

A pause was therefore necessary to await the progress of railway construction, but before our position in the plain could be considered secure it was essential to obtain hold of the one good road which traverses the Judæan range from north to south, from Nablus to Jerusalem.

The Advance into Judæa.

18. The west side of the Judæan range consists of a series of spurs running east and west, and separated from one another by narrow valleys. These spurs are steep, bare and stony for the most part, and in places precipitous. Between the foot of the spur of the main range and the coastal plain is the low range known as the Shephelah.

On our intended line of advance only one good road, the main Jaffa–Jerusalem road, traversed the hills from east to west. For nearly four miles, between Bab el Wad (two and a half miles east of Latron) and Saris, this road passes through a narrow defile, and it had been damaged by the Turks in several places. The other roads were mere tracks on the side of the hill or up the stony beds of wadis, and were impracticable for wheeled transport without improvement. Throughout these hills the water supply was scanty without development.

On **Nov. 17** the Yeomanry had commenced to move from Ramleh through the hills direct on Bireh by Annabeh, Berfilya and Beit ur el Tahta (Lower Bethhoron). By the evening of Nov. 18 one portion of the Yeomanry had reached the last-named place, while another portion had occupied Shilta. The route had been found impossible for wheels beyond Annabeh. (*See* PLATE 17.)

On the **19th** the Infantry commenced its advance. One portion was to advance up the main road as far as Kuryet el Enab, with its right flank protected by Australian mounted troops. From that place, in order to avoid any fighting in the close vicinity of the Holy City, it was to strike north towards Bireh by a track leading through Biddu. The remainder of the infantry was to advance through Berfilya to Beit Likia and Beit Dukka, and thence support the movement of the other portion.

After capturing Latron and Amnas on the morning of the 19th, the remainder of the day was spent in clearing the defile up to Saris, which was defended by hostile rearguards. (*See* PLATE 18.)

On the **20th** Kuryet el Enab was captured with the bayonet in the face of organized opposition, while Beit Dukka was also captured. On the same day the Yeomanry got to within four miles of the Nablus–Jerusalem road, but were stopped by strong opposition about Beitunia.

On the **21st** a body of infantry moved north-east by a track from Kuryet el Enab through Biddu and Kulundia towards Bireh. The track was found impassable for wheels, and was under hostile shell fire. Progress was slow, but by evening the ridge on which stands Neby Samwil was secured. A further body of troops was left at Kuryet el Enab to cover the flank and demonstrate along the main Jerusalem road. It drove hostile parties from Kustul, two and a half miles east of Kuryet el Enab, and secured this ridge.

By the afternoon of the 21st advanced parties of Yeomanry were within two miles of the road, and an attack was being delivered on Beitunia by other mounted troops. (*See* PLATE 19.)

Turkish Counter-Attacks.

19. The positions reached on the evening of the 21st practically marked the limit of progress in this first attempt to gain the Nablus–Jerusalem road. The Yeomanry were heavily counter-attacked and fell back, after bitter fighting, on Beit ur el Foka (Upper Bethhoron). During the **22nd** the enemy made two counter-attacks on the Neby Samwil ridge, which were repulsed. Determined and gallant attacks were made on the **23rd** and on the **24th** on the strong positions to the west of the road held by the enemy, who had brought up reinforcements and numerous machine guns, and could support his infantry by artillery fire from guns placed in positions along the main road. Our artillery, from lack of roads, could not be brought up to give adequate support to our infantry. Both attacks failed, and it was evident that a period of preparation and organization would be necessary before an attack could be delivered in sufficient strength to drive the enemy from his positions west of the road. (*See* PLATE 20.)

Orders were accordingly issued to consolidate the positions gained and prepare for relief.

Though these troops had failed to reach their final objectives, they had achieved invaluable results. The narrow passes from the plain to the plateau of the Judæan range have seldom been forced, and have been fatal to many invading armies. Had the attempt not been made at once, or had it been pressed with less determination, the enemy would have had time to reorganize his defences in the passes lower down, and the conquest of the plateau would then have been slow, costly, and precarious. As it was, positions had been won from which the final attack could be prepared and delivered with good prospects of success.

20. By Dec. 4 all reliefs were complete, and a line was held from Kustul by the Neby Samwil ridge, Beit Izza, and Beit Dukka, to Beit ur el Tahta. (*See* PLATES 22, 23, & 24.)

Fighting on the Auja.

During this period attacks by the enemy along the whole line led to severe local fighting. On **Nov. 25** our advanced posts north of the river Auja were driven back across the river. From the **27th** to the 30th the enemy delivered a series of attacks directed especially against the high ground north and north-east of Jaffa, the left flank of our position in the hills from Beit ur el Foka to El Burj, and the Neby Samwil ridge. An attack on the night of the **29th** succeeded in penetrating our outpost line north-east of Jaffa, but next morning the whole hostile detachment, numbering 150, was surrounded and captured by Australian Light Horse. On the **30th** a similar fate befell a battalion which attacked near El Burj; a counter-attack by Australian Light Horse took 200 prisoners and practically destroyed the attacking battalion. There was particularly heavy fighting between El Burj and Beit ur el Foka, but the Yeomanry and Scottish troops successfully resisted all attacks and inflicted severe losses on the enemy. At Beit ur el Foka one company took 300 prisoners. (*See* PLATE 21.)

Enemy Failure at Neby Samwil.

All efforts by the enemy to drive us off the Neby Samwil ridge were completely repulsed. These attacks cost the Turks very dearly. We took 750 prisoners between Nov. 27 and 30, and the enemy's losses in killed and wounded were undoubtedly heavy. His attacks in no way affected our positions nor impeded the progress of our preparations.

Converging Movement on Jerusalem.

21. Favoured by a continuance of fine weather, preparations for a fresh advance against the Turkish positions west and south of Jerusalem proceeded rapidly. Existing roads and tracks were improved and new ones constructed to enable heavy and field artillery to be placed in position and ammunition and supplies brought up. The water supply was also developed.

The date for the attack was fixed as Dec. 8. Welsh troops, with a Cavalry regiment attached, had advanced from their positions north of Beersheba up the Hebron–Jerusalem road on the **4th.** No opposition was met, and by the evening of the **6th** the head of this column was ten miles north of Hebron. The Infantry were directed to reach the Bethlehem–Beit Jala area by the 7th, and the line Surbahir–Sherafat (about three miles south of Jerusalem) by dawn on the 8th, and no troops were to enter Jerusalem during this operation. (*See* PLATE 25.)

It was recognized that the troops on the extreme right might be delayed on the 7th and fail to reach the positions assigned to them by dawn on the 8th. Arrangements were therefore made to protect the right flank west of Jerusalem, in case such delay occurred.

22. On the **7th** the weather broke, and for three days rain was almost continuous. The hills were covered with mist at frequent intervals, rendering observation from the air and visual signalling impossible. A more serious effect of the rain was to jeopardise the supply arrangements by rendering the roads almost impassable—quite impassable, indeed, for mechanical transport and camels in many places. (*See* PLATE 26.)

The troops moved into positions of assembly by night, and, assaulting at dawn on the 8th, soon carried their first objectives. They then pressed steadily forward. The mere physical difficulty of climbing the steep and rocky hillsides and crossing the deep valleys would have sufficed to render progress slow, and the opposition encountered was considerable. Artillery support was soon difficult, owing to the length of the advance and the difficulty of moving guns forward. But by about noon London troops had already advanced over two miles, and were swinging north-east to gain the Nablus–Jerusalem road; while the Yeomanry had captured the Beit Iksa spur, and were preparing for a further advance.

Surrender of Jerusalem, Dec. 9.

As the right column had been delayed and was still some distance south of Jerusalem, it was necessary for the London troops to throw back their right and form a defensive flank facing east towards Jerusalem, from the western outskirts of which considerable rifle and artillery fire was being experienced. This delayed the advance, and early in the afternoon it was decided to consolidate the line gained and resume the advance next day, when the right column would be in a position to exert its pressure. By nightfall our line ran from Neby Samwil to the east of Beit Iksa, through Lifta to a point about one and a half miles west of Jerusalem, whence it was thrown back facing east. All the enemy's prepared defences west and north-west of Jerusalem had been captured, and our troops were within a short distance of the Nablus–Jerusalem road.

The London troops and Yeomanry had displayed great endurance in difficult conditions. The London troops especially, after a night march in heavy rain to reach their positions of deployment, had made an advance of three to four miles in difficult hills in the face of stubborn opposition.

During the day about 300 prisoners were taken and many Turks killed. Our own casualties were light.

23. Next morning the advance was resumed. The Turks had withdrawn during the night, and the London troops and Yeomanry, driving back rearguards, occupied a line across the Nablus–Jerusalem road four miles north of Jerusalem, while Welsh troops occupied a position east of Jerusalem across the Jericho road. These operations isolated Jerusalem, and at about noon the enemy sent out a *parlementaire* and surrendered the city. (*See* PLATE 27.)

Official Entry.

At noon on the 11th I made my official entry into Jerusalem.

24. In the operations from Oct. 31 to Dec. 9 over 12,000 prisoners were taken. The total captures of material have not yet been fully counted, owing to the large area covered by these operations; but they are known to include about 100 guns of various calibres, many machine guns, more than 20,000,000 rounds of rifle ammunition, and 250,000 rounds of gun ammunition. More than twenty aeroplanes were destroyed by our airmen or burnt by the enemy to avoid capture.

25. My thanks are due to the cordial assistance which I received from his Excellency the High Commissioner, General Sir Francis Wingate, G.C.B., G.C.V.O., K.C.M.G., D.S.O., who has always given me the greatest assistance.

26. During the whole period Rear-Admiral T. Jackson, C.B., M.V.O., has given me most loyal support, and has co-operated with me in a manner which has materially contributed to our success.

27. Brigadier-General Sir G. Macauley, K.C.M.G., C.B., Director of Railway Transport, has given invaluable help in the organisation of my railways.

28. All ranks and services in the Force under my command have acquitted themselves in a manner beyond praise. Fatigue, thirst, heat, and cold have been endured uncomplainingly. The co-operation of all arms has been admirable, and has enabled success in battle to be consummated by irresistible and victorious pursuit.

Leaders and staffs have all done well, and in particular I bring to your Lordship's notice the names of the following officers :—

Major-General (temporary Lieutenant-General) Sir Philip Chetwode, Bart., K.C.M.G., C.B., D.S.O.

My plan of operations was based on his appreciation of the situation and on the scheme which he put forward to me on my arrival in Egypt last summer. To his strategical foresight and tactical skill the success of the campaign is largely due.

Major-General (temporary Lieutenant-General) E. S. Bulfin, C.B., C.V.O.

Has shown great ability as an organizer and leader in high command. To his determination in attack, and his dash and drive in pursuit, is due the swift advance to Jerusalem.

Major-General (temporary Lieutenant-General) Sir Henry Chauvel, K.C.M.G., C.B.

Has commanded my mounted troops with invariable success in attack and pursuit. His co-operation with other arms has always been ready and loyal, and has contributed greatly to the victory won.

Major-General L. J. Bols, C.B., D.S.O., Chief of the General Staff, has done brilliant work. He is a general staff officer of the first rank.

Major-General J. Adye, C.B., Deputy Adjutant-General, has rendered invaluable service.

Major-General Sir Walter Campbell, K.C.M.G., C.B., D.S.O., Deputy Quartermaster-General, has had a difficult task which he has carried out with complete success.

Brevet Lieutenant-Colonel (temporary Brigadier-General) G. P. Dawnay, D.S.O., M.V.O., Reserve of Officers, Brigadier-General, General Staff, has proved himself a strategist and tactician of unusual merit. His work has been of the highest value.

I have the honour to be,
Your Lordship's most obedient servant,

E. H. H. ALLENBY,
General,
Commanding-in-Chief,
Egyptian Expeditionary Force.

General Headquarters,
Egyptian Expeditionary Force,
September 18, 1918.

My Lord,

I have the honour to submit a Report on the operations undertaken since Dec. 11, 1917, by the Force serving in Egypt and Palestine.

1. The operations described in my Despatch of Dec. 16, 1917, had resulted in the enemy's army being broken into two separate parts. One part had retired northwards, and had come to a halt on the hills overlooking the plain which lies to the north of Jaffa and Ramleh. This force consisted of five divisions, four of which had been badly shaken in the recent retreat. Opposite it the XXIst Corps held a line, which starting at the mouth of the Nahr el Auja, three miles north of Jaffa, crossed the Turkish railway from Ludd to Jiljulieh at a point five miles north of Ludd, and thence ran in a south-easterly direction to Midieh. (*See* Plate 28.)

The other part of the enemy's army had retired in an easterly direction towards Jerusalem. Here the remains of six divisions had been concentrated. The XXth Corps, after it had compelled the enemy to evacuate Jerusalem, held a line across the roads leading from Jerusalem to Jericho and Nablus, four miles east and north of the city, and thence westwards through the hills past Beit ur el Foka to Suffa.

The two wings of the Turkish Army were separated by a roadless tract of country, the chief features of which consist of a series of spurs running west. The spurs are bare and rocky, the valleys between them are deep. No operations on a large scale are possible in this country until the tracks have been improved sufficiently to admit of the passage of guns and of wheeled transport. The only lateral communication possible to the Turks lay some thirty miles to the north of the line Tul Keram–Nablus.

2. In order to provide more effectively for the security of Jerusalem and Jaffa, it was essential that the line should be advanced. I therefore ordered the XXth Corps to advance to the line Beitin–Nalin. This involved an advance on a twelve-mile front to a depth of six miles immediately north of Jerusalem. The XXIst Corps on the left I ordered to advance to the line Kibbieh–Rantieh–Mulebbis–Sheikh el Ballutah–El Jelil. When this advance had been carried out the distance between the enemy and Jaffa would be increased to eight miles.

3. Before either of these advances could take place a considerable amount of labour was necessary on the construction of roads and the improvement of communications. Supplies and ammunition had to be brought up, a task which was rendered more difficult by the weather. Heavy rains interfered with the progress of railway construction, and in some places washed away the existing line, while the roads became deep in mud, rendering the use of mechanical transport and camels impossible, and that of horse transport slow and difficult.

4. The operation on the left was the first to be carried out. The chief obstacle lay in the crossing of the Nahr el Auja. This river is only fordable in places, and all approaches to it are overlooked from Sheikh Muannis and Khurbet Hadrah. At these places two spurs running from north to south terminate abruptly in steep slopes some 500 yards from the river.

Before the XXIst Corps could reach its final objectives, it was necessary that the guns should move forward with the infantry. Consequently Sheikh Muannis, Khurbet Hadrah, and the high ground overlooking the river had to be captured as a preliminary to the general advance in order that bridges might be built.

The Passage of the Nahr El Auja, Dec. 20–21.

The chief difficulty lay in concealing the collection and preparation of rafts and bridging material. All preparations were completed, however, without attracting the enemy's attention, and on the night of Dec. 20–21 the 52nd Division crossed the river in three columns. The enemy was taken completely by surprise. The left column, fording the river near its mouth, at this point four feet deep, captured Tell er Rekkeit, 4,000 yards north of the river's mouth; the centre and right columns, crossing on rafts, rushed Sheikh Muannis and Khurbet Hadrah at the point of the bayonet. By dawn a line from Khurbet Hadrah to Tell er Rekkeit had been consolidated, and the enemy deprived of all observation from the north over the valley of the Nahr el Auja.

The successful crossing of the Nahr el Auja reflects great credit on the 52nd (Lowland) Division. It involved considerable preparation, the details of which were thought out with care and precision. The sodden state of the ground, and, on the night of the crossing, the swollen state of the river, added to the difficulties, yet by dawn the whole of the infantry had crossed. The fact that the enemy were taken by surprise, and that all resistance was overcome with the bayonet without a shot being fired, bears testimony to the discipline of this division. Eleven officers, including two battalion commanders, and 305 other ranks, and ten machine guns were captured in this operation.

Dec. 21 was spent in building bridges. Considerable hostile shell fire was experienced during the day, chiefly from the right flank. From Mulebbis the enemy could observe the valley of the Auja. Despite this the bridges were completed, and by dusk the whole of the Divisional Artillery of the 52nd Division had crossed to the right bank, ready to support the advance to the final objectives.

On the morning of **Dec. 22,** the 54th Division on the right drove the enemy from the orchards which surround Mulebbis, and captured the villages of Rantieh and Fejja. On the left the 52nd Division reached all their objectives and consolidated the line Tel el Mukhmar–Arsuf, the latter place, although two miles beyond the allotted objective, being occupied to deny direct observation on Jaffa harbour to the enemy.

During the day the Royal Flying Corps attacked the enemy with bombs and machine-gun fire as he withdrew, inflicting numerous casualties.

Throughout these operations the XXIst Corps received most effective support from the Royal Navy.

This operation, by increasing the distance between the enemy and Jaffa from three to eight miles, rendered Jaffa and its harbour secure, and gained elbow-room for the troops covering Ludd and Ramleh and the main Jaffa–Jerusalem road. (*See* PLATE 29.)

Enemy Attempt to Recover Jerusalem, Dec. 26–27.

5. In the meantime, on XXth Corps front, only minor operations had taken place, resulting in the capture of various points of local tactical importance.

The preparations for the advance to the Beitin–Nalin line were hindered by the weather, heavy rain falling during the week before Christmas. As they were nearing completion, various movements and concentrations of troops on the part of the enemy indicated that he intended to attack, with the object of recovering Jerusalem.

This proved to be the case. On the night of Dec. 26–27, the enemy attacked with great determination astride the Jerusalem–Nablus road. A counter-attack against the right of his attack was carried out immediately by two divisions. As the result of three days' fighting, not only did the enemy's attempt to recapture Jerusalem fail, but by the end of the third day he found himself seven miles further from Jerusalem than when his attack started.

The enemy's attack was launched at 11.30 p.m. on **Dec. 26,** the advanced posts of the 60th Division, east of the Jerusalem road, being driven in. By 1.30 a.m. on **Dec. 27** the 60th Division was engaged along its whole front.

Between 1.30 a.m. and 8 a.m. the outposts of the 60th Division on the ridge north of Beit Hanninah repelled four determined attacks, but the heaviest fighting took place to the east of the Jerusalem–Nablus road. Repeated attacks were made against Tel el Ful; a conspicuous hill from which Jerusalem and the intervening ground can be overlooked. The attacks were made by picked bodies of troops, and were pressed with great determination. At only one point did the enemy succeed in reaching the main line of defence. He was driven out at once by the local reserves. In all these attacks he lost heavily.

In the meantime the enemy had delivered attacks against various points held by the 53rd Division east of Jerusalem. On the extreme right at Kh. Deir Ibn Obeid, a company of Middlesex troops was surrounded by 700 Turks, supported by mountain artillery. Although without artillery support, it offered a most gallant resistance, holding out till relief came on the morning of the 28th. None of the other attacks on this division's front were any more successful.

On the 60th Division front north of Jerusalem, a lull in the fighting occurred after 8 a.m. This lasted till 12.55 p.m., when the enemy launched an attack of unexpected strength against the whole front. In places this attack reached our main line of defence, but these small successes were short-lived, for in each case local counter-attacks, carried out immediately, were successful in restoring the line.

This proved to be the final effort.

At noon the counter-attack by the 74th and 10th Divisions, which had been launched at 6.30 a.m. against the right of the enemy's attack, had made itself felt.

The 74th Division, climbing the western slopes of the Zeitun Ridge, advanced along it in an easterly direction. On their left a brigade of the 10th Division advanced along the neighbouring ridge, the left of the 10th Division advancing in a northerly direction to form a defensive flank.

These divisions met with a determined and stubborn resistance. The ground over which the advance took place was sufficiently rough and broken to render the advance slow and difficult, quite apart from any action of the enemy. In addition, the boulders on the hills rendered it ideal ground in which to fight a delaying action, providing positions for machine guns, which are difficult to locate.

Nevertheless, when night fell the 74th Division had reached the east end of the Zeitun Ridge, opposite Beitunia. On their left the 10th Division overlooked Ain Arik, and further to the left were in possession of Deir Ibzia.

The counter-attack of these two divisions had thus not only resulted in an advance of 4,000 yards on a six-mile front, but, by attracting the enemy's reserves, had prevented the enemy from repeating his attacks on the 60th Division, and, depriving him of the initiative, had forced him to abandon his attempt to capture Jerusalem.

Advance into Mount Ephraim.

Seeing that the Turkish attack was spent I ordered the XXth Corps to make a general advance northwards on **Dec. 28.**

The enemy, after the failure of his attack on Dec. 27, was still holding his original position in front of the 60th Division. This position was of considerable strength, and included Khurbet Adaseh, a high ridge overlooking the approaches from Beit Haninah, while further west it included the villages of Bir Nebala and El Jib, the scene of heavy fighting at the end of November.

El Jib and Bir Nebala were captured by 1 p.m. Khurbet Adaseh was then attacked and captured by 5.30 p.m.

At 6.30 p.m. the advance was resumed and by 9.15 p.m. the 60th Division had reached the line Er Ram–Rafat. Considerable resistance was met with at Er Ram. The right of this advance was protected by the 53rd Division, which extended its left northwards, capturing the villages of Anata and Kh. Almit.

On the left the 74th Division, advancing from the east end of the Zeitun Ridge, captured Beitunia, which was defended with obstinacy, and seized the high ridge east and north of it. Further to the left, the right of the 10th Division, descending into the valley of the Ain Arik, climbed the opposite slopes and captured Kefr Shiyan hill, one mile east of Ain Arik, and the ridge between this hill and Kh. Rubin. Considerable opposition was encountered, and great difficulty was experienced in locating the enemy's machine guns.

The 60th Division continued its advance on **Dec. 29.** At the start no opposition was met with, the enemy having withdrawn to Bireh and the Et Tahuneh ridge just north of the village, leaving a garrison at Shab Salah, a precipitous hill 1,000 yards south of Bireh, overlooking the Jerusalem–Nablus road. As soon as the leading troops came within range of Bireh they were met with heavy rifle and machine-gun fire. Some delay was caused owing to the difficulty experienced in bringing the guns forward.

By 4.15 p.m. the left of the attack reached the Birfeh–Ram Allah road, and then stormed the Tahuneh ridge, the last position from which the enemy could observe the approaches to Bireh.

Simultaneously with this attack the right of the 60th Division had stormed Shab Saleh in face of heavy machine-gun fire, subsequently capturing the ridge east of Bireh.

At 9 p.m. the advance was continued to the line Beitin–El Balua–Kh. El Burj. Little opposition was encountered. On this day the 53rd Division extended its line northwards to protect the right of the 60th Division, occupying Hizmeh Jeba and the high ground north of it overlooking the Wadi el Medineh, with little opposition.

On the left the 74th Division occupied Ram Allah, and the 10th Division advanced without opposition to the line Khurbet Rubin–Ras Kerker–Deir el Kuddis.

The final line occupied by the XXth Corps thus ran from Deir Ibn Obeid, south-east of Jerusalem, northwards past Hizmeh and Jeba to Beitin, and thence westwards through El Burj, Ras Kerker, to Deir el Kuddis.

During these days the Royal Air Force not only gained valuable and timely information, but repeatedly attacked the enemy's troops and transport with bombs and machine-gun fire from low altitudes, inflicting considerable losses.

Results of the Four Days' Fighting.

The Turkish attempt to recapture Jerusalem had thus ended in crushing defeat. He had employed fresh troops who had not participated in the recent retreat of his army from Beersheba and Gaza and had escaped its demoralizing effects. The determination and gallantry with which his attack was carried out only served to increase his losses. The attack had commenced on the night Dec. 26–27. By the evening of Dec. 30, the XXth Corps had advanced on a front of twelve miles to a depth varying from six miles on the right to three miles on the left. This advance had to overcome not only a determined and obstinate resistance, but great natural difficulties as well, which had to be overcome before guns could be brought up to support the infantry.

Seven hundred and fifty prisoners, twenty-four machine guns, and three automatic rifles were captured during these operations, and over 1,000 Turkish dead were buried by us. Our own casualties were considerably less than this number.

As a result of this advance and of that of the XXIst Corps, my force was in a far better position to cover Jerusalem and the towns of Ramleh and Jaffa, and the road, which, running from Jaffa to Jerusalem, formed the chief artery of lateral communication behind my line. (*See* PLATE 30.)

Importance of the Jordan Bridges.

6. Any further advance northwards on my part was out of the question for the time being. Besides the construction of roads and the improvement of communications in the forward areas, stores of supplies and ammunition had to be accumulated. Until the railway had reached a point considerably nearer my front, this was of necessity a difficult task, and one rendered still more difficult by frequent spells of wet weather. Moreover, before a further advance could be made, it was necessary to drive the enemy across the River Jordan to render my right flank secure. (See PLATE 31.) The possession of the crossings over the Jordan offered other advantages. These were:—

(a) The enemy would be prevented from raiding the tract of country to the west of the Dead Sea.

(b) Control of the Dead Sea would be obtained.

(c) A point of departure would be gained for operations eastwards, with a view to interrupting the enemy's line of communication to the Hedjaz, in conjunction with the Arab forces based on Akaba.

7. Before the country around Jericho could be used as a base for operations against Amman, a further advance northwards was necessary to gain sufficient space to the north to render any interruption from that direction impossible.

I had intended to carry out this advance to the north simultaneously with the advance eastwards to the River Jordan. It, however, became apparent that, if this was to be carried into effect the operations against Jericho would have to be postponed for a considerable time to enable preparations for the advance northwards to be completed. I, therefore, decided to carry out the advance to the Jordan as a separate enterprise, the limits of the advance being the Jordan on the east and the Wadi el Auja on the north. This wadi joins the Jordan eight miles north of the point where the Jordan enters the Dead Sea.

For this operation the Australian and New Zealand Mounted Division, less the Mounted Brigade and the Divisional Artillery, was attached to the XXth Corps.

The 60th Division had taken over the line east of Jerusalem some time previously. Opposed to it were some 5,000 rifles, while to the north another 2,000 rifles were in a position from which to act against the left flank of the 60th Division as it advanced.

The chief obstacle to the advance lay in the difficulties of the ground rather than any opposition the enemy might offer.

The descent from the vicinity of Jerusalem to the valley of the Jordan is very steep. The beds of the main wadis run from west to east. Their banks are often precipitous, rendering any crossing from one bank to the other impossible. Numerous tributaries join the main wadis from all directions, breaking up the ridges into a tumbled mass of hills.

The descent to the Jordan Valley from the line then held by the 60th Division is not, however, continuous. It is interrupted by a series of ridges which afforded the enemy strong defensive positions.

Opposite the right of the 60th Division's line El Muntar formed a conspicuous landmark overlooking all the country in the vicinity: opposite the centre the high ground about Ras Umm Deisis and Arak Ibrahim afforded the enemy a strong position, while further north, on the left bank of the wadi es Suweinit, Ras el Tawil formed a dominating feature. After a further fall the ground rose again at Talaat ed Dumm. This rise continued in a south-easterly direction to Jebel Ekteif, thence eastwards to Neby Musa, descending from there to the Jordan Valley, five miles south of Jericho.

To the west of Jericho at Jebel Kuruntul the ground falls sharply in steep cliffs to the Jordan Valley.

The general plan consisted of a direct advance by the 60th Division to the cliffs overlooking Jericho. The Australian and New Zealand Mounted Division was to co-operate on the right flank with a view to entering the Jordan Valley near Neby Musa, thus cutting off the enemy's retreat from Jericho.

The Descent into the Jordan Valley.

The first step of the operation was carried out on **Feb. 19.** By 9 a.m. the 60th Division had captured El Muntar, Arak Ibrahim and Ras et Tawil, the 53rd Division extending its right to include Rummon, thence along the right bank of the Wadi el Asa, in touch with the left of the 60th Division. The greatest opposition was encountered on the left at Rummon by the 53rd Division, and in the vicinity of Ras et Tawil by the 60th Division.

The capture of El Muntar enabled the mounted troops to concentrate behind it, preparatory to operating against the enemy's left on the 20th.

On the left the 53rd Division was now in a position to command the Et Taiyibeh–Jericho road, along which any troops intended to act against the left of the 60th Division would move.

During the day further ground was secured by the 60th Division in face of considerable opposition, to cover the deployment for the attack on Feb. 20. (See PLATE 32.)

During the night of Feb. 19–20 the 60th Division moved into positions of deployment in the Wadi es Sidr. The covering troops of the centre brigade were attacked during the night, but the enemy was repulsed after a sharp struggle. On the morning of the **20th** the centre brigade captured Talat ed Dumm at 7.15 a.m., the enemy resisting with stubbornness. After a pause to enable guns to be brought forward, a further advance of 2,000 yards was made.

The right brigade, advancing on Jebel Ekteif, met with great opposition. Moreover, the ground over which the attack had to take place proved the most rugged and difficult yet met with in this country. Only one approach existed by which the assaulting waves could climb Jebel Ekteif, but by midday it had been stormed.

The left brigade, on the north of the Wadi Farah, advanced four miles, over difficult country, the enemy fighting a rearguard action from ridge to ridge.

Thus by the evening the 60th Division had reached a line running north from Jebel Ekteif, four miles west of the cliffs overlooking Jericho.

In the meantime the mounted troops on the right had encountered considerable opposition, and had been much hampered by the difficulties of the ground.

Two miles south of Neby Musa the enemy held the high ground at Jebel el Kalimum and Tubk el Kaneiterah. Compelled to move in single file over tracks which were exposed to machine-gun fire from the enemy's position, and which had been registered accurately by the enemy's guns at Neby Musa, the progress of the mounted troops was necessarily slow. By 2 p.m., however, the enemy was driven from his position at Jebel el Kalimum and Tubk el Kaneiterah. The further advance of the New Zealand Brigade on Neby Musa was hampered by the ground, and was finally checked at the Wadi Mukelik, the only possible crossing over which was subjected to a heavy fire from Neby Musa. On the right of the New Zealanders an Australian Mounted brigade discovered a crossing over the Wadi Kumran, and entering the Jordan plain reached the Wadi Jufet Zeben by dusk.

The chief feature of the enemy's resistance was the volume of machine-gun fire.

By 6 a.m. the New Zealanders and a battalion of the 60th Division reached Neby Musa, meeting with no opposition.

Occupation of Jericho, Feb. 21.

The Australian Mounted Brigade, advancing along the plain, entered Jericho at 8.20 a.m., the enemy having withdrawn during the night.

The 60th Division advanced to the line Rujm es Shema–Liyeh–Kh. Kakun–Jebel Karuntul, overlooking Jericho.

Meanwhile, patrols from the Australian Mounted Brigade reconnoitred as far as the Wadi el Aujah to the north and the El Ghoraniyeh bridge. The enemy was found to be holding the high ground north of the Aujah, and a bridgehead covering the El Ghoraniyeh bridge with guns on the left bank. (*See* PLATE 33.)

As a direct attack on the bridgehead would have involved heavy losses, without compensating advantages, it was not attempted. On the **22nd** the 60th Division withdrew to the line Jebel Ekteif–Talat ed Dumm–Ras et Tawil, leaving outposts on the cliffs overlooking Jericho. The Mounted Division, leaving one regiment to patrol the Jordan Valley, returning to Bethlehem.

During these operations four officers, 140 other ranks, and six machine guns were captured from the enemy.

On no previous occasions had such difficulties of ground been encountered. As an instance of this, a Field Artillery battery took thirty-six hours to reach Neby Musa, the distance covered, as the crow flies, being only eight miles.

The Royal Air Force rendered valuable service, but mist and low-lying clouds interrupted their work to a great extent.

Improving the Position.

8. This operation, by driving the enemy across the Jordan, had rendered my right flank secure, but the base thus obtained was not sufficiently broad to permit of operations being carried out east of the Jordan against the Hedjaz Railway.

Before any such operation could be undertaken it was essential in the first place to cross the Wadi Aujah and secure the high ground on the north bank covering the approaches to the Jordan Valley by the Beisan–Jericho road, and, secondly, by advancing sufficiently far northwards on either side of the Jerusalem–Nablus road, to deny to the enemy the use of all tracks and roads leading to the lower Jordan Valley. This accomplished, any troops he might determine to transfer from the west to the east bank of the Jordan would have to make a considerable detour to the north.

I therefore ordered the XXth Corps to secure Kh. el Beiyudat and Abu Tellul, in the Jordan Valley, north of the Wadi el Aujah, and further to the west the line Kefr Malik–Kh. Abu Felah, the high ground south of Sinjil, and the ridge north of the Wadi el Jib running through Kh. Aliuta–Jiljilia–Abwein–Arura, thence to Deir es Sudan and Nebi Saleh.

The watershed from which the wadis run, in the one direction to the River Jordan, in the other through the hills to the plain north of Ludd and thence to the sea, runs parallel to and some two miles east of the Jerusalem–Nablus road. The fall to the Jordan Valley is short and sharp, with the result that the beds of the wadis are deep and their sides almost precipitous. The country is so intricate that it cannot be crossed by large bodies of troops. Consequently, there was no danger in leaving a gap between the right of the XXth Corps at Kefr Malik and the detachment in the Jordan Valley at Abu Tellul.

To conform to the advance of the XXth Corps, I ordered the XXIst Corps to advance its right to include the ridge north of the Wadi Ballut, the village of Mejdel Yaba, a conspicuous landmark on a foothill overlooking the plain north of Ludd, Ras el Ain, an old Crusader stronghold on the railway from Ludd to Tul Keram, and El Mirr.

As a result of this advance the XXIst Corps would be placed in a better position for a further advance, should it decide to attack the defensive system constructed by the enemy from Jiljulieh westwards through Tabsor to the sea.

The two Corps were thus advancing on a front, from Kefr Malik to El Mirr, of twenty-six miles, to a maximum depth of seven miles.

The ground over which the advance was to take place is rugged and difficult. A succession of high and rocky ridges, separated by deep valleys, afforded the enemy a series of positions of great natural strength. The slopes of the ridges are in many places precipitous. Ledges of rock confine the descent to definite places, on which the enemy could concentrate his fire. In places the slopes are terraced, and men had to pull or hoist each other up.

It was necessary to reconnoitre each successive position held by the enemy, and the subsequent movement of troops into positions of assembly was of necessity a slow process.

Under these conditions no rapid advance could be looked for.

As soon as supplies and ammunition had been collected and preparations were complete, both Corps made a preliminary advance to enable a closer reconnaissance of the enemy's main positions to be made, and to allow of the construction of roads for the movement of guns and supplies.

By **March 8** the XXth Corps had reached the line En Nejmeh–Et Taiyibeh–Ain Sinia, on the Jerusalem–Nablus road, Hill 2,665 overlooking Bir ez Zeit–Beit Ello, the 53rd Division being on the right, the 74th Division in the centre astride the Jerusalem–Nablus road, and the 10th Division on the left.

On the right of the XXIst Corps the 75th Division had captured Abud and the ridge between the Wadis Barbara and Abud.

In neither case was any serious opposition encountered.

When the subsequent advance began the opposition stiffened considerably on the front of both Corps.

On **March 9** and 10 the XXth Corps had to drive the enemy from ridge after ridge before the final objectives were reached.

During the night of March 8–9, the brigades of the XXth Corps moved forward to their positions of assembly. On the extreme right, in the Jordan Valley, the brigade of the 60th Division entrusted with the task of capturing Kh. el Beiyudat and Abu Tellul experienced some difficulty in crossing the Wadi el Aujah in the dark, and subsequently met with determined resistance. By 3 p.m., however, Kh. el Beiyudat and Abu Tellul had been captured. The occupation of a position astride the Beisan–Jericho road completed this operation. Further west the 53rd, 74th and 10th Divisions had advanced by the evening to a depth varying between 3,000 and 7,000 yards, and had reached a line running east and west through Tell Asur, thence along the ridges overlooking the Wadis En Nimr and El Jib. The 53rd Division on the right had met with considerable opposition and great natural difficulties, especially on the extreme right and at Tell Asur, a conspicuous landmark among a mass of high hills. The importance attached to Tell Asur by the enemy was shown by the number of determined efforts he made to recapture it, all of which were repulsed.

On **March 10** both the enemy's resistance and the difficulties of the ground increased, but during the day and the early hours of the night of March 10–11, an advance of 3,000 yards was made on a front of twelve miles. The line reached ran from Kefr Malik, along the ridge overlooking the Wadi el Kola and the Burj el Kisaneh ridge, past Kh. el Sahlat, Kh. Aliuta, Jiljilia, Abwein, and Arura to its former position at Deir es Sudan and Neby Saleh.

The enemy contested the ridges north of the Wadis en Nirm and El Jib with great obstinacy, while on the extreme left near Neby Saleh he counter-attacked the left of the 10th Division on several occasions. The descent of the slopes leading down to the Wadis en Nimr and El Jib and the ascent on the far side presented great difficulties. The downward slopes were exceptionally steep, almost precipitous in places. It was impossible for companies and platoons to move on a wide front. The slopes were swept by machine-gun and rifle fire and the bottom of the wadis by enfilade fire. The ascent on the far side was steeply terraced. Men had alternately to hoist and pull each other up, under fire, and finally to expel the enemy from the summits in hand-to-hand fighting.

On **March 11** the operation of the XXth Corps was completed by the occupation of Kh. Abu Felah and the heights overlooking Sinjil and the comparatively low-lying country to the north-east. The result of this operation was the capture of a line with great natural facilities for defence, and of eleven officers, 160 other ranks, eleven machine guns and considerable amounts of ammunition and other booty.

The second phase of the operation by the XXIst Corps, the preliminary phase having taken place on March 7, was carried out on **March 12.**

At first the opposition encountered was not serious, but from the time the 75th Division reached the ridge overlooking the Wadi Ballut it stiffened, the enemy contesting the ridge on the far side of the wadi stubbornly, and when driven off making several counter-attacks to regain it. At Benat Burry, a razor-edged ridge north of Kh. Balatah, the top of the ridge is honeycombed with caves and entrances on both sides. Considerable difficulty was experienced in overcoming the enemy's resistance here. Eventually, however, a platoon of Gurkhas worked round to the rear of the ridge. A Lewis gun was brought to bear on the exits. The garrison of the caves, numbering five officers and fifty other ranks, then surrendered.

On the left of the 75th Division the 54th Division captured the villages of El Mezeireh, Kh. Dikerin and Mejdel Yaba in the foothills, and Ras el Ain and El Mirr in the plain. Seven officers, 105 other ranks, and two machine guns were taken by these two divisions.

Sherifian Operations in Moab during January.

9. The Jordan Valley had now been sufficiently cleared of the enemy to enable operations to be carried out against the Turkish line of communication to the Hedjaz, in conjunction with the Arab forces under Sherif Feisal, which were operating in the country to the south-east of the Dead Sea and were under my control.

Sherif Feisal's forces were based on Akaba. In Jan. 1918, he had captured the high ground about Uheida, within seven miles of Maan, his main objective. At the same time a force under Sherif Abdul Magin had occupied the whole of the Hish Forest up to and including Shobek, twenty miles north by west of Maan, destroying thirty-five kilometres of the enemy's light railway which left the main line at Kalaat Aneiza and was used to transport wood as fuel for locomotives. After the capture of Shobek a force under Sherif Nazir raided Jauf ed Derwish, a station on the main line thirty miles north of Maan. This they held for three days, burning the station buildings and destroying two locomotives and some rolling stock. In this successful raid the Turkish losses amounted to over 100 killed, over 200 prisoners, a mountain gun and two machine guns. Further north a separate force of Arab tribesmen under Sherif Nazir captured Tafile, fifteen miles south-east of the south end of the Dead Sea, on Jan. 16. The garrison, which consisted of 100 Turks and the officials of the place, surrendered after a short resistance. Ten days later a Turkish force, consisting of three battalions, with two mountain guns and twenty-seven machine guns, advanced from Kerak to recapture Tafile. An engagement took place on Jan. 26, in which the enemy suffered a crushing defeat. His losses amounted to over 450 in killed and 250 in prisoners. In addition, the whole of his artillery and machine guns fell into the hands of the Arabs. In March the Turks concentrated a considerable force, including a battalion of German infantry, and, advancing from Kutrani and Jauf ed Derwish, re-occupied Tafile, the Arab tribesmen, in face of superior numbers, withdrawing to positions north of Shobek.

The situation to the east of the Jordan thus presented a favourable opportunity for a raid on the enemy's communications with the Hedjaz.

Importance of Amman.

Its immediate effect would be to compel the enemy to recall the force which had recently occupied Tafile. It might, in addition, compel the enemy to call on the garrison of Maan for support. If this should prove to be the case, Sherif Feisal would be afforded his opportunity to attack Maan with some prospects of success. The extent of this opportunity would depend on the amount of damage done to the Hedjaz Railway. Near Amman, the railway crosses a viaduct and passes through a tunnel. If these could be destroyed it would be some weeks before traffic could be resumed. I determined therefore to carry out a raid on Amman, with the object of destroying the viaduct and tunnel and, if this should be found impossible, to damage the railway as much as possible. Even if traffic was only interrupted for a short time, the mere threat of a repetition of this raid would compel the enemy to maintain a considerable force to cover Amman. The troops available to operate against the Arabs would be reduced, and possibly the enemy might transfer a portion of his reserves from the west to the east of the Jordan, thereby weakening his power to make or meet any attack on the main front.

Amman is thirty miles east by north of Jericho as the crow flies. The nature of the intervening country varies to a marked degree. From the banks of the Jordan to the clay ridges, a mile east of the river, the ground is flat, and after rain becomes marshy. Beyond the ridges the country is covered with scrub and intersected by numerous wadis. For the first five miles the total rise is only 500 feet. In the next twelve miles the ground rises some 3,500 feet till the edge of the plateau of Moab is reached. The hills are rugged and steep. The main wadis descend from the plateau to the Jordan in deep valleys. The plateau itself is undulating, the lower portions of it marshy after rain. The hills which rise from it are rocky and covered with scrub. They are isolated features, and only form continuous ridges immediately west of Amman, which lies in a cultivated plain, extending some two miles west and four miles north-west of the town. This plain, which is the site of many ruins, is intersected by numerous deep wadis difficult to cross—especially the Wadi Amman, which runs from south to north, leaving the town of Amman on its right.

The Turks had constructed a metalled road from Ghoraniyeh bridge to Es Salt and Amman. Following the Wadi Nimrin, it enters the hills at Shunet Nimrin and winds round the slopes of the valley of the Wadi Shaib, supported by embankments, in places twenty feet high. At Es Salt, a town of some 15,000 inhabitants, eighteen miles from Ghoraniyeh by road, it is joined by tracks leading from the fords over the Jordan at Umm es Shert and Jisr ed Damieh, and from Jerash to the north. On leaving Es Salt the road runs in a northerly direction for two miles, and then turns east, reaching the edge of the plateau five miles further on. This is the only road, and is in bad repair. Various tracks follow the wadis to the plateau, but are unfit for wheeled transport. One leaves the main road at Shunet Nimrin, and follows the Wadis Jeria and Sir, passing the village of Ain es Sir. Another leads from Ghoraniyeh and Makhadet Hajlah up the Wadi el Kefrein to Naaur, where it joins the main route from Madeba to Amman.

The Amman Raid, March 21–April 2.

11. The force detailed to carry out the raid consisted of the 60th (London) Division, the Australian and New Zealand Mounted Division, the Imperial Camel Brigade, a Mountain Artillery Brigade, the Light Armoured Car Brigade, and a heavy battery. This force was placed under the command of the General Officer Commanding 60th Division. The 60th Division was to force the crossings over the Jordan and advance astride the metalled road to Es Salt, which it was to hold, its left flank being protected by a mounted brigade. The mounted troops and the Camel Brigade, following the 60th Division across the Jordan, were to move direct on Amman by the tracks passing through Ain es Sir and Naaur. On reaching Amman the railway was to be destroyed and the viaduct and tunnel demolished. This having been accomplished, the mounted troops were to withdraw on the 60th Division, the whole force then withdrawing to bridgeheads at the Jordan.

The operations, which started during the night of **March 21–22,** were hampered considerably by rain, which fell during the days preceding the raid and on March 27 and the three following days. The Jordan is unfordable at this time of the year. The current is at all times rapid, and is liable to sudden floods which render the banks boggy and difficult of approach for transport. On March 28 it rose nine feet. The rain which fell during the operations rendered the tracks in the hills slippery and the movement of horses, and especially of camels, slow and difficult. The delay thus caused enabled the enemy to bring up reinforcements. Before Amman could be attacked in strength some 4,000 Turks supported by fifteen guns were in position near Amman, covering the viaduct and tunnel, while another 2,000 were moving on Es Salt from the north. To have driven the enemy from his position, without adequate artillery support, would have entailed very heavy losses. Owing to the marshy nature of the country it was only possible to bring up mountain artillery, and I therefore ordered a withdrawal, which was carried out without serious interruption. Although it had not been possible to effect any permanent demolitions, five miles of railway line, including several large culverts, and the points and crossings at Alanda station, were destroyed to the south of Amman, while to the north of the town a two-arch bridge was blown up.

Considerable losses were inflicted on the enemy, and in addition fifty-three officers and over 900 other ranks were taken prisoner, including several Germans.

The raid also enabled a considerable number of Armenians to escape and find a refuge west of the Jordan.

The Passage of the Jordan, March 22–April 2.

12. The crossing of the Jordan took place during the night of March 21–22. (*See* PLATE 34.)

The crossing was to have been effected by a brigade of the 60th Division at Ghoraniyeh and Makhadet Hajlah. This brigade was then to cover the construction of bridges, the 60th Division crossing at the former, the mounted troops at the latter place. The attempt to cross at Ghoraniyeh failed owing to the strength of the current, which prevented all attempts to cross both by swimming and by means of rafts and pontoons.

At Hajlah, however, the swimmers succeeded in reaching the opposite bank at 1.20 a.m., and by 7.45 a.m. the leading battalion was across. Till dawn this crossing was unperceived by the enemy, but subsequently the troops had to be ferried across, and a bridge constructed under fire. The bridge was completed by 8.30 a.m. Further troops crossed, but it was found impossible to enlarge the bridgehead till dark, owing to the enemy's fire and the thickness of the scrub.

A further attempt to cross at Ghoraniyeh during the night of the **22nd-23rd** was again frustrated by the current and the enemy's fire. Early in the morning, however, a New Zealand regiment crossed at Hajlah, and, galloping northwards, drove back the enemy and formed a bridgehead at Ghoraniyeh. The current having diminished, three bridges were constructed during the day, and by 10 a.m. the whole of the infantry of the 60th Division and the greater part of the mounted troops were east of the Jordan, but owing to the swollen state of the river much valuable time had been lost.

Shunet Nimrin and Es Salt.

On **March 24** the 60th Division attacked the enemy and drove him from his position at El Haud and Shunet Nimrin, covering the entrance to the pass leading to Es Salt. Three guns were captured by a battalion of the London Regiment, the teams being shot down by the fire of the Lewis guns. Following on the heels of the retreating enemy, the 60th Division advanced four miles along the road to Es Salt, which was occupied the following evening without opposition.

In the meantime the mounted troops, followed by the Camel Brigade, made their way along the tracks towards Ain es Sir and Naaur. Early in the day all wheeled transport had to be sent back. Even so, the tracks had been rendered so slippery by rain, which fell continuously on the 25th, that progress was slow. In many places horses had to move in single file, and had to be pulled or pushed up the slippery slopes.

Naaur was reached late in the evening of **March 25.**

The rain continued to fall on **March 26.** At 5 a.m. the New Zealand and Australian Brigades met at Ain es Sir. The Australians moved on to Suweileh, north of the Es Salt–Amman road, capturing 170 Turks there. Both men and horses were, however, too exhausted by their exertions to admit of more than demolition parties being sent on to the railway.

On **March 27** the advance was resumed. The ground favoured the enemy, the rocks and scrub on the hills affording excellent cover to his riflemen. The wadis could only be crossed at a few places, and then only in single file.

Destruction of Railway near Amman.

By evening the New Zealanders had reached the railway south of Amman, their demolition parties working southwards. In the centre the Camel Brigade advanced direct on Amman, but were checked some 1,500 yards west of Amman village. On the left the Australians were unable to reach the railway north of Amman, being heavily counter-attacked; but during the night a demolition party succeeded in blowing up a small bridge seven miles north of Amman.

On March 28 a brigade of the 60th Division arrived from Es Salt accompanied by mountain artillery. The road was too soft to admit of field guns being brought. In fact, twenty-two Turkish motor-lorries and other vehicles found along the road were so embedded in the mud that they had to be destroyed. On its arrival this brigade attacked along the Es Salt–Amman road, the Australians attacking on its left, the Camel Brigade on its right, while the New Zealanders attacked Hill 3,039 just south of Amman.

Enemy Counter-Attacks.

Little progress was made. The enemy made several counter-attacks, especially against the Australians, who were forced back a short distance.

On **March 29** Turkish reinforcements arrived, and the counter-attacks were renewed, but without success. (*See* PLATE 35.)

During the afternoon two more battalions of the 60th Division and a battery of Royal Horse Artillery arrived after a long and arduous march.

The attack on Amman was renewed at 2 a.m. on **March 30.** The New Zealanders captured a portion of Hill 3,039, but were unable to drive the enemy from the northern and eastern ends. Parties of New Zealanders entered the village, but were fired on from the houses. Elsewhere the attack met with only slight success. It was apparent that without greater artillery support further attacks could only succeed at the cost of heavy losses. Moreover, Turkish troops from Jisr ed Damieh and from the north had begun to make their presence felt at Es Salt. Orders were therefore issued for a withdrawal to take place during the night. This was carried out without interruption, after all the wounded had been evacuated.

By the evening of **April 2** the whole force had recrossed the Jordan, with the exception of the troops left to hold the bridgehead on the east bank. (*See* PLATE 36.)

Results of the Raid.

Although no permanent damage had been done to the Hedjaz Railway, the raid had succeeded in drawing northwards and retaining not only the Turkish troops which had been operating against the Arabs, but in addition a portion of the garrison of Maan and the stations further south.

Before the raid was carried out the enemy's strength in the Amman–Es Salt–Shunet Nimrin area was approximately 4,000. By the middle of April it had increased to over 8,000.

13. Taking advantage of this opportunity, Sherif Feisal commenced operations against Maan. The railway was first cut both north and south of Maan at Ghadir el Haj and Jerdun. At these places 270 Turks and three machine guns were captured. On **April 13,** Senna, a Turkish post 4,000 yards south-west of Maan Station, was captured, and on April 17 the station was entered and 100 prisoners made, but the attack was unable to make any impression on the strong Turkish position 400 yards north of the station. This position was of considerable strength, and was provided with concrete machine-gun emplacements. The Arabs then withdrew to a strong position at Senna to await the arrival of further ammunition for their artillery.

In the meantime another column attacked the line between Batn el Ghul and Kalaat et Mudawara, seventy kilometres south of Maan, and destroyed 100 kilometres of line so effectively that at least a month's uninterrupted work will be required to repair it, and then only if large gangs of labourers are available. The damage to the railway north of Maan was not so thorough, but was sufficient to prevent through traffic for several days.

Enemy Attack on Ghoraniyeh Bridgehead.

14. After the troops employed in the last raid had been withdrawn to the west bank of the Jordan, the enemy reoccupied the Shunet Nimrin position, which he held with some 5,000 rifles.

On **April 11** he made simultaneous attacks on the Ghoraniyeh bridgehead and on El Musallabeh, which covers the Beisan–Jericho road west of the Jordan. Both attacks were pressed with considerable determination, but brought him no success, and during the night April 11–12 he withdrew to his positions at Shunet Nimrin, which he commenced to strengthen. His losses in these attacks were heavy. He left three officers and 113 other ranks in our hands as prisoners, while some 500 dead were buried by us or seen to be buried by the enemy.

I determined to seize the first opportunity to cut off and destroy the enemy's force at Shunet Nimrin, and, if successful, to hold Es Salt till the Arabs could advance and relieve my troops. This would have denied the enemy the use of the harvest. I had intended to carry out this operation about the middle of May, when the reorganization of the 1st Mounted Division had been completed. In the meantime, however, a deputation from the Beni Sakhr tribe arrived stating that the tribe was concentrated near Madeba, ready to co-operate with any advance I might make, provided it took place before May 4, after which date their supplies would be finished and the tribe would have to disperse.

The troops available to carry out this raid were the Desert Mounted Corps, less the 1st Mounted Division, the 60th Division, less one brigade, and the Imperial Service Cavalry and Infantry Brigades.

The 60th Division was to attack the enemy's position at Shunet Nimrin, whilst the Mounted Troops, moving northwards from Ghoraniyeh, were to turn east along the tracks leading from Umm es Shert and Jisr ed Damieh, and protect the left flank.

In the former raid the only route found fit for wheeled transport between Amman and Shunet Nimrin had been the metalled road passing through Es Salt. The arrival of the mounted troops at Es Salt would thus sever the main line of communication of the force at Shunet Bimrin, who would be dependent for their supplies on the track further south through Ain es Sir. This track was exposed to attack by the Beni Sakhr tribe.

There appeared every chance therefore of the Turkish force at Shunet Nimrin being compelled to retreat under very difficult conditions, and a fair chance of its being captured.

The Es Salt Raid, April 30–May 4.

The operations were commenced early on the morning of **April 30,** and proceeded according to plan.

The 60th Division captured the advanced works of the Shunet Nimrin position, but were unable to make further progress in face of the stubborn resistance offered by the enemy. (*See* PLATE 37.)

The mounted troops, moving northwards, rode round the right of the Shunet Nimrin position, and by 6 p.m. had captured Es Salt, leaving an Australian Brigade to watch the left flank.

This brigade took up a position facing north-west astride the Jisr ed Damieh–Es Salt track, with patrols watching the Wadi ez Zerka, and with a detachment on the high ground on the east bank of the Jordan, two miles north of Umm es Shert.

At 7.30 a.m. on **May 1** this brigade was attacked by the 3rd Turkish Cavalry Division, and a part of the 24th Division, which had crossed from the west bank of the Jordan during the night at Jisr ed Damieh. The enemy succeeded in penetrating between the left of the brigade and the detachment on the bank of the Jordan. The brigade was driven back through the foothills to the Wadi el Abyad. During its retirement through the hills nine guns and part of its transport had to be abandoned, being unable to traverse the intricate ground.

The Umm es Shert–Es Salt track was thus the only line of supply or retreat left to the mounted troops in Es Salt, till the main road and the Wadi Arseniyet track could be opened by the capture of the Shunet Nimrin position and El Haud. (*See* PLATE 38.)

Arrangements were made for a combined attack to take place on this position on May 2. The 60th Division was to attack from the west and the mounted troops at Es Salt from the north-east.

On **May 2** the mounted troops in Es Salt were attacked by two Turkish battalions which had arrived from Amman accompanied by heavy guns, as well as by cavalry from the north, and troops from Jisr ed Damieh. These attacks were driven off, but the force intended to attack Shunet Nimrin from the north-east had to be weakened and was checked at El Howeij, five miles south of Es Salt. The 60th Division was also unable to make any substantial progress, in spite of determined efforts.

Inactivity of the Beni Sakhr.

As the assistance of the Beni Sakhr tribe had not materialized, the Ain es Sir track was still open to the garrison of Shunet Nimrin. Further Turkish reinforcements were known to be on their way. It was evident that the Shunet Nimrin position could not be captured without losses, which I was not in a position to afford. In these circumstances I ordered the mounted troops to withdraw from Es Salt. Their retirement was accomplished successfully. The enemy, who followed up closely, was held off without difficulty. By the evening of **May 4** all the troops had recrossed the Jordan, bridgeheads being left to cover the bridges at Ghoraniyeh and the crossing at El Auja.

Although the destruction of the Turkish force at Shunet Nimrin had not been effected, the enemy's losses were considerable, the prisoners brought in amounting to fifty officers and 892 other ranks; twenty-nine machine guns and several motor cars and lorries were destroyed by the mounted troops before they left Es Salt.

The raid has undoubtedly rendered the enemy apprehensive of further operations east of the Jordan, and has compelled him to maintain considerable forces in the Amman–Shunet Nimrin area, reducing the forces available to meet the Arab menace.

Despatch of Troops to France.

15. The despatch of troops to France, and the reorganization of the force, has prevented further operations, of any size, being undertaken, and has rendered the adoption of a policy of active defence necessary. During the first week in April the 52nd Division embarked for France, its place being taken by the 7th (Meerut) Division which had arrived from Mesopotamia.

The departure of the 52nd Division was followed by that of the 74th Division, which left Palestine during the second week in April. The 3rd (Lahore) Division was sent from Mesopotamia to replace the 74th Division, but it was not till the middle of June that the last units disembarked. In addition to the 52nd and 74th Divisions, nine Yeomanry regiments, five and a half siege batteries, ten British battalions, and five machine gun companies were withdrawn from the line, preparatory to embarkation for France. (*a*)

By the end of April the Yeomanry regiments had been replaced by Indian Cavalry regiments, which had arrived from France, and the British battalions by Indian battalions despatched from India. These Indian battalions had not, however, seen service during the present war; and, naturally, had not the experience of the battalions they replaced.

(*a*) *See* footnote on following page.

Thus in April the strength of the force had been reduced by one division, five and a half siege batteries and five machine-gun companies; while one mounted division was in process of being reorganized, and was not available for operations.

In May a further fourteen battalions of British infantry were withdrawn and despatched to France. (a) Only two Indian battalions were available to replace them. Thus at the end of May the force had been further reduced by twelve battalions, while the loss of the 74th Division had not yet been fully made good. On the other hand, the reorganization of the mounted division had been completed.

In June the places of the British battalions which had been despatched to France were filled by Indian battalions. Six of the Indian battalions had, however, been formed by withdrawing a company from twenty-four of the Indian battalions already in the Force. As few reinforcements were available for the battalions thus depleted, the Force had been completed in name only.

During July and the first week in August a further ten British battalions were replaced by ten Indian battalions, the personnel of the British battalions being used as reinforcements. (b)

16. During these months of reorganization various minor operations and a number of raids have been carried out.

Advance in the Coastal Sector.

Between April 9 and 11, the right of the line held by the XXIst Corps was advanced on a front of twelve miles, to a maximum depth of three miles; the villages of Kefr Ain, Berukin, El Kefr and Rafat being captured. Considerable resistance was met with, the Turkish troops being stiffened by a German battalion. The enemy made several attempts to recapture Berukin and Rafat. His counter-attacks were broken up by the infantry, ably supported by the artillery, but, in some cases, only after sharp hand-to-hand fighting. The enemy's losses were considerable, over 300 of his dead being counted.

On **June 8** an advance was made on the coast, at the extreme left of my line, with the object of depriving the enemy of observation. The enemy's positions were captured by two battalions—the Black Watch and the Guides. Two counter-attacks were made. In the first the enemy succeeded in reoccupying a portion of the position, but he was expelled. The second counter-attack broke down before it reached our new position. The enemy's losses were considerable, and four officers and 101 other ranks were captured. The capture of these positions not only prevented the enemy from overlooking a considerable length of our defences and the ground in rear, but secured observation of the approaches to the enemy's positions, with the result that his movements, by day, have been considerably restricted.

Successful Indian Raids.

The Indian troops have carried out a number of minor raids with success. On **July 13** a party of the Guides surprised the enemy in his trenches in the middle of the day, bringing back fifteen prisoners and a machine gun. On **July 27** a Pathan company of the 53rd Sikhs F.F. inflicted heavy casualties on the enemy, and brought in thirty-three prisoners and two machine guns.

A raid on a larger scale, carried out on **Aug. 12** by the Leinster Regiment, 54th Sikhs, and 1st Battalion, 101st Grenadiers, was crowned with complete success. The objective was the enemy's defences on the El Burj-Ghurabeh ridge, north-west of Sinjil. This ridge is some 5,000 yards in length, and lies 2,000 yards in front of our line. It was held by 800 rifles and thirty-six machine guns. The defences consisted of strongly-built sangars, protected by thick wire entanglements. The approaches to it are rocky and broken, involving a climb of 900 feet. The position was attacked from both flanks. The enemy was surprised. His losses were heavy, and the raiders brought back 239 prisoners, including a battalion commander and sixteen officers and thirteen machine guns. Great dash was shown by all the troops taking part in it.

In the Jordan Valley the mounted troops have carried out successful raids, and have ambushed a number of hostile patrols. The Indian cavalry have used the lance with good effect on several occasions.

(a) TRANSFERRED.
    Yeomanry.—1/1st Warwicks, South Notts Hussars, 1/1st Bucks., 1/1st Berks., 1/1st Lincs., 1/1st City of London, 1/2nd and 1/3rd County of London, 1/1st East Ridings.
    Siege Batteries.—201st, 292nd, 320th, 322th, 423rd, and 445th.
    Infantry Battalions.—2/4th R. West Surreys, 1/5th Devons, 2/4th Somerset L. I., 1/4th and 1/7th Cheshires, 5th and 6th R. Inniskilling Fusiliers, 1/4th R. Sussex, 2/4th Hampshires, 2nd Loyal North Lancs., 5th R. Irish Fusiliers, 5th Connaught Rangers, 6th Leinsters, 6th R. Munster Fusiliers, 6th and 7th R. Dublin Fusiliers, 2/14, 2/15, 2/16, 2/20, 2/23rd, and 2/24th Londons, 1/1st Herefords.
    Machine Gun Companies.—Nos. 221, 262, 264, 271, and 272.

(b) DISBANDED.
    Infantry Battalions.—2/4th Devons, 1/5th and 1/6th R. Welsh Fusiliers (amalgamated as 5/6th R. Welsh Fusiliers), 2/5th Hampshires, 2/4th Dorsets, 1/4th and 1/5th Welsh (amalgamated as 4/5th Welsh), 2/4th R. West Kents, 2/10th Middlesex, 6th R. Irish Rifles, 2/18th and 2/21st Londons.

17. This activity on our part has not been imitated by the enemy, except in one instance. Then the brunt of the fighting fell on German troops. Early in July movements of troops, and increased artillery and aeroplane activity, foreshadowed an attack on our defences in the Jordan Valley.

On the right bank of the Jordan our defences form a marked salient. The eastern side of the salient faces the ford at Umm esh Shert. The apex is at El Musallabeh, while the western face runs across the north-west slopes of Abu Tellul.

Abu Tellul.

Early on the morning of **July 14** the enemy was seen to be concentrating in the deep wadis north-west of Abu Tellul. At 3.30 a.m. the attack began. The enemy penetrated between the advanced posts and seized Abu Tellul, thus cutting off the posts further north at El Musallabeh. At 4.30 a.m. the 1st Australian Light Horse Brigade counter-attacked. By 5 a.m. Abu Tellul had been regained. The enemy, driven against our advanced posts, which, with one exception, had held their ground, suffered heavily. Two hundred and seventy-six Germans, including twelve officers, and sixty-two Turks were captured, in addition to six machine guns and forty-two automatic rifles. One hundred wounded and many dead were left on the ground. Great credit is due to the Australians for the quickness of their counter-attack and for the determination displayed by the garrisons of the advanced posts in holding out, although surrounded.

El Henu Ford.

While this fighting was in progress a Turkish force of considerable strength was observed to be concentrating to the east of the Jordan, opposite El Henu Ford, which is midway between the El Ghoraniyeh bridgehead and the Dead Sea. A cavalry brigade moved out to counter-attack. Taking advantage of the ground, the cavalry arrived within charging distance before they were observed. In the charge that ensued some ninety Turks were speared; and ninety-one, including six officers, in addition to four machine guns, were captured. It was only by reaching ground impassable for cavalry that the remainder of the Turks effected their escape. The Jodhpur Lancers played a distinguished part in this charge.

The enemy's attack on both banks of the Jordan thus failed ignominiously. His losses, especially those of the German troops, were heavy, and it is probable that the German units which took part will need a long rest before being ready for active operations again. Our casualties were comparatively light.

18. Since April no events of any importance have taken place in the Hedjaz. The Turks have been unable to restore through railway communication between Maan and the north. South of Maan a detachment of the Imperial Camel Corps attacked and captured the station at Kalaat el Mudawara, destroying the water tower and pumps. Thirty-five Turks were killed, six officers and 146 other ranks, two guns and three machine guns were captured.

As a result of this operation, no water supply now exists on the railway for a distance of 150 kilometres south of Maan. Medina has thus been definitely cut off from the north.

Summary of the Operations.

19. The operations, which took place during the first half of the period covered by this despatch, rendered secure the fruits of the fighting, which, commencing with the capture of Beersheba, culminated in the occupation of Jerusalem.

On Dec. 12 the enemy still remained within four miles of Jerusalem. He is now twenty-two miles from the Holy City. (*See* PLATE 39.) To the east he has been driven across the Jordan, and his communications to the Hedjaz raided. His losses between Dec. 12, 1917, and May 31, 1918, were considerable, the number of prisoners amounting to 331 officers and 6,088 other ranks. His one attempt on a large scale to assume the offensive and retake Jerusalem failed, and was turned into a defeat, accompanied by a considerable loss of territory.

In driving back the enemy my troops suffered considerable hardships. The rugged country in which the majority of the fighting took place not only favoured the defence, but demanded great physical exertion on the part of the attackers. In the early months of the year their task was often rendered more difficult by the cold and heavy rains which added greatly to their discomfort. They responded to every call made on them, and proved their superiority over the enemy on every occasion. The second half of the period under review has been spent in reorganization and in training. Although operations have been limited to raids, sixty-nine officers and 1,614 other ranks have been taken from the enemy since June 1.

20. Throughout the whole period, the work of the Royal Air Force has been of great value. Fifty-three hostile aeroplanes have been destroyed, in addition to twenty-three which have been driven down out of control. The enemy's troops, camps, and railways, have been bombed with good results, while very important photographic work has been carried out. Co-operation with the other arms has been excellent.

21. During the early months of the year, whilst the rainy season was still in progress, and before railhead had reached the troops, the supply situation presented great difficulties. The wadis came down in spate, overflowing their banks and flooding the surrounding country. Not only was railway construction hindered, but the country became almost impassable for motor, and extremely difficult for horse transport. Nevertheless, all difficulties were overcome.

The Assistance of Egypt.

22. I am indebted to His Excellency General Sir Francis Wingate, G.C.B., G.C.V.O., K.C.M.G., D.S.O., High Commissioner for Egypt, for the cordial assistance he has given me at all times.

Egypt has provided transport personnel, drivers for the Camel Transport Corps, and men for the Egyptian Labour Corps in large numbers, in addition to several units of the Egyptian Army. These have all done work which, though unostentatious, has been of great value. During the operations in the hills of Judæa, and of Moab, the troops often depended for their supplies on the Camel Transport Corps. The drivers displayed steadiness under fire and devotion to duty in the face of cold and rain, which they had never experienced previously. The Egyptian Labour Corps shared these hardships. The construction and maintenance of roads was a task of considerable importance and difficulty during the rainy season, and threw a great strain on the Egyptian Labour Corps. Its successful accomplishment reflects credit on the Corps. The Egyptian authorities have complied at once with all requests that I have made, and my thanks are due to them for their loyal support.

23. The Army Postal Service has carried out its work efficiently. During the early months of the year, when my troops were far in advance of railhead, the delivery and collection of mails was a matter of considerable difficulty, which was invariably overcome.

24. Throughout the period I have received every help from Rear-Admiral T. Jackson, C.B., M.V.O.

I have the honour to be,
Your Lordship's most obedient servant,

E. H. H. ALLENBY,
General,

Commanding-in-Chief,
Egyptian Expeditionary Force.

General Headquarters,
Egyptian Expeditionary Force,
October 31, 1918.

MY LORD,

I have the honour to forward a despatch describing the operations which, commencing on Sept. 19, resulted in the destruction of the enemy's army, the liberation of Palestine and Syria, and the occupation of Damascus and Aleppo.

1. The latter months of the period covered by my despatch of Sept. 18, 1918, had been spent in the reorganization of my force. The last Indian battalions to arrive had been incorporated in divisions early in August. Some of these battalions had only been formed a few months, and I should have liked to have given them further opportunities to accustom themselves to the conditions prevailing on this front, before calling on them to play a part in arduous operations on a large scale. The rains, however, usually commence at the end of October, rendering the plains of Sharon and Esdraelon impassable for transport, except along the few existing roads. Consequently, operations could not be postponed beyond the middle of September.

Strength of the Enemy.

2. At the beginning of September I estimated the strength of the IVth, VIIth, and VIIIth Turkish Armies to be 23,000 rifles, 3,000 sabres, and 340 guns. The IVth Army—6,000 rifles, 2,000 sabres, and seventy-four guns—faced my forces in the Jordan Valley. The VIIth Army held a front of some twenty miles astride the Jerusalem–Nablus road with 7,000 rifles and 111 guns, while the VIIIth Army front extended from Furkhah to the sea, and was held by 10,000 rifles and 157 guns.

In addition, the garrison of Maan and the posts on the Hejaz Railway north of it, consisted of some 6,000 rifles and thirty guns.

The enemy's general reserve, only 3,000 rifles in strength, with thirty guns, was distributed between Tiberias, Nazareth, and Haifa.

Thus, his total strength amounted to some 4,000 sabres, 32,000 rifles, and 400 guns—representing a ration strength, south of the line Rayak–Beirut, of 104,000.

3. I had at my disposal two cavalry divisions, two mounted divisions, seven infantry divisions, and Indian infantry brigade, four unallotted battalions, and the French detachment (the equivalent of an infantry brigade with other arms attached); a total, in the fighting line, of some 12,000 sabres, 57,000 rifles, and 540 guns.

I had thus a considerable superiority in numbers over the enemy, especially in mounted troops.

4. I was anxious to gain touch with the Arab Forces east of the Dead Sea, but the experience, gained in the raids which I had undertaken against Amman and Es Salt in March and May, had proved that the communications of a force in the hills of Moab were liable to interruption, as long as the enemy was able to transfer troops from the west to the east bank of the Jordan. This he was in a position to do, as he controlled the crossing at Jisr ed Damieh.

The defeat of the VIIth and VIIIth Turkish Armies, west of the Jordan, would enable me to control this crossing. Moreover, the destruction of these armies, which appeared to be within the bounds of possibility, would leave the IVth Army isolated, if it continued to occupy the country south and west of Amman. I determined, therefore, to strike my blow west of the Jordan.

5. With the exception of a small and scattered reserve, the whole of the Turkish Force west of the Jordan was enclosed in a rectangle forty-five miles in length and only twelve miles in depth. The northern edge of this rectangle was a line from Jisr ed Damieh on the Jordan, through Nablus and Tul Keram, to the sea. All the enemy's communications to Damascus ran northwards from the eastern half of this line; converging on El Afule and Beisan, some twenty-five miles to the north. Thence, with the exception of the roads leading from El Afule along the western shore of the Sea of Galilee, his communications ran eastwards up the valley of the Yarmuk to Deraa, the junction of the Palestine and Hejaz railways. (*See* PLATE 41.)

Thus, El Afule, Beisan, and Deraa were the vital points on his communications. If they could be seized, the enemy's retreat would be cut off. Deraa was beyond my reach, but not beyond that of mobile detachments of the Arab Army. It was not to be expected that these detachments could hold this railway junction, but it was within their power to dislocate all traffic.

El Afule, in the Plain of Esdraelon, and Beisan, in the Valley of Jezreel, were within reach of my cavalry, provided the infantry could break through the enemy's defensive systems, and create a gap for the cavalry to pass through. It was essential that this gap should be made at the commencement of operations, so that the cavalry might reach their destinations, forty-five and sixty miles distant, before the enemy could make his escape. Moreover, whichever route the cavalry followed, the hills of Samaria, or their extension towards Mount Carmel, had to be crossed before the Plain of Esdraelon, and the Valley of Jezreel, could be reached; and it was most important that the enemy should not be given time to man the passes.

6. For this reason I decided to make my main attack in the coastal plain, rather than through the hills north of Jerusalem. In the hills the ground afforded the enemy positions of great natural strength, and taxed the physical energy of the attackers to the utmost. The operations in March, astride the Jerusalem–Nablus road, had proved that an advance of five miles in one day, in face of determined opposition, was the most that could be expected. A far more rapid and decisive advance than this was necessary. In addition, the route along the coast would enable the cavalry to pass through the hills of Samaria, into the Plain of Esdraelon, at their narrowest point; thus ensuring greater speed and less likelihood of being checked. The supply of a large force of troops in the plain also presented fewer difficulties.

The Sharon Front.

7. The Coastal Plain at Jiljulieh, the ancient Gilgal, is some ten miles in width. The railway from Jiljulieh to Tul Keram skirts the foothills, running through a slight depression on the eastern edge of the plain. To the west of this depression the Turks had constructed two defensive systems. The first, 14,000 yards in length and 3,000 in depth, ran along a sandy ridge in a north-westerly direction from Bir Adas to the sea. It consisted of a series of works connected by continuous fire trenches. The second, or Et Tireh system, 3,000 yards in rear, ran from the village of that name to the mouth of the Nahr Falik. On the enemy's extreme right the ground, except for a narrow strip along the coast, is marshy and could only be crossed in few places. The defence of the second system did not, therefore, require a large force.

The railway itself was protected by numerous works, and by the fortified villages of Jiljulieh and Kalkilieh. The ground between our front line at Ras el Ain and these villages was open, and was overlooked from the enemy's works on the foothills round Kefr Kasim.

8. By reducing the strength of the troops in the Jordan Valley to a minimum, and by withdrawing my reserves from the hills north of Jerusalem, I was able to concentrate five divisions and the French detachment, with a total of 383 guns, for the attack on these defences. Thus, on the front of attack, I was able to concentrate some 35,000 rifles against 8,000, and 383 guns against 130. In addition, two cavalry and one Australian mounted divisions were available for this front. (*See* PLATE 41.)

The Plan of Campaign.

9. I entrusted the attack on the enemy's defences in the coastal plain to Lieut.-General Sir Edward Bulfin, K.C.B., C.V.O., commanding the XXIst Corps. In addition to the 3rd (Lahore), 7th (Meerut), 54th, and 75th Divisions, which already formed part of the XXIst Corps, I placed at his disposal the 60th Division, the French Detachment, the 5th Australian Light Horse Brigade, two brigades of mountain artillery, and eighteen batteries of heavy and siege artillery.

I ordered him to break through the enemy's defences between the railway and the sea, to open a way for the cavalry, and at the same time, to seize the foothills south-east of Jiljulieh. The XXIst Corps was then to swing to the right, on the line Hableh–Tul Keram, and then advance in a north-easterly direction through the hills, converging on Samaria and Attara, so as to drive the enemy up the Messudie–Jenin road into the arms of the cavalry at El Afule.

I ordered Lieut.-General Sir Harry Chauvel, K.C.B., K.C.M.G., commanding the Desert Mounted Corps, less the Australian and New Zealand Mounted Division, to advance along the coast, directly the infantry had broken through, and had secured the crossings over the Nahr Falik. On reaching the line Jelameh–Hudeira, he was to turn north-east, cross the hills of Samaria, and enter the Plain of Esdraelon at El Lejjun and Abu Shusheh. Riding along the plain, the Desert Mounted Corps was to seize El Afule, sending a detachment to Nazareth. the site of the Yilderim General Headquarters. Sufficient troops were to be left at El Afule to intercept the Turkish retreat there. The remainder of the Corps was to ride down the Valley of Jezreel and seize Beisan.

I ordered Lieut.-General Sir Philip Chetwode, Bart., K.C.B., K.C.M.G., D.S.O., commanding the XXth Corps, to advance his line east of the Bireh–Nablus road, on the night preceding the main attack, so as to place the 53rd Division on his right flank, which was somewhat drawn back, in a more favourable position to advance and block the exits to the lower valley of the Jordan.

I ordered him to be prepared to carry out a further advance with both the 53rd and 10th Divisions, on the evening of the day on which the attack in the coastal plain took place, or later as circumstances demanded.

10. The main difficulties lay in concealing the withdrawal of two cavalry divisions from the Jordan Valley, and in concentrating secretly, a large force in the coastal plain.

To prevent the decrease in strength in the Jordan Valley being discovered by the enemy, I ordered Major-General Sir Edward Chaytor, K.C.M.G., C.B., A.D.C., to carry out with the Australian and New Zealand Mounted Division, the 20th Indian (Imperial Service) Infantry Brigade, the 38th and 39th Battalions Royal Rusiliers, and the 1st and 2nd Battalions British West Indies Regiment, a series of demonstrations with the object of inducing the enemy to believe that an attack east of the Jordan was intended, either in the direction of Madeba or Amman. The enemy was thought to be anticipating an attack in these directions, and every possible step was taken to strengthen his suspicions.

At this time a mobile column of the Arab Army, accompanied by British armoured cars and a French mountain battery, was assembling at Kasr el Azrak, fifty miles east of Amman. The real objective of this column was the railway north, south, and west of Deraa. There was always the possibility, however, that this concentration might be observed. Should this occur, it was hoped that the demonstrations by Chaytor's force would strengthen the enemy's belief that a concerted attack on Amman was intended.

Preparation for the Attack.

The concentration in the coastal plain was carried out by night, and every precaution was taken to prevent any increased movement becoming apparent to the Turks. Full use of the many groves round Ramleh, Ludd, and Jaffa, was made to conceal troops during the day. The chief factor in the secrecy maintained must be attributed, however, to the supremacy in the air which had been obtained by the Royal Air Force. The process of wearing down the enemy's aircraft had been going on all through the summer. During one week in June 100 hostile aeroplanes had crossed our lines. During the last week in August this number had decreased to eighteen. In the next few days a number were shot down, with the result that only four ventured to cross our lines during the period of concentration.

11. That the enemy expected an offensive on my part about this date is probable. That he remained in ignorance of my intention to attack in the coastal plain with overwhelming numbers is certain. On the morning of Sept. 19, when the attack in the coastal plain was launched, his dispositions were normal.

Arab Action.

12. Whilst the concentration in the coastal plain was nearing completion, the enemy's railway communications at Deraa were attacked by the Royal Air Force, and by the mobile column of the Arab Army, which, after concentrating at Kasr el Azrak, fifty miles east of Amman, had moved into the Hauran.

The railway line and station buildings at Deraa were damaged by the Royal Air Force on Sept. 16 and 17. On Sept. 16th the Arab column, which had been joined by the Shalaan Sections of the Rualla, Anazeh, and by a number of Druses, attacked the Hejaz Railway, fifteen miles south of Deraa, destroying a bridge and a section of the railway. On the following day the line was attacked both north and west of Deraa, extensive demolitions being carried out. As the result of these demolitions, all through traffic to Palestine ceased, and a considerable quantity of transport, which had been intended for the Hejaz, was diverted to bridge the break in the railway. (*See* PLATES 41–44.)

The Eastern Front.

13. The concentration in the coastal plain had been completed by the morning of **Sept. 18.** During the night of Sept. 18–19, the XXth Corps swung forward its right on the east of the Bireh–Nablus road. The 53rd Division descended into the basin at the head of the Wadi Samieh, captured Kh. Jibeit, El Mugheir, and the ridge on the far side of the basin, and all its objectives, with the exception of one hill, Kh. Abu Malul. Considerable opposition was encountered; and hand-to-hand fighting took place, in which over 400 prisoners were taken.

In the early hours of **Sept. 19** El Afule and the headquarters of the Turkish VIIth and VIIIth Armies at Nablus and Tul Keram were bombed by the Royal Air Force, with a view to disorganizing their signal communications.

At 0430 the artillery in the coastal plain opened an intense bombardment lasting fifteen minutes, under cover of which the infantry left their positions of deployment. Two torpedo boat destroyers assisted, bringing fire on the coastal road to the north. (*See* PLATE 42.)

14. The operations which followed fall into five phases.

The first phase was of short duration. In thirty-six hours, between 0430 on Sept. 19 and 1700 on Sept. 20, the greater part of the VIIIth Turkish Army had been overwhelmed, and the troops of the VIIth Army were in full retreat, through the hills of Samaria, whose exits were already in the hands of my cavalry. (See PLATES 43–44.)

In the second phase the fruits of this success were reaped. The infantry, pressing relentlessly on the heels of the retreating enemy, drove him into the arms of my cavalry, with the result that practically the whole of the VIIth and VIIIth Turkish Armies were captured, with their guns and transport.

This phase also witnessed the capture of Haifa and Acre, and the occupation of Tiberias, and of the country to the south and west of the Sea of Galilee.

As the result of the rout of the VIIth and VIIIth Armies, the IVth Turkish Army, east of the Jordan, retreated, and Maan was evacuated. (See PLATES 45–46.)

The third phase commenced with the pursuit of this army by Chaytor's force, and closed with the capture of Amman, and the interception of the retreat of the garrison of Maan, which surrendered. (See PLATE 47.)

The fourth phase witnessed the advance by the Desert Mounted Corps to Damascus, the capture of the remnants of the IVth Turkish Army, and the advance by the XXIst Corps along the coast from Haifa to Beirut. (See PLATES 48–52.)

In the fifth phase my troops reached Homs and Tripoli without opposition. My cavalry then advanced on Aleppo, and occupied that city on Oct. 26. (See PLATE 53.)

The Main Attack.

15. The attack in the coastal plain on the morning of Sept. 19 was attended with complete success. On the right, in the foothills, the French Tirailleurs and the Armenians of the Legion d'Orient advanced with great dash, and, in spite of the difficulties of the ground, and the strength of the enemy's defences, had captured the Kh. Deir el Kussis ridge at an early hour. On their left the 54th Division stormed Kefr Kasm village, and wood, and the foothills overlooking the railway from Ras el Ain to Jiljulieh. North of Kefr Kasim the advance was checked for a time at Sivri Tepe, but the enemy's resistance was quickly overcome, and the remaining hills south of the Wadi Kanah captured.

The Battle of Sharon.

In the coastal plain the 3rd (Lahore) Division attacked the enemy's first system between Bir Adas and the Hadrah road. On its left the 75th Division attacked the Tabsor defences, the 7th (Meerut) Division the works west of Tabsor, while the 60th Division attacked along the coast. The enemy replied energetically to our bombardment, but in most cases his barrage fell behind the attacking infantry. The enemy was overwhelmed. After overrunning the first system the three divisions on the left pressed on, without pausing, to the Et Tireh position. On the left the 60th Division reached the Nahr Falik, and moved on Tul Keram, leaving the route along the coast clear for the Desert Mounted Corps. The 7th (Meerut) Division, after passing through the second system, swung to the right, and headed for Et Taiyibeh, leaving Et Tireh, where the 75th Division was still fighting, on its right.

By 1100 the 75th Division had captured Et Tireh, a strongly fortified village standing on a sandy ridge, where the enemy offered a determined resistance. On the right the 3rd (Lahore) Division turned to the east, and attacked Jiljulieh, Railway Redoubt, Kefr Saba, and Kalkilieh, all of which were defended with stubbornness by the enemy. His resistance was, however, broken, and the 3rd (Lahore) Division pressed on eastwards into the foothills near Hableh, joining hands with the 54th Division, north of the Wadi Kanah.

Disorganized bodies of the enemy were now streaming across the plain towards Tul Keram, pursued by the 60th Division and the 5th Australian Light Horse Brigade. This brigade, which had been attached to the XXIst Corps, consisted of two Australian Light Horse Regiments, with a composite regiment of Chasseurs d'Afrique and Spahis attached. Great confusion reigned at Tul Keram. Bodies of troops, guns, motor lorries, and transport of every description were endeavouring to escape along the road leading to Messudie and Nablus. This road, which follows the railway up a narrow valley, was already crowded with troops and transport. The confusion was added to by the persistent attacks of the Royal Air Force, and Australian Flying Corps, from which there was no escape. Great havoc was caused, and, in several places, the road was blocked by overturned lorries and vehicles. Later in the evening an Australian regiment, having made a detour, succeeded in reaching a hill four miles east of Tul Keram, overlooking the road. As a result, a large amount of transport, and many guns, fell into our hands.

In the meantime the 7th (Meerut) Division and 3rd (Lahore) Division had entered the hills, and, in conjunction with the 54th Division, had pressed eastwards. By dusk the line Bidieh-Kh. Kefr Thilth-Jiyus-Felamieh-Taiyibeh had been reached. The 75th Division remained in the vicinity of Et Tireh in Corps reserve. (*See* PLATE 42.)

The Battle of Mount Ephraim.

16. As soon as the success of the initial attack by the XXIst Corps, on the morning of Sept. 19, had become apparent, I ordered the XXth Corps to advance that night on Nablus, and the high ground north-east of that town, in order to close the roads leading to the lower valley of the Jordan, and to drive the enemy from the triangle formed by the Kh. Fusail-Nablus road, our original front line, and the El Funduk-Nablus track, by which the 3rd (Lahore) Division was advancing.

The two divisions of the XXth Corps had been concentrated beforehand, in readiness to carry out this operation; the 53rd Division to the east of the Bireh-Nablus road, the 10th Division on the extreme left of the Corps area, in the vicinity of Berukin and Kefr Ain. The enemy had long anticipated an attack astride the Bireh-Nablus road, and had constructed defences of great strength on successive ridges. For this reason the 10th Division was ordered to attack in a north-easterly direction astride the Furkhah-Selfit and Berukin-Kefr Haris ridges, thus avoiding a direct attack. Even so, the task of the XXth Corps was a difficult one. The enemy in this portion of the field was not disorganized, and was able to oppose a stout resistance to the advance. The country is broken and rugged, demanding great physical exertion on the part of the troops, and preventing the artillery keeping pace with the infantry.

Nevertheless, good progress was made on the night of Sept. 19, and during the following day. The 53rd Division captured Kh. abu Malul, and advanced their line in the centre. On their right Khan Jibeit was heavily counter-attacked on the morning of **Sept. 20.** The Turks succeeded in regaining the hill, but were driven off again after a sharp fight. This incident, and the necessity of making a road, to enable the guns to be brought forward, caused delay.

The 10th Division advanced in two columns, and, by midday on Sept. 20, the right column, after a hard fight at Furkhah, had reached Selfit, and was approaching Iskaka, which was strongly held by the enemy. The left column reached Kefr Haris, which was only captured after heavy fighting. The 10th Division had already driven the enemy back seven miles. The artillery, however, had been unable to keep up with the infantry, and little progress was made during the afternoon.

On the left of the 10th Division the XXIst Corps had continued its advance in three columns. On the right, the 3rd Division advanced up the Wadi Azzun. In the centre, the Meerut Division moved on Kefr Sur and Beit Lid. The 60th Division and the 5th Australian Light Horse Brigade advanced along the Tul Keram-Nablus road on Messudie Station. By evening the line Baka-Beit Lid-Messudie Station-Attara had been reached.

The 3rd (Lahore) and 7th (Meerut) Divisions encountered a determined and well-organized resistance, which stiffened as the Meerut Division approached Beit Lid. The enemy showed no signs of demoralization, and the country was very rugged and difficult.

Considerable confusion existed, however, behind the enemy's rearguards. All day, his transport had been withdrawing. The Messudie-Jenin road was crowded. Its defiles had been bombed continuously by the Royal Air Force, as had long columns of troops and transport moving on Nablus in order to reach the Beisan road. It is probable that the enemy did not yet realize that my cavalry was already in Afule and Beisan, and had blocked his main lines of retreat. (*See* PLATE 43.)

The Advance of the Cavalry.

17. Early on the morning of Sept. 19, before the infantry had advanced to the attack, the 4th and 5th Cavalry Divisions moved out of the groves round Sarona, and formed up in rear of the 7th (Meerut) and 60th Divisions. The Australian Mounted Division, less the 5th Light Horse Brigade, was on its way from Ludd.

Thanks to the rapidity with which the infantry broke through both Turkish systems of defence, the cavalry obtained a good start. By noon the leading troops of the Desert Mounted Corps had reached Jelameh, Tel ed Dhrur, and Hudeira, eighteen miles north of the original front line. After a brief rest, the advance was continued. The 5th Cavalry Division moved north to Ez Zerghaniyeh. It then turned north-east and, riding through the hills of Samaria past Jarak, descended into the Plain of Esdraelon at Abu Shusheh. The 13th Cavalry Brigade was then directed on Nazareth, the 14th on El Afule.

The 4th Cavalry Division turned north-east at Kh. es Sumrah, and followed the valley of the Wadi Arah into the hills. The valley gradually narrows as the pass at Musmus is reached.

The enemy had sent a battalion from El Afule to hold this pass, but only its advanced guard arrived in time. Overcoming its resistance the cavalry encountered the remainder of the battalion at El Lejjun. The 2nd Lancers charged, killed forty-six with the lance, and captured the remainder, some 470 in number.

The 4th Cavalry Division then marched to El Afule, which it reached at 0800, half an hour after its capture by the 14th Cavalry Brigade.

The Nazareth Raid—Sept. 20.

In the meantime the 13th Cavalry Brigade of the 5th Cavalry Division, riding across the Plain of Esdraelon, had reached Nazareth, the site of the Yilderim General Headquarters, at 0530. Fighting took place in the streets, some 2,000 prisoners being captured. Liman von Sanders had already made good his escape, but his papers and some of his staff were taken. This brigade then marched to El Afule, arriving there as the 4th Cavalry Division rode down the Plain of Jezreel to Beisan, which it reached at 1630, having covered some eighty miles in thirty-four hours. The 4th Cavalry Division detached a regiment to seize the railway bridge over the Jordan at Jisr Mejamie.

The Australian Mounted Division, which had followed the 4th Cavalry Division into the Plain of Esdraelon, was directed on Jenin, where the road from Messudie to El Afule leaves the hills. Jenin was reached at 1730, and was captured after a sharp fight, a large number of prisoners being taken.

Thus, within thirty-six hours of the commencement of the battle, all the main outlets of escape remaining to the Turkish VIIth and VIIIth Armies had been closed. They could only avoid capture by using the tracks which run south-east from the vicinity of Nablus to the crossings over the Jordan at Jisr ed Damieh. These were being rapidly denied to them. (*See* PLATE 43.)

The first phase of the operations was over.

Destruction of the Turkish VIIth and VIIIth Armies.

18. The enemy's resistance had been broken on Sept. 20. On **Sept. 21** the Turkish rearguards were driven in early in the morning. All organized resistance ceased. The 5th Australian Light Horse Brigade, with the French cavalry leading, entered Nablus from the west; the 10th Division from the south.

By the evening, the XXth Corps had reached the line Neby Belan, on the high ground north-east of Nablus, and Mount Ebal; the XXIst Corps the line Samaria, Attara, Belah.

Since the early hours of the morning great confusion had reigned in the Turkish rear. Camps and hospitals were being hurriedly evacuated; some were in flames. The roads leading north-east, and east, from Nablus to Beisan, and the Jordan Valley, were congested with transport and troops. Small parties of troops were moving east along the numerous wadis. The disorganization which already existed was increased by the repeated attacks of the Royal Air Force; in particular, on the closely packed column of transport moving north from Balata to Kh. Ferweh, where a road branches off, along the Wadi Farah, to Jisr ed Damieh. Some of the transport continued along the road to Beisan, where it fell into the hands of the 4th Cavalry Division. The greater part made for the Jordan along the Wadi Farah. Nine miles from Kh. Ferweh, at Ain Shibleh, a road branches off to the north to Beisan. A mile beyond this point the Wadi Farah passes through a gorge. The head of the column was heavily bombed at this point. The drivers left their vehicles in panic, wagons were overturned, and in a short time the road was completely blocked. Still attacked by the Royal Air Force, the remainder of the column turned off at Ain Shibleh, and headed for Beisan. (*See* PLATE 45.)

The VIIth Turkish Army was by this time thoroughly disorganized, and was scattered in the area between the Kh. Ferweh-Beisan road, and the Jordan. These parties had now to be collected.

At 0130 on **Sept. 22** the New Zealand Mounted Rifles Brigade, and the British West Indies battalions of Chaytor's Force, seized the bridge at Jisr ed Damieh. All hope of escape for the enemy in that direction had vanished.

In the early hours of the morning, parties of Turks, of strengths varying from fifty to 300, began to approach Beisan, preceded by white flags.

At 0800 a column, with transport and guns, ten miles long, was reported by the Royal Air Force to be moving north along the Ain Shibleh-Beisan road, its head being nine miles south of Beisan. The 4th Cavalry Division was ordered to send detachments towards it, and also to patrol the road, which follows the Jordan on its east bank, to secure any parties which might escape across the Jordan.

At the same time the Worcester Yeomanry of the XXth Corps, supported by infantry, was ordered to advance northwards from Ain Shibleh, and the infantry of the 10th Division along the Tubas-Beisan road, to collect stragglers, and to drive any formed bodies into the hands of the 4th Cavalry Division.

The Royal Air Force had proceeded to attack the Turkish column, which broke up and abandoned its guns and transport. The task of clearing the enemy between the Kh. Ferweh-Beisan road and the Jordan was continued during **Sept. 23.** On this day the XXth Corps Cavalry met with occasional opposition, and its advance was hampered considerably by the large numbers of Turks who surrendered. Great quantities of transport and numerous guns were found abandoned by the roadsides. On one stretch of road, under five miles in length, eighty-seven guns, fifty-five motor lorries, and 842 vehicles were found.

Numerous bodies of Turks surrendered to the 4th Cavalry Division. One column attempted to escape across the Jordan at Makhadet abu Naj, five miles south-east of Beisan, but was intercepted by the 11th Cavalry Brigade. Part of the column had already crossed to the east bank. It was charged by the 36th (Jacob's) Horse, and broken up, few escaping. On the west bank the remainder of the column was charged by the 29th Lancers and Middlesex Yeomanry, who killed many and captured the remainder, together with twenty-five machine guns.

On **Sept. 24** the 11th Cavalry Brigade attacked and dispersed another column in the Wadi el Maleh. The last remnants of the VIIth and VIIIth Turkish Armies had been collected. As armies they had ceased to exist, and but few had escaped.

19. Whilst the 4th Cavalry and the Australian Mounted Divisions were collecting the remnants of the VIIth and VIIIth Turkish Armies, I ordered the Desert Mounted Corps to occupy Acre and Haifa. The roads leading to Haifa from Tul Keram are only country tracks, which, in the event of rain, might become impassable for motor lorries at any time. Any force, advancing northwards from Haifa along the coast, would have to depend on supplies landed at that port. It was necessary, therefore, to occupy the town without delay, in order that the harbour could be swept for mines, and the landing of stores taken in hand. The 13th Cavalry Brigade of the 5th Cavalry Division, which had entered Nazareth on Sept. 20, and had then marched to El Afule, returned to Nazareth the following day.

Part of the garrison of Haifa, which was attempting to reach Tiberias, was intercepted by this brigade on the morning of Sept. 22. At 0130 this column approached the outposts of the 13th Cavalry Brigade. It was attacked in the moonlight by the 18th Lancers, who killed a large number of Turks and captured over 300.

That afternoon Haifa was reconnoitred by a battery of armoured cars. It was held by the enemy. The road was barricaded, and the armoured cars were shelled from the slopes of Mount Carmel.

On Sept. 23 the 5th Cavalry Division, less the 13th Cavalry Brigade, marched from El Afule to capture the town. The 13th Cavalry Brigade marched direct from Nazareth on Acre.

Capture of Acre and Haifa, Sept. 23.

The road from El Afule to Haifa skirts the north-eastern edge of the Mount Carmel range. Some two miles before Haifa is reached, the road is confined between a spur of Mount Carmel on the left, and the marshy banks of the River Kishon and its tributaries on the right. When the 5th Cavalry Division reached this point on Sept. 23 it was shelled from the slopes of Mount Carmel, and found the road and the river crossings defended by numerous machine guns.

Whilst the Mysore Lancers were clearing the rocky slopes of Mount Carmel, the Jodhpur Lancers charged through the defile, and, riding over the enemy's machine guns, galloped into the town, where a number of Turks were speared in the streets. Colonel Thakur Dalpat Singh, M.C., fell, gallantly leading this charge.

In this operation 1,350 prisoners and seventeen guns were taken.

At Acre, the 13th Cavalry Brigade met with little opposition. The small garrison, consisting of 150 men and two guns, attempted to escape to the north, but was overtaken and captured.

Operations East of the Jordan.

20. Interest now turned to the fate of the IVth Turkish Army east of the Jordan. Up till Sept. 22 this army showed no signs of moving from its position on the east bank. (*See* PLATE 45.) On the west bank, the New Zealand Mounted Rifles Brigade and the 1st and 2nd Battalions British West Indies Regiment had advanced northwards on Sept. 21, west of the Jericho-Beisan road, and had reached Khurbet Fusail, four miles in advance of our defences at El Musalabeh. The enemy, however, still held the bridgeheads on the west bank, covering the crossings at Umm es Shert, Red Hill, Mafid Jozeleh, and Jisr ed Damieh. Early in the morning of Sept. 22, the 38th Battalion Royal Fusiliers captured the bridgehead at Umm es Shert. The New Zealand Mounted Rifles placed themselves astride the road which follows the Wadi Farah from Nablus to Jisr ed Damieh, thus closing the last loophole of escape to the Turkish forces west of the Jordan. The crossing at Jisr ed Damieh was captured a few hours later. The bridge was intact. 514 prisoners were taken.

Capture of Amman, Sept. 25.

Thus the west bank of the Jordan had been cleared. As a result of the defeat of the VIIth and VIIIth Armies, the position of the IVth Army east of the Jordan was no longer tenable, and, by the morning of Sept. 23, this army was in full retreat on Es Salt and Amman, pursued by the Australian and New Zealand Mounted Division, and bombed by the Royal Air Force. At 1630 the New Zealanders captured Es Salt, taking 380 prisoners and three guns. The pursuit was continued on a broad front, in face of stout opposition from the enemy's rearguards. On **Sept. 25** Amman was attacked and captured.

The enemy retreated northwards along the Hejaz Railway, and the Pilgrim Route, in a disorganized state, harassed by the Royal Air Force and the Arabs. He was pursued by the Australian and New Zealand Mounted Division, and left over 5,000 prisoners and twenty-eight guns in their hands.

I ordered Chaytor's Force to remain at Amman to intercept the troops of the IInd Turkish Army Corps, who were retreating from the Hejaz. Maan had been evacuated on Sept. 23, and had been occupied by the Arab Army, which then advanced to Jerdun, harassing the rear of the retreating garrison. (*See* PLATE 47.)

Surrender of the Turkish IInd Corps.

On **Sept. 28,** these troops came into contact with the patrols of Chaytor's Force at Leban Station, ten miles south of Amman. The Turkish Commander, seeing that escape was impossible, surrendered on the following day with 5,000 men.

21. In addition to bringing about the retreat of the IVth Turkish Army, the total defeat of the VIIth and VIIIth Armies had removed any serious obstacle to an advance on Damascus. On Sept. 25 I ordered the Desert Mounted Corps to carry out this operation, occupy the city, and intercept the retreat of the remnants of the IVth Turkish Army.

22. The Desert Mounted Corps was to advance on Damascus in two columns; one column by the south end of the Sea of Galilee, *via* Irbid and Deraa, the other round the north end of the Sea, *via* El Kuneitra.

On Sept. 24, Semakh at the south end of the Sea of Galilee, was captured by the 4th Australian Light Horse Brigade, after fierce hand-to-hand fighting, in which 350 Turks and Germans and a gun were captured. Tiberias was occupied on the following afternoon.

Thus, on **Sept. 26,** the Australian Mounted Division was concentrating round Tiberias, and the 5th Cavalry Division was marching from Haifa and Acre to Nazareth. The 4th Cavalry Division was concentrated round Beisan. (*See* PLATE 47.)

The Advance on Damascus.

23. The 4th Cavalry Division started on its 120-mile march that afternoon. The Australian and 5th Cavalry Divisions started the following day, the distance they had to traverse being thirty miles less. Both columns met with opposition. The Australian Mounted Division experienced considerable difficulty in crossing the Jordan on **Sept. 27.** (*See* PLATE 48.) The bridge at Jisr Benat Yakub had been damaged, and Turkish rearguards commanded the crossings. After some delay, the 5th Australian Brigade succeeded in crossing the river a mile south of the bridge; and, working round the enemy's flank, forced him to retire. Opposition was again met with on the eastern side of the Jordan plateau, at El Kuneitra, and the column was continually fired on by the Circassians who dwell on the plateau. Passing through El Kuneitra, the column entered first a plateau covered by boulders and then undulating pasture land, intersected by the numerous streams which rise in Mount Hermon. Fighting took place at Sasa, but the enemy's rearguards were driven back, and, by 1000 on **Sept. 30,** Katana, twelve miles south-west of Damascus, had been reached by the Australian Mounted Division, which was here checked for a time.

At this hour the 14th Cavalry Brigade, on the right of the Australian Mounted Division, was approaching Sahnaya on the old French railway. Further south the 4th Cavalry Division, with the Arab Army on its right, was approaching Kiswe. (*See* PLATE 50.)

Destruction of the Turkish IVth Army.

The route followed by the 4th Cavalry Division across the Jordan plateau had proved difficult, and considerable opposition had been encountered at Irbid, and again at Er Remte, where, after driving the enemy northwards towards Mezerib, the Cavalry gained touch with the Arab Army.

After its raids on the enemy's railways round Deraa between Sept. 16 and 18, the Arab Army had moved into the Hauran. It issued thence to attack the IVth Turkish Army, as the latter passed Mafrak in its retreat northwards, forcing the Turks to abandon guns and transport. Moving rapidly northwards the Arabs then captured the stations of Ezra and Ghazale, between Damascus and Deraa. On Sept. 27 they entrenched themselves at Sheikh Saad, seventeen miles north of Deraa, across the Turkish line of retreat. Sharp fighting took place all day, in which heavy casualties were inflicted on the retreating Turks and Germans, and in which numerous prisoners were taken. After breaking up the retreating columns of the IVth Army, the Arabs captured Deraa, and, on Sept. 28, joined hands with the 4th Cavalry Division near Er Remte.

The cavalry then advanced northwards through Mezerib, and along the old French railway, with the Arabs on its right flank, collecting stragglers, and pressing on the heels of the remnants of the IVth Turkish Army.

In this way a column of Turks some 1,500 strong was driven at noon on Sept. 30 into the arms of the 14th Cavalry Brigade at Sahnaya. (*See* PLATE 50.)

Fall of Damascus.

Shortly after midday on Sept. 30, the Australian Mounted Division overcame the enemy's resistance at Katana. By the evening it had closed the exits from Damascus to the north and north-west, while the 5th Cavalry Division had reached the southern outskirts of the town. (*See* PLATE 51.)

At 0600 on **Oct. 1,** the Desert Mounted Corps and the Arab Army entered Damascus amidst scenes of great enthusiasm. After the German and Turkish troops in the town had been collected, and guards had been posted, our troops were withdrawn. In the meantime, the 3rd Australian Light Horse Brigade had proceeded northwards in pursuit of bodies of the enemy, which had succeeded in leaving the town on the previous day, or had avoided it, and the cordon round it, by making a detour to the east. On **Oct. 2** a column was overtaken at Kubbeth i Asafir, seventeen miles north-east of Damascus. This column was dispersed, 1,500 prisoners and three guns being taken.

Plight of the Enemy.

24. The advance to Damascus, following on the operation in the Plain of Esdraelon and the Valley of Jezreel, had thrown a considerable strain on the Desert Mounted Corps. Great results were, however, achieved.

On Sept. 26, when the advance began, some 45,000 Turks and Germans were still in Damascus or were retreating on it. It is true that all units were in a state of disorganization but, given time, the enemy could have formed a force capable of delaying my advance.

The destruction of the remnants of the IVth Army and the capture of an additional 20,000 prisoners, prevented any possibility of this. The remnants of the Turkish Armies in Palestine and Syria, numbering some 17,000 men, of whom only 4,000 were effective rifles, fled northwards a mass of individuals, without organization, without transport, and without any of the accessories required to enable it to act even on the defensive.

25. I determined to exploit this success, and to advance to the line Rayak–Beirut. The occupation of Beirut would give me a port, with a road and a railway, leading inland to Rayak and Damascus. An alternative and shorter line of supply would thus be obtained.

The Desert Mounted Corps, leaving the Australian Mounted Division at Damascus, moved on Rayak and Zahle on **Oct. 5.** No opposition was encountered, and both places were occupied on the following day.

At Rayak, the junction of the broad gauge railway from the north and the metre gauge lines to Beirut and to Damascus and the Hejaz, were found on the aerodrome the remains of thirty aeroplanes which had been burnt by the enemy before he retired. Large quantities of stores and rolling stock were captured, most of the latter in a damaged condition.

The March of the 7th Division.

In the meantime the 7th (Mereut) Division had marched from Haifa to Beirut. Leaving Haifa on **Oct. 3,** it marched along the coast. Crossing the Ladder of Tyre, it was received by the populace of Tyre and Sidon with enthusiasm. On **Oct. 8** it reached Beirut, where it was warmly welcomed, the inhabitants handing over 660 Turks, including sixty officers, who had surrendered to them. Ships of the French Navy had already entered the harbour. (*See* PLATE 53.)

Occupation of Homs, Tripolis, and Hama.

26. On **Oct. 9** I ordered the Desert Mounted Corps to continue its advance and occupy Homs, leaving one division at Damascus. At the same time I ordered the XXIst Corps to continue its march along the coast to Tripoli. Armoured cars occupied Baalbek on Oct. 9, taking over 500 Turks who had surrendered to the inhabitants. The 5th Cavalry Division, which led the advance, reached Baalbek on **Oct. 11,** and, crossing the watershed between the Nahr Litani on the south and the Orontes on the north, followed up the valley of the latter river, past Lebwe, and reached Homs on **Oct. 15,** having marched over eighty miles since leaving Rayak.

The station buildings at Homs had been burnt by the enemy before he evacuated the town on Oct. 12.

On the coast, Tripoli was occupied by the XXIst Corps Cavalry Regiment and Armoured Cars on **Oct. 13.** No opposition was encountered. The Corps Cavalry Regiment was followed by a brigade of the 7th (Meerut) Division. The occupation of Tripoli provided a shorter route by which the cavalry at Homs could be supplied.

27. Having secured Homs and Tripoli, I determined to seize Aleppo, with the least possible delay. The 5th Cavalry Division and the Armoured Car Batteries were alone available. The Australian Mounted Division at Damascus was over 100 miles distant from Homs, and could not be brought up in time. The 4th Cavalry Division at Baalbek was much reduced in strength by sickness, and needed a rest to reorganize. Time was of importance, and I judged that the 5th Cavalry Division would be strong enough for the purpose. The information available indicated the presence of some 20,000 Turks and Germans at Aleppo. Of these, only some 8,000 were combatants, and they were demoralized. Moreover, reports from all sources showed that considerable numbers of the enemy were leaving the town daily by rail for the north.

The Armoured Cars had reached Hama without opposition on **Oct. 20.** On the following day the 5th Cavalry Division commenced its advance. On **Oct. 22** the Armoured Cars reached Khan Sebil, half-way between Homs and Aleppo, as the enemy's rearguard left the village in lorries. A German armoured car, a lorry, and some prisoners were captured. The enemy was not encountered again till **Oct. 24,** when a body of cavalry was dispersed at Khan Tuman, ten miles south of Aleppo. Five miles further on, the armoured cars were checked by strong Turkish rearguards, and had to remain in observation till the cavalry came up. (*See* PLATE 53.)

On the afternoon of **Oct. 25** the Armoured Cars were joined by the 15th (Imperial Service) Cavalry Brigade. That evening a detachment of the Arab Army reached the eastern outskirts of Aleppo, and during the night forced their way in, inflicting heavy casualties on the enemy.

Early on the morning of **Oct. 26** the Armoured Cars and the 15th Cavalry Brigade, moving round the west side of the town, followed the enemy along the Aleppo-Katma road, and gained touch with him south-east of Haritan. The Turkish rearguard consisted of some 2,500 infantry, 150 cavalry, and eight guns. The Mysore Lancers and two squadrons of the Jodhpur Lancers attacked the enemy's left, covered by the fire of the Armoured Cars, the Machine Gun Squadron, and two dismounted squadrons of the Jodhpur Lancers. The Mysore and Jodhpur Lancers charged most gallantly. A number of Turks were speared, and many threw down their arms, only to pick them up again when the cavalry had passed through, and their weakness had become apparent. The squadrons were not strong enough to complete the victory, and were withdrawn till a larger force could be assembled.

That night the Turkish rearguard withdrew to a position near Deir el Jemel, twenty miles north-west of Aleppo.

The 5th Cavalry Division remained in observation, astride the roads leading from Aleppo to Killis and Katma, and occupied Muslimie Junction.

It was too weak to continue the advance to Alexandretta till the arrival of the Australian Mounted Division, which had already left Damascus to join it.

The Armistice.

Before the latter could arrive, the Armistice between the Allies and Turkey had been concluded, and came into force at noon on **Oct. 31.** (*See* PLATE 56.)

The 5th Cavalry Division captured fifty prisoners and eighteen guns in Aleppo. The Turks had carried out demolitions on the railway at Aleppo and Muslimie Junction before retiring, but had left eight engines and over 100 trucks, which, though damaged, were not beyond repair.

Aleppo is over 300 miles from our former front line. The 5th Cavalry Division covered 500 miles between Sept. 19 and Oct. 26, and captured over 11,000 prisoners and fifty-two guns. During this period the 5th Cavalry Division lost only twenty-one per cent of its horses.

28. Between Sept. 19 and Oct. 26 75,000 prisoners have been captured. Of these, over 200 officers and 3,500 other ranks are Germans or Austrians.

In addition, 360 guns have fallen into our hands, and the transport and equipment of three Turkish armies. It is not yet possible to give accurate figures, owing to the rapidity and the extent of the advance. In the first three phases of the operations, material and equipment were hastily abandoned by the enemy in a mountainous area, extending over 2,500 square miles, while in the remaining phases a further advance of over 300 miles had been made. The captures, however, include over 800 machine guns, 210 motor lorries, forty-four motor cars, some 3,500 animals, eighty-nine railway engines, and 468 carriages and trucks. Of these many are unserviceable, but none have been included that are beyond repair.

29. The plan of operations and the arrangements for the concentration were carefully prepared and well executed by Commanders and staffs. During the subsequent days of fighting, full advantage was taken of every opportunity offered.

Appreciation of Services.

The gallantry and determination of all ranks and of all arms has been most marked. Many units had already made their reputation in this, and other, theatres of the war. Some had yet to gain their first experience of modern warfare. British, French, and Indian troops, and those of the Dominions and Colonies, have all alike done magnificently.

The infantry, in a few hours, broke through the defences, which the enemy had spent months in strengthening, thus enabling the cavalry to accomplish its mission. The subsequent advance through the hills, over most difficult country, and in face of determined and organized resistance by the enemy's rearguards, tried the infantry severely. Nothing, however, stopped its progress, and the relentless pressure maintained on the enemy's rearguards allowed him no time to carry out an organized retreat, and drove him, in disorganized bodies, into the arms of the cavalry.

The Desert Mounted Corps took some 46,000 prisoners during the operations. The complete destruction of the VIIth and VIIIth Turkish Armies depended mainly on the rapidity with which their communications were reached, and on quick decision in dealing with the enemy's columns as they attempted to escape. The vigorous handling of the cavalry by its leaders, and the rapidity of its movements, overcame all attempts to delay its progress. The enemy's columns, after they had outdistanced the pursuing infantry, were given no time to reorganize and fight their way through.

In these brilliant achievements, the regiment of French cavalry took its full share, whilst east of the Jordan the Australian and New Zealand Mounted Division, by its untiring pursuit, threw the IVth Turkish Army into a state of disorganization, intercepted the garrison of Maan, and compelled it to surrender. Chaytor's Force took 10,000 prisoners in the Valley of the Jordan and the Hills of Moab.

The cavalry and infantry received every help from the Royal Artillery and the Royal Engineers, whilst the infantry, in its attack along the coast, was given valuable assistance by the Destroyers "Druid" and "Forester," which Rear-Admiral T. Jackson, C.B., M.V.O., had detailed to assist me.

Of the fighting troops, all have taken their share, and have carried out what was required of them. I would bring to notice the good fighting qualities shown by the newer units. These include the Armenian troops of the Légion d'Orient, the Tirailleurs Algériens, the 1st Battalion Cape Corps, the 38th and 39th (Jewish) Battalions of the Royal Fusiliers, the 1st and 2nd Battalions of the British West Indies Regiment, and all the recently formed battalions of Indian infantry.

The Royal Air Force.

Brilliant work has been done by the Palestine Brigade, Royal Air Force, and the Australian Flying Corps, not only during the actual operations, but in the preceding months. The process of wearing down the enemy's strength in the air had been continuous throughout the summer. Our ascendancy in the air became so marked towards the end of August that only a few of the enemy's aeroplanes were able to fly, with the result that my troops were immune from air attacks during the operations, and the whole strength of the Air Forces could be concentrated on the enemy in his retreat.

Besides taking an active part in the fighting, the Air Forces provided me with full and accurate information as to the enemy's movements.

The Arab Army.

The Arab Army has rendered valuable assistance, both in cutting the enemy's communications, before, and during, the operations, and in co-operating with my cavalry during the advance on Damascus. By throwing itself across the enemy's line of retreat, north of Deraa, it prevented the escape of portions of the IVth Turkish Army, and inflicted heavy casualties on the enemy.

The fighting troops have been loyally assisted by the administrative services and department, who have carried a heavy burden on their shoulders, both in front of, and behind, railhead. The accumulation of ammunition and stores before operations commenced threw a great strain on the railway. The delivery of these stores to the troops during operations proved a difficult task. Supply columns have had long distances to cover, over bad roads, but all difficulties have been overcome.

My thanks are due to the Royal Navy for its assistance in arranging and securing the landing of supplies at the various harbours along my line of advance, and to the French Navy for valuable information gained in the reconnaissance of the northern ports.

The Italian Detachment carried out to my entire satisfaction the task allotted to it, and throughout the operations gave valuable and loyal assistance.

From the first day of operations the Egyptian Labour Corps has followed the troops as they advanced, working hard and successfully to improve the roads. On Sept. 19 companies were working on the roads in front of our original line, while our guns were still firing.

The Camel Transport Corps has rendered valuable services, which have greatly aided in the victorious campaign.

The Signal Service, strained to its utmost, has maintained uninterrupted communication with units of the Army as far east as Amman and as far north as Aleppo.

The rapid advance has rendered difficult the task of evacuating the sick and wounded. The difficulty was increased by the large number of prisoners who, after marching for days, with little food or water, surrendered in a state of extreme weakness, unable to march another day. The care and evacuation of these men has heavily taxed the Medical Services, who have worked untiringly.

I have the honour to be,
Your Lordship's most obedient servant,

E. H. H. ALLENBY,
General,

Commanding-in-Chief,
Egyptian Expeditionary Force.

EGYPTIAN EXPEDITIONARY FORCE.

General Headquarters.

Commander-in-Chief.—Gen. Sir E. H. H. ALLENBY, G.C.B., G.C.M.G., *p.s.c.*

Chief of the General Staff.—Major-Gen. Sir A. LYNDEN-BELL, K.C.M.G., C.B., *p.s.c.* (relinquished, Sept., 1917).
  Major-Gen. Sir L. J. BOLS, K.C.B., K.C.M.G., D.S.O., *p.s.c.*

Brigadier-General, General Staff.—Bt. Lieut.-Col. (temp. Brig.-Gen.) G. P. DAWNAY, C.M.G., D.S.O., M.V.O. (R. of O.) (relinquished, Jan., 1918).
  Bt. Lieut.-Col. (temp. Brig.-Gen.) A. B. ROBERTSON, C.M.G., D.S.O., Cameron Highlanders, *p.s.c.* (relinquished, April, 1918).
  Bt. Col. (temp. Brig.-Gen.) W. H. BARTHOLOMEW, C.M.G., D.S.O., R.A., *p.s.c.*

Brigadier-General, General Staff (I).—Bt. Col. (temp. Brig.-Gen.) B. T. BUCKLEY, C.M.G., Northumberland Fusiliers, *p.s.c.*

Deputy Adjutant-General.—Major-Gen. Sir JOHN ADYE, K.C.M.G., C.B. (relinquished, March, 1918).
  Major-Gen. W. G. B. WESTERN, C.B., *p.s.c.*

Deputy Quartermaster-General.—Major-Gen. Sir WALTER CAMPBELL, K.C.B., K.C.M.G., D.S.O., *p.s.c.*

Assistant to Deputy Quartermaster-General.—Bt. Lieut.-Col. (temp. Brig.-Gen.) E. F. O. GASCOIGNE, C.M.G., D.S.O. (R. of O.) (relinquished, Jan., 1918).
  Bt. Col. (temp. Brig.-Gen.) E. EVANS, C.M.G., D.S.O., Wiltshire Regt., A.D.C.

Major-General, Royal Artillery.—Major-Gen. Sir S. C. U. SMITH, K.C.M.G., C.B.

Engineer-in-Chief.—Col. (temp. Major-Gen.) H. B. H. WRIGHT, C.B., C.M.G., late R.E.

Chief Political Officer.—Major (temp. Brig.-Gen.) G. F. CLAYTON, C.B., C.M.G. (R. of O.)

Chief Administrator, Occupied Enemy Territory Administration.—
  Major (temp. Brig.-Gen.) G. F. CLAYTON, C.B., C.M.G. (R. of O.) (relinquished, April, 1918).
  Major-Gen. Sir A. W. MONEY, K.C.B., C.S.I., *p.s.c.* (O.E.T.A. South).
  Colonel P. de PIÉPAPE, C.B. (O.E.T.A. North).
  ALI RIZA PASHA EL RIKABI (O.E.T.A. East).

Director of Army Signals.—Bt. Col. (temp. Brig.-Gen.) M. G. E. BOWMAN-MANIFOLD, C.B., C.M.G., D.S.O., R.E., *p.s.c.*

Director of Works.—Col. (temp. Brig.-Gen.) E. M. PAUL, C.B., late R.E.

Director of Supplies and Transport.—Bt. Col. (temp. Brig.-Gen.) G. F. DAVIES, C.B., C.M.G., R.A.S.C.

Director of Railway Traffic.—Temp. Brig.-Gen. Sir G. MACAULEY, K.C.M.G., C.B., (R. of O.) (Bt. Major, *r.p.*).

Director of Ordnance Services.—Col. (temp. Brig.-Gen.) P. A. BAINBRIDGE, C.B., C.M.G., R.A.O.C.

R.A.O., Base Depot, Alexandria.—Col. (temp. Brig.-Gen.) R. W. M. JACKSON, C.B., C.M.G., R.A.O.C.

Director of Remounts.—Temp. Brig.-Gen. C. L. BATES, C.B., C.M.G., D.S.O.

Director of Veterinary Services.—Col. (temp. Brig.-Gen.) E. R. C. BUTLER, C.B., C.M.G.

Director of Medical Services.—Col. (temp. Surgeon-Gen.) Sir J. MAHER, K.C.M.G., C.B., *r.p.* (relinquished, Oct., 1917).
  Col. A. E. C. KEBLE, C.B., C.M.G., D.S.O., A.M.S. (relinquished, Feb., 1918).
  Major-Gen. W. T. SWAN, C.B., A.M.S. (relinquished, Sept., 1918).
  Col. (temp. Major-Gen.) R. H. LUCE, C.B., C.M.G., M.B., F.R.C.S., T.F. Reserve.

Director of Labour.—Bt. Lieut.-Col. (temp. Brig.-Gen.) R. C. JELLICOE, D.S.O., R.A.S.C.

Principal Chaplain.—Rev. A. V. C. HORDERN, C.M.G. (relinquished, June, 1918).
  Rev. E. R. DAY, C.M.G.

Director of Inland Water Transport.—Major (temp. Col.) W. H. COYSH, D.S.O., R.E. (relinquished, July, 1918).
Temp. Lieut.-Col. (temp. Brig.-Gen.) W. N. BICKET, R.E.
Brigadier-General Training, E.E.F.—Bt. Lieut.-Col. (temp. Brig.-Gen.) A. B. ROBERTSON, C.M.G., D.S.O., Cameron Highlanders, *p.s.c.*

3rd Echelon.

Deputy Adjutant-General.—Major (temp. Brig.-Gen.) C. P. SCUDAMORE, C.B., C.M.G., D.S.O., *r.p.*

Royal Flying Corps, Middle East Brigade.

Commander.—Bt. Lieut.-Col. (temp. Brig.-Gen.) W. G. H. SALMOND, D.S.O., R.A., *p.s.c.* (relinquished, Oct., 1917).
Col. (temp. Brig.-Gen.) W. S. BRANCKER, R.A., attd. R.F.C., *p.s.c.* (relinquished on reorganization).

Middle East, Royal Air Force.

Commander.—Bt. Lieut.-Col. (temp. Major-Gen.) W. G. H. SALMOND, D.S.O., R.A., *p.s.c.*
Commanding, Palestine Brigade, R.A.F.—Bt. Lieut.-Col. (temp. Brig.-Gen.) A. E. BORTON, C.M.G., D.S.O., A.F.C., Royal Highlanders.
Commanding, Training Brigade, R.A.F.—Bt. Major (temp. Brig.-Gen.) P. L. W. HERBERT, Notts. & Derby Regt.

GENERAL HEADQUARTERS TROOPS.

Palestine Brigade, R.A.F.
"X" Aircraft Park.
"X" Flight.
5th Wing (Corps Wing):—
Nos. 14, 113, 142 Squadrons, R.A.F.
40th Wing (Army Wing):—
Nos. 111, 144, 145 Squadrons, R.A.F.
No. 1 Squadron, A.F.C. (late 67th Squadron, A.F.C.).
No. 21 Balloon Company.
Nos. 49, 50, 57 Balloon Sections.

Mounted Troops.
South Nottinghamshire Hussars (ceased to belong to E.E.F., 19/6/18).

Artillery.
390th and 391st Siege Batteries, R.G.A. (ceased to belong to E.E.F., 18/1/18).

Machine Gun Corps.
Nos. 11 and 12 Light Armoured Car Batteries (L.A.C. Brigade).

Engineers.
Military Printing Section (Government Press, Cairo), R.E.
No. 7 Field Survey Company, R.E.:—
Topographical Section.
Lithographic and Letterpress Section.
Meteorological Section (Stations at G.H.Q. and Jerusalem).
1st Bridging Company, Canadian Railway Troops.

Signal Service.
G.H.Q. Signal Company.
Nos. N 14, N 15, N 23, 42, 61 Airline Sections.
NA, NB, NN, UU, Cable Sections.
No. 6 Wagon W/T, and No. 6 Pack W/T Sections.
Pigeon Section.

Infantry.
38th and 39th Bns. Royal Fusiliers.
1/23rd and 2/23rd Sikh Pioneers.
1st and 2nd Bns. British West Indies Regt.

EGYPTIAN EXPEDITIONARY FORCE

Royal Army Service Corps.

(a) Mechanical Transport:—
  No. 347 M.T. Company (Supply Column).
  No. 644 M.T. Company (Heavy Repair Workshop and Stores Branch).
  Nos. 895 and 972 M.T. Company (Caterpillar Tractor Supply Column).
  No. 956 M.T. Company (Ford Supply Company).
  Nos. 905, 906, 907, 1009, 1010, 1011, 1038, 1039, 1040, M.T. (Auxiliary Petrol) Coys.
  No. 1006, M.T. Company.
  Nos. 4, 6, 9, 10, 11, 16 (Egypt), Mobile Repair Units.
  Advanced M.T. Sub-Depôt, Ludd.

(b) Horse Transport:—
  Nos. 1, 2, 3, 4, Donkey Transport Companies.

(c) Camel Transport Corps:—
  "A," "B," "D," "E," "F," "G," "K," "L," "M," "P," "T," Companies.

Miscellaneous.

Corps of Guides and Interpreters.

Lent to British Mission in Hejaz.

No. 1 L.A.C. Battery.
2—10-pr. B.L. guns on Motor Lorries.
1 Platoon, 1st Garr. Bn. Royal Irish Regt.

Detachments:—
  No. 2 Camel Depôt.
  Egyptian Labour Corps.
  Egyptian Camel Corps.
  R.A.S.C.
  R.A.O.C.

EASTERN FORCE.

(Ceased to exist Aug. 12, 1917.)

Commander.—Major-Gen. (temp. Lieut.-Gen.) Sir PHILIP W. CHETWODE, Bt., K.C.B., K.C.M.G., D.S.O.

Brigadier-General, General Staff.—Bt. Lieut.-Col. (temp. Brig.-Gen.) G. P. DAWNAY, D.S.O., M.V.O. (R. of O.).

Brigadier-General, Royal Artillery.—Col. (temp. Brig.-Gen.) A. H. SHORT, C.B.

Chief Engineer.—Bt. Lieut.-Col. (temp. Brig.-Gen.) R. L. WALLER, R.E.

Deputy Adjutant and Quartermaster-General.—Bt. Lieut.-Col. (temp. Brig.-Gen.) E. F. O. GASCOIGNE, C.M.G., D.S.O. (R. of O.).

DESERT COLUMN.

(Became Desert Mounted Corps Aug. 12, 1917.)

Commander.—Major-Gen. H. G. CHAUVEL, C.B., C.M.G.

Brigadier-General, Royal Artillery.—Col. (temp. Brig.-Gen.) A. D'A. KING, C.B., D.S.O., *r.p.* (R. of O.).

Chief Engineer.—Major (temp. Brig.-Gen.) R. E. M. RUSSELL, D.S.O., R.E.

DESERT MOUNTED CORPS.

Commander.—Major-Gen. (temp. Lieut.-Gen.) Sir H. G. CHAUVEL, K.C.B., K.C.M.G.

Brigadier General, General Staff.—Bt. Lieut.-Col. (temp. Brig.-Gen.) R. G. H. HOWARD-VYSE, C.M.G., D.S.O., Royal Horse Guards, *p.s.c.* (relinquished, July, 1918).
  Bt. Col. (temp. Brig.-Gen.) C. A. C. GODWIN, D.S.O., 23rd Cavalry, I.A., *p.s.c.*

Deputy Adjutant and Quartermaster-General.—Major (temp. Brig.-Gen.) E. F. TREW, C.M.G., D.S.O., Royal Marines, *p.s.c.*

General Officer Commanding, Royal Artillery.—Col. (temp. Brig.-Gen.) A. D'A. KING, C.B., C.M.G., D.S.O., *r.p.* (R. of O.).

HEADQUARTERS.

Mounted Troops.
1/1st Worcester Yeomanry (attached from XXth Corps).

Artillery.
10th (Indian) Mountain Artillery Brigade, R.G.A.
  29th, 32nd, 39th (Indian) Mountain Batteries.

Machine Gun Corps.
Nos. 1, 2, 3, 4, 8, Light Car Patrols.
No. 2 Light Armoured Car Battery.

Signal Service.
"W" Corps Signal Company.
"BS," "KK," "AO," Cable Sections, and "DJ" (Indian) Cable Section.
103rd (Indian) Airline Section.
D.C. Cable Section.
Desert Mounted Corps Wireless Troop (formed from No. 9 Wagon W/T Section and London Pack W/T Section).
Australian Airline Section (disbanded, 23/8/18).
Australian Imperial Force Cable Section (disbanded, 23/8/18).
Australian Mounted Divisional Signal Company (disbanded, 23/8/18).

Engineers.
"D" Field Troop and Bridging Train, Australian Engineers.
Desert Mounted Corps Pontoon Park (8 Pontoons).

Infantry.
20th Indian Infantry Brigade.
2/155th Pioneers.

Royal Army Service Corps.
Nos. 3 and 5, (Egypt), Mobile Repair Units.
Corps Troops Supply Column (Supply details only).

Royal Army Ordnance Corps.
No. 38 Ordnance Mobile Workshop (light).
Corps Troops Supply Column (Ordnance details only).

Miscellaneous.
No. 1032 Area Employment Company.

Brief Record of Service.

Organized on Aug. 12, 1917, from the "Desert Column" which had been engaged throughout the advance from the Suez Canal at Romani, Maghdeba, Rafa and at the 1st and 2nd Battles of Gaza, the Corps has taken a prominent part in the several advances through Palestine and Syria.

The envelopment of the Turkish left flank resulted in the capture of Beersheba by the Australian Mounted Division on Oct. 31, 1917. During the advance through Philistia, the Corps, operating in front of the infantry, captured many important points, such as Deir Sineid and Huj (Nov. 8), Akir and Abu Shusheh (Nov. 15). When the infantry attack swung eastward through the Judæan Hills, Australian and New Zealand troops continued to push northward against ever-stiffening resistance, capturing Ramleh on Nov. 15, and occupying Jaffa and Sarona on Nov. 16 and 17 respectively. The Yeomanry Mounted Division, covering the left flank of the XXIst Corps, advanced up the Valley of Ajalon to Bethhoron. The capture of Neby Musa and Jericho was effected in co-operation with the XXth Corps on Feb. 21, 1918, and two important raids (Amman, March 21 to April 2, and Es Salt, April 29 to May 4), provided heavy fighting, in which infantry of the London Division co-operated. Subsequently, the Desert Mounted Corps was engaged at the Ghoraniyeh bridgehead and at other points in the Jordan Valley.

Hard marching and occasional stiff fighting were experienced in September, resulting in the capture of Jenin (Sept. 20), Nazareth (Sept. 21, after having been successfully raided on Sept. 20), Haifa (Sept. 23), Semakh and Tiberias (Sept 25), and Damascus (Oct. 1), the last-named in conjunction with the Sherifian forces. Rayak was occupied on Oct. 5, and, after a brief halt, the rapid advance was continued, Homs, Hama, and Aleppo being reached on Oct. 15, 22, and 26, respectively.

EGYPTIAN EXPEDITIONARY FORCE

LOCATIONS OF CORPS HEADQUARTERS.

Abasan (three miles east of Khan Yunus)	from	Aug. 12, 1917	Jericho	from	April 30, 1918
Esani (twenty miles south-south-east of Gaza)	,,	Oct. 28, 1917	Talat ed Dumm	,,	May 6, 1918
			Jerisheh (near Sarona)	,,	Sept. 16, 1918
Asluj (fifteen miles south of Beersheba)	,,	Oct. 30, 1917	El Lejjun (six miles west of El Afule)	,,	Sept. 20, 1918
Beersheba	,,	Nov. 1, 1917	Tiberias	,,	Sept. 27, 1918
Tel esh Sheria	,,	Nov. 7, 1917	Rosh Pina (near Safed)	,,	Sept. 28, 1918
Khurbet Muntaret (near Muntaret el Kaneitera)	,,	Nov. 8, 1917	El Kuneitra	,,	Sept. 29, 1918
			Kaukab	,,	Sept. 30, 1918
Hill 331 (near Julis)	,,	Nov. 10, 1917	Damascus	,,	Oct. 1, 1918
Yebna	,,	Nov. 14, 1917	Beirut	,,	Oct. 30, 1918
Khurbet Deiran (near El Kubeibe)	,,	Nov. 16, 1917	Tripolis	,,	Oct. 31, 1918
Talat ed Dumm	,,	April 25, 1918	Homs	,,	Nov. 1, 1918

XXth CORPS.

Commander.—Major-Gen. (temp. Lieut.-Gen.) Sir Philip W. CHETWODE, Bt., K.C.B., K.C.M.G., D.S.O.

Brigadier-General, General Staff.—Bt. Col. (temp. Brig.-Gen.) W. H. BARTHOLOMEW, C.M.G., D.S.O., R.A., *p.s.c.* (relinquished, April, 1918).

Bt. Lieut.-Col. (temp. Brig.-Gen.) A. P. WAVELL, C.M.G., M.C., Royal Highlanders, *p.s.c.*

Deputy Adjutant and Quartermaster-General.—Bt. Col. (temp. Brig.-Gen.) E. EVANS, C.M.G., D.S.O., Wiltshire Regt. A.D.C. (relinquished, Jan., 1918).

Lieut.-Col. (temp. Brig.-Gen.) C. W. PEARLESS, C.M.G., D.S.O., South Wales Borderers, *p.s.c.*

General Office Commanding, Royal Artillery.—Col. (temp. Brig.-Gen.) A. H. SHORT, C.B., C.M.G.

General Officer Commanding, Corps Heavy Artillery.—Lieut.-Col. (temp. Brig.-Gen.) P. de S. BURNEY, C.B. (R. of O.)

Chief Engineer.—Bt. Lieut. Col. (temp. Brig.-Gen.) R. L. WALLER, C.M.G., R.E.

HEADQUARTERS.

Mounted Troops.
1/1st Worcester Yeomanry.

Artillery.
9th Mountain Artillery Brigade, R.G.A.: 10th, 12th, 16th Mountain Batteries.
Hong-Kong and Singapore Mountain Battery, R.G.A.
61st Brigade, R.G.A.; 379th, 420th, 443rd Siege Batteries (ceased to belong to E.E.F., 21/5/18.)
96th Brigade, R.G.A.; 91st Heavy Battery; 300th, 378th, 383rd, 440th, 445th Siege Batteries. (445th Siege Battery ceased to belong to E.E.F., 4/4/18.)
97th Brigade, R.G.A.; 195th Heavy Battery; 134th, 201st, 334th, 421st, 422nd Siege Batteries. (201st Siege Battery ceased to belong to E.E.F., 7/5/18.)
103rd Brigade, R.G.A.; 10th Heavy Battery; 205th, 387th, 392nd Siege Batteries.
Nos. 1, 2, 3 (Medium), Trench Mortar Batteries, R.A.

Machine Gun Corps.
Half Machine Gun Company, Cape Corps.

Engineers.
No. 13 Pontoon Park, R.E.
220th Army Troops Company, R.E.
"V" Section (Sound Ranging) 7th Field Survey Company, R.E.

Signal Troops.
"V" Corps Signal Company, R.E.
N 24 Airline Section, R.E.
"AG," "BQ," "BR," Cable Sections, R.E.
No. 1 Signal Section, Corps Heavy Artillery, R.E.

Royal Army Service Corps.

(a) Mechanical Transport:—
    Nos. 811, 963, 964, 966, 980, 983, 990, 1007, 1008, 1030, 1072 M.T. Companies (attached Heavy Artillery).
    Nos. 12 and 13 (Egypt), Mobile Repair Units.

(b) Horse Transport:—
    Corps Troops Train.

(c) Camel Transport:—
    "N," "U," "V," Companies.

Royal Army Ordnance Corps.

Nos. 52, 58, 60, Ordnance Mobile Workshops (light).
Corps Troops Supply Column (Ordnance details only).

Miscellaneous.

No. 1000 Area Employment Company.

Brief Record of Service.

The Corps was formed on Aug. 2, 1917, and took over the line on the right of the XXIst Corps. In the advance into Philistia, the Turkish defences west and south-west of Beersheba were carried on Oct. 31, and during the following week the enemy was swept from strong positions in the battles of Khuweilfeh, Sheria, and Hareira. At the beginning of December, the XXth Corps relieved the XXIst in the Judæan Hills, captured Jerusalem on Dec. 9, and, in the last days of the year, pushed northward astride the Jerusalem-Nablus road against powerful resistance. Jericho was captured on Feb. 21, 1918, (in co-operation with Desert Mounted Corps), and a northerly advance, entailing stiff fighting over difficult ground, was made in March.

A portion of the Corps co-operated with cavalry of the Desert Mounted Corps in the Amman raid (March-April) and the Es Salt raid (April-May).

The commencement of the final operations of the campaign was a vigorous attack, covered by a feint on the night of Sept. 18-19, and during the following week the XXth Corps drove the Turks northward and westward across the rugged hills of Mount Ephraim, into the areas where enemy resistance had been dislocated and disorganized by the rapid movements of the XXIst and Desert Mounted Corps.

LOCATIONS OF CORPS HEADQUARTERS.

Deir el Belah (beach)	from Aug. 2, 1917	*Junction Station	from	Nov. 23, 1917
Wadi Selka (south-east of Deir el Belah)	„ Aug. 18, 1917	*Latron	„	Nov. 28, 1917
El Fukhari	„ Sept. 3, 1917	Jerusalem	„	Jan. 3, 1918
*El Buggar	„ Oct. 30, 1917	Ram Allah	„	Sept. 19, 1918
*Beersheba	„ Nov. 2, 1917	*Huwarah	„	Sept. 22, 1918
*Gaza (Red House)	„ Nov. 18, 1917	Nablus	„	Sept. 24, 1918
		Haifa	„	Oct. 29, 1918

* Advanced Headquarters.

XXIst CORPS.

Commander.—Major-Gen. (temp. Lieut.-Gen.) Sir Edward S. BULFIN, K.C.B., C.V.O.

Brigadier-General, General Staff.—Bt. Col. (temp. Brig.-Gen.) E. T. HUMPHREYS, D.S.O., Lancashire Fusiliers, p.s.c. (relinquished, Feb., 1918).
    Bt. Lieut.-Col. (temp. Brig.-Gen.) H. F. SALT, D.S.O., R.A., p.s.c.

Deputy Adjutant and Quartermaster-General.—Bt. Col. (temp. Brig.-Gen.) St. G. B. ARMSTRONG, R.M.L.I., p.s.c.

General Officer Commanding, Royal Artillery.—Bt. Col. (temp. Brig.-Gen.) H. A. D. SIMPSON BAIKIE, C.B., C.M.G., R.A., p.s.c.

General Officer Commanding, Corps Heavy Artillery.—Col. (temp. Brig.-Gen.) O. C. WILLIAMSON-OSWALD, C.B., C.M.G., R.G.A.

Chief Engineer.—Major (temp. Brig.-Gen.) R. P. T. HAWKSLEY, C.M.G., D.S.O., R.E.

HEADQUARTERS.

Mounted Troops.
Composite Yeomanry Regiment ("A" Squadron, Duke of Lancaster's Own Yeomanry, and "A" and "B" Squadrons, 1/1st Herts. Yeomanry).
54th Divisional Cyclist Company.

Artillery.
8th Mountain Artillery Brigade, R.G.A.: 11th, 13th, 17th Mountain Batteries.
95th Brigade, R.G.A.; 181st Heavy Battery; 304th, 314th, 320th, 322nd, 394th Siege Batteries. (320th and 322nd Siege Batteries ceased to belong to E.E.F., 4/4/18.)
100th Brigade, R.G.A.; 15th Heavy Battery; 43rd, 292nd, 423rd Siege Batteries. (292nd and 423rd Siege Batteries ceased to belong to E.E.F., 7/5/18.)
102nd Brigade, R.G.A.; 189th, 202nd Heavy Batteries; 209th, 380th, 424th Siege Batteries. (424th Siege Battery ceased to belong to E.E.F., 3/1/18.)
Nos. 55, 121, 123 Anti-Aircraft Sections, R.A.
Nos. 4, 5, 6 (Medium), Trench Mortar Batteries, R.A.

Engineers.
14th A.T. Company, R.E.
"N" and "NN" Sections (Sound Ranging) 7th Field Survey Company, R.E.
28th Observation Group, 7th Field Survey Company, R.E.

Signal Service.
"U" Corps Signal Company, R.E.
N 21 Airline Section, R.E.
"DH" (Indian), "HH" and "GY" Cable Sections, R.E.
No. 12 Pack W/T Section, R.E.
No. 2 Signal Section Corps Heavy Artillery, R.E.

Infantry.
2nd Battalion Loyal North Lancashire Regiment (ceased to belong to E.E.F., 7/5/18).
2/107th Pioneers.

Royal Army Service Corps.
(a) Mechanical Transport:—
   Nos. 810, 904, 951, 952, 955, 965, 967, 982, 984, 988, 989, 1031, 1032, 1073 M.T. Companies (attached Heavy Artillery). (Nos. 810, 1031, 1032 Companies ceased to belong to E.E.F., 21/5/18.)
   Nos. 1 and 2 (Egypt), Mobile Repair Units.
(b) Horse Transport:—
   Corps Troops Train.
(c) Camel Transport:—
   "C," "H," and "R" Companies.

Royal Army Ordnance Corps.
Nos. 37 and 59 Ordnance Mobile Workshops (light).
Corps Troops Supply Column (Ordnance details only).

Miscellaneous.
No. 1031 Area Employment Company.

Brief Record of Service.

The Corps was organized on Aug. 12, 1917, and took over the Coastal and Sheikh Abbas sectors, which it held until the general advance started. Gaza was captured on Nov. 7, and the rapid advance through Philistia into the Judæan hills (in co-operation with the Desert Mounted Corps), carried the troops of the XXIst Corps to within five miles of Jerusalem by Nov. 21. During this advance the nature of the fighting changed from trench warfare to open warfare, and then to hill fighting. In December, on relief by the XXth Corps, the XXIst relieved the Desert Mounted Corps on the new line from Midieh to the sea. The crossing of the Auja, in Dec., 1917, and the difficult hill fighting around the Wadi Ballut, in March and April, 1918, advanced the line to an average depth of six miles.

On Sept. 19, the right of the strong Turkish defensive system was broken in the battle of Sharon, Kefr Kasim, Jiljulieh, Tireh, and Tul Keram were captured, and the flank rolled up to allow the mounted troops to carry out the envelopment required of them.

After a brief halt at Haifa, the advance northward was continued on Oct. 1, and as the result of hard marching, Beirut and Tripolis were occupied on Oct. 8 and 18 respectively.

LOCATIONS OF CORPS HEADQUARTERS.

Deir el Belah ... from Aug. 12, 1917	Jaffa ... from Jan. 4, 1918
*Raspberry Hill (2½ miles east of Deir el Belah) ... „ Nov. 1, 1917	Jerisheh (near Sarona) ... „ April 1, 1918
*Deir Sineid ... „ Nov. 11, 1917	*Sabieh ... „ Sept. 19, 1918
*Jewish Colony (near Beit Duras) ... „ Nov. 14, 1917	*Tul Keram ... „ Sept. 21, 1918
*El Kukab ... „ Nov. 19, 1917	Haifa ... „ Sept. 28, 1918
Bir Salem (German Orphanage, near Ramleh) ... „ Nov. 28, 1917	Beirut ... „ Oct. 8, 1918

* Advanced Headquarters.

CHAYTOR'S FORCE.
(During Operations, Sept. 19 to Oct. 31, 1918).

Commander.—Col. (temp. Major-Gen.) Sir E. W. C. CHAYTOR, K.C.M.G., C.B., *p.s.c.*, A.D.C.
(And Staff of the Australian and New Zealand Mounted Division.)

HEADQUARTERS.

Mounted Troops.

Australian and New Zealand Mounted Division (less one Squadron).

Artillery.

A/263 Battery, R.F.A.
No. 195 Heavy Battery, R.G.A.
29th and 32nd (Indian), Mountain Batteries, R.G.A.
No. 6 (Medium) Trench Mortar Battery, R.A.
Nos. 96, 102, 103 Anti-Aircraft Sections, R.A.

Engineers.

Detachment No. 35 A.T. Company, R.E.

Infantry.

38th and 39th Battalions Royal Fusiliers.
20th Indian Brigade.
1st and 2nd Battalions British West Indies Regiment.

Brief Record of Service.

Sept. 18.—The Force, constituted as above, held the eastern end of the British line, including the Ghoraniyeh bridgehead.

WEST OF JORDAN.

„ 19.—The 2nd British West Indies Regiment captured ridge south of Bakr Ridge, and on the following day

„ 20.—captured Bakr and Chalk Ridges, while 1st British West Indies Regiment captured Grant Hill and Baghalat, and the Auckland Mounted Rifles seized Kh. Fusail and Tel Sh. edh Dhiab.

„ 22.—The 38th Battalion Royal Fusiliers advanced to Mankattat el Mallaha and, with the assistance of two companies of the 39th Battalion, captured the ford at Umm esh Shert.
Further north, the New Zealand Mounted Rifles Brigade captured El Makhruk and Abd el Kadir, taking 500 prisoners, including a Divisional Commander, and blocking the important road *viâ* the bridge at Jisr ed Damieh, between Nablus, west of Jordan, and Es Salt on the east. The bridge itself was captured by the New Zealand Mounted Rifles Brigade and 1st British West Indies Regiment. 1st Light Horse Brigade and 2nd British West Indies Regiment were engaged near Mafid Jozeleh.

„ 23.—All enemy opposition ceased on west bank of Jordan

EAST OF JORDAN.

Sept. 22.—The 2nd Light Horse Brigade captured Tel er Rame, a Turkish strong post seven miles south-east of the Ghoraniyeh bridge.

„ 23.—The 1st Light Horse, with 2nd British West Indies Regiment, captured Mafid Jozeleh, and the 2nd Light Horse took Kabr Mujahid, while the New Zealand Mounted Rifles, having crossed the Jordan, pushed rapidly eastward and seized Es Salt.

„ 24.—Ain es Sir and Ain Hemar occupied by 2nd Light Horse.

„ 25.—The Auckland Mounted Rifles succeeded in cutting the Hejaz Railway near Kalaat ez Zerka, and the 2nd Light Horse and N.Z.M.R. Brigades and the 1st A.L.H. Regt. captured Amman, the Canterbury Mounted Rifles taking a prominent part in this latter engagement.

„ 26.—The 1st Light Horse captured Kalaat ez Zerka, and 2nd Light Horse cut the railway north of Ziza Station.

„ 27.—1st Light Horse engaged a body of the enemy north of Wadi el Hammam, taking 300 prisoners and two machine guns.

„ 29.—The Maan garrison, consisting of 4,066 officers and men, with twelve guns and thirty-five machine guns, surrendered to the 2nd Light Horse Brigade near El Kastal.

EGYPTIAN EXPEDITIONARY FORCE

FRENCH DETACHMENT.
(Détachement Français de Palestine et Syrie.)

Commander.—Col. P. de PIÉPAPE, C.B.

HEADQUARTERS.

Infantry.
  Regiment of Tirailleurs, consisting of 7th Battalion 1st Tirailleurs and 9th Battalion 2nd Tirailleurs, Algerians, with section of 2 guns.
  Regiment Légion d'Orient, consisting of 1st and 2nd Battalions Armenians, and 23rd Company Syrians, with section of 2 guns.
  5th Garrison Battalion of 115th Territorial Regiment.
  3rd Battalion Légion d'Orient.

Cavalry.
  Two Squadrons, 1st Regiment of Spahis.
  Two Squadrons, 4th Regiment Chasseurs d'Afrique.
  One Machine Gun Troop (dismounted).

Artillery Group.
  1st Battery.
  14th Battery of 5th African Field Artillery Group.
  30th Battery of 2nd Mountain Artillery Regiment.
  30th Mixed Munition Section.

Engineers.
  19/6 Company 2nd Engineer Regiment (three sections Sappers and Miners).

Signals.
  Signal Section of 8th Engineer Regiment (4th Section of above Engineer Company).

Artillery and Engineer Services.
  Subsidiary Depôts of the main Artillery and Engineer Base Depôt at Port Said.

Medical Service.
  Nos. 2/P and 3/P Mountain Ambulances.
  Stretcher-Bearer Group.
  No. 2 Field Hospital and C.C.S.
  Advanced Depôt of Medical Stores and Material.

Supply Section of Detachment.

M.T. Section.
  Transport of Material.

Military Police.
  Three mounted, and one dismounted "Brigades."

Brief Record of Service.

1918. CAVALRY.
Sept. 18.—At Jaffa.
  „ 19.—Advanced in co-operation with 5th Australian Light Horse, crossed the Tul Keram–Haifa road, capturing an enemy battery and seizing a convoy of guns, supplies, and a detachment of the Turkish Field Treasury.
  „ 20.—Co-operated with 5th Australian Light Horse in the successful raid to cut the Tul Keram–Jenin railway.
  „ 21.—Entered Nablus in face of determined resistance and captured 700 prisoners, two guns, and nine machine guns.
  „ 27.—Carried out a demonstration against enemy holding the Jordan crossing near the village of Mishmar Hayarden, and forded the river 700 yards south of Jisr Benat Yakub.
  „ 29.—Involved in severe night fighting at Sasa, where two guns and several machine guns were captured.
  „ 30.—Moved, dismounted, along the hills of Kalabet el Mezza, brushing aside all opposition, and blocked the gorge N.W. of Er Rabue, and co-operated with 5th Light Horse Brigade in capture of 4,000 prisoners.
Oct. 19.—Left Damascus for Beirut.

1918. INFANTRY.
Sept. 18.—The infantry of the detachment held the ridge north of the Wadi Ballut, with a front of nearly 6,000 yards, between Rafat and Kh. Umm el Ikba; with 10th Division on its right, and 54th Division on its left.
  „ 19.—0430.—The attack started, and in spite of vigorous resistance, Three Bushes Hill
    0515.—was stormed, and this initial success was followed by the capture of
    0545.—Scurry Hill. In this brief action, 212 prisoners (including sixteen officers) and nine machine guns were taken.
    0700.—Deir el Kussis reached, but as the position was exposed and the situation uncertain, this advanced point was not held.
    1415.—Two Cairns Hill captured and the enemy driven into the Wadi Ayun.
    2350.—Deir el Kussis, which had been reoccupied, again captured and consolidated.
    0500.—Arara and Zawieh captured.
Oct. 8.—Haifa reached and on
Oct. 20.—the Detachment entered Beirut.

ITALIAN DETACHMENT.
(Distaccamento Italiano di Palestina.)

Commander.—Lieut.-Col. Cav. FRANCESCO D'AGOSTINO, Corps of Bersaglieri (relinquished, Sept. 9, 1918).
Lieut.-Col. Cav. GUSTAVO PESENTI, Corps of Alpini.

Headquarters.
Royal Carabinieri Company.
Bersaglieri Company.
Cacciatori Company.
Mounted Carabinieri Platoon.
Port Said Base and Composite Platoon.
Special Platoon.
Ex-Prisoners-of-War Company.

Brief Record of Service.

The Italian Palestine Detachment was formed on July 1, 1917.

On Nov. 8 and following days, it formed part of the mobile column known as the Composite Force, and took part in the capture of the Atawineh Redoubt Trench System and the advance north of Gaza.

The Detachment was present at the fall of Jerusalem, and furnished a Guard of Honour at the official entry of General Allenby on Dec. 11; since when important guard duties have been continuously performed at Jerusalem, Junction Station, Jaffa, and other centres.

4th CAVALRY DIVISION.
(Late 1st Mounted Division, late Yeomanry Mounted Division.)

Commander.—Major-Gen. Sir G. de S. BARROW, K.C.M.G., C.B., *p.s.c.*

10th Cavalry Brigade (late 6th Mounted Brigade, late 1/2nd South Midland Mounted Brigade):—

Commander.—Col. (temp. Brig.-Gen.) T. M. S. Pitt, 2nd County of London Yeomanry (relinquished, July, 1918).
  Bt. Lieut.-Col. (temp. Brig.-Gen.) C. A. C. GODWIN, D.S.O., 23rd Cavalry, I.A. (relinquished, Aug., 1918).
  Bt. Lieut.-Col. (temp. Brig.-Gen.) R. G. H. Howard-Vyse, C.M.G., D.S.O., Royal Horse Guards, *p.s.c.* (relinquished, Sept., 1918).
  Lieut.-Col. (temp. Brig.-Gen.) W. G. K. GREEN, D.S.O., 36th Jacob's Horse, I.A.

1/1st Dorset Yeomanry, 2nd Lancers, 38th Central India Horse.
1/1st Bucks Yeomanry and 1/1st Berks. Yeomanry (ceased to belong to E.E.F., 19/6/18).
10th Cavalry Brigade Signal Troop, R.E.
17th Machine Gun Squadron.

11th Cavalry Brigade (late 8th Mounted Brigade, late 1/1st London Mounted Brigade):—

Commander.—Col. (temp. Brig.-Gen.) A. H. M. TAYLOR, D.S.O., (relinquished, Sept., 1917).
  Bt. Lieut.-Col. (temp. Brig.-Gen.) C. S. ROME, D.S.O., 11th Hussars (relinquished, June, 1918).
  Bt. Col. (temp. Brig.-Gen.) C. L. GREGORY, C.B., 19th Lancers, *p.s.c.*

1/1st County of London Yeomanry, 29th Lancers, 36th Jacob's Horse.
1/1st City of London Yeomanry, and 1/3rd County of London Yeomanry (ceased to belong to E.E.F., 2/7/18).
11th Cavalry Brigade Signal Troop, R.E.
21st Machine Gun Squadron.

12th Cavalry Brigade (late 22nd Mounted Brigade, late 1/1st North Midland Mounted Brigade):—

Commander.—Col. (temp. Brig.-Gen.) F. A. B. FRYER (relinquished, Dec., 1917).
  Bt. Lieut.-Col. (temp. Brig.-Gen.) P. D. FITZGERALD, D.S.O., 11th Hussars, *p.s.c.* (relinquished, April, 1918).
  Lieut.-Col. (temp. Brig.-Gen.) J. T. WIGAN, C.M.G., D.S.O., Berks. Yeomanry.

EGYPTIAN EXPEDITIONARY FORCE

- 1/1st Staffordshire Yeomanry, 6th Cavalry, 19th Lancers.
  1/1st Lincolnshire Yeomanry and 1/1st East Riding Yeomanry (ceased to belong to E.E.F., 2/7/18).
  12th Cavalry Brigade Signal Troop, R.E.
  18th Machine Gun Squadron.

Corps Cavalry Regiment. 1/2nd County of London Yeomanry (ceased to belong to E.E.F., 28/5/18).

Divisional Troops.

20th Brigade, R.H.A. (1/1st Berks., Hamps., and Leicester Batteries, and Brigade Ammunition Column.
4th Field Squadron (late No. 6), R.E.
4th Cavalry Division Signal Squadron, R.E.
4th Cavalry Divisional Train (Nos. 999, 1000, 1001, 1002 Companies, R.A.S.C.).
10th, 11th, 12th Cavalry Brigade Mobile Veterinary Sections.

Brief Record of Service.

The Yeomanry Regiments of which the Yeomanry Division was composed left England in 1915, and served as detached brigades and regiments on the Egyptian, Gallipoli and Salonika fronts: and with Desert Column took part in the advance from the Suez Canal, culminating in the battles of Gaza in March and April, 1917.

On the reorganization in Aug., 1917, it joined the Desert Mounted Corps as the Yeomanry Division. Six regiments were withdrawn in April, 1918, for service as machine-gunners on the Western Front, the vacancies being filled by Indian Cavalry Regiments. The division was renamed "4th Cavalry Division" in July, 1918, and 6th, 8th, and 22nd Mounted Brigades became 10th, 11th, and 12th Cavalry Brigades, respectively.

YEOMANRY MOUNTED DIVISION.

1917.
Oct. 26.—The Division was detached as Army Reserve, and concentrated about Hiseia and Shellal, but 8th Mounted Brigade was lent to Australian Mounted Division and held an outpost line from near El Buggar north-westward to Point 280 near Kh. Umm Rijl, a length of twelve miles. The right of this line was held by 1st County of London (Middlesex) Yeomanry, with 3rd County of London Yeomanry on the left, and City of London Yeomanry in reserve at Karm.

„ 27.—Middlesex Yeomanry were heavily attacked at 0415 by a force of all arms estimated at 3,000–4,000. The garrison at Point 630, although almost surrounded by 0515, defended the position throughout the day against repeated assaults, until relieved by infantry of 158th Brigade at 1600. 3rd Australian Light Horse Brigade were ordered up from Shellal to support the squadron holding the knoll Point 720, but, before they could arrive the post was subjected to concentrated shell-fire and overwhelmed by a combined mounted and dismounted attack. The reserve regiment frustrated an attempt to break through between Points 720 and 630, and at dusk when the enemy withdrew, former position was reoccupied.

Nov. 8.—The division moving north-eastward, as a part of "Barrow's Detachment," encountered stiff resistance at Kh. Mujeidilat. City of London and Middlesex Yeomanry attacked but were unable to dislodge the enemy and orders were received to break off the action and march to Tel esh Sheria.

„ 9 to 11 The division moved via Huj, Zeita, and El Mejdel, and

„ 12.—relieved Australian and New Zealand (Anzac) Division along the Wadi Sukereir between 52nd Division and the sea.

„ 13.—6th and 8th Mounted Brigades occupied Beshshit and Yebnah respectively in conjunction with the infantry attack on Katrah and El Mughar. Patrols found Kubeibeh and Zernukah strongly

1917.
Nov. 13.—held and the infantry advance was checked near El Mughar. 8th Mounted Brigade moved on Zernukah and Kubeibeh; 22nd Brigade was held in readiness to attack Akir as soon as El Muharg was taken; while 6th Brigade were ordered to attack the ridge running north-east from El Mughar. At 1500 Royal Bucks Hussars and Dorset Yeomanry charged the El Mughar ridge from the Wadi Jamus riding 4,500 yards across an open plain devoid of cover, and subjected throughout to galling shell, machine-gun, and rifle fire. The whole hostile position was captured and consolidated by 1530 and 1,096 prisoners, two field guns, and fourteen machine guns taken. (Later in the evening the village was cleared and two squadrons Berkshire Yeomanry captured a further 400 prisoners.)

22nd Mounted Brigade attacked Akir at 1530, but were held up until nightfall. This brigade rounded up seventy-two prisoners and a machine gun retiring from the El Mughar Ridge.

„ 14.—Middlesex Yeomanry (8th Mounted Brigade) occupied Zernukah and Kubeibeh at dawn. Imperial Camel Brigade, attached, remained about Zernukah and Kubeibeh to watch the north, while the division moved east on Kh. Selmeh, Naaneh, and Bir Ghazlun. 22nd Brigade took Naaneh at 1430 with sixty prisoners and one gun, and demolished one mile of railway to the south.

„ 15.—The Sidun–Abu Shusheh Ridge, attacked at 0700 from south-west and north-west by 6th and 22nd Mounted Brigades, with one battalion Imperial Camel Corps Brigade attached, was strongly held. Leicestershire and Berkshire Batteries, R.H.A., assisted by 75th Divisional Artillery, covered the advance, but the position was only taken at 0900 after a stubborn resistance, when a mounted charge by Dorset Yeomanry routed the enemy with the loss of 360 prisoners and one gun. Over 400 Turks were killed in this engagement.

1917.
Nov. 18 to „ 19 Brigades pushed forward into the Judæan Hills, along rock-strewn wadis, and by tracks which existed only in name. Little enemy opposition was encountered but difficulties of terrain rendered rapid movement impossible.

„ 20.—Strong organized resistance was encountered around Beitunia.

„ 21.—6th Mounted Brigade renewed its attack on Beitunia, supported by Lincoln Yeomanry (22nd Brigade), but were opposed by fresh troops brought from Aleppo, numerous and well-trained, who counter-attacked and forced a withdrawal. Meanwhile, East Riding Yeomanry (22nd Brigade) were held up at Ramallah, and the division was ordered to fall back on Beit Ur el Foka and Beit Ur et Tahta.

„ 25.—Leicester Battery, R.H.A., by superhuman efforts man-handled their guns up to Foka, and

„ 26.—Berkshire Battery arrived at Tahta.

„ 27.—An enemy force 400 strong, supported by a howitzer battery, attacked Sh. Abu ez Zeitoun, one mile east of Foka. The garrison (6th Mounted Brigade) held out throughout the day although outnumbered seven to one. At the same time, 200 Turks attacked the left of 8th Mounted Brigade near Beit Dukka, and 2,000 hostile infantry were known to be concentrating at Beitunia. 7th Mounted Brigade (Corps Reserve) were sent up from Zernukah in support, made a forced march, and

„ 28.—arrived at Tahta at 0500. A strong attack was launched against 22nd Brigade at 0630, but Sherwood Rangers and South Notts. Hussars (7th Brigade) reinforced and the attack was held. 155th Brigade (52nd Division), ordered up to cover the left flank of the defence, arrived at 0900. Meanwhile the post at Zeitoun, after a most stubborn resistance, was overwhelmed at 0800, and the brigade was forced to fall back to the ridge between Foka and Tahta. The attack on 7th Mounted Brigade was renewed after dark, but, with assistance from 1/7th Scottish Rifles (52nd Division), the attack was beaten off.

„ 29 to „ 30 Australian Mounted Division came up on the left; 52nd and 74th Divisions relieved the Yeomanry, who, after ten days arduous fighting over difficult ground, went into bivouac for rest and refitting at El Mughar.

Nov. 30 (The division was inspected by the Commander-in-Chief in December; January was spent in refitting and training; and February in salvage work on the old trench lines south of Gaza. In March the division moved up to the Wadi Sukerier, but, on April 2, returned to Belah for reorganization.)

1918.
April 24.—6th Mounted Brigade, with Middlesex Yeomanry and Mysore Imperial Lancers, were ordered to march to Jordan Valley to take part in the Es Salt raid, and reached the point of concentration on April 29.

May 2.—The brigade crossed the Jordan in support of Australian and New Zealand Mounted Troops, who were holding a defensive flank northward to cover the withdrawal from Es Salt. The brigade was not engaged and re-crossed the river during the night May 3-4.

(During the following week the remainder of the division reached the valley; the Indian regiments, to replace the units withdrawn, arrived; and the reorganization was complete.

May to July Constant patrolling and consolidation of defences were carried on in the heat and dust of the Jordan Valley. The enemy was completely dominated; seventy prisoners were captured, and over 400 Turks killed or wounded in patrol encounters.

4TH CAVALRY DIVISION.

1918.
July 19.—The division went into camp at Ras Deiran to rest and recoup.

Aug. 8.—Division returned to the Jordan Valley, and once more took over patrol duties. 29th Lancers and 36th Jacob's Horse (11th Cavalry Brigade) were engaged in successful patrol encounters. Climatic conditions improved and training could be carried on.

Sept. 18.—Concentrated in the orange groves near Selmeh.

„ 19.—Divisional artillery supported the infantry attack, and pioneer parties advanced in rear of 7th Division to cut gaps in the wire and flag the routes for the cavalry through the captured defences.

11th Cavalry Brigade passed through the wire at 0858, and moved rapidly northward to the Kakon-Liktera switch line, where the advanced guard came under fire. The position was galloped by Jacob's Horse and 250 prisoners taken. By 1800 10th Brigade was moving on Kerkur, 12th Brigade was at Jelameh, headquarters and 11th Brigade at Tel ed Dhrur. 2nd Lancers (10th Brigade) advanced up the Kerkur-Lejjun defile, and at 2145 No. 11 Light Armoured Car Battery was attached to the Lancers to reconnoitre the Musmus Pass, which was found clear.

„ 20.—Lejjun was occupied at 0330 and two hours later 2nd Lancers and the armoured cars moved on El Afule. On debouching from the Pass the Turks were encountered in strength astride the road. One squadron and the cars held the enemy in front while the remainder of the regiment charged their left flank, killing or wounding forty-six and capturing 470. 12th Brigade occupied El Afule at 0800, and captured ten locomotives, fifty trucks, and three aeroplanes, while the armoured cars captured twelve lorries driven by Germans endeavouring to escape by Beisan. By 0900 all railway lines radiating from El Afule had been cut, and the division moved on Beisan at 1300, leaving one regiment to hold all roads to the north. 10th Brigade reached Beisan at 1630 (having captured 800 prisoners en route), and galloped over all opposition, taking 100 prisoners and three 15cm. howitzers which were manned to cover the roads to south and east. The division concentrated at Beisan at 1800, and 19th Lancers (12th Brigade) were sent by a difficult mountainous road to hold the Jordan crossing at

„ 21.—Jisr el Mujamia, where they arrived at 0800. South of Beisan 38th Central India Horse (10th Brigade) captured 158 prisoners as the result of a moonlight charge. All roads in the neighbourhood were picquetted and 3,000 were made prisoner or gave themselves up to our patrols during the night.

„ 22.—Jacob's Horse crossed the Jordan at Jisr Esh Sh. Hussein to patrol the east bank and to round up fugitives. No. 11 Light Armoured Car Battery left to join Desert Mounted Corps Headquarters.

„ 23.—Central India Horse relieved 19th Lancers at Jisr el Mujamia. At 0600 11th Brigade moved south along both banks of the Jordan to cut off the retreat of Seventh Turkish Army. Patrols of 29th Lancers were fired on at 0830, from the direction of Makt Abu Naj, by a force covering the ford. Middlesex Yeomanry moved around the enemy's left flank while two squadrons 29th Lancers charged a mound forming the centre of the hostile position and captured

1918.
Sept. 23.—800 prisoners and fifteen machine guns. Two charges by Jacob's Horse on the left bank were held, and the Hampshire Battery was ordered up. The battery came into action in the open, but was immediately subjected to a heavy and accurate fire from two concealed enemy batteries. The situation was cleared by a squadron of Middlesex Yeomanry, who forded the river at Makt. Fatahallah and charged the guns, putting them out of action. The enemy thereupon withdrew, abandoning large quantities of stores and suffering heavy casualties from machine-gun fire.

,, 24.—The march southward continued. Middlesex Yeomanry encountered a hostile advanced guard, estimated at 1,200 with numerous machine guns, in the Wadi Maleh. Hampshire gunners came into action and the Turks were driven back to the Jordan in hopeless rout, exposing the main body to immediate attack. On the west bank 4,000 prisoners (including Rushdi Bey, commanding 16th Division), twenty-nine machine guns and 8,000 rifles were taken, and the few Turks who got away across the river were driven into barren and waterless country. A further 1,000 prisoners were rounded up by Dorset Yeomanry at Ain el Beida.

,, 25.—Division concentrated at Beisan with 10th Brigade at Jisr el Mujamia, in preparation for operations east of Jordan.

,, 26.—10th Brigade engaged enemy holding a line through Zebda–Irbid–Beitras. One squadron 2nd Lancers covered deployment, while remainder of the regiment fought its way round the north flank. Central India Horse captured Zebda, and by nightfall Irbid was closely invested on north, west, and south.

12th Brigade moved to Esh Shuni, and Divisional Headquarters and 11th Brigade to Jisr el Mujamia.

1918.
Sept. 27.—Irbid was evacuated during the night, and 10th Brigade followed up the retreat and forced an action at Er Remte. Dorset Yeomanry attacked from west and south-west at 1035, while remainder of brigade worked round under cover to cut the line of retreat east to Deraa. The enemy counter-attacked Dorset Yeomanry, but the advanced squadron was withdrawn, mounted, and launched upon the counter-attacking force. Twenty-five of the enemy were killed in the charge and the rest fled in disorder to the village. A charge by Central India Horse near Tuiele was equally successful, and by 1150 the Turks were in full retreat leaving 187 prisoners and over twenty machine guns and automatic rifles in our hands.

During the night patrols gained touch with Sherifian troops operating against Deraa.

,, 28.—The Division moved on Deraa which was found to have been occupied by the Sherifian Army. 10th Brigade remained about Deraa and the rest of the division moved to Mezerib.

,, 29.—Division marched north along the Haj road with Sherifian Army on the right.

,, 30.—11th Brigade, acting as advanced guard, reached Khiyara at 1700, where it was shelled from the Jebel el Mania and an enemy column was seen retiring on Kiswe. The village was cleared by a mounted charge, one regiment was sent in pursuit, while the brigade pushed forward on Khan Denun. Some of the enemy escaped up the steep slopes of Jebel el Mania and the rest retired in disorganized rout on Kiswe.

Oct. 1.—The Division camped in the neighbourhood of Daraya, having covered 140 miles over difficult country in six days.

,, 6 to 15 The march was continued viâ Khan Meizelun, Zebdani, and Shtora, to Baalbek, whence 12th Brigade pushed on to Lebwe.

(Total prisoners taken from Sept. 19 to Oct. 15 were approximately 20,000.)

5th CAVALRY DIVISION.

(Late 2nd Mounted Division.)

Commander.—Major-Gen. H. J. M. MACANDREW, C.B., D.S.O.

13th Cavalry Brigade (late 5th Mounted Brigade).

Commander.—Bt. Lieut.-Col. (temp. Brig.-Gen.) P. D. FITZGERALD, D.S.O., 11th Hussars (relinquished, Dec., 1917).

Bt. Lieut.-Col. (temp. Brig.-Gen.) P. J. V. KELLY, C.M.G., D.S.O., 3rd Hussars (relinquished, Oct., 1918).

Bt. Lieut.-Col. (temp. Brig.-Gen.) G. A. WEIR, D.S.O., 3rd Dragoon Guards.

1/1st Warwickshire Yeomanry (ceased to belong to E.E.F., 19/6/18).
1/1st Gloucester Yeomanry, 9th Hodson's Horse, 18th Lancers.
13th Cavalry Brigade Signal Troop, R.E.
19th Machine Gun Squadron.

14th Cavalry Brigade (late 7th Mounted Brigade).

Commander.—Lieut.-Col. (temp. Brig.-Gen.) J. T. WIGAN, C.M.G., D.S.O., Berks. Yeomanry (relinquished, Dec., 1917).

Lieut.-Col. (temp. Brig.-Gen.) G. V. CLARKE, D.S.O., City of London Yeomanry.

1/1st Sherwood Rangers, 20th Deccan Horse, 34th Poona Horse.
14th Cavalry Brigade Signal Troop, R.E.
20th Machine Gun Squadron.

15th (Imperial Service) Cavalry Brigade (late I.S. Cavalry Brigade).

Commander.—Lieut.-Col. (temp. Brig.-Gen.) C. R. HARBORD, D.S.O., 30th Lancers, I.A.

Jodhpore I.S. Lancers, Mysore I.S. Lancers, 1st Hyderabad I.S. Lancers.
15th Kathiawar I.S. Signal Troop.
Imperial Service Machine Gun Squadron.

Divisional Troops.

Essex Battery, R.H.A., and Brigade Ammunition Column (less 2 Sections).
5th Field Squadron (late No. 7), R.E.
5th Cavalry Division Signal Squadron, R.E.
5th Cavalry Divisional Train (Nos. 1103, 1044, 1104, 1105 Companies, R.A.S.C.).
13th, 14th, and 15th (I.S.), Cavalry Brigade Mobile Veterinary Sections.

Brief Record of Service.

5th Cavalry Division, after serving with the British Expeditionary Force in France, landed in Egypt in March, 1918. The Division was brought up to strength by the inclusion of Yeomanry and Imperial Service Cavalry, who had been serving with the Egyptian Expeditionary Force, and joined Desert Mounted Corps on July 2.

1918.
Sept. 18.—Division was concentrated in the orange groves north-west of Sarona, in preparation for the attack.

„ 19.—At 0430 divisional artillery was in action to support the advance of 60th Division.
13th Brigade crossed Nahr el Falik and advanced to the line Tel ed Dhrur-Liktera-the Sea. A column of the enemy was engaged at 1100, and 250 prisoners and four guns captured. At 1815 the brigade left Liktera with Divisional Headquarters for Jarak.
14th Brigade crossed Nahr Iskanderuneh at 1100 and pushed on towards Jarak; while 15th Brigade, with artillery and transport column reached Liktera at 1500.

„ 20.—13th and 14th Brigades reached Jarak at 0100, having left a squadron of 9th Hodson's Horse (13th Brigade) to guard the left flank of troops advancing through the Wadi Arah. The column reached El Mezrah and Nazareth at dawn, after cutting the El Afule-Haifa railway, having marched fifty miles in twenty-two hours. The enemy were attacked north of Nazareth by 13th Brigade, who withdrew to El Afule with 1,200 prisoners. El Afule was attacked from north by 14th Brigade and captured in conjunction with 4th Cavalry Division.

„ 21.—Nazareth was reoccupied by 13th Brigade after a sharp engagement, and reconnoitring patrols were sent out to Kefr Kenna and Sepphoris. 14th Brigade marched to Jenin at 0400, to co-operate with Australian Mounted Division. This Brigade returned to El Afule at 1530, and with 15th Brigade, who had arrived at 0100, picquetted the line El Afule-Shutta Station.

„ 22.—Nazareth was attacked at 0530 by a force of 700 Turks from Haifa. After a sharp fight 18th Lancers (13th Brigade) charged the enemy capturing 311 prisoners and four machine guns.

„ 23.—13th Brigade with No. 11 Light Armoured Car Battery and No. 1 Light Car Patrol, left Nazareth at 0500 and, at 1300, captured Acre after a short engagement, taking 259 prisoners and two guns. 14th and 15th Brigades turned over their line to 3rd Australian Light Horse Brigade and marched on Haifa *viâ* Jebata and Jeida at 0500. 15th Brigade were engaged by Turkish artillery covering Haifa, at 1015; 14th Brigade, with Divisional Headquarters, occupied the Kishon railway bridge and "Harosheth of the

1918.
Sept. 23.—Gentiles" at midday; and at 1400 Jodhpore and Mysore Lancers, supported by "B" Battery, H.A.C., attacked Haifa in face of strong resistance.
The town was captured at 1500, after street fighting, and 1,351 prisoners, seventeen guns, and eleven machine guns fell into our hands.

„ 25.—13th Brigade returned to Kefr Kenna, leaving a squadron of Gloucestershire Yeomanry in Acre.

„ 26.—Division was relieved by 2nd Leicesters (7th Division), and, less 1/1st Sherwood Rangers, left Haifa at 0500 for Kefr Kenna, where it concentrated at 0700.

„ 27.—Left Kefr Kenna (0300) and arrived at Tiberias at 0700. After a halt pushed on to a point north of the road between Mishmar Hayarden and Mahanayim.

„ 28.—Crossed the Jordan at Jisr Benat Yakub and reached El Kuneitra at 2030.

„ 29.—Left El Kuneitra at 1800, in rear of Australian Mounted Division.

„ 30.—Entered Sasa at 0830.
1200.—13th Brigade seized Jebel el Aswad astride Kiswe-Damascus road, engaged the enemy and, having cut their line of retreat, advanced to Kaukab.
1700.—This Brigade captured Kiswe taking 576 prisoners and four guns, and rejoined Division at Kaukab on arrival of 4th Cavalry Division from Deraa.
Night dispositions.—Divisional Headquarters and 13th Brigade at Kaukab; 14th Brigade astride Kiswe-Damascus road, and 15th Brigade about Khan esh Shiha.

Oct. 1.—0600.—Division concentrated and moved into positions east of Damascus, with 13th Brigade on Barada, and Division in touch with Australian Mounted Division on the north.
(During period Sept. 19 to Oct. 1, captures totalled 9,934 prisoners, twenty-seven guns, and twenty machine guns, excluding guns abandoned by the enemy.)

„ 4.—Division (less 1/1st Sherwood Rangers and 1st Hyderabad Lancers), concentrated at El Judeide with No. 12 L.A.C. Battery and No. 7 L.C. Patrol.

„ 5.—Marched *viâ* Katana to Khan Meizelun (sixteen miles) and occupied

„ 6.—Rayak at 1400.—15th Brigade captured Zahle (twenty-one miles) at 1500, with 177 prisoners and two guns.

„ 7.—Armoured car reconnaissance to Beirut.

1918.
Oct. 10.—Armoured car reconnaissance to Baalbek.
" 11.—13th Brigade occupied Baalbek.
" 12.—Remainder of Division arrived at Baalbek and divided into two columns. Column "A," Divisional Headquarters with 15th Brigade and Armoured Cars; Column "B," 13th and 14th Brigades.
Columns marched as follows :—
"A"   "B"
" 13.—Lebwe (twenty miles).
" 14.—El Kaa (sixteen miles).   Lebwe.
" 15.—Kussier (thirteen miles).   El Kaa.
    Armoured Cars entered Homs.
" 16.—Homs (eighteen miles). .   Kusseir.
" 17.—The division concentrated north-west of Homs at midday.
" 19.—15th Brigade, with No. 5 Field Squadron, R.E., advanced to repair the Orontes Bridge at Er Rastan (eleven miles).
" 20.—Divisional Headquarters, with Nos. 2, 11 and 12, L.A.C. Batteries, and Nos. 1 (Australian), 2, and 7 L.C. Patrols joined 15th Brigade at Er Rastan, forming Column "A." Remainder of Division formed Column "B."
" 21.—Column "A" advanced through Hama to Zor Defai (twenty miles).
" 22.—Armoured Cars arrived at Ma'arit en Na'aman at 1230 and two hours later engaged enemy cars near Khan es Sebil. A running fight for fifteen miles ensued, resulting in the capture of twelve prisoners and two cars. A point four miles north of Seraikin was the end of the day's run.
Column "A" reached Khan Shaikhun (twenty-one miles).

1918.
Oct. 23.—The Cars engaged enemy cavalry near Khan Tuman, and at 1000 reached Aleppo and summoned the city to surrender. This was refused.
Column "A" reached Ma'arit en Na'aman (sixteen miles), and Column "B" marched to Khan Shaikhun.
" 24.—Armoured Cars reoccupied Khan Tuman at 0700, reconnoitred towards Aleppo and Turmanin, and withdrew to Zirbe.
Column "A" reached Seraikin (eighteen and a half miles), and Column "B" reached Ma'arit en Na'aman.
" 25.—The Armoured Cars engaged bodies of the enemy near Aleppo and Turmanin during the morning.
Column "A" arrived at Turmanin and 15th Brigade relieved the Cars while Column "B" reached Seraikin.
" 26.—0700.—15th Brigade engaged astride Aleppo-Alexandretta road. Mysore Lancers and two squadrons Jodhpore Lancers charged the enemy.
1000.—Divisional Headquarters with Armoured Cars entered Aleppo (which had surrendered to Sherifian troops) followed at 2030 by 14th Brigade which had pushed on rapidly from Khan Tuman.
" 28.—13th Brigade holding Aleppo-Alexandretta road, and 14th Brigade at Muslimiyeh Junction, having relieved Sherifian troops.
(During operations Oct. 2 to Oct. 28, 821 prisoners, eighteen guns, and much railway and other material were captured.)

AUSTRALIAN MOUNTED DIVISION.

Commander.—Col. (temp. Major-Gen.) H. W. HODGSON, C.V.O., C.B.

3rd Australian Light Horse Brigade.

Commander.—Col. (temp. Brig.-Gen.) J. R. ROYSTON, C.M.G., D.S.O. (relinquished, Oct., 1917).
Lieut.-Col. (temp. Brig.-Gen.) L. C. WILSON, C.M.G., 5th Australian Light Horse Regt.
8th, 9th and 10th Regiments, Australian Light Horse.
3rd Australian Light Horse Signal Troop.
3rd Australian Machine Gun Squadron.

4th Australian Light Horse Brigade.

Commander.—Lieut.-Col. (temp. Brig.-Gen.) J. B. MEREDITH, D.S.O., 1st Australian Light Horse Regt. (relinquished, Sept., 1917).
Lieut.-Col. (temp. Brig.-Gen.) W. GRANT, D.S.O., 11th Australian Light Horse Regt.
4th, 11th and 12th Regiments, Australian Light Horse.
4th Australian Light Horse Signal Troop.
4th Australian Machine Gun Squadron.

5th Australian Light Horse Brigade (late Imperial Camel Corps Brigade).

Commander.—Lieut.-Col. (temp. Brig.-Gen.) G. M. M. Onslow, D.S.O., V.D., 7th Australian Light Horse Regt.
14th, 15th and 16th Regiments, Australian Light Horse.
5th Australian Light Horse Signal Troop.
2nd New Zealand Machine Gun Squadron.

Divisional Troops.

19th Brigade, R.H.A. ("A" and "B" Batteries H.A.C., 1/1st Notts. Battery, and Brigade Ammunition Column).
2nd Field Squadron, Australian Engineers.
2nd Signal Squadron, Australian Engineers.
Australian Mounted Divisional Train (Nos. 35, 36, 37, 38 Companies, Australian A.S.C.).
5th, 8th and 9th Australian Mobile Veterinary Sections.

Brief Record of Service.

In July, 1917, the Australian Mounted Division, at one time known as "The Imperial Mounted Division," consisted of 3rd and 4th Australian Light Horse, and 5th Mounted, Brigades, all of which had served on Gallipoli. The last named became 13th Cavalry Brigade and left the division Aug. 22, 1918, the vacancy being filled by 5th Australian Light Horse (formerly Imperial Camel Corps), Brigade. (See page 72.)

1917.

Sept. 18.—The division relieved Yeomanry Division with an outpost line through Bir el Esani-Kh. Khasif-Abu Shawish.

„ 24 to Oct. 24 } Continual reconnaissances and patrols.

„ 27.—Middlesex Yeomanry (1st County of London) of 8th Mounted Brigade (attached) heavily attacked near El Buggar at dawn by a force estimated at 3,000–4,000. In spite of heavy casualties the attack was temporarily successful and 9th and 10th Regiments (3rd Australian Light Horse Brigade) were sent forward in support. They were ordered not to counter-attack however, and the position was re-taken by infantry of 53rd Division after nightfall.

„ 29.—Concentrated at Khalasa for the attack on Beersheba.

„ 31.—3rd Australian Light Horse Brigade strongly engaged in supporting Australian and New Zealand Mounted (Anzac) Division in attack on Tel el Saba. 4th Australian Light Horse Brigade galloped over strong Turkish positions, demoralized the enemy, and captured Beersheba at 1800 with 1,148 prisoners. 5th and 7th Mounted Brigades came up in support and junction was effected with Anzac Division on the outpost line.

Nov. 2.—3rd Australian Light Horse Brigade rejoined Division, and 5th Mounted Brigade was attached to Anzacs. 8th Regiment (3rd Australian Light Horse Brigade) in action at Khuweilfeh.

„ 4-5.—7th Mounted Brigade attached. Outpost line, Wadi Hanafish-Hiseia, taken over from Yeomanry Division.

„ 7.—Advanced through Irgeig. Stiff fighting at Sheria, where 11th Regiment (4th Australian Light Horse Brigade) pushed the enemy back and beat off a counter-attack, thus assisting the concentration of 60th Division.

„ 8.—Sharp fighting and troop actions by all regiments of 3rd Australian Light Horse Brigade resulted in the capture of several guns. 12th Regiment (4th Australian Light Horse Brigade) effected junction with Imperial Service Cavalry (XXIst Corps) at Beit Hanum as the result of hard riding. One mile west of Huj ten troops of Warwick and Worcester Yeomanry (5th Mounted Brigade) charged a strong position, the garrison of which was delaying the advance of 60th Division. The charge was completely successful and eleven guns and four machine guns were taken.

„ 9.—Marched via Tel el Hesi to Arak el Menshiye where a counter-attack by an enemy column was repulsed.

„ 11.—10th Australian Light Horse Regiment occupied Summeil. Contact was established with 75th Division.

„ 12.—9th Australian Light Horse Regiment occupied Berkusie. The outpost line through Zeita-Berkusie was slightly withdrawn in consequence of a heavy attack against 5th Mounted Brigade and 9th Australian Light Horse Regiment. The 8th and 10th Regiments supported, the attack was held, and the original positions re-occupied during the night. The 2nd Australian Light Horse Brigade temporarily joined the Division and was engaged at Kezaze.

„ 13.—4th Australian Light Horse Brigade advanced, protecting right flank of 75th Division, and occupied Tel et Turmus after sharp fighting. In carrying out this operation the brigade was compelled to move across the enemy's front.

1917.

Nov. 14.—4th Regiment (4th Australian Light Horse Brigade) captured Et Tine with large quantities of ammunition and stores. 7th Mounted Brigade and the 2nd Australian Light Horse Brigade co-operated with 75th Division in the capture of Junction Station.

„ 18.—Operating around Amwas and Latron. In touch with Yeomanry Division on the left (north). (5th Mounted Brigade and 10th Australian Light Horse Regiment, attached to XXIst Corps carried out valuable patrols over most difficult country. Later, on withdrawal of XXIst Corps, these units passed under orders of XXth Corps and were employed to form link between 53rd and 60th Divisions during the final advance to Jerusalem).

„ 28.—4th Australian Light Horse Brigade took over part of line (and came under Yeomanry Division) at Beit ur et Tahta.

„ 29.—3rd Australian Light Horse Brigade relieved the 155th Brigade (52nd Division) at El Burj.

„ 30.—4th Australian Light Horse Brigade and 7th Mounted Brigade rejoined division, which now held the line, El Burj-Beit Sira.

(During the month the division captured 1,804 prisoners, thirty-five guns, and eight machine guns.)

Dec. 1.—A strong enemy attack was checked only when within thirty yards of the line held by 8th Australian Light Horse Regiment. A party of Gloucester Yeomanry (5th Mounted Brigade), and two companies 1/4th Royal Scots Fusiliers (52nd Division) were sent up in support and the attacking force was surrounded and captured. 112 unwounded and sixty wounded prisoners were taken, and over 100 dead were buried. (This attack was made by the 190th Assault Battalion, and a prisoner captured subsequently stated that the whole battalion had been killed or captured.)

„ 26-28.—The line was advanced 1,500 yards with very little opposition. On Dec. 27 patrols assisted the advance of 29th Infantry Brigade by demonstrations against right flank of enemy's positions on Namah Ridge.

1918.

Jan. 1.—Relieved by 10th Division and moved back to Deir el Belah, leaving 4th Australian Light Horse Brigade in the line until Jan. 6 to fill the gap between XXth and XXIst Corps.

Jan. to March } Spent in refitting, extensive training, and salvage work on the old trench systems south of Gaza.

„ 14.—Division inspected by H.R.H. Duke of Connaught, K.G.

Apl.1-26.—Moved via Selmeh and Talaat ed Dumm to Jericho, which was the point of concentration for the projected raid on Es Salt.

„ 30.—5th Mounted Brigade, on the Umm esh Shert-Es Salt track, reached its first objective with little opposition. 4th Australian Light Horse Brigade, in position astride the Jisr ed Damieh-Es Salt track, sent forward 11th Regiment, who found the enemy holding the Jisr ed Damieh Bridgehead in great strength and could not advance, but 1st Regiment (attached) captured Red Hill at 1225. 3rd Australian Light Horse Brigade moving eastward was held up by fire from enemy works covering Es Salt, but these were stormed by 9th and 10th Regiments dismounted, while 8th Regiment galloped along the road and forced its way into Es Salt at 1800 in face of stubborn resistance. One troop pursued the enemy for two miles along teh Amman road, riding down and capturing several

1918.
April 30   parties. 300 prisoners, twenty-nine machine guns, and large quantities of material were taken.

May 1.—Enemy attacked 4th Australian Light Horse Brigade, who inflicted heavy casualties, but were forced to withdraw by overwhelming numbers.

„ 2-3.—10th Australian Light Horse Regiment was attacked four times during the night, but succeeded in beating off the enemy with heavy losses.

„ 3.—An attack was launched at dawn against 8th Regiment supported by one squadron of 5th Regiment. This attack also was repulsed and 319 of the enemy were cut off and captured.

„ 4.—The division was withdrawn west of the river and took over the left sector of the Jordan Valley defences.

May and June } Continual consolidating and active patrolling carried on. Close contact with enemy was maintained throughout, but the weather was very hot and trying and a good deal of sickness ensued.

„ 14 to July 13 } During this period all brigades were withdrawn for a time to the Bethlehem-Solomon's Pools area.

„ 14.—4th Australian Light Horse Brigade assisted Anzac Division to repulse an attack in the Musallabeh Salient.

„ 20.—Australian Mounted Division took over the left sector of Jordan Valley defences from Anzac Division. There was no especial activity, but troops suffered considerably with malaria.

Aug. 23.—Relieved by Anzac Division and moved to the Ludd-Ramleh area.

„ 27 to Sept. 17 } Continuous training was carried out, and the division was armed with swords.

„ 18.—5th Australian Light Horse Brigade, having the French Cavalry attached, was placed under command of 60th Division; the remainder of the division was concentrated south of Selmeh.

„ 19.—Moved (less 5th Australian Light Horse Brigade) to Nahr Iskanderuneh

„ 20.—and Lejjun. 3rd Australian Light Horse Brigade (less 8th Regiment) pushed on to Jenin, where 10th Regiment swept in from the north, demoralising the enemy and capturing 4,000. A German force put up a fight after dark but were caught by machine-gun fire and surrendered. (Total captures in the neighbourhood of Jenin included 8,000 prisoners, five machine guns and much booty; and twenty-four aeroplanes, burned by the enemy, were found in the aerodrome.)

„ 23.—Divisional Headquarters and 4th Australian Light Horse Brigade arrived at El Efule at 0945. A squadron of 9th Regiment reconnoitred to near Beisan and took 80 prisoners.

„ 24.—4th Australian Light Horse Brigade marched viâ Beisan to Jisr Mejamie, and pushed on to

„ 25.—Semakh, reaching the outskirts of that place at 0425. The enemy were found to be in force, but the Brigade Commander decided to attack at once, without waiting for reinforcements. The 11th Regiment attacked from the east supported from the south by the fire of the machine-gun squadron, while one squadron of 12th Regiment worked round and attacked from the west. Several charges were pressed home and the defenders driven back into the town. Desperate hand-to-hand fighting culminated at the railway buildings which were fiercely defended for an hour, but by 0600 Semakh was captured with 389 prisoners (of whom 150 were Germans). The enemy casualties also included seventy killed and fifty wounded. Strong patrols sent up the Yarmuk Valley by the 12th Australian Light Horse Regiment meanwhile had found the enemy occupying strong positions. Tiberias was captured after a sharp fight by squadrons of 3rd and 4th Brigades, who had attacked the town from the west and south simultaneously. Two cars of

1918.
Sept. 25   11th Light Armoured Car Battery co-operated in this engagement.

[Meanwhile 5th Australian Light Horse Brigade with cavalry of the French Palestine Detachment (Regiment Mixte de Marche de Cavalerie) attached, were engaged near Tul Keram where 3,000 prisoners were taken (Sept. 19), and the Tul Keram-Jenin railway was cut near Ajjeh (Sept. 20). On Sept. 21 Nablus was captured 1345 and junction effected with XXth Corps at Balata an hour later. The brigade moved to Zerin to rejoin the division (Sept. 24), and on arrival there sent forward 15th Regiment in support of 4th Brigade at Semakh.]

„ 27.—The march on Damascus commenced. The bridge over the Jordan at Jisr Benat Yakub had been blown up, and enemy held high ground east of the river with many machine guns. A crossing was effected both north and south of the bridge, however, and seventy prisoners and four guns captured.

„ 28.—El Kuneitra reached before nightfall.

„ 29.—4th Australian Light Horse Brigade (less two regiments) remained at El Kuneitra; rest of division moved off with 3rd Australian Light Horse Brigade leading at 1500. Enemy opposition was encountered near Sasa, and the country was very difficult for mounted work, but

„ 30. the brigade forced its way through, capturing twenty-five prisoners, two guns, and seven machine guns. 4th and 12th Regiments (forming Bourchier's Force) continued the pursuit, taking 350 prisoners, one gun, eight machine guns, and 400 rifles, and at 1115 attacked the Kaukab line, which was held by 2,500 rifles and numerous machine guns. After a preliminary bombardment, 4th Light Horse Regiment made a frontal charge on the position while 12.h Regiment attacked the enemy's left flank. This co-operation was entirely successful, and seventy-two prisoners and twelve machine-guns were taken on the spot. The greater proportion of the defenders were ridden down and captured later, in the direction of Daraya. Meanwhile, 5th and 3rd Australian Light Horse Brigades moved rapidly towards north-west of Damascus until held up at El Mezze Heights by heavy shell and machine-gun fire, but the 19th Brigade, R.H.A., silenced most of the opposition. The French Cavalry moving dismounted along the hills of Kalabet el Mezze, blocked the gorge north-west of Er Rabue and captured 4,000 prisoners, in conjunction with 14th Regiment. 3rd Brigade, delayed at Salahiye by heavy opposition, defeated an enemy column and

Oct. 1.—pushed on towards Damascus, captured en route a loaded train with 483 prisoners, eight guns, and thirty machine guns, and passed through the city at 0600. This brigade fought continuously throughout the day, and seized enemy positions at Maraba, Duma, and Kusseir.

„ 2.—3rd Australian Light Horse Brigade pursued a force escaping north-east, and after riding hard for six miles, charged the column before the guns could be unlimbered, or machine guns brought into action. 1,500 prisoners, including a Divisional Commander, three guns, and twenty-six machine guns, were captured within an hour of being sighted.

(Total captures, in the advance on, and occupation of Damascus, were over 25,000 prisoners, thirty-nine guns, 254 machine guns, and nineteen automatic rifles.)

„ 4.—Division concentrated in and around Damascus.

„ 19.—French Cavalry left to rejoin the French Palestine Detachment at Beirut.

„ 27.—Left Damascus for Homs and concentrated there on November 1.

AUSTRALIAN AND NEW ZEALAND MOUNTED DIVISION.

Commander.—Col. (temp. Major-Gen.) Sir E. W. C. CHAYTOR, K.C.M.G., C.B., *p.s.c.*, A.D.C.

1st Australian Light Horse Brigade.

Commander.—Col. (temp. Brig.-Gen.) C. F. Cox, C.B., C.M.G., D.S.O.

> 1st, 2nd and 3rd Regiments, Australian Light Horse.
> 1st Australian Light Horse Signal Troop.
> 1st Australian Machine Gun Squadron.

2nd Australian Light Horse Brigade.

Commander.—Col. (temp. Brig.-Gen.) G. de L. RYRIE, C.B., C.M.G.

> 5th, 6th and 7th Regiments, Australian Light Horse.
> 2nd Australian Light Horse Signal Troop.
> 2nd Australian Machine Gun Squadron.

New Zealand Mounted Rifles Brigade.

Commander.—Lieut.-Col. (temp. Brig.-Gen.) W. MELDRUM, C.M.G., D.S.O., Wellington Mounted Rifles.

> Auckland, Canterbury, and Wellington Mounted Rifles Regiments.
> No. 1 New Zealand Mounted Rifles Signal Troop.
> 1st New Zealand Machine Gun Squadron.

Divisional Troops.

> 18th Brigade, R.H.A. (Inverness, Ayr, and Somerset Batteries, and Brigade Ammunition Column.)
> Australian and New Zealand Field Squadron.
> 1st Signal Squadron, Australian Engineers.
> Australian and New Zealand Mounted Divisional Train (Nos. 32, 33 and 34 Companies, Australian A.S.C., and No. 4 Company, New Zealand A.S.C.).
> 6th and 7th, Australian, and No. 2 New Zealand Mobile Veterinary Sections.

Brief Record of Service.

The Australian and New Zealand Mounted Division, widely known as the "Anzac Mounted Division," was formed in March 1916 of Australian and New Zealand Brigades that had served in Gallipoli and landed in Egypt, December 23–31, 1915.

The Division took part in the advance from the Suez Canal, being engaged at Romani, Maghdaba and Rafa before taking part in the first and second battles of Gaza in March and April, 1917, as part of the Desert Column. It joined Desert Mounted Corps on formation of the latter in August, 1917, and throughout subsequent operations retained its Order of Battle unchanged.

1917.
Oct. 30.—Concentrated at Asluj, fifteen miles south of Beersheba.
" 31.—2nd Australian Brigade struck from east and took its first objectives, Bir el Hammam and Bir Salim Abu Irgeig, by 0800, without encountering serious opposition. Resistance stiffened considerably but Tel es Sakaty was captured at 1300, and the Brigade was astride the Beersheba–Hebron road by 1350. Tel es Saba was strongly held against attacks by 1st Light Horse Brigade and New Zealand Mounted Rifles Brigade, assisted by units of Australian Mounted Division. This position was carried at 1500, and, by 1800, the Division, with 3rd Australian Light Horse Brigade attached, held an outpost line through Bir el Hammam–Bir es Sakaty–just north of Beersheba.
Nov. 1.—179 prisoners and four machine guns were captured as the result of an advance of five miles to the Bir el Makruneh–Towal Abu Jerwal line. 1st Light Horse and New Zealand Brigades were involved in severe fighting in advancing on Tel Khuweilfeh and Ain Kohleh.

1917.
Nov. 2) During this period there was continuous fighting
 to } in difficult country. 2nd Light Horse Brigade
 " 5) supported by Ayrshire Battery, moved on Dhaheriyeh, astride the Hebron road, in continuous touch with Turkish 3rd Cavalry Division.
 1st Light Horse and New Zealand Brigades, with 7th Mounted and Imperial Camel Corps Brigades and 8th Light Horse Regiment attached, were severely engaged in the neighbourhood of Ras en Nagb and Tel Khuweilfeh. 7th Mounted Brigade captured the former, with eleven prisoners and two guns.
" 6) New Zealand Brigade experienced severe fighting
 to } in the capture and subsequent defence of Tel
" 7) Khuweilfeh, in co-operation with 53rd Division.
" 7.—1st Light Horse Brigade captured the station east of Kh. Umm Ameidat (on the Jerusalem–Beersheba line), and took 300 prisoners and much material. Anzac units were also engaged in the neighbourhood of Tel Abu Dilakh. Enemy rearguards fought stubbornly, making full use of machine guns, and progress was slow.
" 8.—Lack of water compelled vigorous action to secure supplies, and the Division (less New Zealand

1917.

Nov. 8 Brigade, but with 7th Mounted Brigade attached), fought its way into the Wadi Jemmameh and took 300 prisoners and two guns. 7th Mounted Brigade was counter-attacked near Tel Hudeiwe, but repulsed the enemy with heavy losses.

„ 9.—An advance of ten miles enabled the Division to occupy a line from Arak el Menshiye through Es Suafir esh Sherkiye to Beit Duras, in close touch with main Turkish rearguard.

„ 10.—Esdud was captured, and

„ 11.—1st Light Horse Brigade and Inverness Battery was engaged with enemy rearguards at the Jisr Esdud bridgehead. 1st Light Horse Regiment was prominent in this fighting, in which the enemy made full use of machine guns, supported by heavy artillery at long range.

„ 12.—1st Light Horse Brigade captured Tel el Murre, and supported 52nd Division in the attack on, and capture of, Burkah. New Zealand Brigade (detached since Nov. 7), rejoined the Division, and the Imperial Camel Brigade temporarily took the place of 2nd Light Horse Brigade, which had joined the Australian Mounted Division, and was engaged near Kezaze on Nov. 12th-13th, and at Junction Station on Nov. 14.

„ 14.—New Zealand Brigade were heavily engaged at Ayun Kara (Richon le Zion). The enemy counter-attacked in force, and were only repulsed by the Auckland and Wellington Regiments at the point of the bayonet.

„ 15.—Ramleh and Ludd were taken by 1st Australian Light Horse Brigade, who captured 360 prisoners.

„ 16.—New Zealand Mounted Rifles occupied Jaffa without opposition ; and

„ 17.—patrols from this brigade passed through Sarona and reached Nahr el Auja, but failed to bring the retreating enemy to action.

„ 19.—Patrols to Rantieh located enemy redoubts at Nebi Tari and trenches at Kh. Hadrah on north bank of Nahr el Auja.

„ 24.—New Zealand Brigade crossed the Auja and captured the advanced line through Kh. Hadrah and Sh. Muannis.

„ 25.—The enemy fiercely counter-attacked Kh. Hadrah at 0300 and at 0800 forced a withdrawal to the old line south of the Auja. Sh. Muannis was also abandoned to an overwhelming force during the morning.

The line Yehudieh-Jerisheh-south bank of the Auja to the sea, held by Anzac Divison (less 1st Light Horse Brigade, but with Imperial Camel and 161st Infantry Brigades attached), was consolidated in expectation of a general hostile attack. The Turks were content, however, to hold their positions, and the attack did not materialize.

Dec. 1 to „ 5 Bald Hill, an important position one mile southwest of Mulebbis, was successfully raided by 2nd Light Horse and Camel Brigades. Sharp fighting and considerable hostile shelling was experienced, particularly by 6th Light Horse Regt.

(The division captured 3,553 prisoners, twenty-one guns, and twenty-one machine guns during the period Oct. 31 to Dec. 7.)

„ 21 to „ 23 1st Light Horse Brigade supported 54th Division in the advance to Mulebbis, and Auckland and Wellington Regiments supported 52nd Division in the crossing of the Auja.

The period for necessary rest and refitting was cut short by the concentration for operations in the Jordan Valley.

1918.
Feb. 18.—Wellington Mounted Rifles were at Deir Ibn Obeid, while Divisional Headquarters with 1st Light Horse Brigade and remainder of New Zealand Brigade were concentrated about Jerusalem and Bethlehem.

1918.
Feb. 19.—Anzac units moved eastward through desolate country to El Muntar, six miles from the Dead Sea.

„ 20.—Tubk el Kaneitera and Jebel el Kahmun were strongly held, and accurate shell and machine-gun fire from the direction of Neby Musa delayed the advance. The first two positions were captured shortly after noon, however, by a dismounted attack along narrow mountain tracks through precipitous country.

„ 20 1st Light Horse Brigade pushed on through the gorge of the Wadi Kumran to the plain on north-west shore of the Dead Sea, and took up a line along the Wadi Jofet Zeben at 1800. New Zealand Brigade, in co-operation with 2/14th London and 10th Mountain Battery, occupied Neby Musa.

„ 21.—1st Light Horse Brigade reached Jericho at 0820, and immediately sent out patrols to El Ghoraniyeh (where the Turks were found holding a bridgehead on the west bank of the Jordan), and to the Wadi Aujah.

One squadron New Zealand Mounted Rifles occupied Rujm el Bahr, a Turkish Base on the northern shore of the Dead Sea.

Mch. 7 to „ 15 1st Light Horse Brigade and Inverness Battery were engaged in the Wadi Samieh, on the right flank of 53rd Division.

„ 23.—Auckland Mounted Rifles crossed the Jordan at Hajlah at 0400, to clear the east bank of the river. Several enemy detachments were galloped down, and the high ground covering Ghoraniyeh secured by noon, with the capture of sixty-eight prisoners and four machine guns. Meanwhile one regiment of 1st Light Horse Brigade also crossed the river at Hajlah, and was engaged in clearing the country to south and south-east.

„ 24.—1st Light Horse Brigade, about one mile north of El Mandesi ford, covered the left flank of 60th Division, while the remainder of the mounted troops moved east and north-east from Hajlah. Infantry turned enemy's right flank, and, with a squadron of Wellington Mounted Rifles in advance, pursued them up the Es Salt road. 2nd Light Horse Brigade reached Rujm el Oshir during the afternoon, but advance was seriously delayed by the state of the track, which was impassable for wheels and almost so for mounted men. New Zealand Brigade advanced by the Wadi Jofet el Ghazlaniye towards Es Sir.

„ 25.—The head of the column arrived at Ain Hekr about 0530 and concentrated there all day, being much delayed by bad tracks and wet. Naaur was reached by 2nd Light Horse Brigade at 1030, and New Zealand troops occupied Es Sir, but progress was very slow on account of the mud. Es Salt, evacuated by the enemy, was occupied by 3rd Light Horse Regiment at 1800.

„ 26.—2nd Light Horse Brigade pushed out patrols north of the Es Salt—Amman road and captured 170 prisoners. It was necessary to rest the greater proportion of the horses, but a raiding party reached the Hejaz Railway, seven miles south of Amman, and blew up a section of the line during the night.

„ 27.—Division left for Amman at 0900. New Zealand Brigade reached Ain Amman at 1030, and 2nd Light Horse Brigade, on their left, were three miles from Amman Station. New Zealand Brigade cut the railway south of Amman at 1500, but 2nd Brigade were held up and only reached the line during the night, when a demolition party succeeded in blowing up a two-arch bridge.

„ 28.—1st Light Horse Brigade engaged an enemy column moving along the Jisr ed Damieh track towards Es Salt. Heavy fighting followed a general attack on Amman, and a determined enemy,

1918.
Mch. 28 well supplied with machine guns, held up our advance in the afternoon and
29.—throughout the following day.
,, 30.—A sudden attack was launched against the whole hostile position at 0200, and at 0430 New Zealand troops captured part of Hill 3039 (a dominating feature south-east of the village), and took six machine guns, but it was found impossible to clear the hill. New Zealand patrols entered the village and some house-to-house fighting ensued. Hill 3039 was heavily counter-attacked at 1100, and, though the attack was broken up, the defence was subjected to continual shelling throughout the day.

Meanwhile strong hostile reinforcements had arrived in the vicinity of Kefr Huda, and were threatening Es Salt from north-west. During the fighting that ensued 3rd Light Horse Regiment captured three machine guns and killed or captured seventeen Turks in a skirmish.

Orders were received for a general retirement, and

,, 31.—2nd Light Horse Brigade covered the withdrawal of 181st Infantry Brigade through Es Sir.

(460 prisoners were taken by the Division during the Amman raid, March 23-31.)

April 3.—1st Light Horse Brigade and 5th Regiment (2nd Brigade) took over the Ghoraniyeh bridgehead from 2/17th and 2/19th London.

,, 11.—Enemy attacked the Ghoraniyeh bridgehead in strength at 0445 and throughout the day. The attacks were launched along the Wadi Nimrin,

1918.
April 11 and were all repulsed with very heavy losses. 3rd Light Horse Regiment attempted to envelope a hostile force from north and south but found the enemy echeloned in depth and, coming under heavy shell and machine-gun fire, withdrew.

2nd Light Horse Brigade (less 5th Regiment) supported Imperial Camel Corps Brigade, who were heavily attacked by German troops at Musallabeh.

,, 30) During the raid on Es Salt, 1st and 2nd Light
to } Horse Brigades, attached to Australian Mounted Division, were involved in heavy fighting around
May 4) Es Salt, while New Zealand Brigade, with other mounted units fought several severe actions on the line Red Hill (east of Jordan) to the foothills.

July 14.—A determined attack on the Musallabeh salient, Abu Tellul-The Bluff, was repulsed by 1st Light Horse Brigade and 5th Regiment, supported by New Zealand Brigade. Wellington Mounted Rifles were prominent in this action. 2nd Light Horse Brigade (less 5th Regiment) also beat off an attack in the Wadi Mellahah.

377 Germans and 71 Turks were captured, and 180 enemy dead counted, as the result of the day's fighting.

Sept. 19) Anzac Division, as part of "Chaytor's Force"
to } (q.v.), was engaged in the Jordan Valley; seized
,, 29) Shunet Nimrin, Es Salt, and Amman; cut the Hejaz Railway; and, in co-operation with other units under General Chaytor's Command, captured 10,000 prisoners, fifty-five guns, 169 machine guns, and 800 tons of ammunition.

3rd (LAHORE) DIVISION.

Commander.—Major-Gen. A. R. HOSKINS, C.M.G., D.S.O., *p.s.c.*

Commanding, Royal Artillery.—Bt. Col. (temp. Brig.-Gen.) H. R. PECK, C.M.G., D.S.O., R.A.

7th Infantry Brigade.
Commander.—Bt. Col. (temp. Brig.-Gen.) S. R. DAVIDSON, C.M.G., 47th Sikhs, I.A.

  1st Battalion Connaught Rangers, 27th and 91st Punjabis, 2/7th Gurkha Rifles.
  7th Light Trench Mortar Battery.

8th Infantry Brigade.
Commander.—Col. (temp. Brig.-Gen.) S. M. EDWARDES, C.B., C.M.G., D.S.O., I.A.

  1st Battalion Manchester Regiment, 47th Sikhs, 59th Scinde Rifles (F.F.), 2/124th Baluchistan Infantry.
  8th Light Trench Mortar Battery.

9th Infantry Brigade.
Commander.—Col. (temp. Brig.-Gen.) C. C. LUARD, C.M.G.

  2nd Battalion Dorset Regiment, 93rd Infantry, 105th Mahratta Light Infantry, 1/1st Gurkha Rifles.
  9th Light Trench Mortar Battery.

Divisional Troops.
  4th Brigade, R.F.A. (7th, 14th and B/69th Batteries).
  8th Brigade, R.F.A. (372nd, 373rd and 428th Batteries).
  53rd Brigade, R.F.A. (66th, 374th and 430th Batteries).
  3rd Divisional Ammunition Column.
  20th and 21st Companies, 3rd Sappers and Miners.
  65th Field Company, R.E.
  3rd Divisional Signal Company, R.E.

3rd Divisional Machine Gun Battalion (Nos. 131, 132, 133 Companies).
1/34th Sikh Pioneers.
3rd Divisional Train (S. & T.).
No. 3 Mobile Veterinary Section.

Brief Record of Service.

The 3rd (Lahore) Division served on the Western Front in 1914-15; in Mesopotamia 1916-17; and landed in Egypt in April, 1918. In June, 1918, the division joined XXIst Corps, and relieved 54th Division in the front line, from Kh. Umm el Ikba to near Tel el Mukhmar, a length of nearly eight miles.

1918.

Aug. 19.—105th Mahratta Light Infantry (9th Brigade), supported by an artillery barrage, raided an enemy post on the west slope of Brown Hill, and killed or captured the whole garrison. The post was stormed at 0225 in face of gallant resistance, particularly on the part of machine-gunners, who stuck to their guns to the last. The raiders returned to the British lines by a circuitous route to avoid the heavy hostile barrage of H.E. put down in front of Brown Hill.

Sept. 19.—The Division attacked on a front of 1,800 yards, with 54th Division on the right and 75th Division on the left. 7th Brigade attacked Bir Adas and Fir Hill; 9th Brigade attacked the strong trench system on Brown Hill; while 8th Brigade moved towards Jiljulieh in reserve. In the right attack 2/7th Gurkhas captured trenches north-west of Bir Adas, and 27th Punjabis were equally successful on the west of Fir Hill, while 1st Connaught Rangers carried the main Fir Hill defences against considerable resistance; and by 0700 the brigade was advancing through Kefr Saba. On the left 2nd Dorsets and 1/1st Gurkhas seized Brown Hill and Hill 283 respectively, and by 0630, having pierced the enemy defences to a depth of two miles, the brigade was swinging eastward towards the foothills.

8th Brigade was ordered to attack Jiljulieh and Railway Redoubt. Both positions were stubbornly defended, but 2/124th Baluchis stormed the Redoubt at 1030, and, at 1100, 1st Manchesters swept the enemy from the village. The whole of the enemy front line positions were captured by 1200, and the Division advanced eastward on a north and south line through Hableh. 9th Brigade on the left was strongly engaged (particularly 105th Mahrattas) in the advance to and capture of Jiyus, and, after being held up for a time, 1/1st Gurkhas advanced in co-operation with right flank of 7th Division.

By nightfall the Division held a line about two miles west of Kh. Kefr Thilth and Azzun on the right, with its left resting on Jiyus.

1918.

Sept. 20.—Brigades moved at 0500, and made steady progress in spite of vigorous resistance by enemy rearguards and howitzer fire from the direction of Kefr Thilth and Azzun. The greatest opposition was experienced along the line of the Wadi Azzun, and 47th Sikhs and 59th Scinde Rifles were heavily engaged on the high ground north and south respectively. Azzun and Kefr Thilth were taken by 1100, and a company of 2/7th Gurkhas was left to clear the former of snipers. A large quantity of war material was abandoned by the enemy along the Azzun road, and at El Funduk Connaught Rangers captured six field guns, five mountain guns, two machine guns, 150 wagons, and 250 animals.

The Division halted for the night on the line El Funduk-Kuryet Jit-Kefr Kaddum.

,, 21.—The advance was continued in a north-easterly direction, the only opposition experienced being from the direction of Nablus on the 9th Brigade front. Kussein was reached about 0730, but 93rd Burma Infantry had a hard fight for Hill 2533, a prominent feature two miles west of Nablus (or Shechem). This important position was captured at 1115 after a stiff climb under fire, and, as it afforded direct observation on Nablus, 3rd Divisional Artillery were able to shell enemy guns in action and transport columns, and assist 5th Australian Light Horse Brigade to capture this hub in the Turkish communications.

By 1915 all the Divisional objectives had been taken, and a line was occupied facing east astride the Tul Keram-Nablus road through Beit Udhen-Zawata-Jennesinia-Nusf Jebil, joining up with 7th (Indian) Division near Samaria.

(During the period Sept. 19-21, 1,366 prisoners and seventy guns were captured and recorded; but the actual numbers taken probably much exceeded these figures.)

,, 24.—7th Brigade marched to Jenin, where it was attached to Desert Mounted Corps, and garrisoned Jenin, El Afule, Nazareth, and Beisan for a week.

,, 29.—Divisional Headquarters, with 8th and 9th Brigades concentrated at Hableh; and 7th Brigade at Semakh.

7th (INDIAN) DIVISION.

Commander.—Major-Gen. Sir V. B. FANE, K.C.I.E., C.B.

Commanding, Royal Artillery.—Lieut.-Col. (temp. Brig.-Gen.) E. C. MASSY, C.B., C.M.G., D.S.O., R.A.

19th Infantry Brigade.

Commander.—Lieut.-Col. (temp. Brig.-Gen.) E. J. M. WOOD, D.S.O., 97th Infantry, I.A. (relinquished, April, 1918).

Bt. Lieut.-Col. (temp. Brig.-Gen.) G. A. WEIR, D.S.O., 3rd Dragoon Guards (relinquished Oct., 1918).

Bt. Col. (temp. Brig.-Gen.) W. S. LESLIE, D.S.O., 31st Punjabis, I.A., *p.s.c.*

1st Battalion Seaforth Highlanders, 28th and 92nd Punjabis, 125th Napier's Rifles.
19th Light Trench Mortar Battery.

21st Infantry Brigade.

Commander.—Lieut.-Col. (temp. Brig.-Gen.) A. G. KEMBALL, 31st Punjabis.

2nd Battalion Black Watch, 1st Guides Infantry, 20th Punjabis, 1/8th Gurkha Rifles.
21st Light Trench Mortar Battery.

28th Infantry Brigade (F.F.).

Commander.—Bt. Col. (temp. Brig.-Gen.) C. H. DAVIES, C.M.G., D.S.O., I.A.

2nd Battalion Leicester Regiment, 51st Sikhs (F.F.), 53rd Sikhs (F.F.), 56th Punjabi Rifles (F.F.).
28th Light Trench Mortar Battery.

Divisional Troops.

9th Brigade, R.F.A. (19th, 20th, 28th and D/69th Batteries).
56th Brigade, R.F.A. ("A," "B," "C" and 527th Batteries). Transferred to 52nd (Lowland) Division in March, 1918.
261st Brigade, R.F.A. ("A," "B" and "C" Batteries). Transferred from the 52nd (Lowland) Division in March, 1918.
262nd Brigade, R.F.A. ("A," "B" and 438th Batteries). Transferred from the 52nd (Lowland) Division in March, 1918.
264th Brigade, R.F.A. (422nd, 423rd and "C" Batteries). Transferred from the 52nd (Lowland) Division in March, 1918.
7th Divisional Ammunition Column. Transferred from the 52nd (Lowland) Division in March, 1918.
3rd and 4th Companies, 1st (King George's Own) Sappers and Miners.
522nd (London) Field Company, R.E.
7th Divisional Signal Company, R.E.
121st Pioneers.
7th Divisional Machine Gun Battalion (Nos. 134, 135, 136 Companies).
272nd Machine Gun Company (ceased to belong to E.E.F., 6/6/18).
7th Divisional Train (S. & T.).
No. 2 Mobile Veterinary Section.

Brief Record of Service.

The 7th (Indian) Division served in France (1914–15), in Mesopotamia (1916–17), landed in Egypt in January, 1918, joined XXIst Corps and relieved 54th Division in the Coastal Sector of the front line (from near Tel el Mukhmar to Arsuf), in March, taking over the Divisional Artillery of the 52nd Division in exchange for its own (see above), which went to France with the 52nd Division.

1918.

May 28–29.—Advanced the line one and a half miles on a seven mile front. 2nd Leicesters and 53rd Sikhs (28th Brigade) were prominent in this fighting, and took over 100 prisoners.

June 8–10.—21st Brigade took the "Sisters" after heavy fighting, in which 2nd Black Watch and 1st Guides Infantry bore the brunt. As the result of this engagement 250 prisoners were taken, and the enemy lost a valuable observation post.

July 13.—A post in the enemy's front system was raided in daylight by Gurkhas of the 1st Guides, who captured fifteen prisoners and three machine guns.

" 27.—A company of 53rd Sikhs raided a portion of the enemy trenches and captured thirty-three prisoners and several machine guns.

(Much of the work in preparation for active operations had to be undertaken by the division, during August and the early part of September, for the divisions that could only be brought into the area immediately before the attack.)

" 19.—Attack on the Tabsor system carried out by two columns. On the right, 92nd and 28th Punjabis were supported by 1st Seaforths and 125th Rifles (19th Brigade); on the left, 2nd Black Watch, supported by 1/8th Gurkhas (21st Brigade). Front line objectives were quickly taken by the attacking troops, and the supporting battalions passed through and seized the support and reserve lines. During the further advance to the Felamieh-Taiyibeh line, the 20th Punjabis captured the village of Felamieh, supported on the left by 2nd Black

1918.

Sept. 19 Watch; while the 92nd Punjabis captured El Mejdel and took a number of prisoners and two machine guns. Further north 56th Rifles and 53rd Sikhs (28th Brigade) stormed the village of Taibiyeh in face of considerable resistance.

" 20.—19th Brigade met with most determined resistance during the advance on Beit Lid (1st Seaforths and 125th Rifles). The village was finally rushed by the Seaforths. 28th Brigade pushed on from El Burj, and seized

" 21.—Messudieh railway station at 0300. 53rd Sikhs were sent round to attack Samaria Hill from the west and occupy the town, while 51st Sikhs attacked the hill from south. Both hill and town were captured by 0500 after a sharp fight, in which 200 prisoners and four machine guns were taken.

" 21.—The division had fought and marched for forty-eight hours, and had covered thirty-four miles over difficult and rocky country, but all objectives had been reached, with the capture of over 2,000 prisoners and twenty guns.

" 23.—19th Brigade marched to Anebta, 21st Brigade to Shuweikeh.

" 24.—21st Brigade moved to Hudeira, 28th Brigade to north of Kakon. 2nd Leicesters left for Haifa in motor lorries, and arrived there on the following morning.

" 26.—Division marched in three brigade groups *via* Zimmarin and Athlit, and on

" 29.—concentrated at Haifa.

Orders were received to continue the march to Beirut along the coast road. A section of

EGYPTIAN EXPEDITIONARY FORCE

1918.
Sept. 29 — this road, upwards of half a mile in length, known as the "Ladder of Tyre," consisted of a narrow rocky track on the side of the cliff with a deep drop to the sea, and at one point became a flight of steps roughly hewn out of the rock. The Sappers and Miners and 121st Pioneers, assisted by infantry, by working continuously for 2½ days, made the road fit for armoured cars, motors, and 60-pounder guns.

The division marched in three columns, as follows :—

Col. "A."—XXIst Corps Cavalry and an Infantry Detachment.

"B."—28th Brigade, 8th Mountain Artillery Brigade, one and a half companies Sappers and Miners, 121st Pioneers, one Machine Gun Company, one Field Ambulance.

"C."—Divisional Headquarters, 19th and 21st Brigades, Composite Brigade, R.F.A., 15th Heavy Battery, R.G.A., No. 522 Field Company, R.E., two sections Sappers and Miners, Machine Gun Battalion (less 1 Company), Divisional Ammunition Column, and two Field Ambulances.

1918.
Sept. 29 — The first day's march was around the Bay of Acre, and, from the high ground near Haifa, the head of the column could be seen moving on to the new camping area, as the rear of the column left the old area, more than ten miles apart.

The division camped as follows :—

	Column "A."	Column "B."	Column "C."
Oct. 3.—	Ras Nakura.	Acre.	Haifa.
,, 4.—	Tyre.	Ras Nakura.	Acre.
,, 5.—	Ain el Burak.	Ras el Ain.	Ras Nakura.
,, 6.—	Sidon.	Nahr el Kasmiye.	Ras el Ain.
,, 7.—	Ed Damur.	El Khidr.	N. el Kasmiye.
,, 8.—	Beirut.	Ed Damur.	Sidon.
,, 9.—	Beirut.	Beirut.	Ed Damur.
,, 10.—	Beirut.	Beirut.	Beirut.

(Column "C" marched 96 miles in eight days.)

,, 14.—19th Brigade left Beirut for Tripolis (fifty-four miles) and

,, 18.—reached the latter town five days later.

,, 21.—Remainder of the division marched northward en route for Tripolis, and concentrated there on

,, 28.—having marched about 270 miles in forty days.

,, 31.—Divisional Headquarters at El Mina, 19th Brigade at Khan Abdi (twelve miles northeast of Tripolis), 21st Brigade at Ras el Lados, and 28th Brigade near Nahr Berid.

10th DIVISION.

Commander.—Major-Gen. J. R. LONGLEY, C.B., C.M.G.

Commanding, Royal Artillery.—Bt. Col. (temp. Brig.-Gen.) W. B. EMERY, C.B., C.M.G., R.A.

29th Infantry Brigade.

Commander.—Bt. Col. (temp. Brig.-Gen.) R. S. VANDELEUR, C.B., C.M.G., Seaforth Highlanders (relinquished, June, 1918).

Bt. Lieut.-Col. (temp. Brig.-Gen.) C. L. SMITH, V.C., M.C., Duke of Cornwall's Light Infantry.

1st Battalion Leinster Regiment, 1/The 101st Grenadiers, 1/54th Sikhs (F.F.), 2/151st Indian Infantry.

5th Battalion Connaught Rangers, and 6th Battalion Leinster Regiment (ceased to belong to E.E.F., 28/5/18).

6th Battalion Royal Irish Rifles (disbanded, 20/5/18).

29th Light Trench Mortar Battery.

30th Infantry Brigade.

Commander.—Lieut.-Col. (temp. Brig.-Gen.) F. A. GREER, C.M.G., D.S.O., Royal Irish Fusiliers.

1st Battalion Royal Irish Regiment, 38th Dogras, 46th Punjabis, 1st Kashmir I.S. Infantry.

6th Battalion Royal Dublin Fusiliers (ceased to belong to E.E.F., 2/7/18), 6th Battalion Royal Munster Fusiliers, and 7th Battalion Royal Dublin Fusiliers (ceased to belong to E.E.F., 28/5/18).

30th Light Trench Mortar Battery.

31st Infantry Brigade.

Commander.—Bt. Col. (temp. Brig.-Gen.) E. M. MORRIS, C.B., C.M.G., Royal Lancaster Regt.

2nd Battalion Royal Irish Fusiliers, 2/42nd Deoli Regiment, 74th Punjabis, 2/The 101st Grenadiers.

5th and 6th Battalions Royal Inniskilling Fusiliers (ceased to belong to E.E.F., 19/6/18 and 28/5/18 respectively), and 5th Battalion Royal Irish Fusiliers (ceased to belong to E.E.F., 20/5/18).

31st Light Trench Mortar Battery.

Divisional Troops.

67th Brigade, R.F.A. ("A," "B" and "C" Batteries).
68th Brigade, R.F.A. ("A," "B" and "C" Batteries).
263rd Brigade R.F.A. (75th, 424th and "C" Batteries).
10th Divisional Ammunition Column.
18th Company, 3rd Sappers and Miners.
66th and 85th Field Companies, R.E.
10th Divisional Signal Company, R.E.
10th Divisional Machine Gun Battalion (Nos. 29, 30, 31 Companies).
10th Divisional Train (Nos. 475, 476, 477, 478 Companies, R.A.S.C.).
25th Mobile Veterinary Section.

Brief Record of Service.

The 10th (Irish) Division, composed originally of Irish Battalions of the New Army ("First Hundred Thousand"), saw service in Gallipoli and Salonika and landed in Egypt in September, 1917. It then consisted of three Regular Battalions (one in each brigade), and nine New Army Battalions. The Division joined XXth Corps during the concentration for the attack on Beersheba. Between May and July, 1918, the New Army Battalions were withdrawn for service in France, and their places filled by Indian units, with the necessary alteration in title.

1917.
Oct. 30.—Concentrated in the Shellal-Tel el Fara area.
Nov. 1.—6th Royal Inniskilling Fusiliers (31st Brigade) captured Abu Irgeig.
 „ 6.—After concentrating on a line north of Irgeig the division participated in the attack on the Kauwukah and Rushdi trench systems, on the left of 53rd Division who were attacking Tel Khuweilfeh. In this fighting, in which 2nd and 5th Royal Irish Fusiliers (31st Brigade) were prominent, all objectives were gained during the afternoon.
 „ 7.—Hareira Tepe Redoubt was stormed by 2nd Royal Irish Fusiliers in face of stubborn resistance and heavy machine-gun fire.
 „ 10 to 30 } Division concentrated at Karm; moved to Deir el Belah a week later; marched northward viâ Beit Duras to Junction Station; and then eastward into the Judæan Hills viâ Latron.
Dec. 2 to 5 } Relieved 52nd Division and 229th and 231st Brigades of 74th Division.
 „ 11.—Occupied the line Beit Dukka-Beit Ur Et Tahta-Suffa.
 „ 27.—1st Leinsters (29th Brigade) captured Deir Ibzia, while the whole line covering Jerusalem on the north and east was furiously engaged in repulsing the general Turkish attack.
 „ 28.—Abu el Ainein and Kh. Rubin Ridge were captured by 1st Royal Irish Regiment and 6th Royal Munster Fusiliers (30th Brigade), while 5th and 6th Royal Inniskilling Fusiliers (31st Brigade) seized Kefr Shiyan.
 „ 29.—Et Tireh Ridge occupied and the line advanced to Batn Harasheh-Ras Kerker-Deir el Kuddis.
1918.
Mar. 9.—After a winter spent in holding the positions gained, operations commenced on a front of 15,000 yards, with 31st and 30th Brigades forming the right column of attack, and 29th Brigade the left column.
Right Attack.—A rapid attack by 2nd Royal Irish Fusiliers forced the enemy to abandon strong positions on Sh. Kalrawany, near Bir ez Zeit and enabled 5th Royal Irish Fusiliers to capture Ras et Tarfu and Attara by 0920. In the evening the latter unit forced the crossing of the Wadi Jib and seized the lower slopes of the hill forming the main defence of Jiljilia. Farther to the left 6th Royal Munster Fusiliers and 1st Royal Irish Regiment pushed back the enemy and captured Ajul.

1918.
Mar. 9 *Left attack.*—5th Connaught Rangers occupied Neby Saleh at 0730, and 1st Leinsters also pushed forward; but progress was slow owing to exceptional difficulties of terrain.
 „ 10.—*Right attack.*—5th Royal Irish Fusiliers, supported by two companies 5th Royal Inniskilling Fusiliers, captured the strong defences south of Jiljilia, and drove the enemy in disorder through the village on to the slopes beyond. A small party, commanded by a German officer, held out to the last, when they were overwhelmed by a bayonet charge. 5th Royal Inniskilling Fusiliers captured Kh. Aliuta against opposition; while 1st Royal Irish Regiment and 6th Royal Dublin Fusiliers captured the ridge west of Jiljilia in face of strong resistance.
 „ 10. *Left attack.*—Extraordinary difficulties were encountered in the attack on Arura and Holywood Hill, owing to precipitous nature of the Wadi Jib, which had to be crossed although swept by heavy oblique fire from numerous machine guns. In spite of this, however, 6th Royal Irish Rifles captured the lower slopes of Holywood Hill and Sh. Redwan by 0730. During the night 5th Connaught Rangers repulsed a counter-attack, and the enemy withdrew his line north of the Wadi Gharib
Mar. 19.—Kefr Tur occupied by 5th Connaught Rangers.
 (During the March operations thirty miles of new roads had to be constructed during the actual fighting, to enable supplies to reach the advancing troops.)
April 9.—Kefr Ain and Kefr Ain Hill were captured to cover the right flank of attack by 75th Division.
Aug.12-13.—1st Leinsters, 1/54th Sikhs, and 1/101st Grenadiers (29th Brigade) successfully raided the El Burj-Ghurabeh Ridge, and annihilated the Turkish 33rd Regiment, while troops of 60th Division carried out a demonstration on the right. In this operation the enemy was surprised, and, though he put up considerable resistance, suffered about 450 casualties.
Sept. 18.—Division held the line Arura to Rafat (exclusive), with 53rd Division on the right and French Palestine Detachment on the left.
 „ 19.—1st Leinsters and 2/151st Infantry (29th Brigade) captured Furkhah Ridge and Topee Hill respectively, while 74th Punjabis (31st Brigade) took Kh. Er Ras, Kh. Mutwy, and Mogg Ridge.

1918.
Sept. 20.—2/151st Infantry and 1/101st Grenadiers (29th Brigade) reached the line Kusr es Sanameh-Selfit, where they were held up, but, supported by 1/54th Sikhs captured all positions in face of determined resistance, and, by 1530, were established on high ground south-west of Iskaka in readiness for further advance.

2/42nd Deolis and 2/101st Grenadiers (31st Brigade) advanced to the line Ras Aish-Kefr Haris, Sh. Othman falling to an attack by the Grenadiers *en route*. 2/42nd Deolis made six desperate but unsuccessful attempts to storm Ras Aish, and the 2/101st Grenadiers were equally unfortunate in their attacks on the Kefr Haris defences. 2nd Royal Irish Fusiliers (31st Brigade) finally rushed the village of right Haris and the enemy, realizing that his Kefr

1918.
Sept. 20 flank was turned, withdrew rapidly from his positions.

During the night of Sept. 20-21, 30th Brigade, moving from Kh. El Mutwy through Huwarah, occupied Neby Belan Heights, north of Nablus, having covered twenty-one miles of very rough going in thirteen hours.

„ 21.—31st Brigade occupied Eslamiyeh, and completed the capture of Nablus.

„ 22 to „ 24 } The area Kh. Ferweh-Tubas-Ain Shibleh was cleared of the enemy, and the fighting was over so far as 10th Division was concerned.

(Between Sept. 19 and 24 6,000 prisoners, 130 guns, and masses of transport and materia were taken on the divisional front; these figures including the captures by Corps Cavalry.)

52nd (LOWLAND) DIVISION (T.).

(Ceased to belong to E.E.F. 21/4/18).

Commander.—Bt. Col. (temp. Major-Gen.) W. E. B. SMITH, C.B., C.M.G. (relinquished, Sept., 1917).
Major-Gen. J. HILL, C.B., D.S.O., I.A., A.D.C.

Commanding, Royal Artillery.—Lieut.-Col. (temp. Brig.-Gen.) E. C. MASSY, C.B., C.M.G., D.S.O., R.A.

155th Infantry Brigade.

Commander.—Lieut.-Col. (temp. Brig.-Gen.) J. B. POLLOK MCCALL, C.M.G., D.S.O. (R. of O.) (relinquished, April, 1918).
Bt. Lieut.-Col. (temp. Brig.-Gen.) P. S. ALLAN, D.S.O., Gordon Highlanders.

1/4th and 1/5th Battalions Royal Scots Fusiliers, 1/4th and 1/5th Battalions King's Own Scottish Borderers.
155th Machine Gun Company, and 155th Light Trench Mortar Battery.

156th Infantry Brigade.

Commander.—Bt. Lieut.-Col. (temp. Brig.-Gen.) A. H. LEGGETT, D.S.O. (R. of O.).

1/4th and 1/7th Battalions Royal Scots, 1/7th and 1/8th Battalions Scottish Rifles.
156th Machine Gun Company, and 156th Light Trench Mortar Battery.

157th Infantry Brigade.

Commander.—Bt. Col. (temp. Brig.-Gen.) C. D. HAMILTON MOORE, C.M.G., D.S.O., Royal Warwickshire Regt., *p.s.c.*

1/5th, 1/6th and 1/7th Battalions Highland Light Infantry, and 1/5th Battalion Argyll and Sutherland Highlanders.
157th Machine Gun Company, and 157th Light Trench Mortar Battery.

Divisional Troops.

52nd Divisional Cyclist Company.
261st Brigade, R.F.A. ("A," "B" and "C" Batteries). Transferred to 7th (Indian) Division in March, 1918.
262nd Brigade, R.F.A. ("A," "B" and 438th Batteries). Transferred to 7th (Indian) Division in March, 1918.
264th Brigade, R.F.A. (422nd, 423rd and "C" Batteries). Transferred to 7th (Indian) Division in March, 1918.
52nd Divisional Ammunition Column. Transferred to 7th (Indian) Division in March, 1918.
133rd and 134th (Medium), Trench Mortar Batteries, R.A.
410th, 412th, 413th (Lowland) Field Companies, R.E.
52nd Divisional Signal Company, R.E.
Pioneer Battalion, 5th Royal Irish Regiment.
211th Machine Gun Company.
52nd Divisional Employment Company.
52nd Divisional Train (Nos. 217, 218, 219 and 220 Companies, R.A.S.C.).
1/1st Lowland Mobile Veterinary Section.

Brief Record of Service.

52nd Division, composed entirely of Lowland Territorial Battalions, served through the Gallipoli campaign, and took part in the advance across the desert from the Suez Canal. It fought in the battle of Romani, and the first and second battles of Gaza, in March and April, 1917.

The annihilation of Sea Post, a strong Turkish redoubt west of Gaza, in June, by 1/5th King's Own Scottish Borderers, inaugurated the series of successful raids that did so much to harass the enemy during the four months prior to the winter campaign.

As a Division of XXIst Corps it played an important part in the final overthrow of the Turks at Gaza and the subsequent advance; but ceased to belong to the Egyptian Expeditionary Force on embarking for France in April, 1918. The Divisional Artillery was transferred to the 7th (Indian) Division in March, 1918, and the Artillery of that Division accompanied the 52nd to France.

1917.

Oct. 31.—The Division held the left sector of the line from the Gaza–Cairo road and along Samson's Ridge to the Sea.

Nov. 1-2.—At 2300, after a heavy bombardment lasting six days, 156th Brigade (temporarily attached to 54th Division) stormed Umbrella Hill, a strong redoubt and the key of the Gaza defences. The position was stubbornly defended, but after a stiff fight in which 1/7th Scottish Rifles were prominent, it was captured and consolidated.

,, 5.—The whole of the defensive system at Gaza was in British hands, and 155th and 157th Brigades advanced along the beach and seized the high ground north of the Wadi Hesi.

,, 8.—The advance was continued in co-operation with Imperial Service Cavalry, and after a trying march over soft sand, the high ground north-west of Deir Sineid was taken. The Turks launched a determined counter-attack from the direction of Ascalon to retake this position and four times drove the Lowlanders off the hill, but at the fifth attempt it was held and consolidated.

,, 9.—The Division captured the line Deir Sineid–Beit Jerjah–Ascalon with little opposition.

,, 10.—Advanced to the Esdud–Mejdel–Herbiah line. The ridge north of Beit Duras was stormed by 157th Brigade after a march of fourteen miles over heavy sand.

,, 12.—Enemy resistance stiffened considerably and a determined stand was made on a line through Brown Hill and Burkah. Several assaults were launched and heavy fighting ensued in which 156th Brigade was heavily engaged. Eventually the whole hostile position was taken late in the afternoon, two battalions of 75th Division co-operating on the right in the last assault.

,, 13.—The enemy continued to fight stubbornly and 155th Brigade met severe opposition in the attack on the Katrah–El Mughar line. The attack had to cross over 4,000 yards of open ground swept by heavy shell and machine-gun fire. Yeomanry co-operation on the left flank, and an infantry charge on the right captured the positions late in the afternoon. King's Own Scottish Borderers dashed up the hill and captured the Mughar defences, while Royal Scots Fusiliers worked their way into Katrah by a series of flank attacks supported by bombers, and rushed the village.

The captures at Katrah included a Turkish infantry battalion, a company of machine-gunners with twenty-six guns, two field guns, and a large store of ammunition.

,, 18.—Division moved up to Ludd and Ramleh, where

,, 19.—it turned to the east towards the Judæan Hills, and occupied Kubab and Annabeh without opposition. The advance was continued with 75th Division on the right and Yeomanry Mounted Division on the left. The tracks were so bad that only three sections of guns accompanied the infantry and they had to be double-horsed.

,, 20.—Beit Dukka was captured by 157th Brigade.

1917.

Nov. 22.—155th Brigade captured Beit Izza, and 156th Brigade relieved 233rd and 234th Brigades (75th Division) at Neby Samwil, where captured positions were extended during the night, in spite of considerable enemy resistance.

,, 24.—The Division attacked with the intention of getting astride the Jerusalem–Nablus road. The first step was to capture El Jib and Bir Nebala, but these commanding positions were strongly held, and the formation of the ground made it impossible to attack from the flanks. 155th Brigade attacked El Jib but could make no headway and the action was broken off.

,, 26.—60th Division relieved 52nd, and the latter were ordered to march to Ludd, but the Turks commenced a series of severe attacks that threatened to cut our communications along the Ramleh–Jerusalem road, and the Lowlanders were hurried back into the line.

,, 28.—155th Brigade took over on the left of the Yeomanry Division, and 156th Brigade went up in support. 1/7th Scottish Rifles (156th Brigade) assisted 8th Mounted Brigade to repulse a strong attack.

,, 29-30.—157th Brigade relieved 22nd and 7th Mounted Brigades during the night, and the whole Division was engaged in stemming hostile attacks.

Dec. 1.—1/4th Royal Scots Fusiliers supported 8th Australian Light Horse Regiment which was attacked in the early morning by a Turkish Assault Battalion. A determined attack was made on the Tahta defences held by 157th Brigade and it was compelled to give ground but recaptured the original line after fierce hand-to-hand fighting.

,, 7.—52nd Division, relieved by 10th, marched to Ramleh, and

,, 12.—concentrated on the left in the coastal sector, between Neby Tari and the sea, covering Selmeh and Sarona.

,, 20 to 21 } The final advance by the Division in Palestine was the crossing of the Auja. The river was swift and swollen by recent rain, and the fords were few and difficult to find. The ground north of the river was entirely unreconnoitred, and the enemy held a strong entrenched line along the high ground overlooking the wide belt of open country through which the river flowed. Light canvas rafts were constructed and concealed in orange groves. These were carried to the river after dark and lashed in position to form a bridge, over which infantry and guns crossed, sound being deadened by use of matting. Meanwhile, some infantry crossed in coracles; others found a possible ford, linked arms and waded over breast deep. Post after post was rushed in silence at the point of the bayonet without a shot being fired. Kh. Hadrah, Sh. Muannis, and Tel er Rekkeit were captured by 155th, 156th, and 157th Brigades respectively, and by dawn all objectives were taken with 316 prisoners and ten machine guns.

,, 22.—The line was further advanced to a depth of one and a half miles by the capture of Tel el Mukhmar and Arsuf; and the Division held this line with two brigades, and one in reserve at Sarona, until relieved by 7th (Indian) Division in March.

EGYPTIAN EXPEDITIONARY FORCE

53rd DIVISION.

Commander.—Major (temp. Major-Gen.) S. F. MOTT, C.B., r.p., p.s.c.

Commanding, Royal Artillery.—Lieut.-Col. (temp. Brig.-Gen.) R. E. A. LE MOTTÉE, R.A. (relinquished, Oct., 1917).
Lieut.-Col. (temp. Brig.-Gen.) J. W. HOPE, D.S.O., R.F.A. (relinquished, Nov., 1917).
Lieut.-Col. (temp. Brig.-Gen.) J. W. WALKER, D.S.O., T.D., R.F.A. (T.F.).

158th Infantry Brigade.

Commander.—Bt. Lieut.-Col. (temp. Brig.-Gen.) C. S. ROME, C.M.G., D.S.O., 11th Hussars (relinquished, Sept., 1917).
Major (temp. Brig.-Gen.) H. A. VERNON, D.S.O., King's Royal Rifle Corps (relinquished, Sept., 1918).
Major (temp. Brig.-Gen.) E. H. WILDBLOOD, D.S.O., 1st Leinster Regt.

5/6th Battalion Royal Welsh Fusiliers (1/5th and 1/6th Battalions amalgamated 3/8/18), 3/153rd Rifles (late Infantry) 3/154th Indian Infantry, 4/11th Gurkha Rifles.
1/1st Battalion Herefordshire Regiment (ceased to belong to E.E.F., 19/6/18).
158th Light Trench Mortar Battery.

159th Infantry Brigade.

Commander.—Col. (temp. Brig.-Gen.) J. H. du B. TRAVERS, C.B. (relinquished, Oct., 1917).
Major (temp. Brig.-Gen.) N. E. MONEY, C.M.G., D.S.O., Shropshire Yeomanry.

4/5th Battalion Welsh Regiment (1/4th and 1/5th Battalions amalgamated 3/8/18), 3/152nd, 1/153rd and 2/153rd Punjabis (late Infantry).
1/4th and 1/7th Battalions Cheshire Regiment (ceased to belong to E.E.F., 19/6/18).
159th Light Trench Mortar Battery.

160th Infantry Brigade.

Commander.—Bt. Lieut.-Col. (temp. Brig.-Gen.) V. L. N. PEARSON, D.S.O., Middlesex Regt. (relinquished, Oct., 1918).
Lieut.-Col. (temp. Brig.-Gen.) F. H. BORTHWICK, D.S.O., 5th Bn. Royal Welsh Fusiliers.

1/7th Battalion Royal Welsh Fusiliers, 1/17th Infantry, 1/21st Punjabis, 1st Battalion Cape Corps.
2/4th Battalion Royal West Kent Regiment (disbanded, 13/9/18), 2/10th Battalion Middlesex Regiment (disbanded, 20/8/18), 2/4th Battalion Queen's Royal West Surrey Regiment and 1/4th Battalion Royal Sussex Regiment (ceased to belong to E.E.F., 19/6/18).
160th Light Trench Mortar Battery.

Divisional Troops.

53rd Divisional Cyclist Company.
265th Brigade, R.F.A. ("A," "B" and "C" Batteries).
266th Brigade, R.F.A. ("A," "B" and "C" Batteries).
267th Brigade, R.F.A. ("A," "B" and 439th Batteries).
53rd Divisional Ammunition Column.
436th and 437th (Welsh), Field Companies, R.E.
72nd Company, 3rd Sappers and Miners.
53rd Divisional Signal Company, R.E.
53rd Divisional Machine Gun Battalion (Nos. 158, 159, 160 Companies).
1/155th Pioneers.
53rd Divisional Train (Nos. 246, 247, 248 and 249 Companies, R.A.S.C.).
53rd Mobile Veterinary Section.

Brief Record of Service.

The 53rd Division was composed originally of Territorial battalions, and landed in Egypt from Gallipoli as a Territorial Division. It took part in the advance from the Suez Canal, the first and second battles of Gaza, and eventually joined the XXth Corps, on its formation in Aug., 1917. Certain Battalions were withdrawn and others were amalgamated or disbanded between June and Aug., 1918, their places being taken by Indian Units and a Battalion of the Cape Corps.

1917.
Oct. 31.—Division concentrated in the neighbourhood of El Buggar, and,

Nov. 1.—after the fall of Beersheba, occupied the line north of the town, from Towal Abu Jerwal to Kh. el Muweileh.

" 3.—Orders were received to attack the heights of Tel Khuweilfeh, and three days and nights of almost continuous fighting ensued. 159th Brigade were heavily engaged, particularly 1/4th and 1/5th Welsh, and 1/7th Cheshires; the first-named carrying a rocky hill at the point of the bayonet.

" 4.—160th Brigade, in an exposed position, suffered considerably from lack of water.

" 5.—265th Brigade, R.F.A., were shelled incessantly throughout the day, but held their ground.

" 6.—158th Brigade, with 1/4th Sussex attached, stormed the Khuweilfeh Heights in the early morning. in conjunction with the main Corps operation, and reached all objectives by dawn. A Company of 1/1st Herefords rushed nine field guns in a ravine, complete with personnel and teams, but had to abandon them later.

Five counter-attacks were launched during the ensuing twenty-four hours, and twice the enemy regained the summit for short periods, but were driven off with heavy losses by 1/7th Royal Welsh Fusiliers, supported by accurate artillery fire.

" 8.—Division concentrated at Khuweilfeh.

Dec. 4.—March towards Jerusalem commenced; Hebron occupied on Dec. 5, and Bethlehem during the night of Dec. 8–9.

" 9.—The division was now in touch with 60th Division, attacking Jerusalem from the west, and the advance was continued at an early hour. Mar Elias was occupied by 1/5th Welsh (159th Brigade) at 0800, and this Battalion was under the walls of the Holy City at 0845, and in action near the cemetery on the Jericho road at 0900. Later in the day 1/4th and 1/5th Welsh captured the Mount of Olives, their advance being assisted by 1/4th Cheshires on the right and troops of 60th Division on the left.

" 11.—Fighting continued, and a line from Abu Dis to El Aziriyeh, astride the Jerusalem–Jericho road was occupied.

" 13.—159th Brigade captured Ras el Kharrubeh.

" 17.—1/4th Sussex and 2/4th Royal West Kents (160th Brigade) seized the ridge east of Abu Dis and took 126 prisoners and two machine guns.

" 21.—Ras ez Zamby and White Hill were captured by 2/4th Queens and 2/10th Middlesex (160th Brigade) after heavy fighting, and these positions were held against a strong counter-attack.

" 27.—The Turks made a series of desperate attacks on the line covering Jerusalem, with the evident intention of retaking the city, but all attacks were repulsed with heavy losses. Deir Ibn Obeid, held by 2/10th Middlesex, was subjected to particularly fierce assaults, but, though surrounded, the position was resolutely defended for several hours and eventually relieved by 1/4th Sussex.

" 28.—Anata was taken by 158th Brigade, and the line further advanced by the capture of Ras Arkub es Suffa (1/7th Royal Welsh Fusiliers) and Khamlit (1/1st Herefords).

1917.
Dec. 29.—159th Brigade captured Hizmeh and Jeba.

Feb. 13.—Early in the year 53rd Division relieved 60th Division astride the Jerusalem–Nablus road (Et Tell-Sh. Abdallah–Arnutieh-Kh. Wady es Serah), 60th Division taking over the line east of Jerusalem in preparation for forthcoming operations towards Jericho.

1918.
Feb. 14.—The right of the line was advanced to Deir Diwan and Kh. Alia to protect the left flank of the attack by 60th Division.

" 19.—2/10th Middlesex captured Rummon, and on the following day,

" 20.—the line Rummon–Garden Hill–Sh. Abdallah was occupied.

Mch. 7.—Nejmeh was captured by 1/7th Cheshires at 0500 after a rapid advance.

" 8–9.—A night advance over difficult ground resulted in the capture of Munatir Ridge by 1/4th Cheshires; and 1/4th Welsh stormed Dar Jerir and Drage's Hill in face of strong opposition. Tell Asur was captured by 1/5th Royal Welsh Fusiliers at the point of the bayonet, and successfully held against three determined counter-attacks; while 1/1st Herefords carried Chipp Hill after heavy fighting.

" 10.—158th and 159th Brigades captured important ridges in rapid succession and Kefr Malik was occupied at 1400.

" 11.—159th Brigade reached the south bank of the Wady Kola by 0900.

" 11–12.—A night advance by the Division secured the line Nejmeh–Rock Park–Kh. Abu Felah–Mezrah el Sherkiyeh. In an attempt to advance beyond this line a company of 2/10th Middlesex were heavily counter-attacked on the slopes of Kh. Amurich, and this attack was not pushed home.

Mch. to Sept. } 53rd Division remained in the same sector of the line throughout the summer.

" 18.—The general attack that was to smash the Turkish Armies in Palestine commenced at 2200, when 1/17th Infantry (160th Brigade) moved north in the direction of Square Hill, followed by the rest of the brigade. Further to the left 159th Brigade captured Round Hill (overlooking Kh. Abu Felah) at 2230.

" 19.—4/5th Welsh (159th Brigade) captured Kew Hill and Pt. 2401 by 0045, and 160th Brigade took Valley View at 0215. Strong enemy positions at Sh. el Azeir, El Mugheir, Boulder Boil, and Pt. 2362, attacked from the rear by 1/7th Royal Welsh Fusiliers, were in our hands by 0300, and the Cape Corps seized Square Hill at 0450. 159th Brigade captured Hindhead (4/5th Welsh), and were heavily engaged near Kh. Abu Malul, where 3/152nd Infantry, after three unsuccessful assaults, stormed the defences at dusk.

" 20.—Kh. Jibeit and Gallows Hill were stormed by the Cape Corps, but a fierce counter-attack by overwhelming numbers, covered by heavy shelling, forced them to withdraw. 1/17th Infantry recaptured Kh. Jibeit at 1230, and took 150 prisoners.

2/153rd Infantry (159th Brigade) captured Ras et Tawil, but 158th Brigade were held up

1918.
Sept. 20   for a time by stubborn opposition south of Kh. Birket el Kusr. At midnight the division continued the advance.
„ 21.—5/6th Royal Welsh Fusiliers and 4/11th Gurkhas (158th Brigade) seized Kh. Birket el Kusr and Pt. 2906 respectively. 159th Brigade advanced rapidly capturing Kusrah (4/5th Welsh) and Akrabeh, at 0400 and 1000 respectively.

1918.
Sept. 21   By nightfall the division had reached Beit Dejan and Beit Furik, having dislodged the enemy from positions of great natural strength and driven the remnant fifteen miles across most difficult country on to the cavalry patrols of Desert Mounted Corps.
„ 26.—Division concentrated in the Sinjil-Tell Asur area.

54th (EAST ANGLIAN) DIVISION (T.).

Commander.—Major-Gen. S. W. HARE, C.B.

Commanding, Royal Artillery.—Lieut.-Col. (temp. Brig.-Gen.) D. B. STEWART, D.S.O., R.A.

161st Infantry Brigade.

Commander.—Bt. Col. (temp. Brig.-Gen.) W. MARRIOTT DODINGTON, Oxford. & Bucks. Light Infantry, p.s.c. (relinquished, Feb., 1918).
Major (temp. Brig.-Gen.) H. B. H. ORPEN PALMER, D.S.O., Royal Irish Fusiliers.

1/4th, 1/5th, 1/6th and 1/7th Battalions Essex Regt.
161st Light Trench Mortar Battery.

162nd Infantry Brigade.

Commander.—Bt. Col. (temp. Brig.-Gen.) A. MUDGE, C.M.G., Queen's Royal West Surrey Regt.

1/5th Battalion Bedfordshire Regiment, 1/4th Battalion Northamptonshire Regiment, 1/10th and 1/11th Battalions London Regiment.
162nd Light Trench Mortar Battery.

163rd Infantry Brigade.

Commander.—Lieut.-Col. (temp. Brig.-Gen.) T. WARD, C.M.G., T.F. Reserve (relinquished, April, 1918).
Lieut.-Col. (temp. Brig.-Gen.) A. J. MCNEILL, D.S.O., Lovat's Scouts Yeomanry.

1/4th and 1/5th Battalions Norfolk Regiment, 1/5th Battalion Suffolk Regiment, 1/8th Battalion Hampshire Regiment.
163rd Light Trench Mortar Battery.

Divisional Troops.

270th Brigade, R.F.A. ("A," "B" and "C" Batteries).
271st Brigade, R.F.A. ("A," "B" and 440th Batteries).
272nd Brigade, R.F.A. ("A," "B" and "C" Batteries).
54th Divisional Ammunition Column.
484th and 486th (East Anglian), and 495th (Kent), Field Companies, R.E.
54th Divisional Signal Company, R.E.
54th Divisional Machine Gun Battalion (Nos. 161, 162, 163 Companies).
54th Divisional Train (Nos. 921, 922, 923 and 924 Companies, R.A.S.C.).
1/1st East Anglian Mobile Veterinary Section.

Brief Record of Service.

54th Division, composed entirely of Territorial Battalions, fought through the Gallipoli campaign; landed in Egypt in December, 1915; and marched across the desert from the Suez Canal.

It took part in the first and second battles of Gaza in March and April, 1917; held the left of the line in front of Gaza in June and July; and eventually was included in XXIst Corps on its formation in August.

Throughout the Palestine campaign 54th Division fought unchanged in its order of battle.

1917.
July 14–15.—The Turkish redoubt known as Beach Post was successfully raided by one company 1/8th Hampshires (163rd Brigade), with one company 2/5th Hampshires (232nd Brigade), attached.
,, 20–21.—1/5th Bedfords (162nd Brigade) successfully raided Umbrella Hill, an important redoubt south of Gaza, and
,, 27–28.—followed this up by a second raid.
Nov. 2.—The Division attacked Gaza with the 156th Brigade of the 52nd Division attached. In the enemy front line system the 156th Brigade captured Umbrella Hill; 1/5th Suffolks and 1/8th Hampshires, assisted by 1/4th and 1/5th Norfolks, stormed El Arish Redoubt; 1/6th and 1/5th Essex captured Beach and Sea Posts and Rafa Redoubt at the point of the bayonet. Zowaiid and Cricket Redoubts also fell to the Essex (161st) Brigade; whilst the 1/5th Bedfords and 1/11th Londons pushed on and seized Sheikh Hassan and Gun Hill respectively, strong points in the Turks' second line of defence. All positions were consolidated and held in spite of determined counter-attacks.
,, 7.—The 162nd Brigade occupied Belah Trench–Turtle Hill. Patrols through Gaza found it evacuated and a defensive line from Sh. Redwan to the sea was occupied and linked up with the line held by 75th Division on the right.
,, 19.—The Division reached Ludd and proceeded to take over a portion of the new line covering Jaffa.
,, 27.—The Turks heavily attacked on the line Beit Nabala–Dear Tureif–Wilhelma, but were repulsed by the 162nd Brigade, particularly stout defence being put up by the 1/4th Northamptons (162nd Brigade) at Wilhelma.
,, 28.—1/5th Essex raided the Turkish trenches on the south bank of the Auja.
,, 30.—1/5th Bedfords repulsed a Turkish attack on Zeifizfiyeh Hill.
Dec. 2.—1/6th Essex repeated the raid on Turkish trenches.
,, 11.—1/4th Norfolks (163rd Brigade) and "C" Battery 272nd Field Artillery Brigade repulsed a second determined Turkish attack on Zeifizfiyeh Hill.
,, 15.—The 163rd Brigade captured Kh. el Bornat (5th Suffolk Regt.) and Et Tireh on the fringe of the Judæan Hills.
,, 22.—The 161st and 162nd Brigades advanced the line to the River Auja, north of Mulebbis, the

1917.
Dec, 22 1/11th Londons storming Bald Hill, which was strongly held, in the course of this engagement.
1918.
March 12.—The 162nd and 163rd Brigades advanced the line further to a depth of four miles, capturing Mezeirah (1/5th Bedfords and 1/11th Londons) Kh. Dikerin (1/4th Northamptons), Mejdel Yaba (1/10th Londons), and Ras el Ain (1/4th Norfolks).
Sept. 18.—161st Brigade at Mejdel Yaba; 162nd Brigade at Mezeirah–Kuleh; and 163rd Brigade, Kuleh–Rantieh.
,, 19.—0420.—Division advanced on a front of 3,000 yards, and by 0700 had captured Crown Hill (1/8th Hampshires), Kefr Kasim and Jevis Tepe (1/4th and 1/5th Essex), strong resistance being experienced by the 161st Brigade at Kasim Wood.
1105.—Oghlu Tepe was stormed by the 1/10th Londons and 1/4th Northamptons. During this action the 1/10th Londons rushed and captured two 5·9-inch howitzers on high ground overlooking the Wadi Kanah.
1115.—Sivri Tepe was captured by 1/5th Essex, after stubborn resistance.
1515.—Kh. Sirisia was taken by 1/4th Norfolks, supported by 1/5th Norfolks.
The Division had to advance over broken and difficult country, but all objectives were taken by nightfall, with 600 prisoners and eleven guns.
A feature of the day's fighting was the use made of captured enemy machine guns. 1/8th Hampshires, in particular, used captured guns with satisfactory results.
,, 20.—The 163rd Brigade occupied north and south line through Bidieh by 0300.
,, 24.—The Division concentrated in the Hableh area;
,, 28.—started the march to Haifa, and on
Oct. 4.—concentrated at Haifa.
,, 23.—The advance northward to Beirut was continued and on
,, 31.—the Division marched through Beirut at the hour that hostilities with Turkey ceased.

60th DIVISION.

Commander.—Major-Gen. E. S. BULFIN, C.B., C.V.O. (relinquished, Aug., 1917).
 Major-Gen. Sir J. S. M. SHEA, K.C.M.G., C.B., D.S.O., I.A., *p.s.c.*
Commanding, Royal Artillery.—Bt. Col. (temp. Brig.-Gen.) H. A. D. SIMPSON-BAIKIE, C.B., R.A. (relinquished, Aug., 1917).
 Lieut.-Col. (temp. Brig.-Gen.) H. M. DRAKE, R.F.A. (relinquished, Oct., 1917).
 Col. (temp. Brig.-Gen.) W. A. ROBINSON, C.B., C.M.G., R.A.

179th Infantry Brigade.

Commander.—Col. (temp. Brig.-Gen.) FITZ J. M. EDWARDS, C.M.G., D.S.O., I.A., A.D.C. (relinquished, Feb., 1918).
 Lieut.-Col. (temp. Brig.-Gen.) E. T. HUMPHREYS, D.S.O., Lancashire Fusiliers, *p.s.c.*

2/13th Battalion London Regiment, 2/19th Punjabis, 2/127th Baluch Light Infantry, 3/151st Punjabi Rifles (late Infantry),
2/14th, 2/15th, 2/16th Battalions London Regiment (ceased to belong to E.E.F., 19/6/18.)
179th Light Trench Mortar Battery.

180th Infantry Brigade.

Commander.—Major (temp. Brig.-Gen.) F. M. CARLETON, D.S.O. (R. of O.), *p.s.c.* (relinquished, Aug., 1917).
    Bt. Col. (temp. Brig.-Gen.) J. HILL, D.S.O., I.A., A.D.C. (relinquished, Sept., 1917).
    Bt. Lieut.-Col. (temp. Brig.-Gen.) C. F. WATSON, C.M.G., D.S.O., Queen's Royal West Surrey Regt.

    2/19th Battalion London Regiment, 2nd Guides Infantry, 2/30th Punjabis, 1/50th Kumaon Rifles.
    2/17th and 2/20th Battalions London Regiment (ceased to belong to E.E.F., 19/6/18 and 2/7/18, respectively), 2/18th Battalion London Regiment (disbanded, 10/7/18).
    180th Light Trench Mortar Battery.

181st Infantry Brigade.

Commander.—Bt. Lieut.-Col. (temp. Brig.-Gen.) E. C. DA COSTA, C.M.G., D.S.O., East Lancashire Regt.

    2/22nd Battalion London Regiment, 1/30th Baluchis, 2/97th Deccan Infantry, 2/152nd Punjabis (late Infantry).
    2/21st Battalion London Regiment (disbanded, 11/6/18), 2/23rd and 2/24th Battalions London Regiment (ceased to belong to E.E.F., 2/7/18).
    181st Light Trench Mortar Battery.

Divisional Troops.

    301st Brigade, R.F.A. ("A," "B" and "C" Batteries).
    302nd Brigade, R.F.A. ("A," "B" and 413th Batteries).
    303rd Brigade, R.F.A. ("A," "B" and "C" Batteries).
    60th Divisional Ammunition Column.
    No. 1 Company, 1st (King George's Own) Sappers and Miners.
    519th and 521st (London) Field Companies, R.E.
    60th Divisional Signal Company, R.E.
    60th Divisional Machine Gun Battalion (Nos. 179, 180, 181 Companies).
    60th Divisional Train (Nos. 517, 518, 519 and 520 Companies, R.A.S.C.).
    2/2nd London Mobile Veterinary Section.

Brief Record of Service.

    60th (London) Division, composed entirely of London Territorial Battalions, served in France from June to December, 1916, was transferred to Salonika, and eventually landed in Egypt in June, 1917. It reached the front in July, and joined XXth Corps in August.

    The Division was reorganized in July, 1918, when seven Battalions were withdrawn for service in France and two were disbanded. The vacancies were filled by Indian units, and the Territorial title was dropped.

1917.
Oct. 30.—Concentrated about the Wadi Mirtaba, six miles south-west of Beersheba.
" 31.—179th and 181st Brigades attacked the Beersheba defences from south-west, on right of 74th Division. 2/14th and 2/15th London broke through by 1230, and twenty minutes later all objectives were taken. 2/13th London were shelled and machine-gunned from direction of Beersheba, so the battalion advanced about a mile and captured two 77mm. guns.
Nov. 6.—Attacked Kauwukah and Rushdi systems at 1230, with 74th on right and 10th on left. 179th and 180th Brigades broke through, after two hours sharp fighting, and occupied Sheria Station.
" 7.—Tel Esh Sheria still held out but the enemy was dislodged after a sharp fight.
" 18.—Division concentrated at Gaza, and marched northward on the following day.
" 24 to 27 Relieved 232nd Brigade (75th Division) and 52nd Division, in the Judæan Hills, on the line Soba–Kustul–Nebi Samwil–Beit Izza.
Dec. 1.—Three determined hostile attacks on Nebi Samwil were beaten off, with a loss to the enemy of 500 killed.

1917.
Dec. 5.—231st Brigade (74th Division) took over the Nebi Samwil–Beit Izza sector, and 60th Divison concentrated about Kustul for the attack on Jerusalem.
" 8.—179th Brigade, with mountain batteries, crossed the Wadi Surar during the night and seized the high ground south of Ain Karim at 0330. The right of the line thus secured, the main attack by the 180th Brigade began at dawn (0515) in heavy rain, and by 0700 the defences on the formidable ridge overhanging the Wadi Surar were captured. Strong resistance was experienced at the "Heart and Liver" redoubts, and the works at Deir Yesin; and the left of the attack was held up until 1530 when a bayonet charge dislodged the enemy. The steep slopes to Lifta were swept by hostile machine-gun fire, but 180th Brigade pushed on and occupied the village at dusk.
" 9.—The Turks evacuated Jerusalem during the night, and the city surrendered to General Shea at 0830.
    Enemy rearguards were engaged and positions were occupied at Tel el Ful and Shafat, four miles north of Jerusalem on the Nablus road.
" 11.—Division occupied the line Tel el Ful–Beit Hannina

1917.
Dec. 23.—2/24th London advanced 800 yards on the left, and 2/18th London stormed Kh. Adaseh, but the main attack was postponed and this advanced position was abandoned.

,, 27.—The Turks attacked along the whole line covering Jerusalem at 0130, and bitter fighting continued throughout the day. A particularly violent attack at dawn enabled them to gain a footing in a portion of our line, but 2/15th London counter-attacked and, in spite of heavy shelling, recaptured the lost ground. Thirteen costly attacks had been delivered by dusk with the net gain to the enemy of the advanced posts on Kh. Ras et Tawil and the quarry north of Tel el Ful, abandoned in the early morning to overwhelming numbers.

,, 28.—181st Brigade occupied El Jib and Bir Nebala, and 180th Brigade took Kh. Adaseh at 1725. 2/20th London captured Er Ram, and the line Er Ram-Rafat was occupied at 1915.

,, 29.—Tel en Nasbeh and the hill north of Kefr Akab were taken by 2/19th and 2/20th London, respectively, and these battalions stormed Shab Salah at 1520. On the right 2/17th and 2/18th seized the ridge immediately north-west of Burkah, and on the left the Tahuneh ridge was carried by 2/22nd and 2/23rd. Beitin and Balua were taken during the night by 180th and 181st Brigades respectively, and the line carried on to near Kh. el Burj where junction was effected with 74th Division.

1918.
Feb. 13.—The Division held the line Deir Ibn Obeid-Ras es Suffa-Hizmeh, taken over from 53rd Division.

,, 14.—181st Brigade occupied Mukhmas and Tel es Suwan.

,, 19.—179th Brigade captured El Muntar; 180th Brigade stormed Arak Ibrahim after severe fighting; and 181st Brigade seized Splash Hill and Ras et Tawil.

,, 20.—Jebel Ekteif and Talaat ed Dumm were captured by 179th and 180th Brigades, respectively, while 181st Brigade advanced four miles along the north of the Wadi Farah. Neby Musa was occupied by 2/14th London, in co-operation with New Zealand Mounted Brigade.

,, 21.—The Division occupied the line Rujm esh Shemaliyeh-Kh. Kakun-Jebel Kuruntul, and, the object of the advance achieved,

,, 22.—withdrew to the line Jebel Ekteif-Talaat ed Dumm-Ras et Tawil, with 144 prisoners and six machine guns.

Mar. 9.—181st Brigade advanced rapidly over rough country and El Madbeh and Kh. el Beiyudat were occupied by 2/24th and 2/22nd London, respectively. With 2/21st astride Wadi Aujah at 0930, 2/24th, supported by Light Armoured Car Batteries, captured Abu Tellul at 1630.

,, 14.—The advance was continued and El Musallabeh captured in spite of opposition.

,, 22.—The first crossing of the Jordan, swollen and unfordable, was effected by swimmers of 2/19th London at Hajlah at 0100, and as the result of their efforts 2/19th and 2/18th Battalions were able to cross on rafts and a light pontoon bridge by 1200.

,, 23.—Swimmers reached the eastern bank at Ghoraniyeh at 1320; rafting and bridge construction commenced, and

,, 24.—The whole force detailed for the Amman raid had crossed the river by 0500.

1918.
Mar. 24 179th Brigade captured El Haud, and 181st Brigade took Shunet Nimrin. 2/22nd London captured three guns in their attack on Tel el Musta.

,, 25.—The advance was delayed by weather conditions but 179th Brigade occupied Es Salt at 2000.

,, 28.—The first attack on Amman commenced at 1300. 2/23rd and 2/21st Battalions were held up 1,000 yards north-west of Amman by intense machine-gun and rifle fire, and 2/17th and 2/18th were ordered up from Es Sir in support.

,, 30.—After thirty-six hours almost continuous fighting a night attack was launched at 0200. 2/22nd London captured 135 prisoners and four machine guns, but were held up 500 yards from their objective (the "Citadel") at 0845. 2/18th on their right were also held up by a heavy frontal fire. 2/21st on the extreme left, though repeatedly counter-attacked, invariably held the advantage in the hand-to-hand fighting that ensued. 2/18th London again tried to storm the "Citadel" at 1500, but were checked by heavy fire from right flank, and shortly after orders were received to withdraw.

Meanwhile the Battalions left to hold Es Salt defeated an enemy attack from the direction of Kefr Huda.

The Division started to withdraw during the night, and

April 3.—the rear units re-crossed the Jordan.

,, 30.—The troops detailed for the Es Salt raid crossed to east of Jordan. 180th Brigade attacked Shunet Nimrin and captured some advanced positions, but the enemy were strongly posted and no further progress was possible. 179th Brigade attacked El Haud but met with no better success.

May 3-4.—The force withdrew west of Jordan after heavy fighting, covered by 181st Brigade, who formed an extended bridgehead.

Sept. 17.—180th Brigade relieved 28th Brigade 7th (Indian Division) in the coastal sector, and the Division concentrated north and north-east of Arsuf.

,, 19.—180th Brigade attacked on a front of 1,500 yards at 0440, with 1/50th Kumaon Rifles (supported by 2/97th Infantry of 181st Brigade) on the right and 2nd Guides Infantry on the left. The objective of this attack was the strong trench system on the extreme right of the Turkish line, consisting of three lines of prepared positions. These were all carried by 0540, and by 0650 2/19th London had forced the Nahr el Falik and established a bridgehead to cover the advance of the cavalry. 181st Brigade pushed forward and 2/22nd London, 130th Baluchis and 2/152nd Punjabis reached a north and south line through Umm Sur at 1400. This Brigade advanced sixteen and a half miles in twelve and a half hours, and 2/22nd London and 2/152nd Punjabis captured Tulkeram and Irtah, respectively, with 835 prisoners. The Punjabis captured seven 77mm. guns in this last engagement, knocking out the teams with Lewis gun-fire.

,, 20.—The Division advanced at 0500 and 3/151st Punjabi Rifles (179th Brigade) captured Anebta and the Bir Asur tunnel.

,, 21.—The line Jebel Bir Asur-Belah-Shuweikeh was occupied,

,, 25.—and the Division concentrated at Rantieh in Army Reserve, less 181st Brigade, which remained at Kakon for escort duty.

74th (YEOMANRY) DIVISION.
(Ceased to belong to E.E.F. 7/5/18.)

Commander.—Bt. Col. (temp. Major-Gen.) E. S. GIRDWOOD, C.B., Scottish Rifles.

Commanding, Royal Artillery.—Lieut.-Col. (temp. Brig.-Gen.) L. J. HEXT, C.M.G., R.A.

229th Infantry Brigade.

Commander.—Col. (temp. Brig.-Gen.) R. HOARE, D.S.O., late 4th Hussars.

16th (Royal 1st Devon and Royal North Devon Yeomanry) Battalion Devonshire Regiment.
12th (West Somerset Yeomanry) Battalion Somerset Light Infantry.
14th (Fife and Forfar Yeomanry) Battalion Black Watch.
12th (Ayr and Lanark Yeomanry) Battalion Royal Scots Fusiliers.
4th Machine Gun Company.
229th Light Trench Mortar Battery.

230th Infantry Brigade.

Commander.—Lieut.-Col. (temp. Brig.-Gen.) A. J. MCNEILL, D.S.O., Lovat's Scouts Yeomanry (relinquished, Dec., 1917).
Bt. Lieut.-Col. (temp. Brig.-Gen.) H. B. H. ORPEN-PALMER, D.S.O., Royal Irish Fusiliers (relinquished, Feb., 1918).
Major (temp. Brig.-Gen.) W. J. BOWKER, C.M.G., D.S.O., Somerset Light Infantry.

10th (Royal East Kent and West Kent Yeomanry) Battalion East Kent Regiment.
16th (Sussex Yeomanry) Battalion Royal Sussex Regiment.
15th (Suffolk Yeomanry) Battalion Suffolk Regiment.
12th (Norfolk Yeomanry) Battalion Norfolk Regiment.
209th Machine Gun Company.
230th Light Trench Mortar Battery.

231st Infantry Brigade.

Commander.—Major (temp. Brig.-Gen.) W. J. BOWKER, C.M.G., D.S.O., Somerset Light Infantry (relinquished, Sept., 1917).
Bt. Lieut.-Col. (temp. Brig.-Gen.) C. E. HEATHCOTE, C.M.G., D.S.O., Yorkshire Light Infantry.

10th (Shropshire and Cheshire Yeomanry) Battalion King's Shropshire Light Infantry.
24th (Denbighshire Yeomanry) Battalion Royal Welsh Fusiliers.
25th (Montgomeryshire and Welsh Horse Yeomanry) Battalion Royal Welsh Fusiliers.
24th (Pembroke and Glamorgan Yeomanry) Battalion Welsh Regiment.
210th Machine Gun Company.
231st Light Trench Mortar Battery.

Divisional Troops.

117th Brigade, R.F.A. ("A," "B," 366th and "D" Batteries).
44th Brigade, R.F.A. (340th, 382nd, 425th and "D" Batteries).
74th Divisional Ammunition Column.
X 74 and Y 74 (Medium), Trench Mortar Batteries, R.A.
No. 5 (Royal Monmouth), No. 5 (Royal Anglesey), 439th (Cheshire) Field Companies, R.E.
74th Divisional Signal Company, R.E.
Pioneer Battalion 1/12th Loyal North Lancashire Regiment.
261st Machine Gun Company.
74th Divisional Employment Company.
74th Divisional Train (Nos. 447, 448, 449 and 450 Companies, R.A.S.C.).
59th Mobile Veterinary Section.

Brief Record of Service.

74th (Yeomanry) Division was formed in January, 1917, of eighteen dismounted Yeomanry regiments, including twelve that had served in Gallipoli. The newly-formed Infantry battalions were brought up to strength with drafts, and reached the front in time for the second battle of Gaza in April.

As an Infantry Division it joined XXth Corps on its formation in August, and, during August and September, Brigades were employed alternately in holding portions of the line and constructing new defences in the left sector.

After taking part in the attack on Beersheba, the capture of Jerusalem, and the subsequent hill-fighting during the winter months, the Division embarked for France in May, 1918, and ceased to belong to the Egyptian Expeditionary Force.

1917.
Oct. 30.—Concentrated south-west of the Wadi Saba.
,, 31.—231st and 230th Brigades attacked Beersheba at 0830 on the left of 60th Division, 10th East Kents (Buffs) and 12th Norfolks leading the attack. Their objectives were the main Turkish trench-line immediately south of the Wadi Saba. Stubborn resistance was met with but all objectives were taken by 1330. Later in the day 230th Brigade crossed the Wadi Saba and rolled up all hostile defences as far north as the Beersheba-Tel el Fara road, while a brigade of 53rd Division threatened them from the west.
Nov. 6.—230th and 229th Brigades attacked the system of trenches and redoubts covering Sheria at dawn, with yeomanry on the right and 60th Division on the left. Stubborn resistance was encountered, but all positions east of the railway were stormed by 1515, and the Division moved to the high ground north of Sheria. Several guns and machine guns were captured and a way cleared for the advance of the cavalry.
,, 17.—Division marched to north of Deir el Belah, and
,, 23.—*viâ* Gaza towards Mejdel and Latron.
,, 28.—A composite Artillery Brigade was sent forward from Latron in support of the Yeomanry Mounted Division, who were heavily attacked on the Beit Ur el Foka-Beit Ur et Tahta-Suffa line.
,, 29.—231st Brigade relieved 8th and 6th Mounted Brigades,
,, 30.—and, throughout the day, was heavily engaged repulsing strong Turkish attacks between Et Tireh and Beit Ur el Foka.
Dec. 3.—16th Devons (229th Brigade) recaptured Beit Ur el Foka, which had been abandoned to the enemy on Nov. 28. Seventeen prisoners and three machine guns were taken in this engagement and several very determined counter-attacks were repulsed with heavy losses to the Turks who left fifty dead in the village alone. The village was again abandoned in the afternoon as it was dominated by high ground and was continually swept by hostile machine-gun fire.
,, 5.—The Division took over the Neby Samwil-Beit Izza Sector from 60th Division, and
,, 7.—extended the line southward to Sh. Abd el Aziz, one mile south-east of Beit Surik.
,, 8.—A general attack along the XXth Corps front was launched just before dawn. 230th Brigade captured Beit Iksa by 1100, but further advance to the Kh. el Burj Ridge was held up by heavy shelling and enfilade machine-gun fire from the right flank.

1917.
Dec. 9.—229th Brigade completed the capture of the Neby Samwil Ridge before dawn, and the right of the line, swinging north towards Beit Hannina linked up with 60th Division astride the Jerusalem-Nablus road. Enemy resistance weakened considerably and the line was advanced to four miles north of Jerusalem.
,, 11.—The Division moved to the left to conform with Corps redistribution, and took over the Neby Samwil-Beit Izza-Beit Dukka line.
,, 26.—24th Welsh Regiment (231st Brigade) stormed Hill 1910, one mile north of Beit Dukka, and beat off a heavy counter-attack.
,, 27.—24th Royal Welsh Fusiliers (231st Brigade) captured Kh. Ed Dreihemeh at 1015, and beat off a counter-attack after withdrawing slightly. 229th Brigade was heavily engaged on the Zeitun Ridge, where the last objective was rushed after dark.
,, 28.—24th Royal Welsh Fusiliers and 24th Welsh Regiment took Hill 2,450 and Kh. El Jufeir respectively, and 229th Brigade captured Beitunia at 1550 against strong resistance.
,, 29.—The enemy made determined efforts to hold Ram Allah, but it was taken, after a stiff fight, by 230th, supported by 229th Brigade.
,, 30.—A night attack by 230th Brigade resulted in the capture of the Kh. Et Tireh-Kh. El Burj line. The captured positions were consolidated, the Division having advanced over five miles in three days, through rugged and difficult country, and against continual and stubborn opposition.

1918.
Mar. 8.—The Division advanced astride the Jerusalem-Nablus road, with 53rd and 10th Divisions on right and left respectively. Ain Sinia was captured by 230th Brigade after a stiff fight.
,, 9.—231st Brigade rushed hostile defences at Selwad by 0525, but two assaults on Yebrud by 230th Brigade were unsuccessful.
,, 10.—The precipitous ridge of Burj el Lisaneh was stormed at 0300 and successfully defended against three counter-attacks, while 230th Brigade reversed the verdict of the previous day by capturing Yebrud and Burj Bardawile after heavy fighting. This Brigade again advanced to a depth of nearly two miles against considerable resistance.
,, 11.—231st Brigade captured Sh. Selim, while 230th Brigade occupied the ridge overlooking Sinjil. This was the final operation of the 74th (Yeomanry) Division in Palestine, and after a few weeks spent in holding the captured line the Division was withdrawn for service in France.

75th DIVISION.

Commander.—Major-Gen. P. C. PALIN, C.B., C.M.G., I.A.

Commanding, Royal Artillery.—Lieut.-Col. (temp. Brig.-Gen.) H. A. BOYCE, D.S.O., R.A.

232nd Infantry Brigade.

Commander.—Bt. Lieut.-Col. (temp. Brig.-Gen.) H. J. HUDDLESTON, C.M.G. D.S.O., M.C., Dorset Regiment.

    1/4th Battalion Wiltshire Regiment, 72nd Punjabis, 2/3rd Gurkha Rifles, 3rd Kashmir I.S. Infantry.
    2/5th Battalion Hampshire Regiment (disbanded, 17/8/18), 2/4th Battalion Somerset Light Infantry, and 1/5th Battalion Devonshire Regiment (ceased to belong to E.E.F., 28/5/18).
    232nd Light Trench Mortar Battery.

233rd Infantry Brigade.

Commander.—Bt. Lieut.-Col. (temp. Brig.-Gen.) Hon. E. M. COLSTON, C.M.G., D.S.O., M.V.O., Grenadier Guards.

1/5th Battalion Somerset Light Infantry, 29th Punjabis, 2/154th Indian Infantry, 3/3rd Gurkha Rifles.
2/4th Battalion Dorset Regiment (disbanded 17/8/18), 2/4th Battalion Hampshire Regiment (ceased to belong to E.E.F., 28/5/18).
233rd Light Trench Mortar Battery.

234th Infantry Brigade.

Commander.—Col. (temp. Brig.-Gen.) F. J. ANLEY, C.B., C.M.G. (relinquished, Nov., 1917).
Bt. Lieut.-Col. (temp. Brig.-Gen.) C. A. H. MACLEAN, D.S.O., Argyll & Sutherland Highlanders (relinquished, Oct., 1918).
Lieut.-Col. (temp. Brig.-Gen.) F. P. H. KEILY, C.M.G., D.S.O., 125th Napier's Rifles, I.A.

1/4th Duke of Cornwall's Light Infantry, 58th Vaughan's Rifles (F.F.), 123rd Outram's Rifles, 1/152nd Punjabis (late Infantry).
2/4th Battalion Devonshire Regiment (disbanded, 17/8/18).
234th Light Trench Mortar Battery.

Divisional Troops.

37th Brigade, R.F.A. (389th, 390th and 405th Batteries.)
172nd Brigade, R.F.A. (391st, 392nd and 406th Batteries).
1st South African Field Artillery Brigade ("A," "B" and "C" Batteries).
75th Divisional Ammunition Column.
496th (Kent) Field Company, R.E.
Nos. 10 and 16 Companies, 2nd (Queen Victoria's Own) Sappers and Miners.
75th Divisional Signal Company, R.E.
75th Divisional Machine Gun Battalion (Nos. 229, 230, 231 Companies).
2/32nd Sikh Pioneers.
75th Divisional Train (Nos. 925, 926, 927 and 928 Companies, R.A.S.C.).
60th Mobile Veterinary Section.

Brief Record of Service.

The 75th Division, made up of units (Territorial and Indian) recently arrived from India, was included in XXIst Corps on its formation, and on

1917.
Oct. 31.—was concentrated in the Mansura area.
Nov. 6-7.—During the night the 233rd Brigade captured Outpost and Middlesex Hills in the trench system south of Gaza, and on the morning of Nov. 7 captured Green Hill, and occupied Australia and Fryer's Hills. The 232nd Brigade had captured The Labyrinth and Ali Muntar, and occupied The Quarry and Delilah's Neck by 1330.
,, 8.—Tank and Atawineh Redoubts were occupied by 234th Brigade and Composite Force.
,, 9.—The advance northward was commenced with 232nd Brigade leading, and this
,, 10.—Brigade occupied Suafir el Gharbiyeh by 1900.
,, 12.—2/5th Hampshires and 2/3rd Gurkhas (of 232nd Brigade) co-operated with 52nd Division in attack on, and capture of, Burkah and Brown Hill.
,, 13.—The 233rd Brigade captured El Mesmiye and, with 232nd Brigade advancing through Yasur, pushed back Turkish rearguards covering Junction Station, taking 292 prisoners and seven machine guns.
,, 14.—123rd Rifles, supported by 58th Rifles (234th Brigade), captured Junction Station.
,, 19.—232nd Brigade captured Amwas and Latron by noon, and, with 58th Rifles attached, pushed on through difficult hill country in face of considerable opposition to within one mile of Saris.
,, 20.—While 2/3rd Gurkhas and 1/5th Devons advanced eastward along the steep hills north of the road,

1917.
Nov. 20 the 2/5th Hampshires and 58th Rifles enveloped Saris, which was stormed by the 2/4th Somersets at 1415. Subsequently, 3/3rd Gurkhas overcame fresh resistance from the enemy; and at 1700 the 2/3rd Gurkhas of 232nd Brigade, with 1/5th Somerset Light Infantry and 1/4th Wiltshires (233rd Brigade), assaulted and carried the final defences of Kuryet el Enab.
,, 21.—232nd Brigade captured Kustul (1130), and 234th Brigade, after occupying Soba, El Kubeibe, and Biddu, sent forward 1/4th D.C.L.I. and 123rd Rifles to attack Neby Samwil. The 2/4th Hampshires and 3/3rd Gurkhas (233rd Brigade) co-operated in the last-named engagement, and this strong position was stormed late in the day.
,, 22.—Neby Samwil heavily counter-attacked. Severe fighting around El Jib by 1/5th Somersets and 1/4th Wiltshires of 233rd Brigade, with 1/5th Devons and 2/3rd Gurkhas of 232nd Brigade attached.
,, 23.—Attack on El Jib by the same units, in face of heavy shell and machine-gun fire.
,, 23-25.—233rd and 234th Brigades relieved by 52nd Division, and 232nd Brigade by 179th Brigade of 60th Division. Intermittent fighting continued during this relief.
,, 30 } Attack on Sh. el Gharbawy repulsed by 2/4th
,, 1. } Hampshires supported by one company 3/3rd Gurkhas (attached 54th Division).

1917.
Dec. 11.—Occupied line Midieh-Zebdah-Kh. Hamid-Budrus-Sh. Obeid Rahil (232nd Brigade).
„ 15.—Captured Kibbieh (2/3rd Gurkhas); Dathrah (2/5th Hampshires); Kh. Ibanneh (58th Rifles). Kh. el Bornat occupied by 2/4th Somersets.
„ 22.—Kh. el Beida and Kh. el Bireh occupied by 232nd Brigade, with 58th Rifles attached.

1918.
Mar. 8.—2/3rd Gurkhas (232nd Brigade) captured Deir Abu Meshal, Abud and Abud Ridge.
„ 11-12.—2/4th Somersets (232nd Brigade) occupied Rentis.
„ 12.—Fighting in Wadi Ballut; 232nd Brigade occupied Rijal Sufah, and captured Mughair Ahmeh (2/4th Somersets); Benat Burry (2/3rd Gurkhas); Deir Kulah (2/5th Hampshires); Kh. el Emir (1/5th Devons); 2/3rd Gurkhas captured sixty enemy who had fortified a cave and were holding up the attack with machine guns. 234th Brigade (co-operating with 54th Division on their left), occupied the Kh. Bara'aish-Kefr Insha ridge, crossed the Wadi Ballut and seized the Ballut ridge, the 1/4th D.C.L.I. capturing Ballut village at 1430.
April 9.—El Kefr, Sh. Nafukh-Toogood Hill, Berukin, and Tin Hat Hill were stormed by 2/3rd Gurkhas, 2/5th Hampshires, 1/5th Devons, and 2/4th Somersets respectively, in face of considerable opposition. The 1/5th Somersets, and 2/4th Dorsets subsequently reinforced by 123rd Rifles, carried Rafat village and Three Bushes Hill respectively, while 1/4th D.C.L.I. captured Rafat Ridge. Later in the day, 2/4th Dorsets and 123rd Rifles were heavily counter-attacked on Three Bushes Hill.

1918.
April 10.—Severe fighting around Berukin, Arara, and Rafat, in which units of 232nd and 233rd Brigades were heavily engaged against German and Turkish troops.
„ 11.—123rd Rifles of 234th Brigade were involved in severe fighting on Three Bushes Hill.
„ 27.—Attempted raid on 1/4th D.C.L.I. at Rafat repulsed. Determined night attacks on 2/4th Dorsets (Tin Hat Hill) and 58th Rifles (Rafat), and an attempted raid on 2/5th Hampshires (Toogood Hill) were beaten off.
„ 30 / May 1 }
July 13.—Attack by German assault troops on 3/3rd Gurkhas at Rafat, after an intense bombardment, was broken up and heavy casualties inflicted on the enemy.
Aug. 31 to Sept. 13. } After having been continuously in the line since April, the division was relieved by the French Palestine Detachment and 10th Division, and moved to Beit Nabala and thence to Mulebbis.
„ 19.—0700.—1/4th Wiltshires of 232nd Brigade captured Miskeh.
0800.—58th and 123rd Rifles (234th Brigade) captured enemy defensive system west of Et Tireh.
1100.—232nd Brigade, assisted by 1/152nd Punjabis of 234th Brigade, carried Et Tireh after stubborn resistance.
"A" Squadron, XXIst Corps Cavalry, and No. 2 L.A.C. Battery, under orders of G.O.C., 75th Division, pressed on and attacked Turkish columns retreating on Tul Keram.
At midnight the division came into Corps Reserve, concentrated about Et Tireh and Miskeh.

BRIGADES (Non-Divisional).
IMPERIAL CAMEL CORPS BRIGADE.

Commander.—Bt. Lieut.-Col. (temp. Brig.-Gen.) C. L. SMITH, V.C., M.C., D.C.L.I. (relinquished, June, 1918).
Bt. Lieut.-Col. (temp. Brig.-Gen.) C. S. ROME, D.S.O., 11th Hussars.

1st (Anzac) Battalion. Four Australian Companies.
2nd Battalion. Four British Companies.
3rd (Anzac) Battalion. Four Australian Companies.
4th (Anzac) Battalion). Two Australian and two New Zealand Companies.
Two Detached Companies (British).
No. 26 Machine Gun Squadron (late Scottish Horse).
Hong Kong and Singapore Mountain Battery, R.G.A.
Brigade Ammunition Column.
Field Troop, R.E.
Signal Section, R.E.
Detachment, R.A.S.C.
Australian Camel Field Ambulance.

Brief Record of Service.

The Imperial Camel Corps Brigade, which had been engaged at Maghdaba, Rafa, and in the 1st and 2nd Battles of Gaza, constituted as above, took part in the attack on Beersheba; the subsequent advance into Philistia; the Amman Raid; and co-operated in the Es Salt Raid. It was reorganized as a cavalry force at the end of June, 1918, Headquarters and six companies (later reduced to four) being retained, and joined the Australian Mounted Division as the 5th Australian Light Horse Brigade on Aug. 22. 1918.

1917.
Oct. 31.—Engaged near the Wadi Saba, west of Beersheba.
Nov. 1.—In action at Towal Abu Jerwal in co-operation with the Australian and New Zealand Mounted Division.
„ 6.—Engaged in repulsing a determined counter-attack near Tel Khuweilfeh.

1917.
Nov. 12.—Occupied Yebnah in conjunction with Yeomanry Mounted Division.
„ 15.—Co-operated with Yeomanry Division in the attack on, and capture of, the Abu Shusheh Ridge.
„ 27 to Dec. 6 } Engaged in operations around Jaffa.

EGYPTIAN EXPEDITIONARY FORCE.

1918.
Mch. 27.—The brigade, having crossed the Jordan at Hajlah, moved directly on Amman, over difficult country rendered almost impassable by bad weather.

,, 28.—The enemy, holding Amman in strength, checked the advance, but demolition parties were able to destroy a section of the line near Libben.

,, 29.—Heavily engaged on the right of the attack on Amman and,

,, 30.—captured two trenches, but were held up by enfilade fire.

,, 31.—The withdrawal having been ordered the brigade reached Es Sir at 0715, and eventually withdrew to the west bank of the Jordan.

1918.
April 9 to ,, 11 } The enemy launched a series of strong attacks (led by a German storm battalion), after a heavy artillery bombardment, against the posts in the Musallabeh salient, held by 1st (Anzac) Battalion, but they were repulsed after hard fighting, with considerable losses to the enemy.

May 1 to ,, 3 } Co-operated in the Es Salt Raid by carrying out demonstrations on the west bank of the Jordan.

July to Aug. } Headquarters and two companies carried out operations in northern Hejaz including capture of Mudawara station with 133 prisoners. This force returned to Beersheba on Sept. 6 having covered 930 miles.

20th INDIAN INFANTRY BRIGADE.

Commander.—Col. (temp. Brig.-Gen.) H. D. WATSON, C.M.G., C.I.E., M.V.O., I.A. (relinquished, Jan., 1918).

Lieut.-Col. (temp. Brig.-Gen.) E. R. B. MURRAY, 90th Punjabis, I.A.

110th Mahratta Light Infantry.
Alwar I.S. Infantry.
Gwalior I.S. Infantry.
Patiala I.S. Infantry.
Signal Section (British), R.E.
20th Indian Infantry Brigade Train.

Brief Record of Service.

The 20th (Indian) Infantry Brigade arrived in Egypt from India in Nov., 1914; was engaged in repelling the Turkish attacks on the El Ferdan Sector of the Suez Canal in 1915; and took part in the advance into Palestine in 1917.

The Brigade operated in the Gaza–Mendur sector during Oct. and Nov., 1917; held the Ghoraniyeh Bridgehead from April to Sept., 1918; and, finally, took part in the advance on Amman in September as part of Chaytor's Force (*q.v.*).

49th INDIAN INFANTRY BRIGADE.

Commander.—Lieut.-Col. (temp. Brig.-Gen.) E. R. B. MURRAY, 90th Punjabis, I.A.

1/The 101st Grenadiers.
2/The 101st Grenadiers.
Signal Service (British), R.E.

Brief Record of Service.

The 101st Grenadiers landed in Egypt from East Africa on Sept. 4, 1916, and joined 29th (Indian) Infantry Brigade on Canal Defences. The battalion was formed into two battalions on Feb. 3, 1917, and the Brigade became 49th (Indian) Infantry Brigade (two battalions only), on April 15.

The brigade was in support to 54th Division on Samson's Ridge (April 1917), and, later, took over the Canal, and Rafa, defences.

In Jan. 1918, the brigade was disbanded and the battalions composing it joined 20th (Indian) Infantry Brigade, and, on May 1, 29th Infantry Brigade of 10th Division (*q.v.*).

PALESTINE LINES OF COMMUNICATION.

HEADQUARTERS.

Commander.—Bt. Lieut.-Col. (temp. Brig.-Gen.) E. N. BROADBENT, C.M.G., D.S.O., King's Own Scottish Borderers.

Canal Zone.

Commander.—Lieut.-Col. (temp. Brig.-Gen.) A. H. O. LLOYD, C.B., C.M.G., M.V.O., Shropshire Yeomanry.

Australian and New Zealand Training Centre (Moascar).

Mounted Troops.

"C" Squadron Royal Glasgow Yeomanry (less one troop).
Camel Coastal Patrol.
Nos. 5, 7, 8, 9, 10 Companies, Imperial Camel Corps.
Nos. 1, 3, 6 Companies, Bikanir Camel Corps.
Arab Scouts (taken over by F.D.A.).
1st Squadron Cavalry, Egyptian Army (employed under O.E.T.A.).
No. 1 Company Egyptian Camel Corps (employed under O.E.T.A.).
Indian Cavalry Base Depôt.

Artillery.

Anti-Aircraft Group, R.A.
Nos. 30, 38, 85, 96, 102, 103, 119, 120, 122, 124, 125, 126, 151, 152 Anti-Aircraft Sections, R.A.
No. 204 (Calcutta) Battery, R.G.A.

Armoured Trains.

Nos. 1 and 3.

Machine Gun Corps.

221st, 262nd, 264th Machine Gun Companies (ceased to belong to E.E.F., 7/5/18).

Engineers.

35th A.T. Company, R.E.
357th, 359th, 360th Companies, R.E. (Water Units).
555th (Lancashire), 569th, 570th, 571st (Devon), A.T. Companies, R.E.
Nos. 1 and 2 Egyptian Sapper Companies.

Infantry.

1st Garrison Battalion Royal Warwickshire Regiment, 1st Garrison Battalion Devonshire Regiment, 1st Garrison Battalion Essex Regiment. 1st Garrison Battalion Northamptonshire Regiment, 2nd Garrison Battalion Cheshire Regiment, 19th (Western) Battalion The Rifle Brigade, T.F.
2nd Battalion West India Regiment, 2/18th Infantry, 2nd (Reserve) Half Battalion Cape Corps, 1st, 2nd, 3rd Egyptian Infantry Battalions, Egyptian Detachment Palestine Gendarmerie (2 Companies employed under O.E.T.A.).
Nos. 1, 2, General, and Indian Infantry, Base Depôts.

Royal Army Veterinary Corps.

Nos. 16 (Acts as Base Depôt) and 31 Veterinary Hospitals.
Advanced Depôts of Veterinary Stores, Ludd and Jerusalem.
No. 3 Base Depôt, Veterinary Stores.
Nos. 2, 3, 4 Camel Hospitals.
Nos. 1 and 2 Field Veterinary Detachments, and No. 23 (Indian) Field Veterinary Section.

Royal Army Service Corps.

(a) Mechanical Transport :—
  No. 7 (Egypt) Mobile Repair Unit.
  493rd M.T. Company (Supply Column).
  1080th M.T. Company (No. 3 Motor Ambulance Transport Company).
  Advanced M.T. Sub-Depôt, Kantara.

(b) Horse Transport :—
  No. 900 Company A.S.C. (23rd Auxiliary H.T. Company).

(c) Supply Companies :—
  Nos. 18 and 27 Field Bakeries.
  Nos. 18, 19, 20, 21, 36, 37 L. of C. Supply Companies.
  No. 17 Field Butchery (ceased to exist 21/3/18).

(d) Camel Transport Corps :—
  "O," "Q" and "S" Companies.

EGYPTIAN EXPEDITIONARY FORCE.

Area Employment Groups.

No. 3 Group :—
Nos. 809, 810, 811, 812, 813 Companies.

No. 4 Group :—
No. 808, 814 and 815 Companies.

Postal Units.

British :—
Advanced Base Army Post Offices, SZ 8 and SZ 9.
Army Post Offices—SZ 2, SZ 7, SZ 14, SZ 17, SZ 18, SZ 23, SZ 27, SZ 32, SZ 34, SZ 38, SZ 43, SZ 47, SZ 48, SZ 49, SZ 57, SZ 58, SZ 59.
Travelling Post Offices (Railway Trains)—DAL, KAL, LAD, LAK, LAP, PAL, RAB, BAR, JAP PAJ.

LINES OF COMMUNICATION UNITS.
(Controlled by General Headquarters.)

COMMAND DEPOT.

Mounted Troops.

Headquarters and Administrative Centre Imperial Camel Corps (Abbassia).

Engineers.

389th Advanced Park Company, R.E.
46th Base Park Company, R.E.
5 Railway Transportation Sections, R.E.
Railway Operating Division.—Nos. 71, 72, 73, 74, 75, 76, 77, 94, 95, 99, 100, 101, 102, 103, 104 and 105 Sections, R.E.
98th Light Railway Train Crew Company, R.E.
115th, 116th, 265th, 266th Railway Companies, R.E.
272nd Railway Construction Company, R.E.
Light Railway Survey Section, R.E.
299th (Indian) Railway Construction Company.

Signal Service.

L. of C. Signal Companies, R.E. " M," Sinai, South Palestine, North Palestine.
Airline Sections, R.E. Nos. 12, 62, 68, 69 and 105 (Indian).
Northern W/T Section, R.E.
No. 6 Light Railway Signal Section, R.E.
Egyptian Construction Section.
Base Signal Depôt, R.E.

Schools of Instruction.

Imperial School of Instruction (Zeitoun).
Senior Officers School (Heliopolis).
Officer Cadet Battalion, Egypt.
Branch School (El Arish).
School of Cookery (Ismailia).
Central Gas School (Rafa).
M.T. Drivers Training School (Lorries).

Royal Army Service Corps.

(a) Horse Transport :—

137th Company (2nd Base Horse Transport Depôt), Kantara.
973rd Company (Advanced Horse Transport Depôt), Ludd.
Indian Transport Depôt, Richon-le-Zion.

(b) Camel Transport Corps :—

No. 1 Camel Depôt, Kantara, No. 2 Camel Depôt, Ramleh.

(c) Harbour Transport :—
   R.A.S.C. Motor Boat Company.

(d) Supply Companies :—
   Nos. 22, 34, 35 (L. of C.) Supply Companies.
   19th Field Bakery (less detachment).

Labour.

(a) Inspectorate of Recruiting (Cairo) :—
   Recruiting Camps (Sohag, Assiut, Cairo).

(b) Military Labour Bureaux (Alexandria, Port Said, Cairo, Ismailia, Jaffa, Jerusalem, Haifa).

(c) Egyptian Labour Corps :—
   Headquarters and Advanced Depôt, Ludd.
   Base Depôt, Kantara.
   Nos. 1, 2, 3, 4, 5, 6, 7, 8, 9, 11, 12, 21, 23, 24, 25, 26, 27, 29, 30, 31, 32, 33, 34, 35, 36, 37, 38, 39, 40, 41, 42, 43, 44, 45, 46, 47, 48, 49, 50, 51, 52, 53, 54, 55, 56, 57, 58, 59, 60, 61, 62, 63, 64, 65, 66, 67, 68, 69, 70, 71, 72, 73, 74, 75, 76, 77, 78, 79, 80, 81, 82, 83, 84, 85, 86, 87, 88, 89, 90, 91, 92, 93, 94, 95, 96, 97, 98, 99, 100, 101, 102, 103, 104, 105, 106, 107, 108, 109, 110, 111, 112, 113, 114, 115, 116, 117, 118, 119, 120 Companies.

Remounts.

No. 1 Remount Depôt (40th and 47th Squadrons).
No. 2 Remount Depôt (44th Squadron).
No. 3 Remount Depôt (46th Squadron).
No. 4 Remount Depôt (Australian Remount Unit).
Nos. 1 and 2, Camel Remount Depôts.
Nos. 1 and 2, Field Remount Sections.
No. 1 Camel Field Remount Section.
No. 1 Syce Remount Corps.

Royal Army Veterinary Corps.

Veterinary Hospitals Nos. 20, 21 and 26.
Convalescent Horse Depôt.
Advanced Base Depôt of Veterinary Stores.
No. 1 Camel Hospital.
Indian Veterinary Hospital.

Ordnance.

Nos. 9, 11, 24, 25, 26, 27, 31, 123, Detachment 136, 138 and 139 Companies R.A.O.C. and Detachment No. 140 Boot Repairing Company.
Nos. 16, 32, 38, 39, 44, 56, 113, and 141 Companies, R.A.O.C. and Headquarters No. 140 Boot Repairing Company, R.A.O.C. (employed with R.A.O. Base Depôt).
Nos. 22, 23, 24 (Medium), and No. 39 (Light) R.A.O. Mobile Workshops.
Nos. 1 and 2, Ammunition Depôts, L. of C., R.A.O.C.
Nos. 1, 2 and 3, Advanced Ammunition Railheads, R.A.O.C.

Postal Units.

British :—
   Base Army Post Offices K., T., Z.
   Advanced Base Army Post Office SZ 10.
   Army Post Offices—SZ 4, SZ 5, SZ 6, SZ 11, SZ 12, SZ 15, SZ 16, SZ 20, SZ 22, SZ 24 SZ 25, SZ 26, SZ 50, SZ 55, SZ 56.
   Travelling Post Offices (Railway Trains)—CAT, TAC.

Australian :—
   Base Army Post Office SZ 3.

EGYPTIAN EXPEDITIONARY FORCE.

New Zealand :—
    Base Army Post Office SZ 1.

Indian :—
    Base Army Post Office " E."

Miscellaneous.

    H.Q. Army Printing and Stationery Services (Egypt and Salonika).
    Commission of Graves Registration and Enquiries.
    Central Claims Bureau.

FORCE IN EGYPT.

HEADQUARTERS.

Commander.—Col. (temp. Major-Gen.) H. D. WATSON, C.B., C.M.G., C.I.E., M.V.O., I.A.

Sollum Section.

Commander.—Lieut.-Col. (temp. Brig.-Gen.) R. M. YORKE, C.M.G., D.S.O., Gloucestershire Regiment.

Mounted Troops.

    Royal Glasgow Yeomanry (One Troop " C " Squadron).
    Imperial Camel Corps (No. 6 Company).
    Bikanir Camel Corps (No. 7 Company).

Infantry.

    1st Garrison Battalion Notts. and Derby Regiment, 1st Garrison Battalion Liverpool Regiment, 1st Garrison Battalion Royal Irish Regiment, 2nd Garrison Battalion Royal Welsh Fusiliers, 20th Garrison Battalion Rifle Brigade, 21st Garrison Battalion Rifle Brigade (to India, 28/9/18), 40th (Palistinian) Battalion Royal Fusiliers, 3rd Egyptian Infantry Battalion, one Company.

Machine Gun Corps.

    Machine Gun Corps, Base Depôt.
    Machine Gun Section, Egyptian Army.

Armoured Cars.

    Light Armoured Car Brigade (less 3 Batteries) :—
        Headquarters.
        No. 3 Light Armoured Car Battery.
        Nos. 5, 6, 7, 9 Light Car Patrols (Ford Cars).
        Heavy Armoured Car.

Armoured Trains.

    No. 2 Armoured Train.

Royal Army Service Corps.

    (a) Mechanical Transport :—
        H.Q. and Sollum Detachment, 790 Company (Western Force M.T. Supply Column).
        No. 1079 M.T. Company (No. 2 Motor Ambulance Transport Company).
        Nos. 14 and 15 (Egypt) Mobile Repair Units.
        Advanced M.T. Sub-Depôt, Cairo.
        Training School for M.T. drivers (Lorry), Helmich.

(b) Horse Transport :—
  313 H.T. Company (6th Auxiliary Horse Company).
  Matruh Detachment, 671 Company (Auxiliary Horse Transport Company).

(c) Supply Companies :—
  23rd L. of C. Supply Company.
  2/3rd "D" Supply Company.
  Detachment No. 19 Field Bakery.
  No. 26 Field Bakery.

(d) Camel Transport Corps :—
  Detachment from No. 1 Camel Depôt.

Area Employment Group. (No. 2.)
  Nos. 804, 805, 806 and 807 Companies.

Miscellaneous.
  Command Depôt (Abbassia).
  Egyptian Army Transport Corps (Tel-el-Kebir).

ALEXANDRIA DISTRICT.

HEADQUARTERS.
Commander.—Col. (temp. Brig.-Gen.) R. C. BOYLE, C.B., C.M.G.

Mounted Troops.
  Bikanir Camel Corps, Nos. 2, 4, 5, 8, 9, 10 Companies.

Coast Defence Artillery.
  103rd (Local) Company, R.G.A.
  Royal Malta Artillery Detachment.

Royal Engineers.
  13th Base Park Company, R.E.

Infantry.
  1st Garrison Battalion Royal Scots (2 Companies), 5th (Reserve) Battalion British West India Regiment, 1/70th Burma Rifles.

Royal Army Service Corps.
  (a) Mechanical Transport :—
    No. 8 (Egypt) Mobile Repair Unit.
    No. 303 M.T. Company (Divisional Ammunition Park).
    No. 500 M.T. Company (Base M.T. Depôt).
    No. 644 M.T. Company (Heavy Repair Workshop and Stores Branch).
    No. 1078 M.T. Company (No. 1 Motor Ambulance Transport Company).

  (b) Horse Transport :—
    No. 671 Company (9th Auxiliary Horse Transport Company).
    No. 930 Company (24th Auxiliary Horse Transport Company).

  (c) Camel Transport :—
    Detachment No. 1 Camel Depôt.

  (d) Supply Companies :—
    Nos. 24 and 25 L. of C. Supply Companies.
    H.Q. and 1/3rd "D" Supply Company.

Area Employment Group. (No. 1.)
  Nos. 800, 810, 802 and 803 Companies.

Miscellaneous.
  Command Depôt (Sidi Bishr).

EGYPTIAN EXPEDITIONARY FORCE.

DELTA AND WESTERN FORCE.

(Ceased to exist, April 8, 1918.)

Commander.—Col. (temp. Brig.-Gen.) H. G. CASSON, C.B., C.M.G.

25th Motor Machine Gun Battery (disbanded, 18/1/18).

ARMY MEDICAL SERVICES.

DIVISIONAL FIELD AMBULANCES.

4th Cavalry Division.
10th Cavalry Brigade Combined Field Ambulance (formerly 6th Mounted Brigade Field Ambulance, formerly 1/2nd South Midland Mounted Brigade Field Ambulance).
11th Cavalry Brigade Combined Field Ambulance (formerly 8th Mounted Brigade Field Ambulance, formerly 1/1st London Mounted Brigade Field Ambulance).
12th Cavalry Brigade Combined Field Ambulance (formerly 22nd Mounted Brigade Field Ambulance, formerly 1/1st North Midland Mounted Brigade Field Ambulance).

5th Cavalry Division.
13th Cavalry Brigade Combined Field Ambulance (formerly 5th Mounted Brigade Field Ambulance, formerly 1/1st South Midland Mounted Brigade Field Ambulance).
14th Cavalry Brigade Combined Field Ambulance (formerly 7th Mounted Brigade Field Ambulance, formerly 1/1st Notts and Derby Mounted Brigade Field Ambulance).
15th Cavalry Brigade Combined Field Ambulance (formerly 124th Indian Cavalry Field Ambulance).

Australian Mounted Division.
3rd, 4th, and 5th (formerly Australian Camel Brigade Field Ambulance) Light Horse Field Ambulances.

Australian and New Zealand Mounted Division.
1st and 2nd Light Horse, and New Zealand Mounted Brigade Field Ambulances.

3rd (Lahore) Division.
110th, 111th, and 112th Indian Combined Field Ambulances.

7th (Indian) Division.
128th, 129th, and 130th Indian Combined Field Ambulances.

10th Division.
154th Indian Combined Field Ambulance (formerly 32nd Field Ambulance).
165th Indian Combined Field Ambulance (30th Field Ambulance disbanded).
166th Indian Combined Field Ambulance (formerly 31st Field Ambulance).

52nd Division.
1/1st, 1/2nd, and 1/3rd Lowland Field Ambulances (ceased to belong to E.E.F., 21/4/18).

53rd Division.
1/1st Welsh Field Ambulance.
113th, 170th (formerly 1/2nd Welsh), and 171st (formerly 1/3rd Welsh), Indian Combined Field Ambulances.

54th Division.
2/1st, 1/2nd, and 1/3rd East Anglian Field Ambulances.

60th Division.
121st Indian Combined Field Ambulance (2/4th London Field Ambulance disbanded).
160th Indian Combined Field Ambulance (formerly 2/5th London Field Ambulance).
179th Indian Combined Field Ambulance (formerly 2/6th London Field Ambulance).

74th Division.
>229th, 230th, and 231st Field Ambulances (ceased to belong to E.E.F., 7/5/18).

75th Division.
>123rd Indian Combined Field Ambulance (formerly 147th Field Ambulance).
>127th Indian Combined Field Ambulance (145th Field Ambulance disbanded).
>163rd Indian Combined Field Ambulance (formerly 146th Field Ambulance).

20th Indian Infantry Brigade.
>157th (formerly 110th) Indian Field Ambulance.

Palestine Lines of Communication.
>Scottish Horse Field Ambulance.

CASUALTY CLEARING STATIONS AND CLEARING HOSPITALS.

Palestine Lines of Communication.
>26th, 35th, 66th, 74th, 76th Casualty Clearing Stations (35th Casualty Clearing Station ceased to belong to E.E.F., April, 1918).
>24th Indian Clearing Hospital.
>31st Indian Clearing Hospital (formerly 31st Combined Clearing Hospital).
>15th Combined Clearing Hospital.
>32nd Combined Clearing Hospital (formerly 75th Casualty Clearing Station).
>33rd Combined Clearing Hospital (formerly 77th Casualty Clearing Station).
>34th Combined Clearing Hospital (formerly 65th Casualty Clearing Station).

STATIONARY HOSPITALS, etc.

Palestine Lines of Communication.
>24th, 26th, 36th, 43rd, 44th, 45th, 47th, and 48th Stationary Hospitals (43rd Stationary Hospital disbanded, 45th Stationary Hospital ceased to belong to E.E.F., April, 1918).
>No. 2 (Australian) and 137th (Indian) Stationary Hospitals.

Medical Store Depôts.
>Levant Medical Store Depôt (Alexandria).
>No. 5 Base Depôt Medical Store (Alexandria).
>Base Depôt Medical Stores (Abbassia).
>No. 8 Base Depôt Medical Stores.
>Nos. 4, 5, 6, 7, and 8 Advanced Depôts Medical Stores.

Laboratories.
>Military Bacteriological Laboratory (formerly Central Bacteriological Laboratory).
>Nos. 1, 2, 3, 4, 5, and 6 Field Laboratories.
>32nd, 37th, and 38th Mobile Laboratories.
>Anzac Field Laboratory (Desert Mounted Corps).

Sanitary Sections.
>5th Cavalry Division (formerly 5th Indian Cavalry) Sanitary Section.
>18th, 19th, 24th, 29th, 30th, 31st (formerly 4th Indian Cavalry), 52nd, 53rd, 54th, 60th, 80th, 85th, 87th, 88th, 89th, 90th, 91st, 92nd, 93rd, 94th, 95th, 107th, 108th, 113th, 114th, 115th, 116th, 121st, 122nd, 123rd, and 124th Sanitary Sections (52nd and 87th Sections ceased to belong to E.E.F. on 21/4/18 and 7/5/18 respectively).
>7th and 8th Australian Sanitary Sections.
>11th and 12th Indian Sanitary Sections.

Hospital Trains.
>(Former numbers shown in brackets).
>>Nos. 40, 44 (1), 45 (2), 46 (3), 47 (5), 48 (43), 50 (45), 51 (46), 56 (47).
>>Nos. 49 (44) and 57 (11) (Egyptian).

Hospital Barge.
>"Niagara."

EGYPTIAN EXPEDITIONARY FORCE.

HOSPITALS AND CONVALESCENT DEPOTS.

Palestine Lines of Communication.

69th and 78th General Hospitals.
No. 14 Australian General Hospital.
Nos. 5, 30, 32, 39, 41, 44, 50 (formerly "Indian Base Hospital"), 54th, and Mhow, Indian General Hospitals.
Nos. 3, 4, and 5 Prisoners-of-War Hospitals.
Nos. 1 (formerly No. 6), 2, 3, and 4 Egyptian Stationary Hospitals.
Nos. 1, 3, 4, 5, 6, 7, 8, 9, 10, 11, and 12 Egyptian Detention Hospitals.

Force in Egypt.

27th, 31st, and 71st General Hospitals.
Nos. 31 and 45 (formerly 70th General) Indian General Hospitals.
Citadel and Nasrieh Hospitals.
Infectious Hospital, Choubra, and Orthopædic Hospital, Helwan.
Nos. 1, 2, 6, 7, 8, and 9 Prisoners-of-War Hospitals.
No. 13 Egyptian Detention (formerly No. 1 Egyptian Stationary) Hospital.

Alexandria District.

15th, 17th, 19th, 21st, and 87th General Hospitals (15th General Hospital ceased to belong to E.E.F. April, 1918).
Ras el Tin Military Hospital.
No. 10 Prisoners-of-War Hospital.
Nos. 2 and 14 (formerly No. 5 Egyptian Stationary) Egyptian Detention Hospitals.

Convalescent Depôts.

Abbassia, Boulac, Montazah, Mustapha.
Aotea New Zealand Convalescent Home.
Indian Convalescent Depôt.
Reception Station, Mustapha.

THE ANTI-AIRCRAFT SECTIONS.

In July, 1917, there were in the Egyptian Expeditionary Force only seven Anti-Aircraft Sections, of which two had only lately arrived. Owing to the small number of sections available, it was impossible to do more at that time than protect points of vital importance, such as railheads, dumps, and aerodromes.

With the arrival in October and November of eight new sections, equipped with more modern guns (two additional sections were formed later for the protection of important bases) and the formation of Anti-Aircraft Group Headquarters to co-ordinate the work of the sections, it became possible for a more comprehensive scheme of defence to be formulated. During the operations of Nov. and Dec., 1917, Anti-Aircraft Sections followed up the advance as closely as transport facilities and the state of the roads would permit.

When the line had been stabilized, a front line barrage was established—except on a few miles of front where the country, on account of its mountainous and broken character, became unsuitable for anti-aircraft positions—with the object of preventing hostile aircraft from crossing our line without being observed and engaged. Secondary, but most important considerations in establishing this barrage, were the protection of our front line trenches and the prevention of co-operation between enemy artillery and their aircraft. (*See* inset PLATE 52.)

In the earlier months of the present year, there was a considerable amount of hostile air activity, and most of the sections were kept pretty fully occupied. For example, in April one section was in action seventy-six times and fired an average of just under 100 rounds per day.

A more elaborate scheme of co-operation with the Royal Air Force was gradually evolved, and with a view to giving immediate warning of the approach of enemy machines, wireless telegraphy stations were placed at the positions of several of the more advanced sections. A system of directional shots was arranged to point out the position of hostile machines to our air patrols, ground arrow signals were put out, and the course of every aeroplane, from the time it appeared till it finally went out of sight behind its own lines, was charted and reported.

The result of this, together with the increasing number and improved types of our own machines, was that enemy planes crossed our lines at an ever-increasing height until very few flew lower than from 14,000 to 18,000 feet. There was also a gradual decrease in the number of hostile 'planes seen, and from Sept. 6 to 17 inclusive, only two machines crossed our lines, and these were at too great a height to get information of any value, as their reports, which have since been captured, show.

The last machine to be engaged was one which flew over the Jordan Valley on Sept. 21. The section which engaged it were immediately shelled out of their position by artillery fire—an interesting sidelight on the absence of knowledge on the part of the enemy forces in that area as to the true position of affairs on that date. (*See* PLATE 45.)

Owing to the entire absence of enemy machines during the September (1918) advance, the Anti-Aircraft Sections took no active part in the operations. Sections were, however, pushed forward rapidly in case they should be required. By Oct. 31 three of them had made the long journey to Beirut by road. One of these was on its way north from there when the Armistice came into effect and it was recalled.

Protection has also been afforded throughout the whole campaign to the more important points on the lines of communication.

That anti-aircraft did something towards fulfilling its functions on this front is testified to by the constantly recurring entries in the captured diaries of the enemy Flying Corps Headquarters and squadrons, which shew that machines were continually being damaged and reconnaissances prevented by anti-aircraft fire. The following are typical extracts:—

"20/3/18. Machines hit at Ramleh at height of 4,700 metres."

"13-19/4/18. Anti-aircraft defence still very strong and makes things difficult for our working machines in the near reconnaissances."

"20/5/18. Wadi Auja. 1240. Reconnaissance here was impossible in spite of much turning, in consequence of a storm and extraordinarily lively anti-aircraft fire. Shooting extraordinarily violent."

"2/6/18–8/6/18. Enemy anti-aircraft fire was lively and as good as ever."

"19/7/18. Machine of 300 Squadron was seriously damaged in the elevator* by anti-aircraft hits. Glided down to 500 metres and broke up on the ground."

"22/8/18. Machine of 301 Squadron considerably damaged by anti-aircraft fire."

"27/8/18. Very strong anti-aircraft fire over Ramleh, whereby there were several hits in the machine and petrol tank shot through."

---

* The "elevator" here referred to is part of the lifting gear in the wings of the machine.

THE ROYAL ENGINEERS.

1.—Water Supply.

The army, which crossed the Sinai Desert into Palestine and then deploying on a broad front, enveloped the Turkish position extending from Beersheba to Gaza, demanded much of its engineers.

During its deliberate advance it was followed by a broad guage railway and a piped supply of filtered water from Kantara, on the Suez Canal, into the field of battle near Beersheba, a distance of 147 miles.

It would be an exaggeration to say that there is no water in the Sinai Peninsula, which separates Egypt from Palestine, but the supplies are so scanty and bad that the desert has always been a very formidable obstacle to the passage of troops.

The only practicable route across the desert runs along its northern edge where scanty supplies of water are found in small wells on the caravan route, or by digging new wells in the sand dunes, but, nearly all water in these wells is brackish and unpalatable and as a supply it is quite inadequate for a large force, followed by an army of labourers constructing a railway. It was therefore necessary to provide the army with water from a source outside Sinai.

The water supply system, as originally planned, was only intended to supply 500,000 gallons a day for a force of one mounted and two infantry divisions detailed to recapture the Egyptian town of El Arish, which was in the hands of the Turks, but, as it was extended beyond there and proved to be an important factor in subsequent operations it must be briefly described.

On the west bank of the Suez Canal, at its northern end, runs the Port Said branch of the Sweet water Canal which carries the water of the Nile to that town. In the autumn of 1916, plant to filter 600,000 gallons of water per day was installed on this sweet water canal at Kantara, and the purified water was pumped through syphons under the Suez Canal into masonry reservoirs on the east bank. From Kantara East a water supply main of twelve inch, ten inch, and eight inch steel screw-jointed pipes was laid into El Arish, in four sections each about twenty-four miles long. Duplicate engines and pumps drove the water from the reservoir at Kantara to a reservoir at the end of the first section and thence it was again pumped forward through the next section of pipe and so forward, section by section, until it reached El Arish.

To explain the work done on water supply it is necessary to describe briefly the system adopted for the distribution of water by rail and camel convoys and the clearest way to do this is to start from the beginning.

Before the pipe-line from Kantara was laid and supplying water, the army had started on the march forward covering the railway construction parties and water had to be carried forward in trains of water trucks.

These water trains were filled at a special siding, where twenty or more trucks could be dealt with simultaneously, and on arrival at railhead were emptied into a long row of canvas reservoirs laid beside the rails. Here small camel tanks, called fantasses, were filled up and these were carried forward by camel convoys for distribution to the troops beyond railhead.

When the first section of pipe-line was completed a new water siding was provided and the railway was relieved of carrying water for the first stage and so on until water was finally pumped to railhead.

Once El Arish had been reached the army passed into a country where, within certain limits, the troops could be supplied with water from local resources. The railway engineers, however, rejected local water as unfit for use in its locomotives on account of its salinity and hardness : the railway, therefore, became the principal consumer of the piped supply : it was, however, also used by the troops to a considerable extent to supplement local supplies and in the final operations was a very valuable asset.

The army continued its advance from El Arish to Khan Yunis on a narrow front, along the caravan route, near the coast where the only water which can be found in the district is from wells in the sand dune area and in the villages of El Burj, Sheikh Zowaid, Rafa, and Khan Yunis. At Khan Yunis two good wells about 100 feet deep and at Beni Sela, an adjoining village on a higher site, a well 210 feet deep were found.

These three wells, when provided with pumps and engines, eventually supplied 130,000 gallons a day.

From Khan Yunis forward it became possible to extend on to a wider front, as water can be got in some parts of the bed of the Wadi Ghuzze and in its tributary valleys, from springs or in pools or by sinking shallow wells, while further to the right lay Beersheba, whose wells have been famous since the days Abraham watered his flocks there.

On the left front lay the village of Deir el Belah, with several good wells twenty to thirty feet deep, the Wadi Ghuzze, and, further forward, the town of Gaza with abundant supplies of water from deep wells.

The Turks abandoned to us Deir el Belah and Shellal, where the best supplies of water in the Wadi Ghuzze are found, but held on to Gaza and Beersheba.

For a time the army advanced no further but utilised the next few months in preparations and during this period much useful work was done in the development of local supplies and in laying pipe-lines forward and to the right flank to enable troops to be concentrated where required.

The railway was extended to Rafa and thence to Gamli and Shellal on the right and to Deir el Belah on the left. The water from Kantara followed the railway to Rafa, in six-inch and twin four-inch pipes, and to Shellal, supplying the requirements of General Headquarters and El Fukhari on the way. A pipe-line was also laid from the wells at Khan Yunis, *via* Abasan el Kebir and Abu Sitta, to Abu Bakra, and this was cross-connected from Abu Sitta to Abu Khatli so that water could be distributed either from Rafa or Khan Yunis to any point. (*See* PLATE 2.)

At Shellal springs, yielding about 14,000 gallons per hour, of somewhat saline water, had been cleaned out, covered in, and the water was led through pipes to a water distributing area. A natural rock basin had been improved by a masonry dam and provided storage for some 500,000 gallons of water. A pipe-line had been laid forward from Shellal to Imara and three sets of twenty-five horsepower engines and centrifugal pumps were installed for local distribution and to pump water forward if required. The capacity of each of these pumping sets was 4,800 gallons per hour against a 200 feet head and the pumps were arranged so that any two sets could work "in series" to pump against a 400 feet head, keeping one set spare in reserve.

At Abu Bakra several miles of piping were held ready to extend the pipe-line beyond the Wadi Ghuzze if required.

At Mendur and at Dorset House deep bore wells had been sunk and provided with pumping engines.

The Deir el Belah wells were connected up and, from these, water was pumped into the trenches south of Gaza, while further to the left there was another smaller piped supply from the Red House wells. Along the Wadi Ghuzze and in the sand dunes near the coast wherever water could be got and was required wells had been dug.

Between March and Oct., 1917, the force in this area gradually grew to three mounted divisions, a brigade of the Imperial Camel Corps, seven infantry divisions, and a composite brigade of Allied and Indian Imperial Service troops. General Headquarters moved into the area in Aug., 1917, and preparations were made for an enveloping attack on the Turkish position at Beersheba, combined with a frontal attack on Gaza.

On PLATE 31 (*see* INSET) an attempt has been made to indicate the arrangement of the water supply up to and during the operations which commenced on Oct. 22.

The supply of water which could be brought into the area by rail and delivered at Shellal or Gamli was some 100,000 gallons.

The El Arish–Rafa pipe-line, after meeting railway requirements at Rasum, could supply some 156,000 gallons per day to Rafa, whence 60,000 gallons per day could be delivered through Fukhari and Sheikh Nuran to Shellal or Abu Sitta.

The Khan Yunis well and pumping station could supply some 100,000 gallons per day to Abu Sitta and thence by the cross line to Sheikh Nuran and Shellal, or direct to Abu Bakra.

These transferable supplies from the rear, amounting to 260,000 gallons were controlled by General Headquarters during the course of the operations and deliveries at the various watering points were regulated according to the daily movements of the troops.

The development of water supplies east of Esani was allotted to the Desert Mounted Corps, but could not be commenced until the date fixed for the first movement of troops into the area (Oct. 22).

Preparations had to be made at once to collect suitable engines, pumps and plant to restore and develop water supplies in an area which had not yet been occupied.

The development of water supplies in the Sheikh Nuran–Gamli–Shellal–Hescia area, and east, including the improvement and restoration of the water supplies in Beersheba, when captured, was allotted to the XXth Corps, but no work east of the Wadi Ghuzze was to be taken in hand until Oct. 22.

The arrangements for the distribution of water in the Gamli–Shellal–Hiseia area, from which three mounted and four infantry divisions, accompanied by large convoys of camels for carrying water, were to start for the attack on the Turkish position, was of first importance.

There is a considerable amount of water in springs and in pools in the bed of the Wadi Ghuzze within the limits indicated, but to make it available for rapid distribution involved a great deal of preparatory organization and work.

At intervals along the valley a total of over 3,000 running feet of masonry and wood troughs were provided for watering horses and camels.

In addition to the main road crossings, for use by transport, and roads for use of the troops moving out from the concentration area, special tracks across the wadi had been arranged for animals going to and returning from water and others again for camel convoys carrying fanatis to and from the fantasse filling areas. All these roads were placarded with notice boards showing what formations had to use them, and where they led to.

At Shellal, a fantasse filling area, in which 2,000 fanatis could be filled and loaded on camels every hour, was organized, and the piping for the line to be laid forward, canvas tanks, watering troughs, and everything which was likely to be required for water distribution forward, was also collected here.

At both Gamli and Hiseia pumping engines were erected to fill high level storage tanks, supplying water by gravity to fantasse filling areas, capable of filling 250 fanatis per hour.

The engines, pumps, and plant for work in Beersheba had to be collected, loaded on tractor trains and held ready to push forward without delay when the town had been captured.

The maintenance and enlargement of the water supply in the area Mendur to Sheikh Ajlin, on the sea, and back to Deir el Belah, was allotted to the XXIst Corps.

Until Oct. 22 no troops or animals watered east of the Wadi Ghuzze. After this date troops began to move eastward to take up their position for the attack on Beersheba.

The following is a brief summary of the work done between Oct. 22 and Nov. 1 :—

Desert Mounted Corps.

Abu Ghalyun was occupied at dawn on Oct. 22 and work on water development started at once. An old well was cleaned out but failed to produce a satisfactory supply. Work on a second well was started but was abandoned. Meanwhile, an officer of the Australian Engineers "divined" water in the wadi bed not far away. Two wells, sunk at the places indicated by him, reached an abundant supply of water at 13ft. depth.

Malaga was occupied the same day and here trenches dug in the wadi bed provided a good supply.

Khalassa was occupied by the Camel Brigade on the night of the 22nd/23rd and working parties started at dawn of the 23rd to restore two wells which had been effectively blown in by the enemy. These parties, relieved every two hours, worked continuously until finally the wells had been cleaned out to a depth of forty-two and thirty-six feet respectively. Pumps and engines with a capacity of 4,500 gallons per hour were installed and water sufficient for a division of mounted troops was stored.

Asluj was occupied on the night of Oct. 25-26 and work started at once on the restoration of wells which the enemy had thoroughly destroyed. After a great deal of heavy work including the installation of machinery, Asluj on the 30th was in a position to water a mounted division, Corps Headquarters, and a considerable concentration of friendly Arabs.

XXth Corps.

Esani.—Was occupied by one mounted brigade and one infantry brigade on the night of Oct. 22-23. A party of 1,000 men of the Egyptian Labour Corps accompanied this force for work under the Royal Engineers, and work began on the morning of the 23rd. Two portable power-driven pumping sets, with a combined capacity of 8,000 gallons per hour, canvas storage tanks with a capacity of 150,000 gallons, and water distribution gear were installed. Two hundred wood horse troughs filled by lift and force pumps were also provided in the wadi bed. Work was completed within three days, when a yield of 100,000 gallons per day had been attained.

Imara.—On Oct. 25, storage capacity for 80,000 gallons was erected at Imara, and the water was pumped forward to Imara, from Shellal.

Karm.—Work on the pipe-line from Imara to Karm was started on the 23rd. On this day, five kilometres of pipe were laid out and screwed up in ten sections. On the 24th, these ten sections were connected through the pipe, was tested and washed out and storage tanks and distribution arrangements were completed at Karm. During the night of the 24th-25th the water was being pumped from Shellal through Imara to Karm and was available on the morning of the 25th, for the use of the troops. Later, additional storage and a second water distribution area were provided at Karm for water brought by the rail from El Arish, and when the railway extension had been completed, 80,000 gallons per day were delivered for some days.

Khasif.—At Khasif, the cisterns were cleaned out and filled with 60,000 gallons of water, carried there by two camel convoys of 1,000 camels each on Oct. 29 and 30. This provided an additional advanced reserve of water.

The water problem at Beersheba, after its capture, was not confined to the immediate provision of water sufficient for the minimum daily needs of the cavalry corps and two infantry divisions, in itself a large order, but it was necessary, with as little delay as possible, to make such preparations as would allow the second phase of the operations to begin. This could only happen when it was possible for the force to march out with a day's rations of water in hand for troops, and every animal to drink its fill before starting.

The water question ahead of Beersheba was, at best, a doubtful one, and it was essential that when the advance from Beersheba began, the force employed should be in a position to face a long waterless period.

The Turks only destroyed a few of the wells before leaving, though all the principal wells had been prepared for demolition. This neglect, while most fortunate for us, was not creditable to the Turkish engineers, for, however sudden the attack, it was only the work of a moment to light the fuses which were ready in position.

Of the seventeen wells in Beersheba, only two were thoroughly demolished, and two partly damaged. In three wells the pumps were in a workable condition though the engines had been put out of action. In three other wells, *saqqias** were found in at least a workable condition, and though two of these *saqqias* were discarded as unprofitable and replaced by pumps and engines, the third was put in good working order in a few hours and was able to cope with the full yield of the well. In addition, the Turks had left intact two reservoirs containing some 90,000 gallons, a very useful legacy.

It was at once clear that the source of water in Beersheba was a large one and likely to provide nearly the whole needs of that part of the force which was temporarily based on the town—a force requiring in all about 400,000 gallons per day.

---

* A Saqqia is a wheel fitted with buckets for raising water. It is worked as a rule by an animal pacing round in a circle on the principle of an old fashioned mill.

It was not to be expected that this volume of water would be available at once, but horses can subsist without water for forty-eight hours, and men can do with less than a gallon per day if the weather is at all favourable as one might hope it would be in the beginning of November.

However, the three or four days after the capture of Beersheba were among the hottest of the year— a strong *khamsin* wind blew without intermission, and the whole of the district was enveloped in fine dust.

Of the plant carried by the tractor train, five engines and three pumps were erected and parts of the sixth engine were used to replace similar parts in a duplicate engine left by the Turks. The three pumps left by the Turks were put in good working order. Four pumping sets brought in from Asluj were erected, one *saqqia* was put in order and used continually, and from two wells water was raised by bucket and rope.

Several of the wells were concealed in houses and gardens; two were not found until the third day and one on the fourth day. On the third day, in the afternoon, the water situation was most acute. Every available gallon of water stored during the previous night having been consumed.

The output was just equal to the demand and it was expected that watering animals for the day would be finished by midnight.

At 1600 a mounted brigade of some 2,000 men and horses with forty-eight hours thirst, arrived unexpectedly.

A new well, with *saqqia*, had fortunately been found about noon on this day, the *saqqia* was being repaired and troughs were being erected, but there was no means of knowing what the yield of the well would be. This well was at work by 1700 and proved a good one, yielding about 1,500 gallons per hour, just enough to provide water by midnight for the mounted brigade.

During the first two days, some water had been found in shallow pools and in pits dug in the wadi bed to the west of the town. This supply, however, was nothing more than surface water left from a storm which had occurred about a week before, and it was soon exhausted.

By the morning of the fourth day, the water development had reached its maximum, the total output was about 390,000 gallons per day. After this there was no further great anxiety.

As an extreme measure, an attempt was made to cut down the ration of water to horses by imposing a time limit for each batch of horses as it came to the troughs. Such rationing might be effective where the control of the watering area was very perfect and where animals had not been without water for an undue time. In the exceptional circumstances at Beersheba, the famished horses got out of control and rushed the troughs as soon as they got near them and then while some drank greedily, it was a difficult matter to get others to drink. There is no difficulty in limiting the ration of water for camels, as the camel habitually d.ink in two "bouts" with an interval of about ten minutes.

The provision of a stout guard rail to every line of troughing was well worth the extra time and labour, as it prevented animals from breaking down the troughing in their eagerness to drink.

(*See* text facing PLATE 39 for continuation of above.)

2.—Signal Service.

A branch of the Royal Engineers that merits a separate chapter is the Signal Service. The nature of the operations, the rapid and wide movements, and the great distances traversed, which have been special features of our operations in Palestine, made the problems of intercommunication peculiarly difficult. The sharp changes from soft sandy deserts to rolling pasture land passable by wheels, and then to mountain tracks where lines could be laid only by hand, and material conveyed by pack animals, called for much elasticity in transport, and ingenuity in methods of building telegraph lines. The necessity for long distance speech from the front to the base required the provision of telephone trunk lines as long as from London to Aberdeen. The volume of traffic to be dealt with has involved the use of delicate apparatus for high-speed automatic telegraphy, under very trying conditions of dust and damp; and its successful employment is entirely due to skilful handling by the telegraphists, and to the watchful tending of the instrument mechanics.

An expeditionary force operating in such varying circumstances necessarily has to undergo many changes in organization, and each alteration in the organization of a force involves corresponding changes in the means of communication. Not only does this apply to actual lines and offices, but to the organization of signal personnel. On the formation of the XXth and XXIst-Corps, new companies and sections to meet the demands of these headquarters were necessary, and to a great extent were improvised locally. This improvisation has certain advantages, *e.g.* the officers and men are accustomed to local conditions but, on the other hand, the older units have to suffer from the withdrawal of officers and men. Besides these major changes in organization, there are always others going on, due chiefly to an ever-extending line of communication, but also to additional means of signalling such as pigeons or "trench" wireless and to the re-grouping of units and formations. This all means, that, while the Signal Service is functioning as a whole, the parts are constantly being altered and improved, and the smooth working of the machine must go on owing to elasticity of the organization and the adaptability of individual members.

The system of intercommunication built up to July, 1917, consisted of : (1) the tactical cable and airlines between East Force Headquarters and the battle front, which included special artillery, Royal Flying Corps and other circuits ; (2) the main backbone of semi-permanent lines connecting East Force Headquarters (near Deir el Belah) with the Kantara base (about 140 miles away) ; (3) the permanent lines within Egypt connecting Kantara to Cairo, Alexandria, Port Said, Suez, and to our cables to Europe, India, and Australia.

During September and October of 1917, with the prospect of an advance, signal units were very busy—in addition many had only recently been formed, and still had to continue training. Behind the battle area, the increase in administrative services and the doubling of the railway line entailed an expansion of the Lines of Communication Signals. Not only were the local telephone systems continually growing, but means of maintaining telephonic communication with Egypt as the force advanced required the previous building of heavier trunk wires. To economise men, as the lines lengthened, the old Turkish desert telegraph lines had to be replaced by new lines along the railway, where maintenance is easier. Forward units with the assistance of infantry and artillery were engaged on elaborate buried telephone systems in the shelled areas. Alternative routes were so developed that any battery, for example, could always ring up any observation post or artillery commander, even if some of the main lines were cut. Preparations for the attack on Beersheba and the maintenance of communication with the cavalry on their long march of envelopment also involved much careful preliminary work and training. Material for airlines and cables was laid out and concealed ready for rapid laying when the flag fell. Three cables accompanied the cavalry and these were patrolled constantly by horsemen left at test points every five or six miles. Although the lines were cut one or more of the three were always in working order and communication was preserved throughout the enveloping attack.

When " Z " day arrived and Beersheba was captured, rapidly erected permanent wires were substituted for the long cable lines which had been laid round by way of Asluj. A network of cables spread out from Beersheba to the north and north-west as the flank attacks on the main Turkish positions progressed. When mounted troops advanced, wireless communication came into use to keep touch with the rear. When Gaza fell, lines were rapidly extended up the main road and along the railway. Gaza, Beit Hanun, Deir Sineid, Mejdel, each in turn became railhead where local telephonic systems were rapidly installed. Among the troops advancing, divisional and corps signal units were ever at work coping with the constant forward jumps of their headquarters. For two months this process continued in difficult country and during severe climatic changes. Then, as warfare became less mobile, more elaborate forms of forward communications grew, involving alternative means of all sorts. In rear the railway and its telegraphs advanced, and as Ludd became railhead there grew up the usual telephone system. Jerusalem, Ramleh, and Jaffa were all linked up, and became important centres ; while Jericho served as the focus of intercommunication for the operations across the Jordan.

During the summer of 1918, while big changes in the constitution of the force were in progress some signal units had largely to help units of other arms who were short of trained signallers in maintaining their telephonic systems. Assistance was also given in the training on a large scale of regimental signallers in Corps Signal Schools. A very large increase in the number of signallers was effected in Indian Army units. The more prosaic side, such as the improvement, and in some instances multiplication of lines in rear, and the transmission of masses of telegrams, numerous telephone calls, and messages by despatch rider went on continuously through 1918.

Early in September, preparations had to be made for the final battle of the war with the Turk. The wonderful secrecy of all the preliminary arrangements necessitated limitations to the amount of work that could be done in certain directions. On the other hand, considerable scope to ingenuity was given by opportunities for misleading the enemy. For instance, the leaving of signal stations in their old places, the continuation of work as usual and the building out of dummy lines, and special telephone exchanges built only for purposes of deception, helped to mask our intentions.

Finally, when the cavalry had moved across to the left flank and all was ready, the " break through " was effected. As is well known, the advance of the cavalry averaged some sixty miles during the first twenty-four hours. As soon as the cavalry divisions got to their positions across the line of retreat of the Turks at Afule and Beisan, telegraphic communication was established between these points and General Headquarters near Ramleh by rapid building and repairs to Turkish lines. Thus, the movements of cavalry working northwards from Ghoraniyeh and southwards from Beisan—closing the ring—could be co-ordinated. It must not be forgotten that other forms of telegraphy—visual and wireless—and motor cyclist despatch riders were also playing their important part.

To resume, after the major portion of the Turkish army had been surrounded the freer movements of the cavalry made still greater calls on their signal units. One day's march from Afule led to the capture of Haifa, and, though this was an advance of about thirty miles over new territory the capture was reported from just outside the town by telephone to the Desert Corps Headquarters at Megiddo (Lejjun) the same afternoon.

During the subsequent advances to Damascus and Aleppo, telegraphic communication to advanced troops was usually obtained as soon as these halted. The method employed was to mount parties of linemen in motor cars with the necessary material and implements, and so effect rapid repairs to existing wires. Subsequently, the patched-up lines have to be thoroughly overhauled, and for many weeks after the army is at rest the cable and airline sections of the Signal Service are kept hard at work re-building and adding to the telegraph system in the occupied territory.

For those who appreciate figures, it may be of interest to picture the " traffic " dealt with at various places :—

Average number of words telegraphed daily at (a) Divisional Headquarters 12,000
,, ,, ,, ,, ,, ,, (b) Corps Headquarters ... 25,000
,, ,, ,, ,, ,, ,, (c) General Headquarters ... 90,000
,, ,, ,, ,, ,, ,, (d) Kantara... 60,000

3.—Survey Company.

The work of the 7th Field Survey Company, Royal Engineers, may be summarized under the headings : Field survey, compilation and reproduction of maps and photographs and letterpress printing, sound ranging sections and observation group, meteorological section.

A series of contoured maps on the scale of 1 : 40,000 of the coastal belt of Northern Sinai up to Rafa had been issued before July, 1917. Work on this scale was continued up to the Gaza–Beersheba line, and a series on the scale of 1 : 10,000 was started, showing the enemy trenches, barbed wire, and gun positions in greater detail. The work of the field parties consisted chiefly of triangulation, detailed survey with plane tables showing contours, intersecting points in and beyond the enemy's lines, and fixing battery positions and datum points for the artillery. Survey parties also accompanied all reconnaissances in force towards the more easterly trench systems and Beersheba, and did such survey work as time permitted on these occasions, fixing points ahead which were of great use to the artillery and in the compilation of the maps from aeroplane photographs. Officers in charge of sections in the field also kept in close touch with divisions and brigades and supplied them with advanced tracings of new or special areas surveyed.

The Royal Air Force and Australian Flying Corps took aeroplane photographs regularly over the enemy trench lines and country beyond. Copies were supplied to the Field Survey Company, and from these many maps were compiled wholly ; intersected points or good detail on the existing maps forming the basis. An officer was appointed under G.S.I. to study all photographs and indicate all enemy defence works and details of military importance which were then plotted by the Survey Company on the maps. Enemy battery positions and other important targets were plotted at once, and co-ordinates supplied to this officer for communication to the artillery.

The compilation of maps from survey and photographs, and fair drawing ready for reproduction were done at headquarters, and in June, 1917, a power-driven lithographic printing machine was installed at Rafa for printing maps with a minimum loss of time. In this way up to about the middle of Aug., 1917, all the country from the sea near Gaza to south of Beersheba was mapped in more or less detail, including all enemy trenches, and published in nine sheets on the 1 : 40,000 scale, and seventeen sheets on the 1 : 10,000 scale, in all thirty-seven editions.

Owing to the large number of 1 : 10,000 scale sheets required to cover the whole line of trench systems the scale of 1 : 20,000 was adopted and eighteen sheets were prepared, and twenty-eight editions printed, nineteen of them by the Survey Company, Printing Section, and nine by the Survey of Egypt, Cairo. Of the area covered by these sheets, 282 square miles were surveyed, and 403 square miles were compiled from aeroplane photographs. Over 3,000 photographs of the Gaza area and its communications were dealt with.

When the Turks evacuated their Gaza–Beersheba positions and retreated to the Jaffa–Jerusalem line, the survey parties continued the triangulation through the intervening country in two belts, one through the coastal plain and thence to Jerusalem, the other along the Beersheba–Hebron–Jerusalem road in the hills. Points were thus established for the continuation of detailed ground survey along the new lines of defence, and for laying out new bases for sound ranging sections without delay. At the same time a limited amount of contoured detailed survey of immediate importance was done.

The rate of advance of our troops during periods of open warfare was too great to allow detailed survey of all the country traversed at the time, but as soon as the enemy held a defensive line again, detailed survey was resumed by the field sections and continued with the gradual British advances, comprising a belt across the front from the sea to the River Jordan averaging fifteen miles in depth. This survey was carried practically up to the enemy's lines and a large number of points such as prominent hills, trees, and buildings in and beyond the enemy line were fixed by intersection. A check base line measured near Jaffa, and connected with the triangulation, showed that a satisfactory standard of accuracy was being maintained.

The scale of 1 : 20,000 was continued for a time, but in consideration of the extent of the country to be mapped and the steep mountainous character of the greater part of it, the scale of 1 : 40,000 was adopted again for the general map, while shortly before the British attack in September, five sheets were printed on the more open scale of 1 : 20,000, covering those areas where the enemy trench and communication systems were most complicated and extensive—that is, upon the coastal plain and the foothills. The operations maps of the 1 : 40,000 scale series were printed in four colours ; the wadis, roads, railways, villages, wells, and such topographical features, the lettering and also the numbered reference grid, were in black, contours in brown, trees in green, and enemy trenches, gun emplacements, barbed wire, and such works in red over black. Different classes of roads were also indicated in red. Contours were surveyed at twenty metres (about sixty-six feet) vertical interval in the hilly country and at ten metres on the plain, with spot heights on the hills. A small number of sheets were also overprinted with a special grid sub-division and enemy battery numbers in blue, for the use of the artillery in counter-battery work.

The Royal Air Force photographed the whole of the enemy trench line, and country in the rear of it to a distance of roughly twenty-five miles, and in addition the main roads and railways leading into this area from the north. From Jan. 1, 1918, to the cessation of hostilities, 15,690 photographs were dealt with, and the topographical information published in map form.

The Photographic Section of the Royal Air Force has shown the greatest willingness to co-operate with, and meet the somewhat exacting requirements of, the Survey Company in the matter of aeroplane photographs, with the result that these photographs have been used in the compilation of topographical detail maps in this force to a relatively greater extent, perhaps, than on any other front.

After the survey in the neighbourhood of the line had been completed, a number of topographers were available for surveying the country passed over in the rapid advance from Gaza. The area between the sea and three miles east of the Jerusalem–Beersheba road, and back to the area surveyed before the Gaza–Beersheba line, has now been completed for the Occupied Enemy Territory Administration. This area covers 1,473 square miles. After the British advance in September field sections continued the triangulation northwards, one party along the Nablus road, another along the plain and foothills to near Messudieh railway junction, whence a single belt was continued beyond Nazareth to Damascus, thus connecting Damascus with the Survey in Egypt.

Astronomical observations have been made at Baalbek, Hama, and Aleppo, determining the latitudes and longitudes of these places.

A small party proceeded to the Hedjaz and determined by star observations the geographical positions of several places, including Maan and Shahm on the railway. The wireless time signals of Paris and Berlin were received.

In addition to the regular sheets of the principal series of maps a considerable number of other miscellaneous maps were produced and new information from aeroplane photographs added to sheets of the one inch to one mile series. Maps showing the disposition of enemy forces to accompany "Intelligence Summaries" were printed periodically. During active operations these maps showing the situation up to 1,800 or 2,200 were printed at night for despatch to units in the field before the commencement of following day's operations. These maps were issued for some sixty days.

Sun printing and photography were also used for reproducing maps and plans when small numbers only were required.

Twenty-six telephoto panoramas were taken from a number of positions commanding good views over the enemy's ground, and enlarged copies supplied to the corps and divisions concerned.

Two Topographical Sections were formed in Aug., 1918, to work in closer touch with the headquarters of the XXth and XXIst Corps, and to compile and print small maps of the enemy's defence line as required, showing information from the latest air photographs and Intelligence reports, more frequently than the regular full sheets of the Survey Company could be issued. The maps of the Survey Company were used as a basis, and new work was added or enlargements of limited areas were made to show smaller details. Maps measuring fourteen and a half inches by nine inches were reproduced in five colours if necessary, on duplicators, and in this way several hundred copies could be produced within twenty-four hours of the taking of the photographs. The short time required to get out a map with a suitable amount of detail, made this a very useful supplementary method, especially in the case of raids. In the short period of seven weeks, during which the topographical sections were in action, thirty-two of these sketch maps in all were produced, and over 8,800 copies distributed.

THE LETTERPRESS SECTION OF THE COMPANY.

Periodical "Intelligence Summaries," Topographical Handbooks, and other reports were printed at Ramleh.

Sound Ranging Sections.

Two Sound Ranging Sections were added to the establishment of the Field Survey Company in Aug., 1917. Their work was to locate enemy guns and bursts of shells by sound, and also to conduct shoots on certain of the more active gun positions located. It should be noted that the sound ranging here spoken of is carried out by an application of advanced electrical science, and should not be confused with what are known as " sound bearings "—a rough and ready method, where direction is judged by hearing. On the Gaza–Beersheba line two bases were surveyed and occupied, one by each section, between the coast and Mendur. In this way the whole of the enemy's front line from the sea to Atawineh was covered —approximately ten miles. In this position 629 gun locations were made and twenty-four shoots conducted.

With open warfare these sections came out of action, but with the commencement of trench warfare bases were once more established and occupied. The sections moved with the advance of our line until the Arsuf–Sinjil line was reached, where three bases were occupied by one section on the hills and two bases by the other section on the plain. In Aug., 1918, a third sound ranging section was formed locally to occupy a sixth base on the foothills. In this way the whole of the enemy line, approximately thirty-six and a half miles in length to a depth of five miles, was covered.

Sound ranging sections are able to locate guns by day or night with considerable accuracy, except in strong adverse winds, and at the same time to give the calibre of the guns located. In conjunction with aeroplane photographs sound ranging succeeded in locating practically all the enemy gun positions, and shoots on the majority of the locations were so effective that the enemy was forced to vacate occupied pits or their guns were silenced at will by our artillery.

From Sept., 1917, to Sept., 1918, over 3,000 gun locations were made, and over seventy shoots by our artillery were conducted.

Observation Group.

This group came into action in the foothill area in Aug., 1918. Its work consisted in locating enemy guns by flash spotting and reporting enemy activity behind the line, for example, concentration of troops, movements along roads, etc., The group required four accurately fixed observation posts, for which the necessary survey was done by the field sections of the company. During the short time the group was in action, however, enemy artillery activity on its front was slight, and very little opportunity was given for locating guns in this way.

Meteorological Section.

Regular meteorological observations have been made by this section of the company. Readings of maximum and minimum temperatures, humidity, barometric pressure, evaporation, wind, and rainfall were recorded four times a day. A daily weather report was issued comprising the observations at General Headquarters and at Jerusalem, and also a weekly summary of the observations at these two places. The necessary observations were telegraphed every morning to the Physical Service, Cairo, where they were combined with data from other places and used in making the forecast for the Palestine front. This forecast was issued daily except during the settled summer season. Recently a daily report has been issued giving weather and road conditions at a number of places throughout Syria.

Measurements of the direction and velocity of upper air currents were made by the observation of the flight of small pilot balloons. From these observations corrections were computed for the use of the artillery and communicated usually once daily. During artillery activity balloon flights were observed at intervals of four hours during the day and night. These upper air reports were also issued to the Royal Air Force, and to the Sound Ranging Sections. Special balloons flights were observed, when required by the Royal Air Force, before long distance aeroplane flights.

The second meteorological station was established at Jerusalem in April, 1918, and later pilot balloon work was conducted there and the results sent to the artillery on that part of the front.

The Meteorological Section also undertook the checking and calibration of instruments, such as aneroid barometers, compasses, thermometers, etc., for other units as required.

4.—Military Railways.

Previous to the operations against the Gaza position in 1917, the main line had been laid to kilometre 226·2 and was operated as far as Belah Station.

From Rafa (kilometre 200), a branch line had been laid in the direction of Beersheba as far as kilometre 28 from Rafa, and was operated as far as Shellal Junction from which point a short line of about seven kilometres in length ran southwards to Gamli.

During the same period the double tracking of the main line from Kantara East to Rafa had advanced as far as kilometre 137·5, that is to say, to Maadan Station. This length of double line enabled considerable economies to be effected in time, engines, trucks, and operating staff.

In order to economise transport immediately in front of Belah, for the purpose of increasing the amount available in the Beersheba area, a two-foot six-inch gauge light railway was run from Belah Station to various points but little west of the Wadi Ghuzze. Before operations commenced this line had attained a length of nineteen kilometres and was eventually extended another four kilometres. A large part of this line was in direct view from the Turkish position, but no material damage resulted. This line enabled large reserves of supplies and ammunition to be placed before-hand well up towards the front line and proved to be of considerable value.

In connection with the Gaza operations the following programme was arranged. The Beersheba branch was to be extended to Karm Station at kilometre 36·8. This necessitated track being laid at a rate approaching two miles per day. At the same time it was arranged to extend the main line in front of Gaza, across the Wadi Ghuzze, and then construct a dummy station on the west side of the wadi. In spite of heavy rains both parts of the programme were carried out successfully; Karm Station being opened for traffic one day ahead of the scheduled date, *viz.* Oct. 28. During the operations the Beersheba line was extended to about kilometre 39.

In view of the successful development of the attack, work was stopped on the Beersheba line, and the construction of the main line towards Gaza was recommenced on Nov. 10.

Up to this date the light railways were constructed and operated by the Railway Operating Division of the standard gauge. Owing to the rapid advance after the capture of Gaza and the necessity for operating the captured Turkish railways (at this time isolated from the standard gauge system), a Light Railway Organization was formed which moved up to Deir Sineid to take over and operate the three-foot six-inch lines taken from the Turks. The useful part of this line extended from Beit Hanun to Jerusalem (eighty-nine kilometres), with a branch from Junction Station (Wadi Surar Junction) to Ludd (nineteen kilometres). At first the line was only available for use as far as Artuf on the Jerusalem line on account of the destruction of bridges. On the branch towards Ludd the bridge over the Wadi Surar had been destroyed, but a temporary deviation was soon constructed which made this line available for traffic.

On the line between Artuf and Jerusalem four steel bridges had been destroyed, *viz.*: two of thirty metres span, one of ten metres span, and one of sixteen metres span. The work of reconstruction was immediately commenced.

Further advances by our troops and the possibility of unloading stores at Jaffa rendered the construction of railway communications with that port necessary. The light railway staff was therefore transferred to Jaffa about the middle of December and construction commenced on lines north of Jaffa and towards Ludd to connect with the existing three-foot six-inch line. To enable this to be done the three-foot six-inch lines were taken over by the Railway Operating Division.

The reconstruction of the bridges on the Jerusalem line was much hampered by the narrowness and rocky nature of the gorge which prevented much material being taken forward to any bridge until those in rear were completed.

The four bridges were finally completed and the whole of the line to Jerusalem opened to traffic on Jan. 27, 1918.

During this period the narrow gauge suffered severely from rains. The line from Deir Sineid to Tineh was constructed on new earthworks with inadequate drainage. Numerous washouts occurred, and the line was closed on this account on several occasions for periods varying from three to ten days. Meanwhile, the standard gauge was progressing northwards through Gaza, and Deir Sineid Station, with ample facilities for transhipment to the three-foot six-inch line, was opened for traffic on Nov. 28, 1917. The opening of this station enabled additional rolling stock for the narrow gauge to be brought up with consequent increase of capacity.

North of Deir Sineid the standard gauge line runs through long stretches of brown cotton soil which caused endless trouble during the winter. The heavy rains caused subsidences of the new earthwork and washouts were frequent. The unfavourable nature of the soil not only caused trouble on the railway but greatly hampered the camel transport during wet weather. Indeed movement of any sort of transport was at times impossible. Considerable relief was afforded when the railway reached the sandy hills which stretched from south of Jaffa towards Wadi Surar Junction. To effect this a temporary supply railhead was opened at Deiran (kilometre 293) on Jan. 8, 1918. Besides taking supplies for troops to the north, this station was used for supplies to the Jerusalem region, as Ramleh (about seven miles distant) was connected to Jerusalem by a fairly good metalled road and by the older portion of the three-foot six-inch line, which was made available for through traffic by the completion of the bridges on Jan. 27, 1918. Ludd Station, with extensive railway facilities, and unloading sidings for all departments, was opened for traffic on Feb. 4, 1918. Ample transhipment facilities to the three-foot six-inch line were soon available for all services, which reduced the handling of goods destined for Jerusalem to a minimum.

Construction of the line north of Ludd was continued as far as kilometre 315, just beyond Rantieh Station, which was as far as the military situation then permitted.

It soon became evident that traffic demands to Jerusalem could not be met by the narrow gauge line. The first stage of relief was the laying of the standard gauge from Ludd to Artuf and the construction of transhipment sidings at the latter place. This portion of the line was laid with three rails, so as to allow the narrow gauge trains to run at night while construction work was not in progress. This work was commenced on Feb. 27, 1918, and finished on March 31. It was then possible to concentrate all the narrow gauge rolling stock on the Artuf-Jerusalem section, thus increasing the capacity of the line.

Shortly after this, it was decided to push the standard gauge on to Jerusalem and, as the amount of rockwork necessary to permit the passage of the larger rolling stock was not excessive, the work was put in hand on April 22. Except for eight hours per day, while construction work was in progress, the narrow gauge line was open for traffic, and was worked to its maximum capacity. The daily programme of work consisted of taking up a length of narrow gauge, levelling and removing the ballast, laying the standard gauge, laying the narrow gauge rails inside the new ones and finally joining up the narrow gauge to permit traffic to continue. This is probably the best laid and most permanent section of the whole system. During the alteration of this section the average daily tonnage taken into Jerusalem by rail exceeded 740 tons, and as a maximum reached 1,051 tons on May 24. Jerusalem was reached on June 9, and the station opened for standard-gauge traffic on June 15.

The construction of the standard gauge line to Beersheba had been going on intermittently during the spring and was finished on May 3, 1918.

In accordance with the demands of the military situation the standard gauge was laid on the old Turkish formation between Irgeig, on the Beersheba line, and Wadi Surar Junction, thus giving an alternative line north of Rafa to Ludd, Wadi Surar, and Jerusalem. This was carried out between May 14 and July 8.

The construction of the double line, which was temporarily stopped near Maadan, was recommenced by a small construction party on Nov. 1, 1917, and was completed through to Rafa on April 17, 1918.

Following up the successful operations of Sept., 1918, railway construction was again commenced on the 20th. On Sept. 28 the standard gauge alignment swung on to the old Turkish formation north of Ras el Ain, thus enabling construction to be carried out at an increased rate (two kilometres per day).

Tul Keram Station was reached on Oct. 15, enabling direct transhipment to take place between the standard gauge and the narrow gauge running towards Haifa and Damascus. Continuing northwards from Tul Keram, by way of Tanturah and the western end of Mount Carmel, the line reached Haifa, and was opened for traffic early in Jan., 1919.

From Dec., 1917, light railways were constructed and operated for the supply of our more advanced lines :—

    From Jaffa to Ludd.
     " Sarona to Jelil.
     " Sheikh Muannis to Carrick Hill.
    From Ludd to Ras el Ain.
     " Kafr Jinnis to Lubban.
     " Jerusalem to Bireh.

a total of some 115 kilometres, exclusive of sidings.

The following figures are of interest in connection with the standard gauge lines :—

Total length of track laid	kilos. 1,009 (includes Haifa Station).	Number of locomotives	169
Number of turnouts laid	748	Number of wagons	2,573
Number of stations	86	Number of passenger vehicles	50
		Number of hospital coaches	98

The Units which have taken part in the construction and operation of military railways of all gauges are :—

Railway Operating Division, R.E. (eighteen sections, about 5,500 all ranks).
96th Light Railway Operating Company, R.E.
98th Light Railway Train Crew Company, R.E.
115th Railway Construction Company, R.E.
116th Railway Construction Company, R.E.
265th Railway Construction Company, R.E.
266th Railway Construction Company, R.E.
272nd Light Railway Construction Company, R.E.
1st Bridging Company, Canadian Railway Troops.
299th (Indian) Railway Construction Company.
1/23rd Sikh Pioneers.
2/23rd Sikh Pioneers.
2/32nd Sikh Pioneers.
121st Sikh Pioneers.
Egyptian Army Reserve (about 2,800).
Egyptian Labour Corps (eventually about 26,000).

EGYPTIAN EXPEDITIONARY FORCE

5.—The Army Postal Service.

The Army Postal Service of the Egyptian Expeditionary Force was formed of British, Australian, New Zealand, and Indian sections, and served an area stretching from Mersina to Assiut, and from Sollum to Amman, through 140 army post offices. The personnel of all sections totals: British, twenty-five officers, 564 men; Australian, one officer, fifty-seven men; New Zealand, twelve men; Indian, eighteen British officers, twenty-nine other ranks, and 257 Indian officers and other ranks. The average number of bags received weekly for the troops from overseas reached:—

		Letters.	Parcels.	Total.
British	bags	2,500	2,350	4,850
Australian	,,	632	1,339	1,971
New Zealand	,,	130	270	400
Indian	,,	20	20	40

The maximum number of bags received in one calendar week at one port totalled 24,810 bags. Every bag, from its despatch to this force to its receipt at railhead, has to be handled and re-handled not less than twenty-five times.

The average number of letters sent weekly to the home countries was: British, 500,000; Australian, 42,000; New Zealand, 8,400; Indian, 15,000. The totals for the period are: British, 36,000,000; Australian, 3,000,000; New Zealand, 600,000; Indian, 950,000. Letters received from home are received in sealed bags and amount for the period to many millions, exceeding these figures. 173,750 letters circulate weekly within the forces, and 47,000 letters are posted weekly by the Egyptian Expeditionary Force for Egypt. The combined Army Returned Letter Offices dealt with 4,548,000 items. Registered letters dealt with by the combined services during the period total 600,000 received and 297,000 despatched.

Postal Orders and Money Orders have been issued to a value of £476,000 and paid to a value of £165,000 by the British post offices, while the Indian post offices have issued Money Orders to a value of £256,250. War Savings Certificates recently issued total £4,180.

In addition to normal Army post office work, Egyptian civil mails have been embarked and disembarked, and mails in transit from India, China, and the East, to England and the Continent, have been handled over land and re-embarked.

Civil Mails in Occupied Enemy Territory.

In the Occupied Enemy Territory, postal services for civilians have been carried on at fifteen post offices. Postal Orders have been issued and paid to a value of £12,000 in each case, and Money Orders to a value of £2,250 and £3,900 respectively.

Special stamps were issued on Feb. 10, 1918, for use in this area. At first only one piastre and five milliemes overprinted on one piastre were available; but other values were added from time to time, and the complete set now consists of the issues described hereunder:—

Current Stamps.

All these are gummed and perforated. They were printed in England and have no control numbers:—

Denomination.	Date of Issue.	Colour.
1 millieme	July 16, 1918	brown.
2 milliemes	July 16, 1918	green.
3 ,,	Dec. 17, 1918	pale chocolate
4 ,,	July 16, 1918	scarlet.
5 ,,	Sept. 25, 1918	orange
1 piastre	Nov. 9, 1918	dark indigo.
2 piastres	July 16, 1918	olive.
5 ,,	July 16, 1918	purple.
9 ,,	Dec. 17, 1918	bistre.
10 ,,	Dec. 17, 1918	blue.
20 ,,	Dec. 27, 1918	grey.

Obsolete Stamps.

Denomination.	Date of Issue.	Colour.	Description.	Control Number.	Number Issued.	Where Printed.
5 milliemes (a)	Feb. 16, 1918	blue	rouletted and ungummed	B 18 A	6,000	Egypt.
,, (b)	March 5, 1918	blue	rouletted	C 18 B	55,560	Egypt.
,, (c)	May 13, 1918	blue	rouletted	D 18 C	54,120	Egypt.
1 piastre (a)	Feb. 10, 1918	dark indigo	rouletted and ungummed	A 18	21,000	Egypt.
,, (b)	March 5, 1918	blue	rouletted	C 18	338,000	Egypt.

ROYAL ARMY SERVICE CORPS.
1.—Establishment and Supplies.

NUMBER OF R.A.S.C. OFFICERS IN THE EGYPTIAN EXPEDITIONARY FORCE.

The Royal Army Service Corps in the Egyptian Expeditionary Force is divided into four main branches, *viz.*: mechanical transport, horse transport, supply, and camel transport, and the number of officers employed with these branches is as under:—

Mechanical transport, 273; horse transport, 174; supply, 256; camel transport, 234.

In addition there are the following:—

Supply and transport Directorate, 23; Staff of G.H.Q., corps, divisions, etc., 19; attached to Infantry, 76; attached to R.A.F., 12; duty with O.E.T.A., 17; duty with Egyptian Army, 2; miscellaneous (non-R.A.S.C. duties), 8. In all, 1,094.

This total of 1,094 officers comprises the following:—

Regulars, 39; Indian S. & T. Corps, 33; Territorials, 110; Australians, 49 (serving with C.T.C.); Anglo-Egyptians, 51; New Army, 783; Regular Quartermasters, 29.

CIVIL PROFESSIONS.

Of the 168 recorded professions followed by New Army officers in civil life, the chief are as under:—

Accountants (includes 11 Chartered)	50
Assurance and Insurance	16
Auctioneers and Valuers	5
Agents and Travellers	59
Bankers, Bank Managers, etc.	19
Brewers and Distillers	11
Brokers	16
Civil Servants	35
Clerks	73
Clergymen	3
Commercial Directors and Secretaries	22
Contractors and Builders	13
Egyptian Ministry Officials	20
Carried forward	342
Brought forward	342
Engineers	154
Farmers, Graziers, Cattle and Sheep Men	75
Journalists and Lecturers	11
Manufacturers	16
Merchants	51
Planters	15
Schoolmasters and Educational Officials	32
Solicitors	30
Students	21
Surveyors	10
Theatrical Managers and Actors	6
TOTAL	763

STRENGTH OF OTHER RANKS IN THE EGYPTIAN EXPEDITIONARY FORCE.

	BRITISH.								INDIANS.	EGYPTIANS.				GRAND TOTAL.
	H.T. DRIVER CLASS.	M.T. DRIVER CLASS.	ARTIFICERS.	BAKERS.	BUTCHERS.	CLERKS.	LOADERS.	TOTAL.	E.A., H.T. DRIVERS.	EGYPTIAN DRIVERS.	EGYPTIAN CAMEL DRIVERS.	TOTAL.		
(1) Horse Transport	4705	—	685	—	—	—	—	5390	2725	3677	4799	—	8476	16591
(2) Supply	—	—	—	734	1354	1752	433	4273	—	—	—	—	—	4273
(3) Mechanical Transport	—	6558	1298	—	—	—	—	7856	—	—	977	—	977	8833
(4) Camel Transport	218	—	—	—	—	20	—	238	—	—	—	19423	19423	19661
(5) Donkey Transport	56	—	—	—	—	4	—	60	—	—	—	3868	3868	3928
TOTAL	4979	6558	1983	734	1354	1776	433	17817	2725	3677	5776	23291	32744	53286

SUPPLIES—EGYPTIAN EXPEDITIONARY FORCE.

(1) *Approximate Ration Strength Sept. 19, 1918:—*

British	226,900	Horses		74,800
Indians	111,800	Mules		39,100
Egyptians	128,950	Camels		35,000
		Donkeys		11,000
TOTAL	467,650	TOTAL		159,900

The daily cost of feeding the above Ration Strength amounts to £43,385.

(2) *Sources of origin of principal supplies* :—

Article.	Origin.	Daily requirements.	Article.	Origin.	Daily requirements.
Meat Frozen or	Australia, South Africa, Argentine	70 tons	Potatoes	Egypt and Cyprus	25 tons
Meat preserved	America, Australia	52 „	Lentils and beans	Egypt	16 „
Flour	Australia, India, Canada	90 „	Onions	Egypt	25 „
Atta, or	India	230 „	Matches	Japan	100,800 boxes
Biscuit	England and Egypt	250 „	Barley	Egypt and India	
Bacon	England, Australia	24 „	Maize	Egypt	grain 800 tons
Cheese	Australia	20 „	Gram	India	
Jam	Australia, Egypt	24 „	Millet	Sudan	
Tea	Ceylon	6 „	Tibben	Egypt	
Milk	England, America	17 „	Bhoosa	India	
Sugar	Egypt	25 „	Hay	India	Haystuffs 900 tons
Salt	Egypt	7 „	Dries	Egypt	
Rice	Rangoon	31 „	Sucrepaille	Egypt	
Dried fruit	Cyprus, Egypt, India, Basra	8 „	Green forage	Egypt	
Fuel wood	Egypt and Cyprus	250 „	Petrol	Sumatra, Red Sea wells (refined at Suez)	Avtn. 8,000 galls. Tspt. 15,000 „
Sheep and goats	Sudan and Cyprus	300 head	Kerosene	„ „	5,000 „

(3) *Supplies produced and Establishments managed by R.A.S.C., or under R.A.S.C. supervision* :—

Compressed forage	In cotton presses at Alexandria.	Grain crushers	Kantara, Port Said, and Cairo.
Compressed tibben Compressed dries	In cotton presses at Alexandria, Zagazig, Mansura, Barrage, and Assiut.	Dairy farm	Wilholma, Palestine—milk, butter, eggs.
Biscuit	Cairo, Alexandria.	Bakeries	Alexandria, Cairo, Port Said, Bir Salem, Ludd, Jerusalem, Haifa, Beirut, Tripoli, Rayak.
Margarine	Cairo.		
Rum	Alexandria.	Cold storage premises	Three at Port Said. One W.D. property with capacity for 4,500 tons; two requisitioned premises, each with capacity of about 500 tons.
Pickles	Cairo.		
Jam	Alexandria.		
Cured fish	Port Said, Kantara.		
Ice	Port Said, Jaffa, Jerusalem.		
Flour mills	Cairo and Zagazig.		

(4) *Average daily tonnage of supplies despatched by rail via Egypt, Port Said, and Kantara to Palestine* :—

June, 1,615 tons; July, 2,026 tons; Aug., 2,317 tons; Sept., 1,732 tons; Oct., 806 tons;

2.—Mechanical Transport.

The great value of mechanical transport in this force may be said to have commenced in connection with the operations resulting in the capture of Beersheba and Gaza, and the advance through Southern Palestine to the Jaffa–Ramleh–Jerusalem line in the months of Nov. and Dec., 1917.

Prior to this date mechanical transport was almost entirely localized in station transport in Egypt, with the exception of a certain number of light ambulances and Ford vans and Light Car Patrols, used in the Western Desert and in the advance across the desert to Sinai, it being impossible at this stage of the proceedings to use heavier types of vehicles, except caterpillar tractors of which there were then only some half dozen, and these were engaged in pipe laying.

Once the desert was crossed, it was possible to use heavy transport in the Palestine operations. The roads in most cases were bad—little more than tracks—but nevertheless, with care, it was possible to make use of lorry transport. The immediate result of this change was that units, hitherto only equipped with horse and camel transport, had their War Establishments amended to provide for the use of mechanical transport, resulting in a greatly increased mobility on the part of the whole force in Palestine, and enabling operations to be carried out at a much greater distance in advance of railhead.

To give some idea of the great increase in mechanical transport in this force subsequent to July, 1917, it is only necessary to point out that between that date and Nov. 30, 1918, the mechanical transport of the whole force had more than doubled, and if that portion which has been employed in the Palestine operations were taken alone, it would be safe to say that, whereas, in the summer of 1917 we had only a few hundred mechanical transport vehicles in Palestine, we have now thousands.

Just before the Armistice the following mechanical transport vehicles were employed in this force, these figures being exclusive of Royal Air Force vehicles and those of Allied contingents, which if included would considerably augment the numbers shewn:—

Motor cycles	1523
Touring cars	617
Motor ambulances	586
Lorries, including gun, workshop, store lorries, etc.	1579
Vans	670
Caterpillar tractors	281
Caterpillar trucks and other trailers	612
Motor boats	37
TOTAL	5905

There are in the force between sixty and seventy distinct Army Service Corps Mechanical Transport Units, in addition to which must be added mechanical transport which is attached to almost every other branch of the service, e.g. Corps, Divisional and Brigade Headquarters, Heavy Artillery, Light Car Patrols, Armoured Batteries, Signal Companies, Sanitary Sections, Postal Service, Bridging Companies, Ordnance Workshops, Army Troops Companies, R.E., Railway Construction and Operating Companies, Hospitals, and Casualty Clearing Stations, etc.

Mechanical transport may be divided into various branches, of which the following are a few:—

Workshops.—Those at the Base being for heavy work, while others, which are mobile, follow the troops from place to place and are employed for carrying out repairs in the field.

Stores.—This branch deals with the demand for spare parts from the United Kingdom, with the local purchase of parts which can be obtained in Egypt, and with the distribution of spares to all units employing mechanical transport.

Convoy Work.—Embracing supply convoys, transport of ammunition for heavy artillery, Ordnance, and Royal Engineer material and troops. Convoys have largely been made up of lorries, but caterpillar tractors have also been used where the nature of the ground precludes the use of lorries and Ford van convoys also have been run.

Motor Boats.—There is attached to this force what I believe is a unique unit in the Army Service Corps work, viz.: Motor Boat Company, A.S.C. This unit consists of thirty-seven motor boats of different sizes, the bulk of which are employed on the Suez Canal and ports, but with detachments at Cairo, Alexandria, Dead Sea, and the Palestinian ports. Subsequent to the operations in the autumn of 1917, it was decided to send motor boats to the Dead Sea. The only means of transport from railhead, then at Ludd, was by hauling the boats on specially constructed drags from Ludd to the Dead Sea, a work of no small magnitude when one realizes the excessive gradients to be negotiated, the hair-pin bends and, in many cases, the narrowness of the roads at such bends but still four boats were safely taken to the Dead Sea. After the recent advance it was decided to send two boats to Lake Tiberias, the larger of the two boats selected being forty feet in length, standing sixteen feet from the ground, and weighing twenty-one tons with its drag. The journey from the Dead Sea was commenced on Sept. 29 via Jerusalem, Nablus, Jenin, Nazareth, Tiberias being reached on Oct. 12. Shortly after the boats had been launched, the rapidity of the advance made their retention on the Lake of Tiberias unnecessary. Orders were therefore given for them to be withdrawn and taken by caterpillar tractor to Haifa. The difficulties of the transport of these boats were very great. They were accompanied by a guard of British West Indians and by Egyptian Labour Corps personnel. In many cases the sides of the roads had to be built up to permit the passage of the boats. In other cases culverts had to be strengthened en route. Wadis with from three to four feet of water had to be crossed. In other places abandoned German lorries had to be pushed over the side of the road. In some sections difficulties of travelling were so great that only three miles were accomplished in the twenty-four hours.

Fighting Units.—These are principally comprised of Armoured Car Batteries and Light Car Patrols. These units perform important functions in scouting and reconnaissance work, particularly in the case of an advance such as those which took place in 1917 and recently. They were also employed in outlying work on the Western Desert along the Tripolitan frontier. Practically the whole of the Heavy and Siege Artillery of this force is moved by caterpillar tractors. During the operations which resulted in the capture of Jerusalem the strain on this branch of the service was extremely heavy. Owing to it being the winter season, the country was largely composed of one vast bog through which the tractors had to haul the guns; and they had also to get the ammunition up to the dumps once the guns were in position. Notwithstanding the difficulties the caterpillar tractors had to contend with the heavy guns, throughout the operations, were kept up with the advance.

Tyre Presses.—These form an important adjunct to the mechanical transport in this country. The standard life of a lorry tyre is based at 10,000 miles. Needless to say owing to the difficulties under which lorries have to work in Palestine (in many cases over roads, which are roads in name only), the heavy gradients, etc., the life rarely, if ever, exceeds 2,000 miles, and in some instances, such as the run from Samakh to Damascus, the life of a lorry tyre does not exceed 700 miles. Tyres are taken off and new ones put on by means of hydraulic presses, which work at a pressure up to eighty tons. In order to cope with the difficulties of retyring lorries during the recent advance, two tyre presses were built on to German lorries (captured in the Beersheba operations of 1917), and followed the lorry companies throughout the advance, thereby reducing the time the lorries were kept off the road to a minimum.

Man Power.—During 1918 it has been with the greatest difficulty that personnel has been found for the ever-growing needs of transport. Early in the year the question of substitution of the "A" class personnel by men of lower category was considered by the War Office. In view of the climatic conditions, the length of the journeys to be performed, the dust, etc., it was considered by this force that it was of the utmost importance that as many of the personnel in Palestine should be "A" class, and that substitution was inadvisable. This was finally agreed to by the War Office, and it is safe to say that the heavy and continuous work which has devolved on the mechanical transport in Palestine during the summer and autumn of 1918 has fully upheld the action taken some twelve months ago. Even in spite of the fact that as many "A" class personnel as possible were employed, the number of men in hospital has increased from about four per cent in June, 1918, to ten per cent at the present time. In order to assist the supply of drivers, War Office was informed early in 1918, that as far as possible, this force would be self-contained as regards drivers and artificers. In consequence of this in Jan. 1918, a School of Instruction for lorry drivers was formed at Cairo for training Egyptians. Recruits were given ten weeks training in the school and then drafted into lorry companies employed in Egypt and the Canal Zone, the British personnel thereby released being sent to Palestine to take over additional lorries, etc., which were being received from the United Kingdom, and also to replace casualties. Further Egyptians were trained at the garages in Cairo, Alexandria, and Kantara as drivers for light cars and motor ambulances in Egypt. Egyptian artificers have been also taken on in the workshops in Egypt and trained and given instruction in mechanical transport shops. At the present time there are upwards of 800 Egyptian drivers and about 200 Egyptian artificers employed in this force in the mechanical transport. In order to further assist matters, in the autumn of this year a certain number of Jewish women were taken on at the Advanced Base M.T. Sub-Depôt, Palestine, to release men and were employed in the stores department, vulcanizing shops, and on clerical work. Another source from which drivers were provided was by obtaining "B" class personnel from the infantry and other branches of the service for instruction in mechanical transport; in fact every possible source from which drivers could be obtained was tapped.

Repairs.—At times great difficulty has been experienced in keeping mechanical transport on the road owing to the lack of spare parts. This arose from various causes. Some of the principal makes of vehicles employed in this force, *e.g.* Peerless lorries, Ford cars, van and ambulances, Holt caterpillar tractors, are American, and the spares for these vehicles had to be brought first from America to England and then sent on to this force. Also the supply was curtailed owing to the demands from other theatres of war. Again in many instances transports with consignments of spare parts were sunk owing to enemy action, causing delay often of months before the spares could be replaced. Various expedients had to be resorted to, the chief being the manufacture of parts in the Army Service Corps workshops, local purchase of parts made by engineering firms in Egypt, adapting parts for other uses than those for which they were originally intended; and temporarily disassembling vehicles and employing the parts removed to keep other vehicles on the road.

During all the operations east of Gaza, the mainstay of the army for supplies has been the mechanical transport, until the broad gauge railway had been built or the narrow gauge Turkish lines repaired. In the case of the operations in 1917, the troops were fed over sixty miles ahead of railhead by means of mechanical transport. Ever since the occupation of Jericho all troops in the Jordan Valley and on the east of the Jordan at Es Salt and Amman have been fed by means of mechanical transport.

In the recent operations resulting in the capture of Damascus, Aleppo, and Alexandretta, the whole of the supplies and ammunition were taken from railhead by the mechanical transport, until such time as Syrian ports at Haifa, Beirut, Tripolis, and Alexandretta were opened. To give instances how the troops were maintained, it is only necessary to point out that troops were fed at Tiberias by lorries working from Ras el Ain, a distance of some eighty miles, and that until the Turkish railways could be put in order they were fed at Damascus from lorries based at Samakh, the return journey occupying three to four days. Again in the advance on Aleppo, the troops were fed and ammunition conveyed by lorries based at Beirut and Tripolis. In fact, without the extensive employment of mechanical transport, it is difficult to see how the services of maintenance could have been carried out in the operations which resulted in the capture of Jerusalem in 1917, Damascus and Aleppo in 1918.

The whole work of the mechanical transport officers and men of all ranks has been consistently maintained at a very high standard. In order to maintain vehicles on the road and to meet the demands made on them during the last eighteen months, the strain on the workshop and store personnel has been exceptionally heavy. To maintain the troops at the front the drivers of lorries, cars, and caterpillar tractors had continuously to work long hours under trying conditions of heat and dust or wet, according to the season of the year. Every branch of the service however, rose to each emergency as it came along, and it is impossible to appreciate too highly the work done by this branch of the service during the past eighteen months.

3.—Camel and Donkey Transport.

In July, 1917, the Camel Transport Corps consisted of sixteen companies and two depôts, the total strength of burden camels being 32,712. Eleven of these companies (2,000 camels per company) were heavy burden camels and were attached to East Force. Five light burden companies (2,000 camels per company) were employed on lines of communication with detachments on the western front at Matrûh, Sollum, and Baharia.

During the following months of August and September, the companies of the Corps were allocated to the army formations as follows:—

	Camels.	Duty.
XXth Army Corps	8,000	1st line transport.
XXIst Army Corps	8,000	1st line transport.
Desert Mounted Corps	8,000	Convoy.
General Headquarters	4,000	Convoy.

The remaining camels of the corps were employed on lines of communication and the western front.

In October a further re-distribution of camels was made to the formations. The XXth Corps had 20,000 camels allotted, 8,000 being attached to divisions for first line work and the remaining 12,000 were employed on convoy duty.

The XXIst Corps had 6,000 camels allotted to divisions for first line work and Desert Mounted Corps received 6,000 for convoy duty.

The total strength of burden camels including those working on lines of communication and those on the western front was 35,000. Transport work during the preceding months had been comparatively light and the camels were remarkably fit when operations commenced.

During the actual period of operations, i.e. from October to December all companies were very hard worked. The troops were operating in areas in advance of the railheads and long convoys were necessary to maintain them in water, rations, and ammunition.

In the Beersheba area large convoys marched out daily from the railhead, but as the tracks were suitable for camels and the weather remained mild and open, camel wastage was very low.

In early December severe weather set in. Heavy rain storms made the going difficult and the piercing cold had a telling effect both on animals and personnel. In the XXth Corps area the conditions were particularly bad. The troops were then operating in the hills. To keep in touch, long camel convoys had to wind their way over the stony hill sides where there were no definite tracks, the roads up the valleys being reserved for other forms of transport. Camel camps were frequently pitched on the wind-swept hills, often at an altitude of 3,000 feet. The biting night winds and the showers of ice-cold rain militated severely against the camels and their drivers, both of which were entirely new to such climatic conditions.

In the central area the conditions were equally difficult. Desert Mounted Corps convoys were working from the railhead at Deir Seneid, Esdud, and Sukereir to Ramleh. The intervening country consisted of tilled land across which there were no permanent roads. The heavy rains soon reduced the whole area to one vast spongy quagmire, crossed here and there by broad wadies, which were difficult to negotiate. In places camels sank up to the girth in the mud and many had to be abandoned. This was probably the first occasion on which camel transport had been called upon to work under such adverse conditions.

The XXIst Corps camels operating in the sandy area along the coast worked under much easier conditions.

The camels in the XXth and XXIst Corps areas were very short of forage during the period Dec., 1917, to Feb., 1918; five pounds of grain being the maximum ration for long periods and during this period full rations of grain and tibbin were exceptional.

Towards the end of January conditions as to forage for animals, and clothing and equipment for personnel were much improved.

The following table gives a list of casualties (from all causes) sustained in animals and personnel during the 1917 operations:—

	Killed.	Died of Wounds.	Wounded.	Missing.	Died of Exposure.	Captured.	TOTAL.
British	—	1	6	—	—	—	7
Egyptians	38	8	158	125	209	1	539
Camels	574	27	310	29	2090	3	3033
Horses	1	—	—	1	4	—	6

During the months of Feb. and March, 1918, camel transport was reorganized on a basis of 1,200 camels per company. The reasons for this change were:—

(a) A reduction in size of command for despite standard of efficiency maintained, competent authorities were convinced that a 2,000 camel unit was too big for continuous efficient control.

(b) As only 1,200 camels were required for the first line transport of infantry divisions, that number constituted a complete unit.

(c) Uniformity of organization and consequent interchangeability of first line transport and convoy companies.

The strength of the Corps at latter part of March, 1918, was 29,000 camels. Distribution was as follows:—

XXth Army Corps	13,200 camels
XXIst Army Corps	6,000 ,,
Desert Mounted Corps	1,200 ,,
Lines of Communication	2,400 ,,

The remaining camels were at kilo. 298 in reserve and employed on convoys at Ramleh. Camels with the XXth Corps were doing heavy convoys from railhead and depôts to various points. The tracks and weather conditions were still very bad.

During the Amman operations (from March 23) in practically every instance the ground over which the camels worked was of the worst possible nature, being extremely hilly and stony. The Anzac convoys marched by routes which were simply goat tracks in the sides of the hills—only wide enough in many places for one string of camels to pass at a time. (See PLATE 35.)

At Ain Sir village three broad rough terraces had to be crossed. The country was everywhere difficult, time was limited and officers in charge of convoys had to exercise the greatest care in negotiating the hills. The stony nature of the ground injured the camels' feet and the heavy rains rendered the narrow tracks down the inclines very difficult. Nos. 1 and 2 convoys, 1,100 camels, based on Shunet Nimrin worked to Ain Sir, a distance of sixteen miles. No. 3 convoy working from Ain Sir forward, had to traverse extremely bad and difficult ground, which was in many places marshy. The camels were often long hours under their loads owing to existing situation and fluctuation of battle, and coupled with this fact they had to work at night. This same convoy had a most trying time during the withdrawal marching from 1600 on March 31 until 1400 on April 1 when they reached Shunet Nimrin. The most difficult part of the journey had to be done in complete darkness with heavy rain falling and the ground thick with mud and exceedingly slippery. The convoy was greatly harassed and broken by other units of the retiring column on the single track. In all convoys fifty per cent of the camels were overloaded owing to nature of supplies and size of bales and sacks. The good work performed was fully recognized and appreciated by the XXth Corps and the divisions concerned. Two thousand camels were used in the two convoys out of which number, 100 were killed in action and ninety-two had to be destroyed on account of injuries received on the march.

In the latter part of April, 1918, the strength of the Corps was 27,800 camels.

XXth Army Corps had 3,600 with divisions.

XXIst Army Corps had 2,400 with divisions.

Desert Mounted Corps and General Headquarters had the remaining camels on convoy excepting 3,800 on Palestine Lines of Communication and in depôts.

In May, strenuous work was done by camels in the second Amman operations. Weather conditions had improved and tracks were better.

The months of June, July, and August were comparatively quiet, the camels working on ordinary duties of first line with divisions and convoys from railhead to Wadi Surar and Latron. Rations and water were good, and camels recovered condition.

Camels have also been supplied for work in the Hejaz. In March, 1918, 700 light burden camels fully equipped were sent from "Q" Company to Akaba to operate with the Egyptian army in the Hejaz. These camels were under the command of, and worked by, Camel Transport personnel.

In April, 1918, a further detachment of 2,000 camels was despatched from No. 2 depôt at kilo. 298 to Beersheba, where they were handed over to the representative of the Hejaz forces.

At the commencement of the operations in Sept., 1918, the strength of the Corps in camels was 25,700. They were allotted to formations as follows:—

Formation.	No. of Camels
XXth Corps, 1st Line with divisions	3,600
Convoy	1,400
XXIst Corps, 1st Line with divisions	3,600
Convoy	9,600
Desert Mounted Corps, Convoys	2,600
Palestine Lines of Communication, W.F.F. and Depôts	4,900

Four of the convoy companies working with the XXIst Corps were used for carrying water and the remaining four carried rations.

Compared with the 1917 operations the work of the camels was exceedingly light.

The distances covered were very small; the weather conditions were excellent, the country in which the majority of the companies were working was fairly open. Consequently casualties were very few.

The following table shews the total casualties sustained in animals and personnel:—

	Killed.	Wounded.	Missing.	Died of Exhaustion and exposure.	TOTAL.
Egyptians	7	19	38	—	64
Camels	25	5	15	37	82

In the later stages of operations when the troops moved up country north of Haifa, seven of the XXIst Corps camel companies were employed on convoy duties until Beirut and Tripolis were reached.

Donkeys.—During Sept. and Oct., 1917, the formation of donkey transport companies was in progress, the establishment being 2,000 donkeys to a company. In November of 1917 the first of the donkey transport companies, No. 1 D.T.C. moved from Rafa to the front and this company was employed during the whole of the winter under the most arduous conditions.

No. 2 D.T.C. moved up early in 1918 followed by Nos. 3 and 4. These companies comprised 2,000 donkeys in each and during the summer of 1918 were largely employed in road making and were distributed over the whole forward area from Jericho to Jaffa. The donkeys, allowing for the casualties in No. 1 Company caused by abnormal conditions of work in the winter of 1917, and lack of proper rations at times have been kept in remarkably good condition.

The following table shews the casualties sustained by the donkeys during the operations:—

	Killed.	Wounded.	Died of Wounds.	Died of Exposure.	TOTAL.
1917	5	5	2	233	245
1918	9	12	—	2	23
Total	14	17	2	235	268

It will thus be seen that the camel transport drivers whose sky blue galabiehs added a very welcome touch of colour to the drabness of our khaki and of the country side, together with their trusty "oonts", besides increasing our knowledge of natural history, took a very considerable share in operations, and were not wanting in pluck when occasion required. The camel, by the way, proved to be impervious to shell-fire and the drivers stood their ground repeatedly under difficult circumstances, showing themselves well-endowed with the fatalistic courage of the East. The same may be said of the Donkey Corps, and, in addition, these plucky little beasts made fast friends of all who had to deal with them.

ORDNANCE WORK IN THE PALESTINE AND SYRIA CAMPAIGNS.
A Brief Review.

The work of the Army Ordnance Department, with its scale of supply to a fighting force, ranging from big guns to bootlaces, has been arduous and interesting during the Palestine and Syria campaigns. Many problems have been encountered, in addition to routine duties, since warfare in the desert, combined with an advance into enemy country at a pace unequalled in any other theatre of war, has presented many special difficulties. Seemingly small things tell; and it is not too much to say, for instance, that had not many thousands of *fanatis*, or water-tanks, of different sizes, been provided for the Expeditionary Force, its advance across the Sinai desert from the Canal and onwards into Palestine would not have been possible.

If departmental responsibilities may be roughly defined, it should be understood that while other authorities feed the soldier and his animals and consider both in sickness, the Royal Army Ordnance Corps provides a fighting force with its guns, rifles, and ammunition, the clothes it wears, the tentage that shelters it, the vehicles for its transport, the oil and grease for the maintenance of its implements, its sanitary and cooking utensils, its office furniture, its soap and dubbin, its pails, spades and shovels, its tools, timber, metals, repair material of all kinds, signalling implements and telephones, its harness and saddlery, its entrenching tools and dial sights—in fact, the full equipment of a fighting force which enables it to fight. And, whatever the special conditions of campaign, the speed of advance, the nature of country or weather, these stores must be adequately supplied, and guns, vehicles, tents, rifles, harness, and so forth, must be kept in repair. To achieve this was the first principle of Ordnance policy in the Palestine and Syria campaigns.

The position of Ordnance services by the late summer of 1917 may be briefly defined. The summer months had been busy with expansion in men, arms, guns, transport, ammunition, aeroplanes, hospitals. The channel of Ordnance supplies was simple and as expeditious as the Desert Railway could make it. Alexandria was, as always, the Base. A Depôt at Cairo, working hand in hand with the Base, looked after the troops in Egypt, the Western Frontier, the stores for the Hejaz operations, the rapidly increasing training camps, cadet schools, hospitals, and flying grounds, which Egypt with its wide areas, its good railways and its healthy climate was so admirably adapted to entertain. On the Canal itself were useful Ordnance posts at Port Said, Suez, and Moascar (Ismailia), while the main work of Ordnance supply for the fighting force was done by the Field Depôt at Kantara, on the east bank of the Canal and at the terminus of the Desert Railway.

The development of the Ordnance Depôt at Kantara has been characteristic of the general activity of the Egyptian Expeditionary Force and of its Ordnance Services. A bare patch of sand in the autumn of 1916, this area has now become a highly organized Ordnance Depôt covering in all many acres, with a working personnel little short of 3,000, extensive offices, areas for the different "groups" of stores, for salvage and transit, large workshops, armouries, and magazines, sidings from the broad gauge railway and an internal narrow gauge system. It has wharves on the Canal itself, at which in one month alone fifteen ocean-going steamships and nineteen Inland Water Transport craft were discharged. In the autumn of 1918 no fewer than 976 Royal Army Ordnance Corps troops were at work, while over 700 men of the Egyptian Labour Corps and over 700 prisoners-of-war were daily employed on unskilled work, and no fewer than 558 Egyptian Labour Corps, civilian, and prisoners-of-war tradesmen, tentmenders, carpenters, saddlers, tinsmiths, wheelers, blacksmiths, were kept busy in the big workshops. Here, too, in one autumn month, over 19,000 indents for Ordnance stores for units were dealt with and over 19,000 tons of ammunition handled.

During 1917, up the line, and in preparation for operations, advanced posts had been established at El Arish, Rafa, Deir el Belah, and later at Karm. (*See* PLATE 2.) These were steadily fed by Kantara, and in order to make for greater efficiency, the El Arish Depôt was closed down and pushed forward on Oct. 27, 1917, to make contact with the Light Railway that led from Deir el Belah directly to our troops in the positions before Gaza. Thus, at Deir el Belah and Karm, emergency depôts were quickly established, holding for urgent issue to troops during the earlier stages of the operations such stores as clothing and boots, picketing gear, horse-shoes and nails, mess-tins, nose-bags, dubbin, soap, oil and grease for rifles and guns, ground sheets and blankets. On Oct. 27 the operations against Gaza began.

It may be well to record that the wide scope and variety of Ordnance supply had now to embrace the daily needs of a force of some 250,000 British and over 18,000 Indian troops, together with 100,000 Egyptians, and some 150,000 horses, mules and camels, and that, from the Ordnance standpoint, the position was complicated by the fact that the force was very heterogeneous, so that special stores of many kinds, over and above stores peculiar to Egyptian and desert conditions, had to be provided for French and Italian contingents, Indians, units of the Egyptian Army, British West Indian regiments, natives of the Egyptian Labour Corps, and Camel Transport personnel.

When, after the successful onslaught on the Gaza–Beersheba positions, the force was advancing rapidly into Palestine, new problems at once presented themselves. Of these the chief were transport and the weather. The troops had left the railway behind and practically every available channel of motor or pack transport was required for food, while ammunition was hastened forward by coastal steamer. Great difficulty was experienced in getting important stores up to the troops, for the Turkish railway was constantly breaking down under stress of weather, and roads became impassable. Nevertheless a Railhead Ordnance Post was established as early as Dec. 6 at Junction Station, and a depôt was formed temporarily at Deir Sineid, to be pushed forward to Ludd and greatly expanded directly the broad gauge railway giving direct communication with Kantara was available. Railhead Ordnance posts kept pace with the broad gauge railway as it advanced, and on Feb. 6 the Ordnance post at Junction Station was moved up to Jerusalem itself. Throughout these very difficult weeks of the quick dash of the fighting force up to the Jaffa-Jerusalem line the heavy wear and tear on Ordnance stores of many kinds gave a great deal of hard work to depôts and workshops. The line of communications, it must be remembered, began in the hot, dry sand of Sinai and extended through the moist lowlands of Gaza and Deir Sineid to the arid and barren highlands of Judæa. It is not easy to conceive more exacting contrasts of climate and natural conditions than those of Kantara and Jerusalem. It is easy to realize the strain upon troops passing through such varied conditions in so short a time in the wet season. The wear and tear of material in a swift campaign over such varied areas—especially, for instance, of wheels, harness, clothing, and boots—is necessarily very great.

Jaffa had fallen on Nov. 16, 1917. Jerusalem had surrendered on Dec. 9. The later operations, while establishing our positions north of both places, and securing the lateral communications from east to west and working into, and across, the Jordan valley, so as to get into touch with the Sherifian troops and protect our extended right flank, did not involve any great advance, but enabled the railway to get up to the troops and the Ordnance to reorganize its system of supply. So far as general stores were concerned, the Advanced Base Depôt at Kantara, the depôt at Ludd, and the Railhead post at Jerusalem constituted a quick and accurate channel. A similar policy had been adopted for two most essential Ordnance duties, the supply of ammunition and the never-ending task of salvage and repair.

The principle adopted in every branch of Ordnance work has been that supply must keep pace with the troops, whatever the difficulties of transport and local conditions. During the summer of 1917 ammunition was steadily concentrated near the scene of operations. Magazines at El Arish and Rafa covered each some 26,000 square feet. Large stocks were massed at these places, at Belah and at Karm. During operations approximately 250 tons of ammunition were sent daily up the line. During the summer of 1918 advanced magazines were established at Ludd, Jerusalem, and Sarona, to meet the requirements of the campaign which was to come and the minor but important operations which established our preliminary positions and safeguarded our earlier gains.

Immediate work of repair to guns, vehicles, etc., is done by Light Travelling Workshops, while heavier jobs are sent back to medium shops or down to depôts, or the Base, where larger plant has been established and greater facilities exist. The Mobile Workshops advance on the heels of troops and are thus immediately ready for any task that offers. A line of these shops had, by the end of Dec. 1917, reached Jaffa, Ramleh, Junction Station, Latron, and Jerusalem. They were subsequently pushed further forward still and then concentrated into two groups centring upon Jerusalem and Jaffa, thus meeting the requirements of each flank.

These travelling workshops had by no means an easy time during the stormy winter months in Palestine. They had been thrown almost entirely on their own resources in motor lorries and cars as it was quite impracticable, on the one hand, to get spare parts, and so forth, up to the shops near the line by any other means; or, on the other hand, to send guns, etc., needing heavy repair, to shops farther back. It is not to be wondered at that on arrival at captured cities such as Jerusalem and Jaffa the Ordnance workshops made the most of everything that could be requisitioned in the way of plant and premises. At Jerusalem, Turkish armourer's, blacksmith's, and instrument shops were promptly absorbed and plant was taken over in various parts of the city, including a spacious and well-equipped shop in a Franciscan Monastery. Shops were established for bootmakers since boots had suffered severely in the change from use in summer on the hot desert sand to winter conditions among the wet and rocky mountains of Judæa. To help in these new Ordnance workshops, on whose capacity very heavy demands were at once made, native tradesmen of several trades were brought in.

A great deal of work was thus at once undertaken in repairs to guns, vehicles, etc. The busy activity and elastic scope of the Jerusalem Ordnance workshops was reproduced at Jaffa. It is interesting to record that at Jaffa a foundry was established and captured Turkish gun cartridge cases were used for casting pipe boxes of wagon wheels . . . . a development which illustrates the extreme technical isolation of the whole front of the force in the earlier part of the year. In advance of these workshops at Jerusalem and Ludd mobile shops were suitably posted. Behind them were well-equipped shops at Ludd and the large, still steadily expanding shops at Kantara.

The thoroughness of this workshop organization, as it got into its stride for the summer, enabled it to cope effectively with the serious situation which arose owing to the effect on vehicles in summer of the great heat and dryness of the Jordan Valley. A vehicle repair shop was established in Jericho and did good work under very trying conditions. In the ten weeks prior to the autumn operations the mobile shops forward of Kantara repaired no fewer than 2,500 vehicles and, including Kantara, over 14,000 wheels.

The reconstruction of the fighting force which took place in the summer of 1918, involving the despatch to France of many British troops and their replacement in Egypt and Palestine by Indian units from India, Mesopotamia, and France, gave more work to the Ordnance authorities than is perhaps fully realized. Arrangements had to be made for troops leaving the country to hand in large quantities of stores and vehicles, and the units arriving had to be equipped according to the Egyptian scale, while suitable provision had to be made for them to be regularly supplied with the stores peculiar to their race or religion. All this, on a considerable scale, meant careful organization; a marked extra strain was thrown upon the Ordnance organizations at Ludd and Kantara; and to meet the needs of Indian units a busy temporary depôt was opened at Tel el Kebir.

The time now approached for the beginning of a second autumn campaign. Ordnance preparations of all kinds—the establishment of ammunition supplies, the repair of guns and vehicles, the expansion of hospitals, and the supply of tentage for reinforcement camps—were accelerated. For various reasons it had been decided to close down the Ordnance Depôt at Ludd and the channel of supply now ran direct from Kantara to railheads. Both depôt and railway proved adequate to the emergency. The development of sea-going traffic direct to Kantara from England, Taranto, Alexandria, and India, must be noted as having an important bearing on the supply and handling of stores during and after the Syria operations. Nor must the bridging of the Suez Canal itself be ignored, establishing direct railway communication with Egypt, for the first through train from Jerusalem to Cairo left on July 15.

The autumn operations presented problems very similar to those of the preceding campaign. Again troops went "into the blue" and means of supply to them, over difficult country, became sparse and uncertain. But this time the weather held and the very rapidity of the advance into Syria enabled a new system of supply to be quickly brought into operation. This was supply by sea from Kantara direct to such ports as Haifa, Beirut, Tripolis, and Alexandretta, as they successively came within the area occupied by the Egyptian Expeditionary Force. Thus the curious, but thoroughly economical phenomenon was now witnessed of important Ordnance stores which had been collected in Palestine being sent all the way down the line again to Kantara for shipment to Syrian ports. Ordnance personnel was promptly sent up to these ports and new channels of supply were thus established; while such divisions as were later on returned down the line to Egypt found the old system ready to meet their needs. Meanwhile a similar policy had been followed with the Mobile Workshops which had been promptly moved up in accordance with their accepted principle of working as near as practicable to the troops. (*See* PLATE 54.)

Next, the Ordnance system again confronted two of the great problems which successful operations in war always involve. These are salvage and the accommodation of prisoners-of-war. Salvage in these operations was immense in quantity and much of the material was very difficult to get at and bring to the collecting depôts at railhead. So salvage posts were at once established at important centres, such as Jelil, Kalkilieh, Ras el Ain, Tul Keram, Ram Allah, Afule, and Damascus, and the disposal of salved stores, thousands of tons in bulk, will come under the final control of Kantara and Alexandria. Extensive areas have been prepared for the reception not only of captured and salved stores from the last operations but also of an immense amount of Ordnance stores, including especially, camp equipment from hospitals and standing camps in Egypt. In Palestine itself large quantities of vehicles have been sold through the O.E.T.A. to the local population at reasonable prices. The salvage of guns necessarily depends on the capacity of the broad gauge railway, and it is only fair to record that, at every point and throughout their system, the railway authorities have always endeavoured to meet Ordnance requirements as fully and fairly as possible.

A further task was that of providing accommodation for the thousands of prisoners-of-war who now thronged into Egypt and had to be provided with camps and hospitals, the latter, especially, calling for urgent attention as the percentage of sickness was very high; and that not only amongst the prisoners-of-war, but also amongst our own British and Indian troops and Egyptians. It should be noted that the ration strength of the fighting force had steadily increased from the figures above-quoted for 1917, until, at the time of the Armistice it amounted to: British and Indians, 341,000; Egyptians, 133,000; animals, 160,000; and in addition some 90,000 prisoners-of-war Ordnance work consequently at this stage was greatly extended, the strain falling chiefly upon Cairo, Kantara, and the Base. Tentage, camp equipment, and clothing had to be provided—for example, at Belbeis for 30,000 prisoners-of-war, at Tel el Kebir for 19,000, and at Salhia for 10,000—whilst five large hospitals had to be formed and six hospitals largely expanded, as the condition of the prisoners on arrival was generally deplorable.

We have now traced the main current of Ordnance Services during the two campaigns and the intervening summer of 1918. The full scope of Ordnance work can, indeed, only be outlined—the immense developments at Kantara; the gun-repair work done at Jaffa and Jerusalem; shipping, ammunition and railhead work up and down the line; the establishment of laundries, boot and clothing-repair shops; experimental work on pack-saddlery, covers for machine guns in the desert, ped-rails and cacolets; the steady provision of desert stores, involving a trustworthy and absolutely indispensable water supply; the fine work on dial sights and range-finders; the exacting work on vehicles which had suffered so severely under the rough Palestine conditions—all these and a hundred other daily tasks have been duly and painstakingly performed. There have been difficult questions of personnel, of local labour, of health, and above all of the extremely heavy strain thrown upon Ordnance organization at a period of such great pressure in a hot summer by the substitution for their trained personnel of utterly inexperienced men generally less capable and always of inferior physique. It is hoped, however, that in general, whatever the conditions, the daily job has been done and the very wide Ordnance requirements of the troops fully and fairly met.

THE WORK OF THE MEDICAL SERVICES.

The arrival of General Sir Edmund Allenby in July, 1917, was followed almost immediately by a reorganization of the Egyptian Expeditionary Force. This necessitated considerable changes in the medical service. The front line had been for some months on the southern boundary of Palestine, and our field ambulances were already provided with motor ambulances, sand-carts and camel cacolets. A motor ambulance convoy arrived in time for the Gaza operations, and from then until now has done excellent service. The expansion of the force necessitated the addition of five new casualty clearing stations and one Indian clearing hospital—previously there had been but two all told. Five new stationary hospitals were provided, making eight in all, and four 1,040 bedded general hospitals were added to the seven already in the country. With these new medical units to hand, the extensive preparations for the Gaza–Beersheba operations were commenced. Three casualty clearing stations, with a total accommodation for 3,000 patients were allotted to serve the right flank and these were placed at Imara; the two at Belah dealt with the evacuations from the Gaza sector.

Imara was in full, though distant, view of the Turkish positions and orders forbade the pitching of any tents until after dusk of the evening preceding the attack. Many readers will remember the appearance next morning of the erstwhile bare plain with its whole town of tents. To these advanced hospitals extra surgeons were sent up from the Base so that there should be no delay in surgical treatment, and hospital trains were able to evacuate the wounded direct to El Arish and Kantara.

The casualties during these early operations, though not as heavy as had been prepared for, were quite enough to keep the medical department busy in all its branches. From Oct. 28 to Nov. 11, 1917, Desert Mounted and XXth Corps had 245 officers and 4,674 other ranks wounded, and XXIst Corps 126 officers and 2,947 other ranks. During the same period an equal number of sick was dealt with.

The pursuit taken up by the Desert Mounted and XXIst Corps, which did not cease until Jaffa had been taken and Jerusalem was in sight, taxed the medical services to their utmost. All medical transport which could be spared from XXth Corps was temporarily transferred to the other two Corps to enable them to get their sick and wounded away. As it was impossible to move forward a casualty clearing station for some time, two field ambulances were also lent them to string out their long line of evacuation, and to provide resting and feeding places for the patients coming down. The weather during this period of the fighting was very bad and greatly increased the difficulties of the medical service. The work of the front line units, especially the field ambulances of the 52nd, 74th, and Yeomanry Divisions in the Judæan Hills, was at this time very arduous.

The pause which occurred before the attack on Jerusalem enabled three casualty clearing stations to be brought up; one to Gaza, another to Deir Seneid, and the third to Junction Station, to which point the Turkish railway was by this time fitfully running. On the capture of Jerusalem it was necessary to hold up the sick and wounded there in order to save them the long journey in the bad weather which still persisted. A casualty clearing station was soon opened in Jerusalem, to be followed later by two others. Meanwhile, a fourth had been opened at Jaffa, and on the arrival of the railway at Ludd, this latter place became the centre for evacuation from the whole front.

The strain was not confined to the front line and lines of communication, and mention must be made of the good work done by the hospitals at the Base, which, although depleted of many of their staff in order to fill gaps in the front line, were called upon to work for a time at very high pressure.

The raid on Es Salt and Amman was from the medical point of view exceptionally arduous. The closely-pressed retirement from Amman, over ground so deep in mud as to be almost impassable for camels and wheeled transport, made the evacuation of the wounded a task of considerable magnitude.

In April came the reorganization of the force owing to the demands for man-power from France. The substitution of Indian for British regiments necessitated a complete remodelling of the Divisional field ambulances, which became combined units capable of dealing with both British and Indian troops. Casualty clearing stations were similarly converted into combined clearing hospitals. Five new Indian general hospitals were opened, two British being at the same time closed. These alterations entailed drastic changes in the personnel. India were able to supply but a very limited number of medical officers, and many of the units, on arrival, consisted simply of equipment and very partially-trained Indian personnel. The few weeks remaining before operations began were devoted to " intensive training ", and it is greatly to the credit of all concerned that, when put to the test, these hastily-formed units fulfilled their functions with credit to themselves and their service.

In the final operations, the casualties from wounds were fortunately not heavy and well within the numbers anticipated. The speed of the pursuit and the consequent rapid lengthening of the line of evacuation accentuated the transport difficulties. With the capture of Haifa the pressure was relieved by the opening of a casualty clearing station there which was able to despatch cases by hospital ship direct to Alexandria. Later on, this hospital ship service was extended to the other Syrian ports, where casualty clearing stations have been opened. Damascus also was supplied with a casualty clearing station the moment transport became available. The total number of wounded in these operations has been 239 officers and 4,854 other ranks.

No sooner had we reached a breathing space in dealing with our own wounded than we were overwhelmed with sick and wounded prisoners-of-war. The captured Turks were in a deplorable condition of health, owing to prolonged shortage of food, to malaria, and finally to a serious epidemic of influenza. Of the 100,000 captured, more than 20,000 passed into medical charge. For their accommodation three large 2,000 bedded hospitals were rapidly prepared in Egypt and the permanent prisoners-of-war hospitals were also greatly expanded. Several of the Egyptian Hospitals—a service which has done splendid work throughout the campaign—were also devoted to their treatment, and for a short time the British General Hospital at Giza was set free for the accommodation of the more serious cases.

The flood of prisoners had subsided, and now a new trouble had to be faced. Our own sick rate began to show an alarming increase, the daily average of hospital admissions rising from 600 to 1,000 and even to 1,400 per day. This was mainly due to malaria contracted in the newly-occupied districts and to influenza. Superhuman efforts were made in Cairo and Alexandria to open new hospitals and expand existing ones. By these means it was found just possible to keep pace with the increasing sickness.

From a medical point of view, the most important problem of this campaign—as of all previous campaigns in this country—has been that of malaria. During 1917 this disease was easily controlled by dealing with the localized mosquito-breeding areas in the Wadi Ghuzzee. In 1918 it was a very different story. Palestine is notoriously malarious, and, during the summer months some localities such as the Jordan Valley, the coastal plain, and the Vale of Esdraelon have the reputation of being barely habitable. Practically all the perennial streams produce marshes which are infested with mosquitoes, including many anopheline varieties. Even the hill country is by no means free, and every well, cistern, and streamlet is a potential breeding place for these pests.

Directly our front line was definitely established in the early spring, the campaign against mosquitoes began in earnest. Each division was made responsible for its own areas. Their sanitary sections soon got to work, and with the aid of the Royal Engineers and Egyptian labour, marshes were drained, streams canalised, and wells and cisterns oiled. Each regiment was further expected to provide a malaria squad to deal with the vicinity of its own camp. By mid-summer, the result of this combined offensive became apparent, and the mosquito had been driven even from areas which in early summer had been its most formidable strongholds. The slightest relaxation of effort was immediately followed by a counter-offensive on the part of the anophelines, who missed no chance of re-establishing their position in any unguarded water area. Even the Jordan Valley was so satisfactorily dealt with that troops were enabled to live through the worst season of the year in this poisonous locality without any alarming amount of sickness. In order to assist in the early detection of malaria cases, small " diagnosis stations " were scattered along the front line in easily accessible positions. Each consisted of one medical officer and two trained orderlies with microscopes and a diagnosis was made on the spot. No less than 40,000 blood slides were examined in these units and have been the means of saving hundreds of lives.

With the advent of active operations and the passage of the troops into an untreated area, it was inevitable that the incidence of malaria should rise for a time. Within a fortnight of the opening day the number of malaria admissions began to increase, most of the cases being of the malignant type. The average sick rate, which had been 2·85 per cent for the four weeks preceding operations, increased to 5·51 per cent for the period of the third to sixth week of operations. This was a proof, if any were needed of the efficacy of our previous anti-malarial measures. There is little doubt that had not the problem been energetically grappled with from the first, and had malaria been allowed to exact its toll throughout the summer months, the efficiency of the troops would have been very seriously taxed. What effect such a state of affairs might have had upon the campaign gives opportunity for interesting speculation.

Typhus, enteric, relapsing fever, and cholera have been kept in check by inoculation, cleanliness and sanitation. It may well be said that the incinerator and disinfector have helped to win this war. A small outbreak of cholera among the civil population at Tiberias was soon got under control with only a single case of infection among the troops. The only other epidemic of any serious aspect has been that of pellagra among the Turkish prisoners. This obscure disease has been responsible for many deaths among them and is at present the subject of an exhaustive enquiry by a special medical commission. No case has occurred among British troops and only one German prisoner has been found suffering from it.

Ophthalmia, which in Napoleon's Egyptian and Palestine expeditions proved so formidable a bugbear, has, thanks to the cleanly habits of the British soldier, been practically absent from our ranks. In the case of the Turks, however, both before and after capture, its ravages have been severe.

With the arrival of the armistice, further problems await the medical service. Sick repatriated prisoners have to be looked after, and, in this " half-way house," from India, no doubt many sick will find a hospital lodging on their way to and fro.

Within the limits of a short article it is possible to enumerate but a few of the multifarious activities of a medical service called upon to safeguard the health and tend the sick and wounded of a force larger than the peace-time British Army. Altogether the force may be congratulated on the state of its health during the campaign, and the short period following the opening of operations which provided so much sickness may perhaps be considered part of the inevitable price to be paid for one of the most complete victories in the history of British arms.

ROYAL ARMY VETERINARY CORPS.

At the beginning of the period now under review, the veterinary service of the force found itself already organized and equipped on a basis which provided for the efficient performance of its duties at the moment, and at the same time permitted of considerable expansion, if necessary, without dislocating existing arrangements.

To its formation, Australia, New Zealand, India, Egypt, and the Mediterranean Expeditionary Force, had contributed varied units, and to these had been added two veterinary hospitals originally intended for another theatre of war; but the organization and equipment of the various components differed, and even the British units were not uniform in either particular.

It had been at once evident that satisfactory service could hardly be rendered under such conditions and a complete reorganization had been carried out; a reorganization which was rendered comparatively easy by the enthusiasm and co-operation of all concerned. The adherence of the Australian and New Zealand authorities to the idea of a universal organization was especially fortunate, and in consequence all Colonial divisions which were transferred to France, landed in that country with a veterinary organization similar to the other formations of the British Expeditionary Force.

While speaking of Australian and New Zealand units it may here be remarked that the high professional standard of veterinary officers of the forces of these Dominions, their devotion to duty and loyalty to the Directorate, has been a marked and pleasing feature in the veterinary history of the Egyptian Expeditionary Force.

Veterinary hospitals were established at centres where rail connection and the possibility of obtaining green fodder combined to make transit easy and the forage supply suitable for sick animals. In these line of communication establishments Egyptians were employed as much as possible in order to economise British personnel. Field veterinary units with divisions were brought to a uniform establishment and equipped similarly to those in France, the possibility of their being required overseas having been realized.

So far as horses, mules, and donkeys were concerned it was also necessary to establish a trustworthy system of mallein inoculation throughout the army in order to detect cases of glanders and endeavour to prevent extension of the disease when introduced. This equine scourge may easily become one of the great sources of loss among the animals of armies in the field, and consequently every animal in the force was tested. Subsequently every entry to a veterinary hospital or issue to a remount depôt was retested, and, although many isolated cases and local outbreaks occurred, the disease has always been kept under control, and the losses have been very slight. More cases indeed were detected among captured Turkish animals than occurred among the entire army during the campaign.

The raising of Camel Corps on a large scale naturally called for a special organization on the part of the veterinary service. However successful previous camel campaigns may have been from the military point of view, they have generally resulted in the rapid extinction of the animals, and the maintenance of numbers has only been possible by renewing them *in toto*.

In one of the Central Asian campaigns of the Russian Army for instance, a force under General Skobeleff, with a transport of 12,000 camels, returned after some months with one camel only; and in our own Afghan campaign of 1879-80 we lost 70,000 transport animals of which a high proportion were camels, the necessary numbers of which could hardly have been maintained for a longer period. The animal mortality of a camel corps, therefore, might be confidently anticipated at a very high figure, and the large numbers it was proposed to employ called for special effort to keep losses at the minimum possible.

In its endeavours to assist in the creation and maintenance of this branch of the army the veterinary service was again fortunate: its recommendations received due consideration and the spirit in which the camel veterinary duties were undertaken both by officers and other ranks was worthy of every commendation. Camel hospitals were established for the reception of serious casualties, and a considerable veterinary personnel was specially trained to deal with cases which could be retained with their units. This included a comprehensive scheme for the treatment of camel mange, a disease which, if allowed to run its course unchecked, will destroy a camel corps on service in from three to six months. Since practically every adult camel in Egypt has the disease, and as all suitable Egyptian camels were employed, it is easy to understand that extensive preparations were necessary in order to combat its ravages successfully. The losses in camels have proved to be about thirty per cent per annum. This is, of course, a high percentage, but when it is considered that an average of some 40,000 camels has been maintained in the field for between two and three years it represents a great advance on previous similar campaigns. Many factors which do not come altogether within the purview of this article were naturally concerned in the successful accomplishment of the work of the camel corps with this force, but the efficient manner in which the veterinary duties were carried out undoubtedly contributed to the result.

The operations which began in Oct., 1917 (Beersheba-Gaza-Jerusalem) were of the most strenuous nature for all animals of the army. The weather conditions varied from a heat wave to frost, and from a drought to torrential rain. During the heat many horses were without water for forty to eighty hours, while military requirements combined with floods and mud prevented the regular supply of full quantities of forage. The resulting casualties were perforce heavy, and only the unremitting attention of all formations and all ranks concerned prevented more serious loss. During this period the work of the Mobile Veterinary Sections and Field Veterinary Detachments calls for special notice, and through their agency very many animals which would otherwise have perished were saved and subsequently restored to the service.

The continuous work demanded from all animals of the army during the summer and autumn of 1918 was such as to keep veterinary hospitals full; and although they were organized and prepared to deal with a further increase had it been necessary as a result of the operations, viz. the advance from Haifa to Aleppo, this was not requisite. Though considerable casualties were sustained during this advance they were the unavoidable outcome of war, out of all proportion small, when compared with the results achieved, and the general health of animals remains good up to the period of writing.

In such a brief review it is impossible to give statistics of the contagious diseases encountered and dealt with, but glanders, anthrax, mange, piroplasmosis (tick fever), and epizootic lymphangitis, may be mentioned as affecting horses and mules, while trypanosomiasis (surra, debab), and mange, have been the most frequent among camels.

The last-mentioned conditions combined with insufficient food supply are said to have been the cause of the breakdown of the Turkish camel transport in 1916-17, their losses of these animals during that period in the Jordan Valley, being estimated by their own officers at 40,000. Whatever may have been the real numbers, the skeletons everywhere in evidence on our arrival in the area mentioned, warrant its being placed at a very high figure.

During the period under review (July, 1917–Oct., 1918), over 63,000 horses, mules or donkeys, and 31,000 camels were received into veterinary hospitals, while the number of less serious casualties attended to in the field greatly exceeded these figures.

The percentage of animals returned from hospitals to the Remount Department as fit for re-issue to the service has been eighty per cent in the case of horses, and seventy per cent in the case of camels.

The total losses during the entire campaign calculated on the average strength of the animals of the army have not exceeded sixteen per cent of horses, mules and donkeys, and thirty per cent of camels, per annum.

LABOUR IN THE EGYPTIAN EXPEDITIONARY FORCE.

General Remarks.

Under the above heading was included all the unskilled Egyptian personnel and a large proportion of the skilled and semi-skilled personnel which Egypt was called on to furnish towards the needs of the Egyptian Expeditionary Force. It fell to the Directorate of Labour to arrange for its provision and distribution.

The numbers involved eventually reached a total of 135,000 men, engaged on six months' contracts giving an annual turn-over of some 270,000 men, apart from replacement of casualties. The figures before the attack on Gaza in 1917 and the figures reached during 1918 were as under in the various corps:—

	1917	1918
Egyptian Labour Corps	48,472	*100,002 labourers
Camel Transport Corps	20,000	23,452 drivers
Donkey Transport Corps	—	1,992 ,,
Horse Transport (A.S.C.)	3,200	4,349 ,,
Remount Service	1,200	1,433 syces
Veterinary Service	1,100	3,496 ,,
Imperial Camel Corps	280	247 drivers
TOTALS	74,252	134,971

Recruiting.

The modest needs of the Mediterranean Expeditionary Force in 1915–16 in unskilled Egyptian personnel had been adequately met by collecting the men required in the large cities and sending a few recruiting agents to Upper Egypt at intervals. Towards the end of 1916, however, demands for Egyptian personnel, especially for Camel Transport Corps, became insistent and it was found necessary to set up a small recruiting staff in Upper Egypt to provide for Camel Transport Corps, leaving the hitherto untapped Delta as a field for Egyptian Labour Corps recruiting. Early in 1917, between calls

---

* Includes 6,406 skilled or semi-skilled Egyptians.

for Egyptian labour for service in France, Mesopotamia, and Salonika, and the rapidly growing needs of the Egyptian Expeditionary Force, it became obvious that provision for recruiting on an extensive scale should be made. An Inspectorate of Recruiting (Directorate of Labour) was therefore established consisting of twenty-six officers whose activities extended throughout Egypt from Alexandria to Assouan. A strict system of medical inspection and examination was enforced and an advance of L.E. 3 made to all recruits accepted to enable them to provide for their dependents.

The appointment of Inspector of Recruiting was filled by a senior Inspector of the Ministry of the Interior, whose services were placed at the disposal of the Egyptian Expeditionary Force by the Egyptian Government; this arrangement subsequently proved to be of very great assistance and was attended with most successful results.

Recruiting camps for the reception of Egyptians were opened at Sohag, Assiut, and Roda Island, Cairo, whence special trains, conveying 2,000 recruits at a time were run to the respective Base Depôts on the Suez Canal (Kantara) where the men were disinfected, clothed, equipped, and organized into companies or detachments. The Inspectorate of Recruiting also made provision for some 6,000 skilled or semi-skilled personnel constantly required in the Egyptian Labour Corps.

Organization of Labour.

Apart from the recruitment of Egyptian personnel generally, the allotment of labour to employers was dealt with by authorized demands being put forward locally by services and departments to Assistant Directors or Deputy Assistant Directors of Labour.

The following table shows the chain of responsibility :—

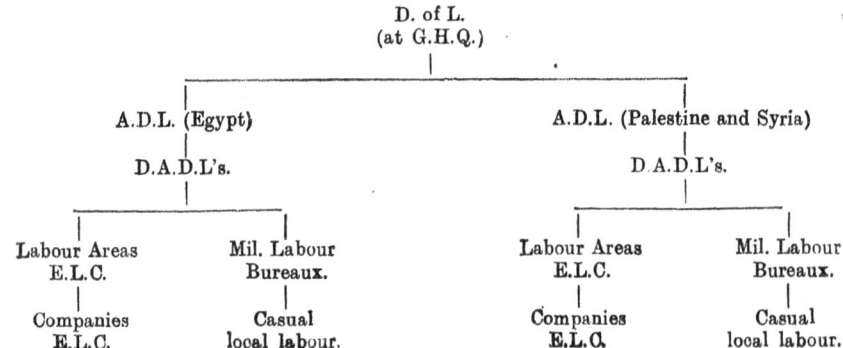

(The Inspector of Recruiting and Inspector, Egyptian Labour Corps, were in direct communication with Director of Labour, G.H.Q.)

The system outlined above, whilst ensuring decentralized control, did away to a great extent with the practice of and necessity for employers holding reserves of labour at their own disposal; it enabled a "pool" of labour to be established at various centres of activity and especially at the base ports of Alexandria, Port Said, Suez, and Kantara, and subsequently at Jaffa, Haifa, Beirut, Tripoli, and Alexandretta.

Very great savings, financially and otherwise, were effected thereby.

Egyptian Labour Corps.

The strength of the corps was as under :—

	Officers.	Men.
In Jan., 1916	39	2,973
In Aug., 1916	88	24,838
In Aug., 1917	292	55,592
In Aug., 1918	418	85,547
In Nov., 1918	504	100,002*

In 1916, 10,463 Egyptian Labour Corps were sent to France; 8,280 to Mesopotamia; 600 to Salonika; whilst in Oct., 1918, 7,000 labourers were held ready for despatch to Salonika before Turkey had capitulated.

Among many difficulties experienced, but successfully overcome, in dealing with the above extraordinarily rapid expansion, was the question of finding suitable officers. Egypt had been thoroughly tapped by the spring of 1916 in order to furnish Arabic-speaking officers for the various local corps and for Intelligence duties. The original and experienced officers of the Egyptian Labour Corps who had done excellent service in Mudros, Egypt, and elsewhere were required for senior appointments in the corps, and they represented only a fraction of the increased numbers now necessary. Consequently, if

---

* Includes 6,406 skilled or semi-skilled E.L.C.

Egyptian labour was to be properly organized it became essential to draw suitable officers with a knowledge of discipline from some other source. The problem was solved by offering temporary commissions to selected candidates from the ranks of British units, and ensuring them facilities for the acquisition of Arabic with extra duty pay on becoming proficient. Only those candidates who showed an aptitude in the handling of Egyptians, after a thorough practical test extending over several weeks, were accepted, and it is of interest to state that out of over 800 candidates dealt with 401 have been commissioned.

Although Egypt could make no further provision in officers, it could still produce large numbers of local subjects of European descent, who by their knowledge of the fellahin and their proficiency in languages proved to be most valuable material for foremen. Advantage was taken of this fact to engage and train large numbers as serjeant-foremen and corporal-foremen. Meanwhile, practical experience in working Egyptian Labour Corps in the field had led to the evolution of the organization best suited to its many and varied activities.

The smallest unit in the corps is the gang. It consists of fifty men, viz. a reis and forty-nine labourers. The reis, usually, is personally known to all the men in his gang, and frequently all come from the same village or markaz. Thus in a company of 600 labourers there are twelve gangs, and in a double company of 1,200 labourers, twenty-four gangs. To such companies skilled personnel were frequently attached. The proportion of officers handling labour is one officer to each section of 200 men.

The organization of the Egyptian Labour Corps was as follows on Sept. 19, 1918 :—

Headquarters (Inspector, E.L.C.)	Ludd
Base Depôt, E.L.C.	Kantara
Advanced Depôt, E.L.C.	Ludd
Double companies	24
Single companies	75

"Labour areas" for purposes of administration, and consisting of the requisite number of companies, were formed as circumstances demanded.

It is not possible in a short survey to enter into particulars as regards the detailed employment of 100,000 men; therefore it must suffice to enumerate the main classes of work on which these considerable numbers were engaged:—

(a) Railway construction and maintenance (broad and narrow gauge), and bridge building.

(b) Roadmaking and metalling; constructing and laying "wire roads"; clearing tracks.

(c) Laying pipe-lines.

(d) Construction of buildings and reservoirs; carpentry and general Royal Engineer work.

(e) Quarrying stone.

(f) Well-boring.

(g) Formation of supply depôts and general Army Service Corps labour.

(h) Stretcher bearing and conservancy; drainage of malarial areas.

(i) Ammunition depôts and general Ordnance labour.

(j) Loading and discharging ships; stevedoring, including working winches and derricks.

(k) Boatmen—manning surf boats landing stores along the coasts of Palestine and Syria.

(l) Labour for Royal Air Force, for "Signals," and for salvage.

To all members of the force the Egyptian Labour Corps were well-known in small detachments; it was given to few to observe them at work where large numbers were employed; but those who have seen many thousands of Egyptian Labour Corps labourers on task work, either driving a cutting with pick and fasse through Palestine clay, or in their thousands carrying baskets of earth to pile up some railway embankment, will long remember such examples of intensive labour. No less striking was it to watch the line of laden boats leaving the storeships off the coast and making their way through the surf to the beach, there to be hauled high up by teams of cheerful Egyptians working to whistle signal under their own officers.

Nor must their equally important work at the base ports of Alexandria, Port Said, Suez, and Kantara be forgotten. Trained stevedore gangs under Egyptian Labour Corps officers were always in readiness to board incoming ocean-going steamers, work their discharging gear, and empty the holds as rapidly as had hitherto been done by skilled contractor's personnel; or, conversely, to load outgoing vessels with supplies, ammunition, and stores required for operations on the Syrian coast or in Salonika.

It stands to the lasting credit of the officers of the Egyptian Labour Corps, that certain companies, under selected Egyptian Labour Corps officers, reached such a high standard in connection with work on roads, railways, pipe-line, and other services, that they were able to make satisfactory progress without constant expert supervision.

Among the skilled trades represented by over 6,000 Egyptians in the Egyptian Labour Corps, the following are examples:—

Basket-menders; blacksmiths; carpenters; fitters; hammermen; masons; plasterers; quarrymen; saddlers; stevedores; stokers; tentmenders; tinsmiths; well-borers; wheelwrights; winchmen.

The accompanying maps (inset on PLATES 44 and 52) show in a general way the distribution of the Egyptian Labour Corps throughout Palestine and Syria in connection with the advance of the force, but it should be borne in mind that equally large numbers were employed in Egypt particularly in the Suez Canal Zone and at Alexandria.

Military Labour Bureaux.

In order to effect economy and utilize all local sources of casual labour, Military Labour Bureaux had been successfully established at Alexandria and Port Said in 1916.

Concurrently with the advance from Gaza–Beersheba in 1917, immediate steps were taken by the Directorate of Labour to collect and organize the labour resources of the newly occupied territory in conformity to the military requirements.

The first Military Labour Bureau in Palestine was opened at Jaffa shortly after the town was occupied. Labour requirements to clear the streets, repair roads, and prepare the quay for the arrival of shipping were immediate and any labour that could be utilized at once was of especial value.

Certain notables, sheikhs, and muktars were called together, the situation explained and notices issued calling for volunteers.

The chief difficulty at the onset was the natural tendency of the population to hold aloof until they understood the new régime and government, and this was augmented by the necessity of their becoming accustomed to receive wages in a new currency. In fact, at every Labour Bureau opened, the initial work was largely concerned in creating confidence in the local inhabitants with totally new conditions and in every case such confidence was uniformly and quickly established.

Payment initially was made in coin to each separate labourer at the finish of each day's work. As soon as confidence was assured and the number of employees consequently increased, a weekly system of payment—partly in paper and partly in coin—was instituted. Each labourer had a numbered green armlet and a pay-slip which was marked up and checked at least twice a day.

It soon became necessary to open a Bureau at Jerusalem, and very shortly some 10,000 local labourers were engaged on work extending from Hebron to Jerusalem and Jerusalem to Jaffa, controlled and organized by two bureaux.

These large numbers had absorbed most of the available able-bodied men and both women and boys were then allowed to volunteer for certain classes of work on which they could be suitably employed.

Where food was scarce millet was issued in part payment to individual labourers, at their option.

The Military Labour Bureaux ensured that regular work was provided in Palestine for thousands of people who in many cases would otherwise have been destitute.

The currency question was thus very materially helped, both by the circulation of large sums in the new coinage as wages and because every case of trafficking or depreciating the official paper currency was immediately taken up by the Labour Bureaux officers whenever one of the employees reported that he could not obtain full value for his wages when paid in notes.

In addition to the labourers, some 1,500 skilled men were registered and engaged on casual employment by these bureaux, boatmen from Jaffa and stone dressers from Jerusalem being particularly successful and freely volunteering for work in any locality required.

Similar steps were taken for opening labour bureaux currently with the advance of 1918. Within seven days of the commencement of operations, labour Bureaux were opened at Tul Keram, at Haifa, and shortly afterwards at Beirut.

All Bureaux were organized on the same lines as proved successful at Jaffa and Jerusalem, and the rates of pay of casual labour were standardized throughout Palestine and Syria.

THE NAVY AND ARMY CANTEEN BOARD.

Under the title of the Army Canteen Committee, an organization was established by the War Office in April, 1916, to control the operations of Army Canteens managed by Contractors. In Dec., 1916, the actual conduct of canteens was vested in this Committee. Its functions were subsequently enlarged to include the operation of Naval Canteens ashore and on board His Majesty's Ships, and the name was changed to the Navy and Army Canteen Board.

In June, 1917, a Commission under Major-General Sir G. C. Kitson, appointed by the Quartermaster-General, arrived in Egypt and at once proceeded to take over the canteens previously managed by civilian contractors west of the Suez Canal and in the Sudan.

In Sept., 1917, the Board took over the control of the forty-one canteens on the Canal and to the east of it, formerly provided by the Expeditionary Force Canteens (a temporary organization).

Then came the advance of Oct., 1917, and it was during this difficult period that the Board's activities, so far as the advanced sections were concerned, commenced. At that time the canteen organization was not provided with its own transport, and was insufficiently staffed, but, nevertheless, by the time the troops had settled down north of the Jaffa–Jerusalem line canteen facilities were available at Jaffa, Ludd, Bir Salem, Latron, and Jerusalem. During the spring of 1918 these facilities were extended by the provision of canteens at Sheikh Muannis, Sarona, Bir ez Ziet, Mulebbis, Wilhelma, Hot Corner, in the Wady Ballut, Khurbetha ibn Harith, Ain Sinia, Ramallah, Jericho, and on the Auja.

The summer of 1918 was a time of preparation, during which upwards of sixty motor vehicles arrived, and at the moment of the advance in September arrangements were complete by which it was hoped that the advancing infantry would never be out of touch with an Army Canteen. In pursuance of this object army canteens were opened at Tul Keram on Sept. 25, Nablus on Sept. 28, Haifa on Oct. 2, Beirut on Oct. 19, Tripolis on Oct. 23, Aleppo on Nov. 6, and at Damascus. The previously existing canteens at Ras el Ain, Jiljulieh, and Messudieh supplied the wants of those divisions that were withdrawn. One division was accompanied during its advance to Tiberias by a mobile canteen comprising five lorries.

It is of interest to study a few points in connection with the administration of the Navy and Army Canteen Board in the area of the Egyptian Expeditionary Force.

The unit forms a section of the Royal Army Service Corps and has an establishment of twenty-seven officers and 372 other ranks, with 135 personnel attached. It employs upwards of 800 European and Egyptian civilians.

It is charged with the supply and conduct of all Army canteens, now ninety-eight in number. In addition it operates four mineral water factories, the Jerusalem Hotel, the Summer Camp Hotel at Alexandria, and the Winter Camp Hotel, Cairo.

It has, or has had, bakeries at Cairo, Alexandria, Jerusalem, Jaffa, and Beirut, and it maintains refreshment tents or rooms for officers and men at railhead and intermediate stations on the Palestine Military Railway.

In Egypt, where Egyptian personnel is available, each Canteen consists, as at home, of a coffee bar, a grocery bar, and a beer bar, and in addition, in some cases, of a recreation room and a wholesale grocery bar. Owing to the shortage of personnel it was not found possible in the advanced sections to provide more than wholesale and retail grocery bars with, where possible, refreshment rooms for officers and men. During the summer of 1918, however, a number of kiosks containing soda fountains where such articles as cigarettes, sweets, and cakes, were available, were provided as near to the line as possible. Among such kiosks were those opened at Sheikh Muannis, Hot Corner, Bir ez Zeit, and Ain Sinia.

In the Egyptian Expeditionary Force the canteen sales amount to a yearly total of upwards of four and a half million sterling, and the approximate value of the canteen stores in Egypt is one million pounds. Regimental and other funds are largely maintained by means of a rebate or discount of eight per cent on all cash sales to soldiers, and the Christmas issue of half a pound of plum pudding per man, in addition to many other amenities, was provided by the Army Council out of an additional two per cent which is paid by the Board to it.

THE ROYAL AIR FORCE.

In July, 1917, the Royal Air Force on this front consisted only of two squadrons, of which one was Australian. The Australian Squadron was chiefly employed in long distance reconnaissance, bomb-dropping and photography; while the other carried out the tactical work and artillery co-operation. The machines with which these squadrons were equipped were of an old type and much inferior to those used by the enemy. As a result, little could be achieved towards acquiring the superiority in the air.

Shortly before the attack on the Gaza-Beersheba front, a second artillery squadron arrived, thus enabling the nucleus of a fighting squadron to be formed. The machines of the latter included one flight of Bristol fighters, which were held in reserve until a few days prior to the attack. One memorable morning four Bristols left the ground in response to a hostile aircraft alarm; they met and engaged an enemy formation, and, for the first time on this front, shot down an enemy machine in our lines. The German pilot who was captured stated that he had been taken completely by surprise, never having doubted that his own machine was superior to anything that we had.

From that day onward the tables were turned in our favour, and during the next few weeks other German machines shared the fate of the first. In all ninety-three enemy machines were brought down, fifty-nine of them behind the enemy's lines, eleven in our own lines, and twenty-eight out of control. Our long distance reconnaissance machines, which on previous occasions had been attacked on sight by the enemy, were now carefully avoided by him.

On Sept. 29, 1917, the Commander of the Sinai Front informed the Yilderim Group Command that, "The mastery of the air has unfortunately for some weeks completely passed over to the British." He adds that, "Our aviators estimate the number of British aircraft at from thirty to forty." Though the enemy considered our Bristol fighter as far superior to their own machine, and were fond of attributing their want of success to the "machine," the following remark indicates that there were also other factors :—

"The shooting down of a second fighting plane, which again was fighting alone, points to the necessity of an experienced O.C., Aircraft." (Von Papen, 16/10/17.)

During the Gaza operations, formations of slow aeroplanes escorted by one or two Bristols, bombed and fired upon the retreating enemy without interference on the part of the German Flying Corps.

Late in November the Bristol fighters were reinforced by S.E.5 scouts, a faster machine than any on this front; and this type, with the Bristol fighters, gained for us the complete superiority in the air, which we held until the end.

By the time our troops had taken up the Jerusalem-Jaffa line, the position of the Royal Air Force as regards machines and personnel rendered possible a continuous policy of offensive action against enemy aircraft, which were in all cases, without exception, attacked whenever met and in whatever numbers. The following extracts from captured enemy documents show the cumulative effect of this policy on the moral of the German Air Forces :—

"25/8/18-31/8/18.
"In consequence of lively hostile flying activity, no reconnaissances could be carried out."
"1/9/18-7/9/18.
"No flights over enemy country."
"8/9/18-14/9/18.
"No flights over enemy country."

This was confirmed in the weekly reports from enemy Air Force Headquarters, as follows :—

"25/8/18-31/8/18.
"The loss of two more machines of 301st Abteilung compelled the suspension of all reconnaissance in front of VIIIth Army.
"An attempt will be made to continue flights on the remainder of the front occasionally."

Thus it will be seen that the enemy was unable to obtain any information from aerial reconnaissance at a period when this was of vital importance.

This is even more remarkable when it is realized that at the commencement of the advance in Sept., 1918, the enemy Air Force was in considerable strength and equipped with up-to-date types of machines, which, if properly handled, were greatly superior in performance to our artillery machines.

On the night of Sept. 18-19, a Handley-Page, carrying over half-a-ton of bombs flew over enemy country and attacked Afuleh Station and Aerodrome. This machine, which had previously flown all the way from England, started the offensive as far as the Royal Air Force is concerned.

At dawn the next morning, that is, "Z" day, a perfect orgy of bombing took place. A special squadron, detailed solely for bombing, had arrived a few weeks before operations commenced. This squadron attacked all telephone and telegraph exchanges far behind the line; while the Corps squadrons bombed the smaller exchanges just behind the trenches, with the result that enemy communication by telephone or telegraph was completely deranged.

EGYPTIAN EXPEDITIONARY FORCE

To ensure that the enemy should not be aware of the massing of our cavalry just before the attack and their subsequent movements after the infantry had broken through, it was necessary to prevent enemy machines from leaving the ground. With this objective, two scouts at a time patrolled over Jenin aerodrome. Each machine carried four bombs, which were dropped on any sign of activity on the aerodrome. Each pair was relieved while still patrolling over the aerodrome and on relief came down and fired machine guns into the hangars, with the result that enemy aircraft were prevented from taking any part in the battle.

During the infantry attack, three artillery machines continually patrolled the front of the XXIst Corps and, co-operating with the artillery, located and engaged thirty-two active batteries.

On Sept. 20 and 21, every available machine was used for bombing the retreating enemy. Of these, the column retreating on the Nablus–Kh. Ferweh road on the 21st sustained the greatest losses. Early on the morning of the 21st a column of enemy troops and transport was reported by a strategical reconnaissance machine moving along the Nablus–Wadi Farah road, just south of Kh. Ferweh. It was of the utmost importance that this movement should be stopped, as, although the cavalry had blocked the enemy retreat by way of Beisan, the road to the bridge over the Jordan, at Jisr ed Damieh could not possibly be closed by our troops for some hours; nor could the crossings over the Jordan between that place and Beisan be guarded in time. All available machines were at once mobilized for this attack, and departures were so timed that two machines should arrive over the objective every three minutes, and that an additional formation of six machines should come into action every half hour. These attacks were maintained from 0800 till noon, by which time our troops were in touch with the column. The road was completely blocked and was strewn with a mass of debris of wrecked wagons, guns and motor lorries, totalling in all eighty-seven guns, fifty-five motor lorries, four motor cars, and 932 wagons.

Very few flights took place in the air during operations, for the simple reason that practically no enemy machines were met with; but, just prior to the capture of Aleppo, an interesting combat occurred. Two Bristol fighters belonging to the Australian Flying Corps met an enemy aeroplane and after a running fight drove him down, forcing him to land behind his own lines. The occupants left the stricken machine, seeing which, the Bristol landed beside it and, while our observer held up the two German airmen, the pilot set fire to the hostile machine. Owing to the soft nature of the ground, he was prevented from bringing back the two Germans as prisoners, who were released and left where they were.

A comparison of the strength of the Royal Air Force in Palestine in July, 1917, and Sept., 1918, is interesting. On the former date it consisted of one Wing, with two Squadrons, and a Balloon Company; whilst in Sept., 1918, it consisted of a Brigade, with two Wings, seven Squadrons, and a Balloon Company.

EXPLANATORY NOTE TO THE MAPS ILLUSTRATING OPERATIONS.

The movements of troops during any fixed period are frequently so complex that it is not possible to illustrate such moves in detail on maps of a scale which is, of necessity, small in order to include the wide area of country over which the troops were disposed.

Consequently, the following maps, with a few exceptions, show the dispositions of our forces and those of the enemy as they were known at General Headquarters at certain fixed times, and are based on the situation maps which were issued nightly during the major operations. Considerable information has been added, such as the location of heavy artillery and aerodromes, and alterations made where later information proved the original maps to be incorrect.

In order to avoid overcrowding the maps, the words " division " and " brigade " have been omitted except where brigades have been acting separately from their divisions; and in all cases the positions are approximate only. Thus, in the case of the heavy artillery, it has frequently been impossible to show each battery, or even the Royal Garrison Artillery brigade, in the actual position occupied, and the conventional sign has been placed close to the headquarters of the formation with or under which it was operating.

Regiments and battalions are only shown when acting apart from their higher command, and then only when space permits.

It should be realised that the Turkish regiment (*i.e.* three battalions) is a similar formation to our brigade, and is the enemy's principal fighting formation. This fact, and the number of odd units on the front, especially east of the Jordan, tends to make the Turkish troops appear on the maps in an undue preponderance.

Throughout, the activities of the Egyptian Expeditionary Force are shown in red, and those of the enemy in green.

For details of the moves of any particular unit reference should be made to the "Brief Record of Service" of the formation concerned.

Owing to the abnormal weather conditions in Cairo during the period in which the maps were printed, the unequal expansion and contraction of the paper caused unusual difficulty in obtaining correct colour registration, and the paper shortage in Egypt and the limited time in which delivery was required, made reprinting impossible.

LINES OF COMMUNICATION, 1917.
British.

In June, 1917, the "Palestine Lines of Communication" comprised the bases Port Said and Kantara, and a single line of railway track from Kantara to Deir el Belah, the railhead station which had been opened in April, 1917. (*See* Plate 2.)

Great stress was thrown upon all departments by the erection of efficient railway, ordnance, and engineer workshops, the construction of wharves along the Canal bank, the laying out of thirty miles of metalled roads, the development of the terminus of the military railway, and the transfer of all the more

REFERENCE
TO CONVENTIONAL SIGNS

PLATE 1

Railways	—•—•—•—
Main Roads	————
Other Roads	————
Good Tracks	
Telegraph Lines	·—·—·—·—
Jewish Colonies	✡
Heights in feet above Sea Level	5020
,, ,, ,, below ,, ,,	−1254

BRITISH

Infantry { Division	7	▪
Infantry { Brigade	161	▪
Cavalry		◰
Arab Army		◰
Army H.Q.		▭
Corps H.Q.	XVI	✕
Arab Army H.Q.		☾
Divisional H.Q.	60	▰
Patrols, Cav. & Inf.		• •
Heavy or Siege Artillery		⚔
Armoured Car		🚗
Motor Transport Columns		🚚

AERIAL

Aerodrome and Advanced Landing Ground ✈ ○ AFULE

Areas bombed ⋯

TURKISH

Infantry { Division	53	▪
Infantry { Regiment	72	▪
German Infantry		▪
Cavalry		◰
Army H.Q.	VII	▭
Corps H.Q.	II	✕
Divisional H.Q.	26	▸
Heavy Artillery		⚔
Disorganised retreating Columns		⋯
Motor Transport Columns		🚚
Horse Transport Columns		🐎
Lines of Retreat		⤳

AERIAL

Aerodrome ✈

Areas bombed ⋯

FORMATIONS ARE SHOWN THUS:

 Concentrated    in Line   ▮ in Column of Route

Front Line 18-9-18 — — —

important base depôts from Egypt to Kantara; all performed against time, in order that the army in front might derive full benefit from these works when active operations should be opened.

In the most difficult and most important work of all, that is to say, in transforming Kantara into a port at which many ocean-going steamers can discharge, the Suez Canal Company gave its fullest and most effective support. Essential as these works were for the army in the field, the Canal was not constructed with a view to such developments, and the harbour works might well have been regarded by the Company as of doubtful value. Nevertheless, the Company entered sympathetically into the programme, and, not content with giving its formal consent to the proposed works, technical advice and assistance were freely placed at the disposal of the army.

While the work was going forward at the main base of the lines of communication during the summer of 1917, developments were also taking place further east. El Arish was made into a hospital centre in order to ease the transference of sick and wounded from railhead to the base hospitals; advanced depôts of supplies, stores, and ammunition were established at Rafa, Khan Yunis, and at Deir el Belah; while the work of doubling the railway track across Sinai was pushed forward rapidly, the double track to El Arish being opened for traffic by mid-November. Two months previously the lines of communication had been extended to include the new railhead at Shellal on the Rafa–Shellal branch.

The operations which began in October resulted in the extension of the lines of communication, first to Beersheba to the east and to Mejdel to the north. This was quickly followed by the inclusion of Ramleh (Dec. 24), Jaffa (Jan. 30) and Jerusalem (Feb. 4). In the meantime the defence and administration of the lines of communication were placed under one commander.

During this period and until the arrival of railhead in the neighbourhood of Ramleh, there were many periods of anxiety and difficulty owing to the weather conditions.

The movement of supplies, reinforcements, and remounts was seriously interrupted both by rail and road, as owing to the heavy floods during November and December, the railway track was repeatedly breached in the low-lying coastal plain, and this made the movement of all forms of transport impossible for days together. No metalled road existed across this plain between the Wadi Ghuzze and Julis, a distance of over twenty miles, and parties of reinforcements marching from the ever-advancing railhead to the front line found themselves isolated in a waste of mud and water, unable to move forward or back, and suffered considerable hardships before arriving in the front line. It was due to the persistent efforts of the railway construction parties and of engineers, who did what could be done with the "roads," such as they were, that the lines of communication were kept open under the difficult conditions which prevailed.

Turkish.

The Turkish lines of communication, which extended from Bozanti to Beersheba (see PLATE 2), were under the Syrian Western Arabia Command, and the G.O.C. (Ahmed Jemal Pasha) did not work harmoniously with the Yildirim Army group as he was jealous because his command had been taken over by a foreigner.

The task of keeping up supplies, even under the best of conditions, was not an easy one, for at this time the Amanus and Taurus tunnels were incomplete, and all supplies from west of Bozanti had to be unloaded, and either re-loaded into narrow-gauge trucks, which were drawn by engines driven by compressed air, or transported by motor lorry or pack animals to the east end of the tunnels. The same procedure was adopted over the Amanus range, thus entailing four separate transhipments of all supplies. A further transhipment took place at Rayak owing to the change from the normal guage line to the metre gauge of the Hejaz and Palestine railways. (See PLATE 2.)

Thus the only means of communication for the Turkish force in Palestine with their main base at Haidar Pasha (Constantinople Station in Asia), was by a single line of rail about 1,275 miles in length, which had in addition to carry all ordnance stores for the force in Mesopotamia, as far as Muslimie, and for the Hejaz, as far as Deraa. (See PLATE 2.)

The rolling stock was neither good nor numerous, and the wood fuel which was used in place of coal did not tend to accelerate the service. An instance occurred of a train being stopped between stations so that the wood fuel could be chopped into pieces small enough to feed the fire. Numerous short lines were constructed for the purpose of bringing the requisite wood from the timbered areas. In order to release rolling stock, reinforcements frequently marched from Rayak to the front line, a distance of about 250 miles.

In addition to the above difficulties, the inefficiency of Turkish officials and their amenity to bribery, made the supply and equipment of the Yildirim armies no easy problem.

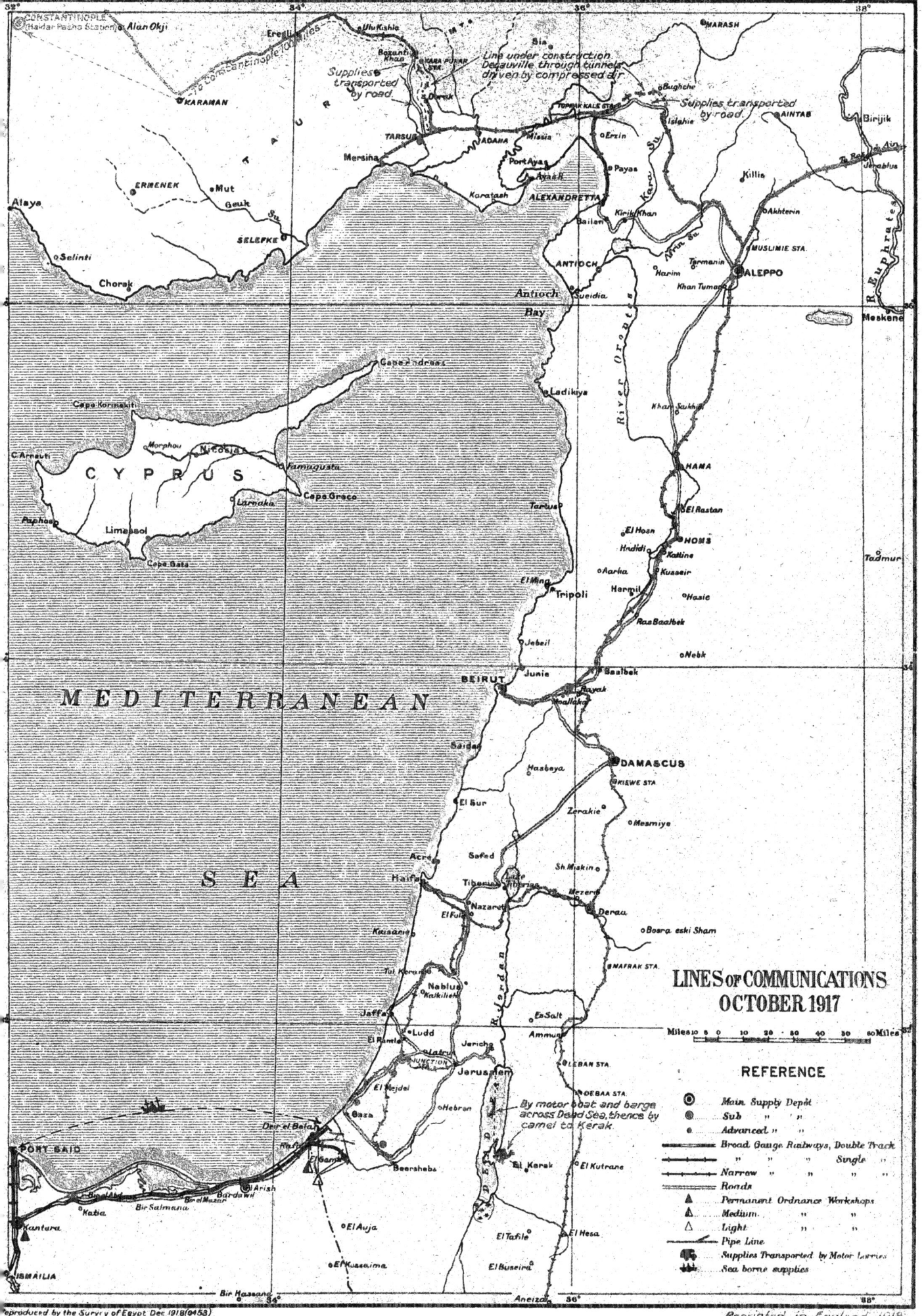

October 28.

The concentration for the attack on Beersheba had been proceeding for a week past, and troops were gradually moving to their concentration areas. On Oct. 27 the line of observation (the Rashid Bek–El Buggar–Point 720–Point 630 ridge), was held by the 8th Mounted Brigade, and at dawn the enemy launched a determined attack on Points 630 and 720, and eventually succeeded in occupying the crests of both hills, despite the very gallant and determined resistance of the 1st County of London (Middlesex) Yeomanry. The garrison on Point 720 were, save for three men, all killed or wounded, and that on Point 630 held on in a support trench close behind the crest, in spite of heavy casualties and though almost surrounded. It was eventually relieved by 158th Brigade, and the whole line re-occupied in the evening, on the enemy withdrawing.

Much work on the ever-pressing question of water supply was necessary, wells being developed and water stored at Esani, Asluj, Khalasa for the cavalry, and at Abu Ghalyun and Maalaga for the infantry.

On Oct. 28, the outpost line was held by the 53rd Division, plus the 229th Brigade (74th Division), covering the construction of the railway to Karm. The remainder of the XXth Corps was concentrating about Tel el Fara, while Desert Mounted Corps was moving to its concentration area about Khalasa and Asluj.

It is not uninteresting to review the enemy situation at this period:—

The German Staff in Sinai had, so far back as August, decided that the British would make another effort to break through on that front, and with such forces that, unless the Turks were heavily reinforced, the result could only be in favour of the British. That the weaknesses of their position were its extent and the exposed left flank at Beersheba, was fully realized by the Command in the field, and during August and September repeated requests were made to the Higher Command for a shortening of the line by withdrawing from Beersheba, or generous reinforcements so that Beersheba could be held *à l'outrance*.

The soundness of these demands was fully realized by the German advisers of the Turks, but there existed a policy which was a veritable millstone to those who wished to conduct the operations in accordance with clear strategic principles. This policy was directed towards the recovery of Baghdad. Baghdad, a former capital of the Khalifs, and therefore important to the pan-Islamic party, was ever before the Young Turk, soldier, and politician, and the plan had received the backing of Berlin. A composite German force had been formed and one of the first of German soldiers, Marshal Erich von Falkenhayn, lent for the carrying through of this undertaking. If Baghdad was to be retaken, every man and gun must be sent to Irak and every man sent to Sinai decreased the chance of success. But to this was the unanswerable argument of those who asked that reinforcements should be sent to Sinai: "If the Sinai front is broken, Palestine and Syria will fall into the enemy's hands, and not only will Baghdad not be retaken, but the armies in Irak will be caught like a rat in a trap, with the British across their lines of communication at Aleppo." It was not until mid-October that this argument prevailed and then it was too late. Troops being diverted from Mesopotamia were still on the lines of communication and the aircraft were still being unpacked and put together on their aerodromes, when the British troops attacked and captured Beersheba on Oct. 31, 1917.

The German Command had, however, estimated the date of the British attack with fair accuracy, which they considered would take place, owing to weather conditions, early in November. But they were totally incorrect in their estimate of its direction.

Various circumstances made them believe that it would consist of a third and final assault on Gaza, combined with a landing to the north, which would turn their right flank and enable the British to occupy the fertile coastal plain. To meet this primarily, all defensive work was concentrated for many weeks on the Gaza sector, and their main reserves—the 7th and 19th Infantry Divisions—were concentrated behind Gaza.

Von Falkenhayn proposed, by a concentration of forces, to deliver an attack on the British right flank, and so drive back General Allenby out of Palestine into the waterless and difficult country east of the Wadi el Arish. In addition to its strategical effect, this would have had the political result of clearing that portion of the Turkish Empire from the invader.

This attack was originally timed for the latter half of October, to precede and forestall the British attack. Owing, however, to indecision, general procrastination, poor transport facilities, and, above all, to the jealousy and opposition of Ahmed Jemal Pasha, G.O.C. of the Fourth Army and Governor of Syria, it had to be postponed, and was eventually timed for early December.

By Oct. 28 the organization of the Turkish forces under the Yildirim Army Group into the seventh and eighth armies was nearing completion. The headquarters of General Kress von Kressenstein (G.O.C., Eighth Army) had moved back from Huj to Huleikat so that the former, now connected to the main railway by a light line, might be used as a reserve area, and Fevzi Pasha (G.O.C., Seventh Army) was about to move forward his headquarters from Hebron to near Beersheba, finally to take over the troops allotted to his command. Marshal von Falkenhayn was at Aleppo *en route* for Jerusalem.

The front had been strengthened by three fresh divisions—the 19th (Sedad Bey), 24th (Wilmer Bey, a German), and 26th (Fakhr-ed-Din Bey), and the 20th Division was moving towards the front on the lines of communication, south of Aleppo.

ADVANCE THROUGH PHILISTIA

PLATE 3

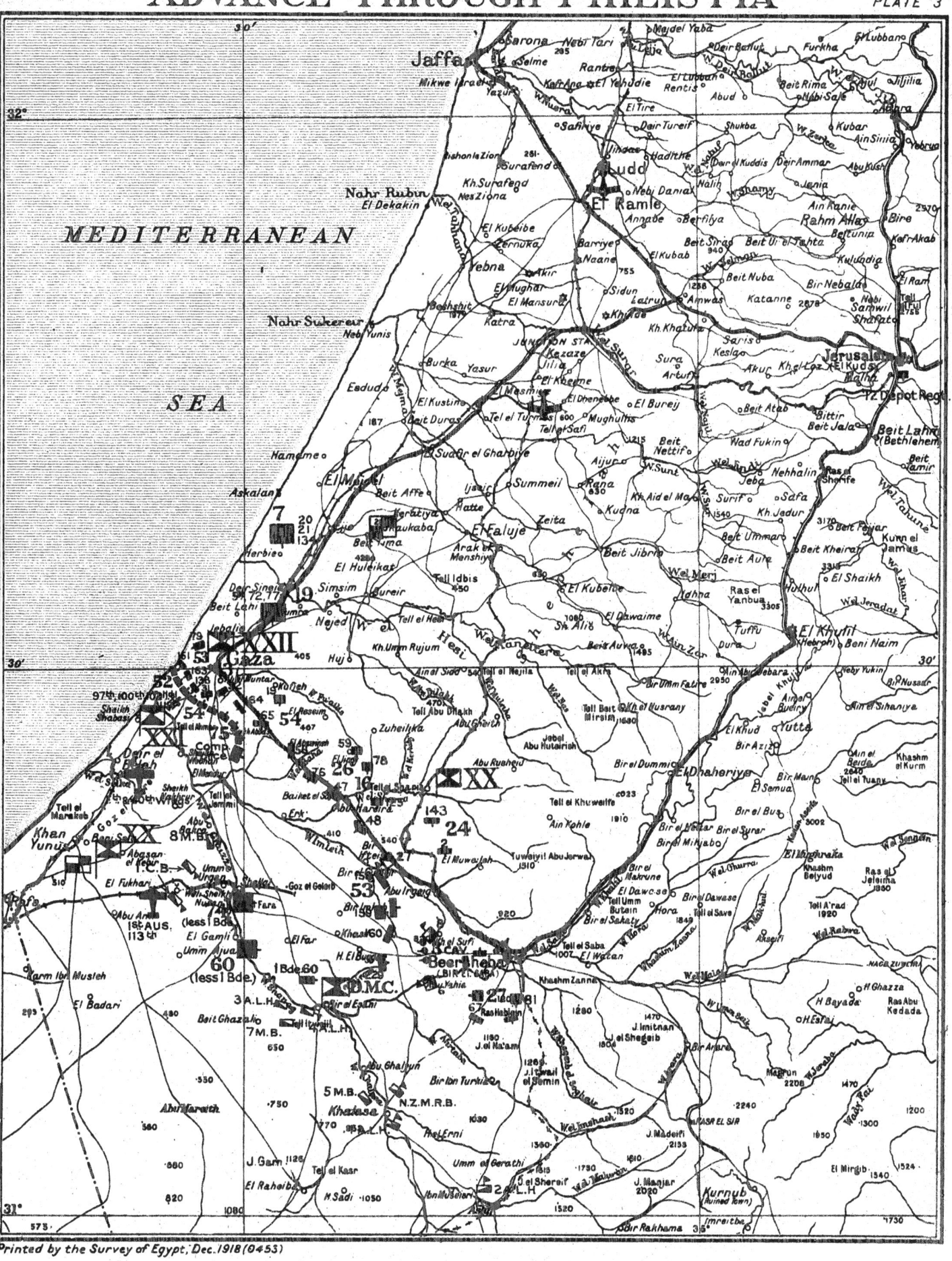

Situation at 6 p.m. on 28-10-17 as known at G.H.Q. E.E.F.

OCTOBER 28TH—*continued.*

The Gaza sector was a network of trenches, wire entanglements, and strongly fortified posts, conveniently sited for mutual support and cross fire, which extended to the south-east until the defences of Beersheba were reached. The German Staff appears to have been very well satisfied as to the security of the line against frontal attack and any second-line system of defence had been almost totally neglected. A wide turning movement on the east was considered impossible owing to the broken nature of the country and lack of water. Although the possibility of a landing on the coast north of Gaza had always been considered, the following telegram, despatched on Oct. 24 to the Yildirim Army Group Headquarters by Major von Papen (of espionage notoriety in the U.S.A.), Liaison officer between the armies and the group, is indicative of the accepted views on this point :—

> "Reconnaissance undertaken to-day along the coastal sector shows that sufficient positions for local defence are in existence near Askalon and Wadi Hesy. Disembarkation, which might be tactically possible, could not, from the nature of the country, take place north of Wadi Hesy. Employment of naval guns and a few machine guns seems desirable for local defence."

October 29.

On Oct. 29 the process of concentration continued. The Desert Mounted Corps continued its move towards Khalasa and Asluj. In the XXth Corps area, the 53rd Division continued to cover the front and left flank of the concentration, and the enemy made no further attempt to interfere with or to reconnoitre the movement. The 60th Division moved up from Tel el Fara to Bir el Esani, the advanced brigade moving to a point south of Maalaga. One brigade of the 74th Division moved forward to link up the 60th and 53rd Divisions, while the 10th Division commenced to move from Rafa to Tel el Fara.

The enemy were still unaware of the real British intentions :—

> "An outflanking attack on Beersheba, with about one infantry and one cavalry division is indicated, but the main attack, as before, must be expected on the Gaza front."

So ran the enemy appreciation, based on reports of our tactical deployment for the offensive as received from their air service.

The standing camps left in the whole area around Deir el Belah, and inhabited by only a few details, also misled the enemy, who, about this period, estimated that there were "six infantry Divisions in the Gaza sector, deeply echeloned."

To face Plate 4.

ADVANCE THROUGH PHILISTIA

PLATE 4

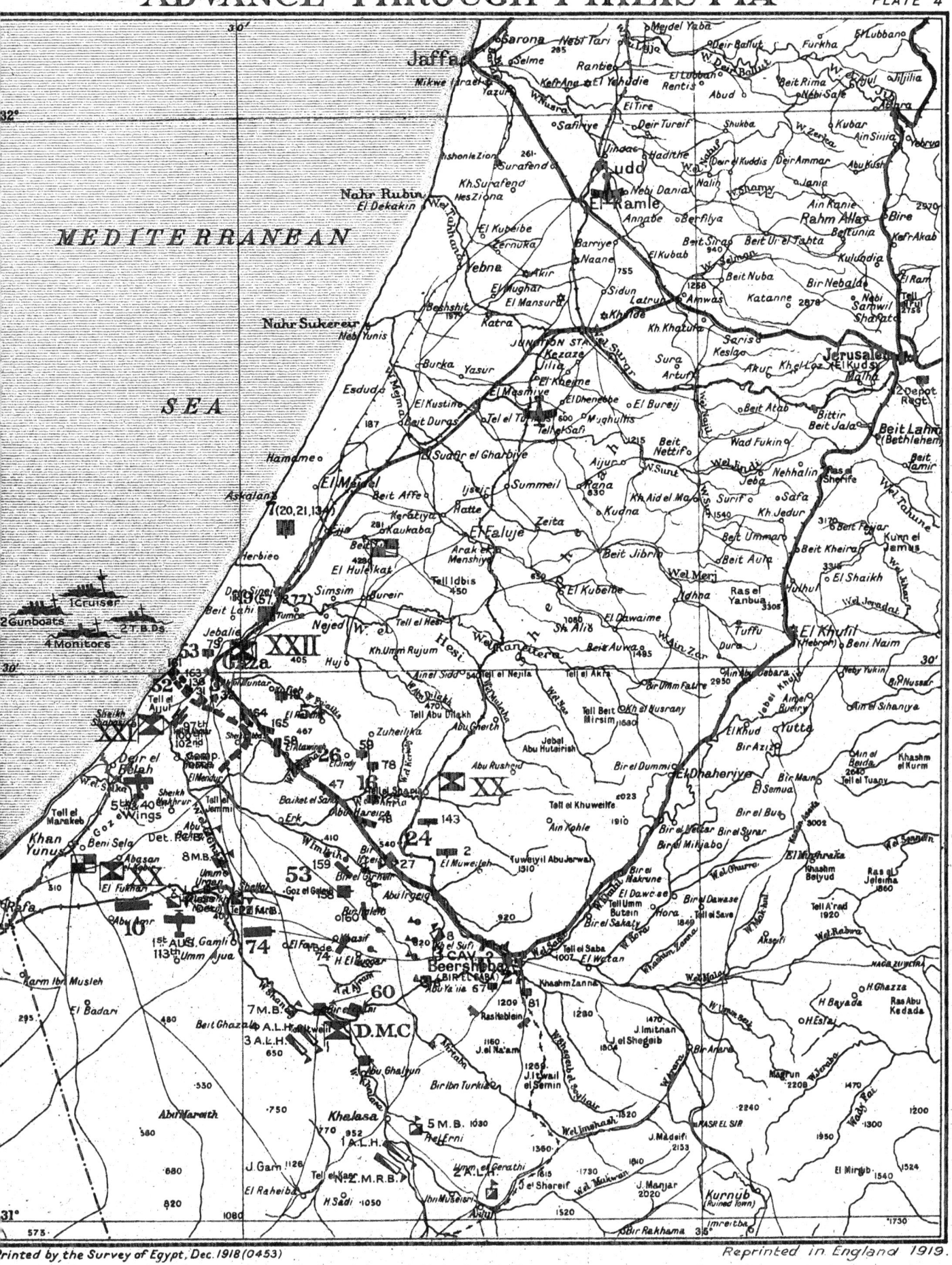

Situation at 6 p.m. on 29-10-17 as known at G.H.Q. E.E.F.

October 30-31.

On the night of Oct. 30-31, the XXth Corps moved forward to positions of deployment, and by dawn was in position ready for the attack. At the same time, the Desert Mounted Corps (less the Yeomanry Mounted Division) moved from its concentration area about Khalasa and Asluj to positions about Khashim Zanna ready to attack Beersheba from the east, in co-operation with the XXth Corps. The moves to the final positions were aided by the bright moon, which rose shortly after sunset.

The plan of attack was for the 60th and 74th Divisions to seize the enemy works between the Khalasa road and the Wadi Saba, while the defences north of the wadi were masked by the Imperial Camel Corps Brigade and two battalions of the 53rd Division. The Anzac Mounted Division, Australian Mounted Division, and 7th Mounted Brigade were to attack the defences of the town from the north-east, east, and south-east.

At 0555 on the morning of Oct. 31, the artillery of the 60th and 74th Divisions commenced to bombard the enemy's positions on a front of some 4,500 yards. Some 100 field guns and howitzers took part in the bombardment, while twenty heavy guns were engaged mainly in counter-battery work. At 0830, the 181st Infantry Brigade advanced to the assault of Point 1070, an advanced enemy work which was captured within ten minutes. The guns now moved forward in order to cut the wire of the enemy's main line of defence, and at 1215 the main assault was launched, the attacking troops from right to left being the 179th, 181st, 231st, and 230th Brigades. By 1330, all objectives had been gained and soon after an outpost line was established.

The enemy was, however, still holding out in his positions north of the Wadi Saba. While a brigade of the 53rd Division threatened these from the west, the 230th Brigade, 74th Division, attacked them from the south at 1900 and found no difficulty in occupying the works, as the enemy had evacuated them during the preliminary bombardment.

Meanwhile, the Anzac Mounted Division reached Bir el Hammam and Bir Salim abu Irgeig, their first objective, with only slight opposition, by about 0800. Resistance now stiffened considerably, but Tel es Sakaty was captured by 1300 by the 2nd Australian Light Horse Brigade and by 1350 this brigade was astride the Hebron road. The strongly held position of Tel es Saba was captured by the New Zealand Mounted Rifles Brigade, assisted by the 1st Australian Light Horse Brigade by 1500. By 1800 the Anzac Mounted Division, plus the 3rd Australian Light Horse Brigade (Australian Mounted Division) attached, reached the line Bir el Hammam–Bir es Sakaty–Point 1020–Point 970.

The Australian Mounted Division reached Iswaiwin by 1100 and at 1600 the 4th Australian Light Horse Brigade moved forward to attack Beersheba. The brigade galloped over successive lines of trenches in the face of severe machine-gun and rifle fire, and succeeded in occupying the town by about 1800.

The 7th Mounted Brigade assisted in turning the defences on Ras Ghannam and reached Beersheba about 1830.

The enemy troops holding Beersheba consisted of the 27th Division, an Arab formation of poor moral, but stiffened by battalions from the 16th and 24th Divisions.

The defence of Beersheba had been entrusted to the IIIrd Corps, and of its tactical handling by its commander, Ismet Bey, the following criticism by a German staff officer is of interest:—

"The battle control of the IIIrd Corps appeared deplorable: even before the commencement of the decisive infantry attack, all reserves had been thrown in."

To face Plate 5.

ADVANCE THROUGH PHILISTIA

PLATE 5

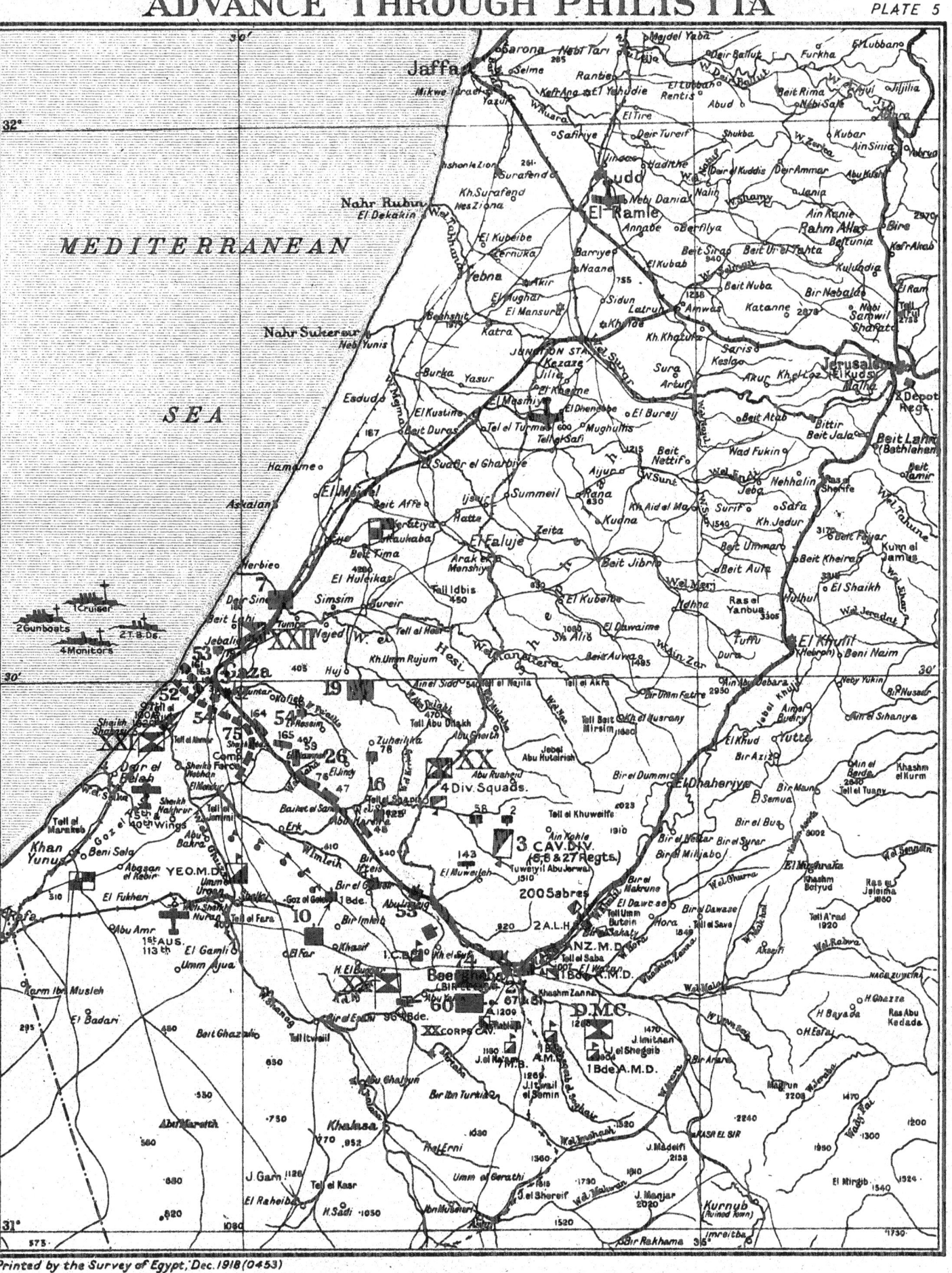

Situation at 6 p.m. on 31-10-17 as known at G.H.Q. E.E.F.

November 1.

After the capture of Beersheba, preparations were at once commenced for the attack on the Kauwukah and Rushdi trench systems covering Tel esh Sheria and Abu Hareira. Accordingly, on the morning of Nov. 1, the 53rd Division, with the Imperial Camel Corps Brigade on its right, moved to Towal abu Jerwal in order to protect the flank of the corps during the coming attack.

The question of water supply for mounted units raised great difficulties, as the surface water remaining after the thunderstorm of Oct. 25 had dried up, and the supply from the Beersheba wells was not equal to the demand. Accordingly, on Nov. 1 the Australian Mounted Division was withdrawn into reserve, and the Anzac Mounted Division advanced, and, after a certain amount of opposition, occupied the line Bir el Marruneh–Towal abu Jerwal, capturing 179 prisoners and four machine guns.

To assist in completing the rout of the Turkish troops retiring from Beersheba, a small mobile force on camels, consisting of Lewis gunners, machine gunners, and a few Sudanese Arab scouts, under Lieut.-Col. S. F. Newcombe, R.E., D.S.O., left Asluj on Oct. 30. It had a number of machine guns and Lewis guns, a large quantity of small arms ammunition, and carried three days' rations. Moving rapidly, it established its headquarters at Yutta, and on Oct. 31 occupied some high ground west of and commanding the road between Dhaheriyeh and Hebron. It was hoped that the Turks retiring by night from Beersheba would encounter this force, which, taking them by surprise, would by its large fire power put them to rout, and cause a general débâcle on the Turkish left wing. However, as the Anzac Mounted Division had cut the road further south, the Turkish forces from Beersheba retired north to Tel esh Sheria. The force, nevertheless, succeeded in intercepting and capturing the motor transport with supplies which was endeavouring to reach Beersheba from Jerusalem.

The Turks were surprised by the appearance of this force, and having no idea of its numbers, despatched the 12th Depôt Regiment from Hebron, and the 143rd Regiment from Tel esh Sheria—six battalions in all—to dislodge it. It held out resolutely, but, after sustaining heavy casualties and having exhausted all its ammunition, was obliged to surrender on Nov. 2 or 3.

ADVANCE THROUGH PHILISTIA

PLATE 6

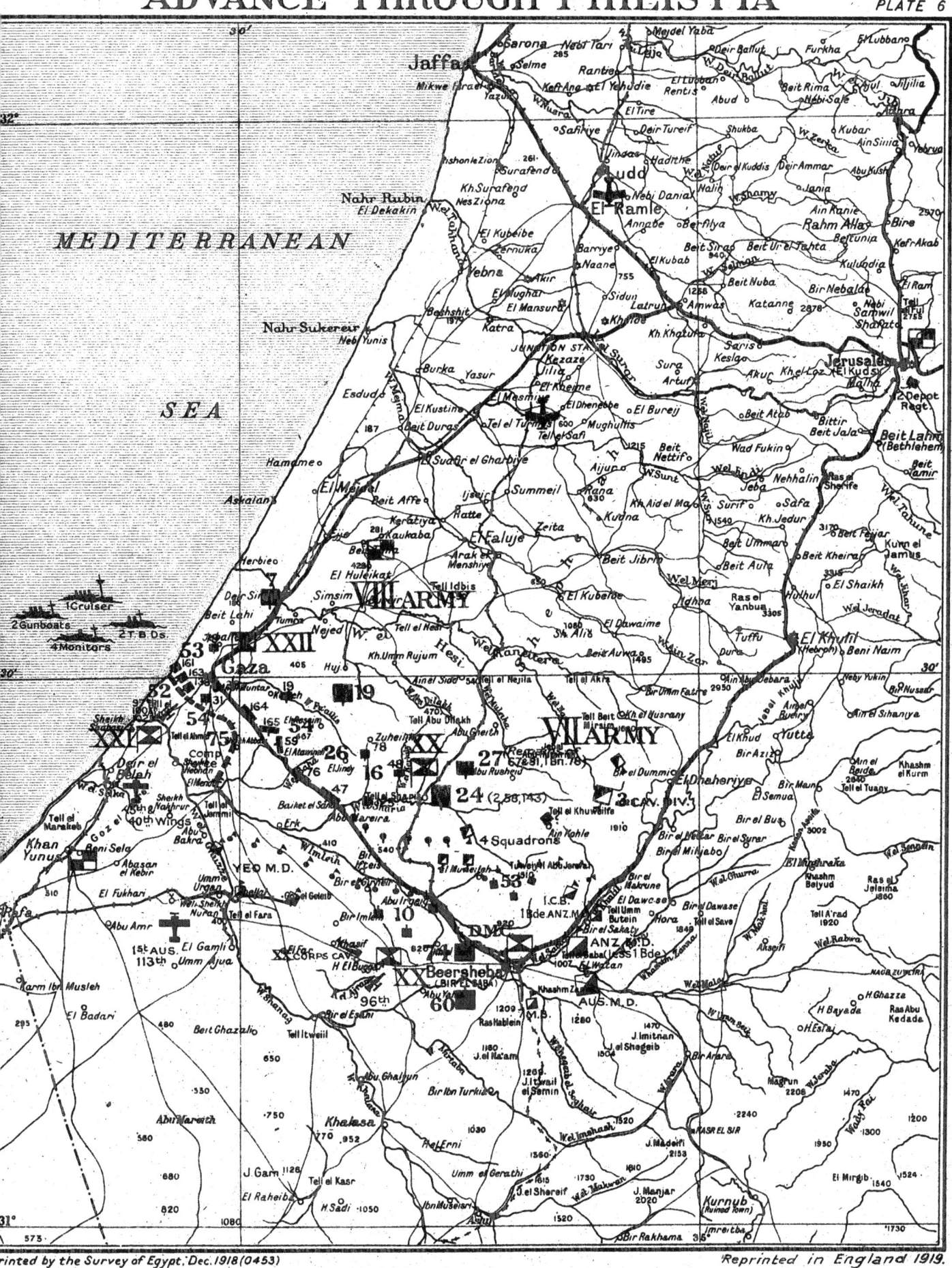

Situation at 6 p.m. on 1-11-17 as known at G.H.Q. E.E.F.

November 2.

The rôle which had been allotted to the XXIst Corps in the operations of Oct.-Nov., 1917, was to pin down as many enemy troops as possible in the coastal sector, and to endeavour to attract his reserves to this neighbourhood. In order to accomplish this, it was decided, while holding the line in sufficient strength, to repulse any attack made by the enemy to relieve the pressure of the Beersheba operations, to attack the works in front of Gaza and, eventually, if possible, to capture the town.

To carry out this plan, it was first of all essential to smash the elaborate system of defences which the enemy had spent the past six months in constructing. Accordingly, on Oct. 27 the bombardment commenced, increasing day by day, and carried out by two 60-pounder batteries, five and a half 6-inch howitzer batteries, one 8-inch howitzer battery and the divisional artillery of the 52nd, 54th, and 75th Divisions. On the 29th the Navy joined in with H.M.S. "Grafton," and H.M.M. 15, 29, 31, and 32. The river gunboats "Ladybird," and "Amphis," and the destroyers "Staunch" and "Comet" also co-operated. The bombardment was highly successful, as prisoners and captured documents testify.

Owing to the great width of " No man's land," averaging 1,000 yards, it was necessary to carry out the attack by night. Accordingly, on the night of Nov. 1–2 at 2300, the 156th Brigade assaulted and captured Umbrella Hill. At 0300 on Nov. 2 the enemy's front-line trenches were treated to an intense bombardment, and the 161st and 162nd Brigades attacked, capturing the whole of the front line system at once. The 163rd Brigade were not so successful in their assault on the support trenches at 0345, meeting with stiff resistance, the 5th Suffolk Regt. alone being able to secure all its objectives. The 162nd Brigade carried on the attack and by 0630 had reached Sheikh Hassan. Six tanks participated in the later parts of the attack, rendering material assistance.

During the afternoon of Nov. 2, the enemy launched three counter-attacks, two on Sheikh Hassan, the first of which was broken up by naval and heavy artillery fire with severe loss to the enemy, and one from the direction of Crested Rock. All were successfully repulsed.

Some 650 prisoners were taken and over 1,000 Turkish dead were buried in the positions. The enemy also lost three guns, one Hotchkiss, twenty-nine machine guns, seven trench mortars, and a large quantity of rifles, ammunition, and stores.

Meanwhile, on the right flank the XXth Corps moved its headquarters to Beersheba. The left of the 53rd Division's line was taken over by the 229th Brigade, while the remainder of the 74th Division moved to the neighbourhood of Point 910. The 10th Division occupied Abu Irgeig without opposition, and was in touch with the 74th Division on the right.

The 2nd Australian Light Horse Brigade and 7th Mounted Brigade advanced towards Dhaheriyeh and the Khuweilfeh area respectively. Stiff opposition was met in very difficult country, but by nightfall the line Bir en Nettar–Deir el Hawa–Ras en Nagb -Point 1580, had been reached, linking up with the Imperial Camel Corps Brigade about one mile NNE. of Towal Abu Jerwal. The position of Ras en Nagb, to which the enemy attached great importance was captured by the 7th Mounted Brigade, which took eleven prisoners and two guns.

To face Plate 7

ADVANCE THROUGH PHILISTIA

PLATE 7.

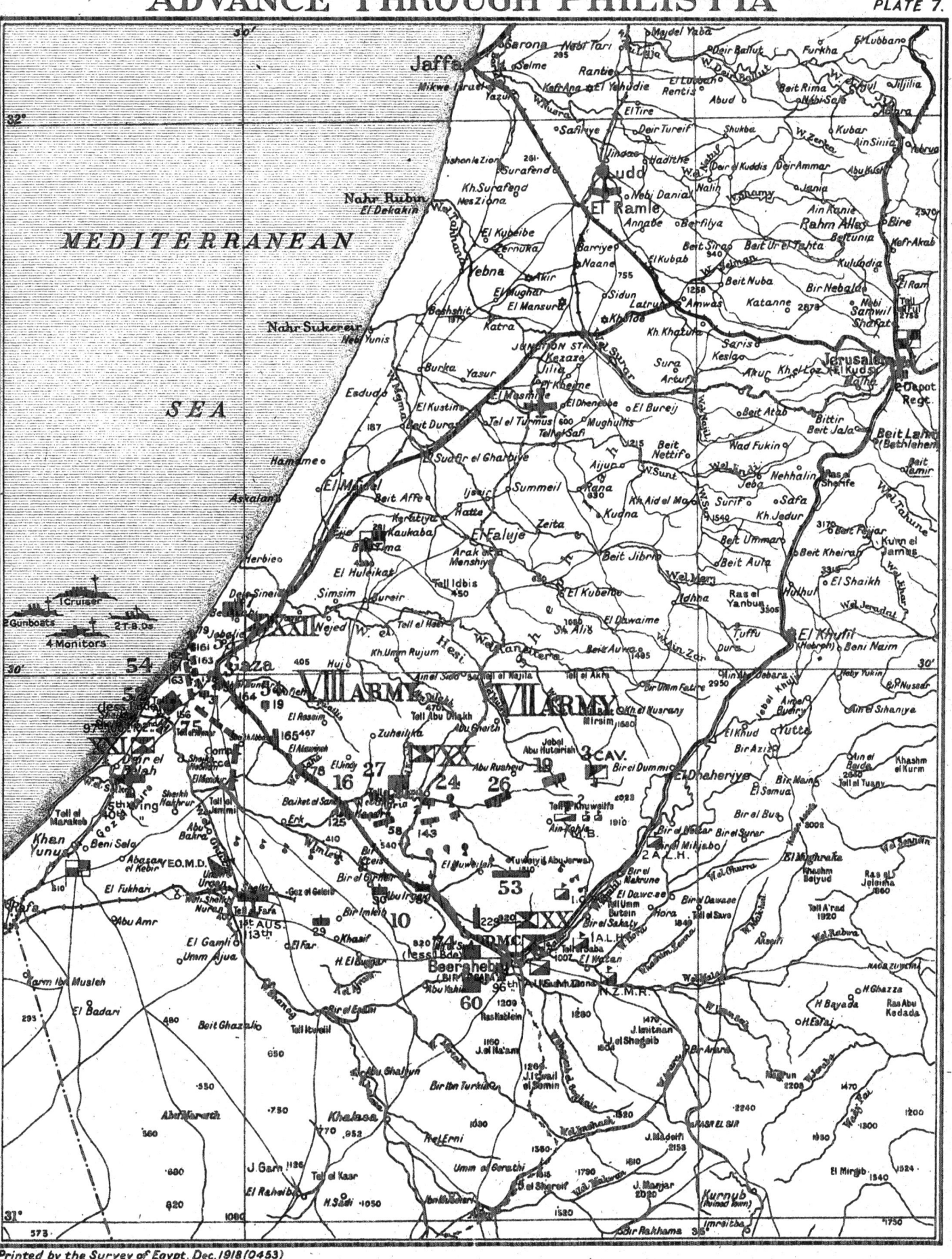

Situation at 6 p.m. on 2-11-17 as known at G.H.Q. E.E.F.

November 3 to 6.

On Nov. 3 the 53rd Division attacked the Khuweilfeh lines but was only able to occupy part of the position in view of the stout resistance made by the enemy who had diverted a considerable proportion of his reserves to this sector of the front. He was by this time probably under the impression that a wide outflanking movement was to be undertaken rather than a break-through. This attack continued day and night against superior forces and the division was at last able to capture Tel el Khuweilfeh on Nov. 6. Once the enemy succeeded in regaining the position with a great counter-attack but was again dislodged with the loss of many hundred prisoners and some guns. There is no doubt that the obstinate fighting of the 53rd Division, which came temporarily under the G.O.C., Desert Mounted Corps from XXth Corps did much to confirm the enemy in his erroneous estimate of our intentions, and by attracting his reserves to the Khuweilfeh area to contribute to the subsequent success of the 10th, 60th, and 74th Divisions at Kauwukah, although such action naturally increased the difficulty of its own attack.

Meanwhile the lack of water in the operations area occupied by our right and right centre made it necessary for the Australian Mounted Division, which had passed into reserve on Nov. 1, to return to Karm for water. The 2nd Australian Light Horse Brigade which was manœuvring against the Turkish 3rd Cavalry Division and his 12th Depôt Regiment in front of Dhaheriyeh, was able to draw sufficient water locally. From this point, the extreme right of our line, there was a good deal of cavalry fighting during these days in which the 5th Mounted, the New Zealand Mounted Rifle, and Imperial Camel Brigades, repulsed determined enemy counter-attacks, inflicting satisfactory losses in the process. The 5th Mounted Brigade was withdrawn to the Tel el Saba area after the first day, when the 2nd Australian Light Horse Brigade came south-west from Dhaheriyeh, and on Nov. 6 the New Zealand Mounted Rifle Brigade also came out of the line. Meanwhile the Yeomanry Division came right round the back of the front from near Shellal on Nov. 3 and during the night of the 5th came into line on the right of the 74th Division two miles south of Ain Kohleh in order to free the infantry for movement into its position for deploying for the Kauwukah operations. The horses were then sent back to Beersheba.

In order to facilitate the operations of Nov. 6 a detachment for the defence of the right flank of the army was formed under Major-General G. de S. Barrow, C.B., consisting of the Imperial Camel Corps Brigade, the 53rd Division, the Yeomanry Mounted Division, the New Zealand Mounted Rifle Brigade, and part of the 2nd Australian Light Horse Brigade. At the same time the 60th Division was temporarily attached to the Desert Mounted Corps which was rejoined by the Australian Mounted Division on its return from Karm to Bir Imleih.

On Nov. 6 at dawn the three infantry divisions, 10th, 60th, and 74th, with the Yeomanry on the extreme right, attacked the series of Kauwukah positions held in strength by the Turkish VIIth Army under Fevzi Pasha. The 74th Division met with obstinate resistance on its extreme right, but was able to capture all its objectives by 1315. Wire cutting was sufficiently far advanced for the attack on the main Kauwukah system to be launched at 1230, and two hours later the 60th and 10th Divisions had broken through. The 60th Division then advanced to Sheria and occupied the station but was much delayed in its further advance by the explosion of a Turkish ammunition depôt at the station which caused a large fire which unduly exposed its movements. In consequence of this the division was unable to cross the Wadi Sheria that night. After the break-through at Kauwukah a Brigade of the 10th Division took over the captured works while the remainder of the division passed into Corps reserve near Samarra Bridge and the 74th Division faced north-east.

To face Plate 8.

ADVANCE THROUGH PHILISTIA

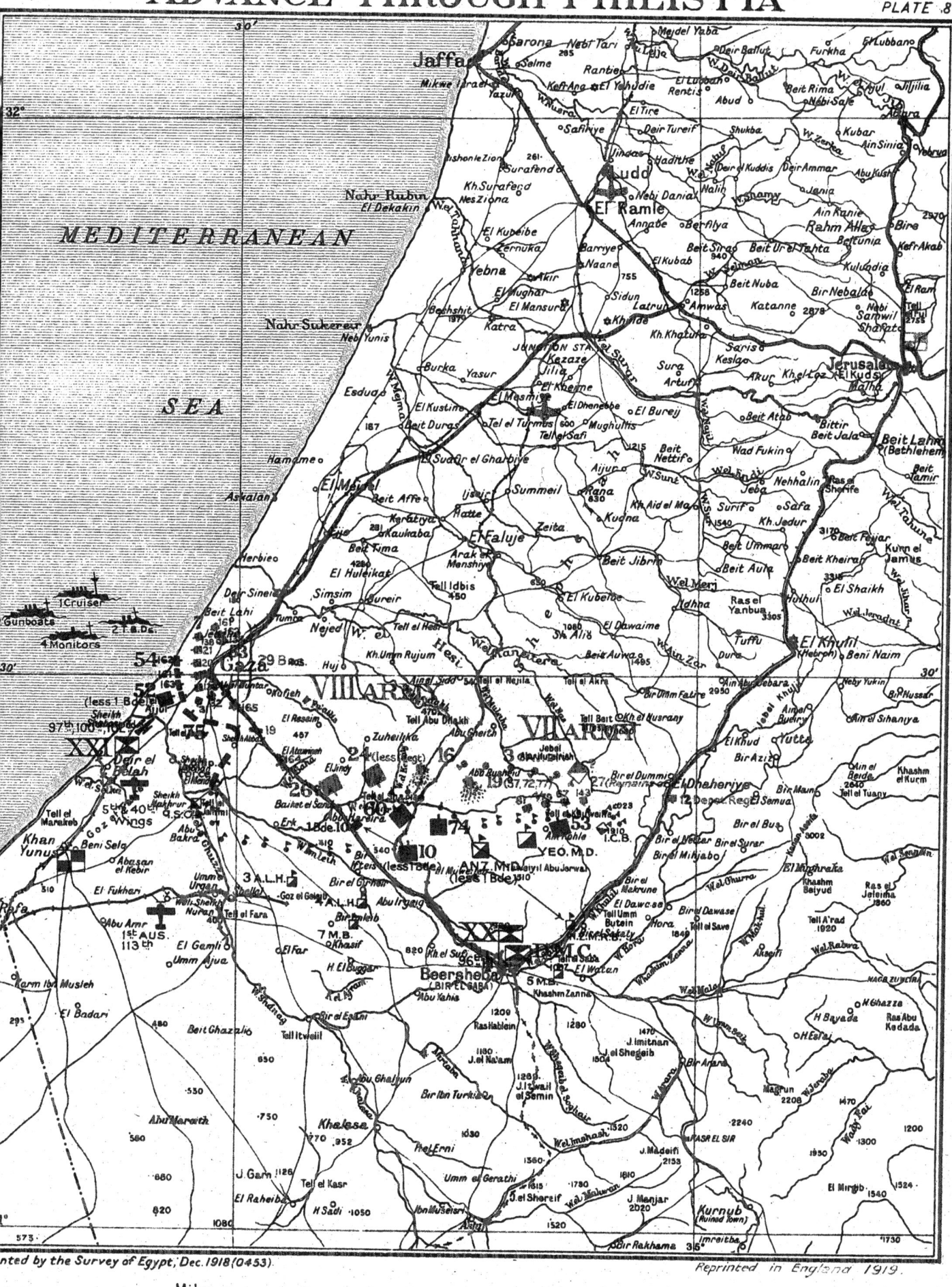

Situation at 6 p.m. on 6-11-17 as known at G.H.Q.E.E.F.

November 7.

On Nov. 7 the main interest shifts to the coastal sector, where the intense bombardment carried out by the Navy and the XXIst Corps on the 5th and 6th, had produced so strong a feeling of unease among the Turks that a considerable part of their forces were carefully withdrawn. To such an extent had this retirement been carried out, that British attacks during the night of Nov. 6–7 on Outpost Hill and Middlesex Hill, met with only half-hearted opposition, and the occupation of Ali Muntar itself was effected by the 75th Division at 0740 without much trouble. A little before this, at 0700, the 54th Division was able to establish a line from Sheikh Redwan to the sea, and two squadrons had passed up the beach at 0630, to push patrols up to the Wadi Hesi. The Imperial Service Cavalry Brigade advanced towards Beit Hanun, after passing right through the ruins of Gaza at 0900. Two brigades of the 52nd Division, withdrawn from the trenches, moved off at 1000 and, after advancing under cover of the cliffs along the beach, seized the high ground on the right bank of the Wadi Hesi, in the face of considerable resistance on the part of the 53rd Turkish Division (Mehmet Salah-ed-Din Bey). The 52nd Division by this move passed behind the 54th and formed the extreme left of the British line.

Gaza itself was found to be in a deplorable condition. Its civilian population had been evacuated and the greater part of the wood-work of the houses, floors, roofs, doors, and fittings, window sashes and shutters, removed to be used either for the revetting of Turkish trenches in the sandy soil, or for firewood. Many trees had been cut down and immense damage effected by the explosions of the Turkish ammunition stored in prominent buildings and detonated by British gun fire. The place was, in consequence, entirely ruinous and destitute of any economic value to the victor. On the other hand, General Allenby was not called upon to make arrangements for the feeding of a large civilian population.

Away on the right, the 10th Division captured the Hareira Tepe redoubt, in face of considerable machine-gun fire, thereby making it possible for a junction to be effected with the extreme right of the XXIst Corps near the Wadi Baha. The intention had been for the Desert Mounted Corps to pass immediately through the gap in the Turkish line made by the three Infantry Divisions at Kauwukah, but the Turks were not yet too disorganized to offer sturdy resistance in places, and the 60th Division had some difficulty in dislodging them from Tell esh Sheria at 0600 as a necessary preliminary to an advance of two miles beyond the Wadi Sheria. This cleared the way finally for the cavalry. Passing through the gap, the 1st Australian Light Horse Brigade captured the station east of Kh. Um Ameidat, four and a half miles north of Tell esh Sheria, with 300 prisoners and much material. The Australian and New Zealand Mounted Division was then engaged with enemy rear-guards and was only able to advance to the positions shown—a distance of two and a half miles—by nightfall. The Australian Mounted Division filled the gap between the advanced cavalry and the 60th Division to the north of the Wadi Sheria. The lack of water in this area was severely felt.

To face Plate 9.

ADVANCE THROUGH PHILISTIA

PLATE 9

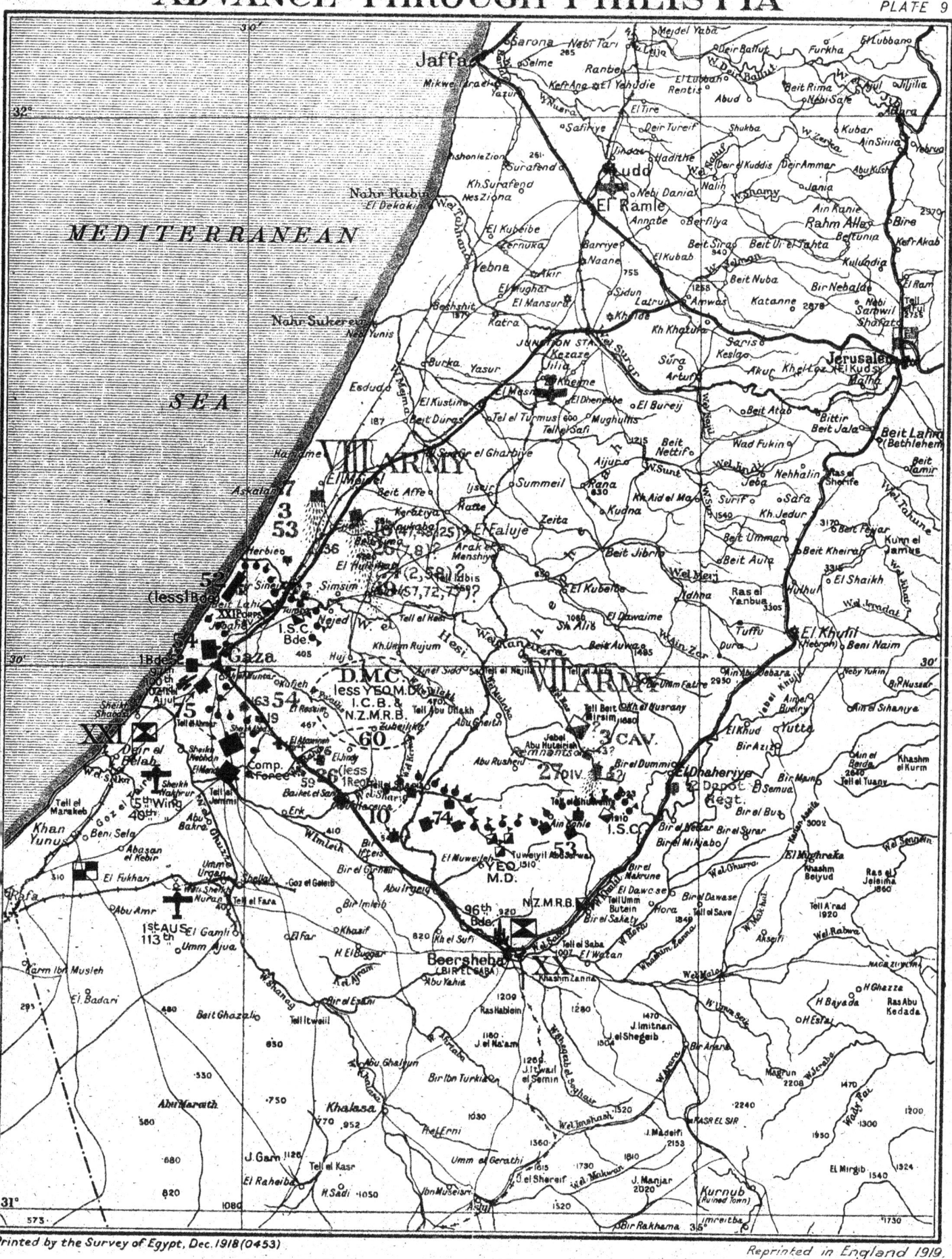

Situation at 6 p.m. on 7-11-17 as known at G.H.Q. E.E.F.

November 8.

The desperate resistance made by the enemy and the lack of water had delayed the Desert Mounted Corps during the few hours required by the Turks to withdraw the greater part of their 26th and 54th Divisions, commanded respectively by Fakhr-ed-Din Bey and Nasuhi Bey, through the gap which still remained between the XXIst Corps at Beit Hanun and the newly-won positions to the west. The Desert Mounted Corps, however, was in bad country and the "break through" after the Battle of Sheria was vastly handicapped by natural as well as human obstacles in comparison with the "break through" after the Battle of Sharon ten months later. During this day, Nov. 8, the Australian and New Zealand Mounted Division fought its way to water at the Wadi Jemmameh, capturing 300 prisoners and two guns. The 7th Mounted Brigade heartily repulsed a Turkish counter-attack near Tell Hudeiwe, while the Australian Mounted Division came up on the left and occupied a line from Umm Rujum to the north side of Huj, which, with its large accumulations of ammunition was occupied by the 60th Division after an advance of ten miles, during which the enemy had been defeated in three successive rearguard actions. In one of these at 1500 ten troops of 1/1st Worcester and 1/1st Warwick Yeomanry of the 5th Mounted Brigade (Australian Mounted Division) charged a detachment of Turks holding a position one mile west of Huj, with complete success in spite of the stout resistance of the enemy who served his guns until the last moment. Further west the 4th Australian Light Horse Brigade got into touch with the XXIst Corps at Beit Hanun.

Meanwhile the XXIst Corps had been actively pushing forward, and the 75th Division was able to link up with the 10th after occupying the Beer Trenches, Tank Redoubt, and Atawineh, which had been found to be lightly held by the enemy, by patrols from the Composite Force, early in the morning. In the afternoon the Composite Force relieved the 75th Division which moved on the 9th to Beit Hanun. Here the Imperial Service Cavalry Brigade had established itself, after considerable difficulty, on the ridge to the east whence it was able to link up with the 4th Australian Light Horse Brigade, and then pursue the enemy to Tumrah and Deir Sineid. Between the cavalry and sea the 52nd Division continued to advance, toiling in heavy sand, and opposed strongly by the Turks, who made a formidable counter-attack from the direction of Ascalon. Four times did the enemy drive the Lowlanders off the high ground north-west of Deir Sineid only to lose it once more and find our men arrayed a fifth time against them on the top of the hill.

This sweeping advance on nearly the whole front appears to have contributed much to the breakdown of the Turkish moral. In places the enemy was still dangerous and made sturdy resistance but many of his people became increasingly anxious to remove themselves from the unpleasant vicinity of the front. This frame of mind betrayed itself in the behaviour of certain units, and aerial reports gave warning that the enemy was becoming disorganized.

To face Plate 10.

ADVANCE THROUGH PHILISTIA

PLATE 10

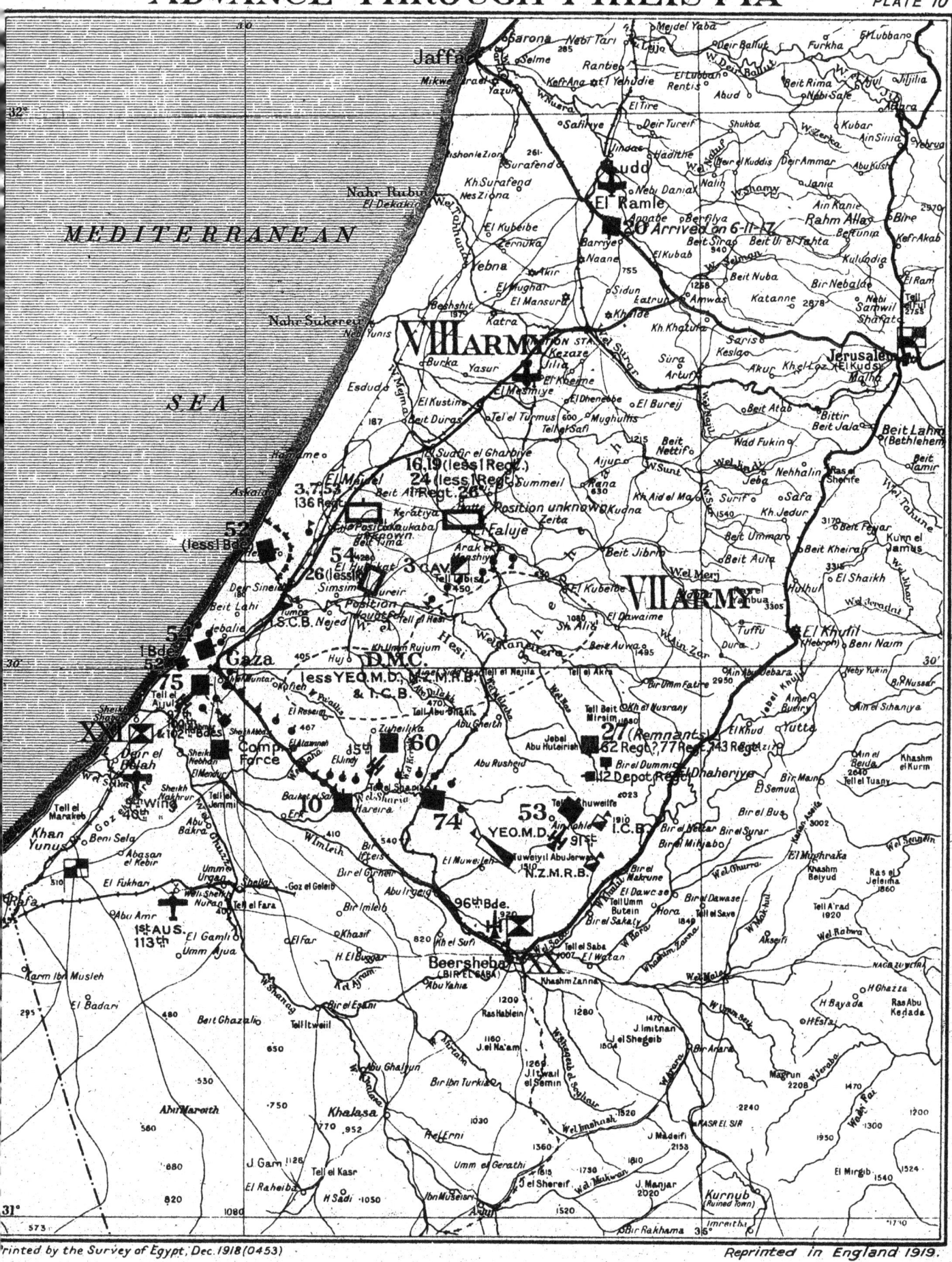

Situation at 6 p.m. on 8-11-17 as known at G.H.Q. E.E.F.

November 9.

On this day the 52nd Division continued its advance, and by noon had occupied the line Deir Sineid–Beit Jerjah–Ascalon. At 1400 Hamame, the northern point of the Mejdel oasis among the sand dunes, was reached, and the cavalry located the Turkish rearguard at 1830 in the Suafir group of villages about seven miles away. During the night the 75th Division arrived at Deir Sineid and the Imperial Service Cavalry returned to the Gaza area. Further inland the cavalry was beginning to feel the want of water. The Yeomanry Division, which had been engaged on the previous day in the pursuit of the enemy retreating on Hebron, had been called across to the more important front and rejoined the Desert Mounted Corps at Huj, where it was delayed in consequence of the difficulties in watering described in para. 13 of No. 1 Despatch. The same cause prevented the Australian Mounted Division from moving far, and only the Australian and New Zealand Mounted Division with the 7th Mounted Brigade could advance. By night they had reached the line Arak–El Menshiye–Suafir esh Sherkiye–Beit Duras, and were close up to the Turkish main rearguard, in advance of the positions shewn on the map which are those reported up to 1800 at General Headquarters.

To face Plate 11.

ADVANCE THROUGH PHILISTIA

PLATE 11.

Situation at 6 p.m. on 9-11-17 as known at G.H.Q. E.E.F.

November 10.

A *khamsin*, or *sciroque*, as it is often called in Palestine, began to blow on Nov. 10, lasting two days. This hot wind was an additional trial to all troops, particularly to the cavalry already suffering from water-shortage. The Australian and New Zealand Division, however, was able to capture Esdud, the Ashdod of the Philistines, and its bridgehead before being brought to a halt owing to the water difficulty. During the previous night the Australian Mounted Division had marched north-east from Huj *viâ* Tell el Hesi (the Lachish of the *Old Testament*), and linked up on the right of the line at Arak el Menshiye on Nov. 10. It was joined soon afterwards by the Yeomanry Division which had left Huj early in the morning. Thus, with the exception of the New Zealand Mounted Rifle Brigade and the Imperial Service Cavalry Brigade, the whole Desert Mounted Corps was now in position for further pursuit across the open country of Philistia and the foothills, after having captured over 1,000 prisoners and sixteen guns in the two days. During the day the 52nd Division moved into the Esdud–Mejdel–Herbiah area, and the 157th Brigade engaged the enemy north of Beit Duras, capturing the position and three machine guns with a bayonet charge in spite of having already marched fourteen miles over heavy sand in a *khamsin*.

The 75th Division advanced into the Es Suafir–Julis–Burberah–Beit Jerjah area, and the 10th and 60th Divisions (which latter rejoined the XXth Corps) began to fall back on Karm and the railway to facilitate supply work. The 54th Division, at Gaza, gave up all its transport to assist in the forward move, and was able to maintain itself without transport on a supply of five days' rations in depôts close at hand.

To face Plate 12.

ADVANCE THROUGH PHILISTIA

PLATE 12

Situation at 6 p.m. on 10-11-17 as known at G.H.Q. E.E.F.

November 11 and 12.

During these two days XXIst Corps Advanced Headquarters moved up to Deir Sineid (Nov. 11) and two important actions were fought on the banks of the Nahr Sukereir. In one of these, the 1st Australian Light Horse Brigade drove back the enemy, forced the passage of the stream, and captured Tel el Murre. This was an important step towards securing control of the mouth of the river, which was afterwards most useful as a temporary landing-place for stores. In the other the 52nd Division, with two battalions of the 75th Division, the 1st Australian Light Horse Brigade, and the 8th Mounted Brigade, assaulted and captured Burkah, in spite of determined resistance and a strong counter-attack. On the right of the 75th Division, the Australian Mounted Division, after hard fighting succeeded in advancing as far as Berkusie on a general line running south-eastwards to Zeita ; but under pressure of a determined counter-attack by an enemy force, estimated at 5,000 men of the 19th and 53rd Turkish Divisions (commanded by Sedad Bey and Mehmet Salah ed Din Bey respectively), the cavalry had to retire two or three miles to Arak el Mensbiye and Summeil.

During the night of the 12th, the 1st Australian Light Horse Brigade was relieved by the Yeomanry Mounted Division, which had been brought right across from one end of the line to the other, by way of Mejdel, and now took over the country to the north of the mouth of the Nahr el Sukerier, advancing almost to Tell el Kharrube and Beshshit. The New Zealand Mounted Rifles had now rejoined the division, which was also reinforced by the Imperial Camel Corps Brigade, which had rejoined the Desert Mounted Corps at Julis on Nov. 11. Owing to the exhaustion of their horses on account of the lack of water, the 7th Mounted and the 2nd Australian Light Horse Brigades had to be withdrawn into corps reserve.

The enemy was beginning to show signs of recovery and made efforts to reconstruct his line of resistance, and make a front in hopes of maintaining control of the lateral line of communications along the railway from Ludd to Jerusalem. This is clearly shewn on the map, and the importance of a further advance before the line could harden into a prepared front, is obvious.

To face Plate 13.

ADVANCE THROUGH PHILISTIA

PLATE 13

Situation at 6 p.m. on 11-11-17 as known at G.H.Q. E.E.F.

November 13.

Up to the evening of Nov. 12 the advance of XXIst Corps had been northward, but on the morning of Nov. 13 it was necessary for the proper execution of the Commander-in-Chief's plans to advance eastward. The 52nd Division on the left flank was thrown well forward and the 75th Division wheeled on its right. To guard the northern flank of the troops advancing eastward, two battalions and a battery of Royal Field Artillery occupied Yebna (the Jamnia of the *New Testament* period, the Ibelin of the Crusades) which had been captured at 1100 by the Yeomanry and Imperial Camel Corps. A similar force was subsequently detailed to hold the high ground north of Mughar, and one battalion and a battery of Royal Field Artillery held Akir after its capture early next morning. All these detachments were furnished by the 52nd Division until the arrival of the 54th Division several days later.

The enemy position on the ridge to the north-east of El Mughar was captured by infantry of the 52nd Division and the 6th Mounted Brigade of the Yeomanry Division. The attack had to pass over 4,500 yards of open ground near Katrah. It was entirely successful and resulted in the capture of 1,096 prisoners, two guns, and fourteen machine guns. Over 400 dead Turks were counted in one field. The village of El Mughar itself was captured in the evening by two squadrons of the 1/1st Berkshire Yeomanry who entered the village on foot and took 400 prisoners. The 75th Division had a good deal of trouble with the Turks along the line from Mesmiyeh to Kh. Sallujeh. The 232nd Brigade, advancing through Yasur, was engaged on the left, while the 233rd, advancing just to the north of Kustine, was engaged on the right. This brigade finally stormed Mesmiyeh from the south, and the division took 292 prisoners and seven machine guns. The 234th Brigade then came through in the centre as far as Kh. el Mugharah on the railway, where it was strongly counter-attacked during the night by the Turks covering Junction Station less than two miles distant. The 6th Mounted Brigade operating towards Akir captured seventy-two prisoners, one gun and two machine guns. XXIst Corps advanced headquarters moved up to a point near Beit Duras.

To face Plate 14.

ADVANCE THROUGH PHILISTIA

PLATE 14

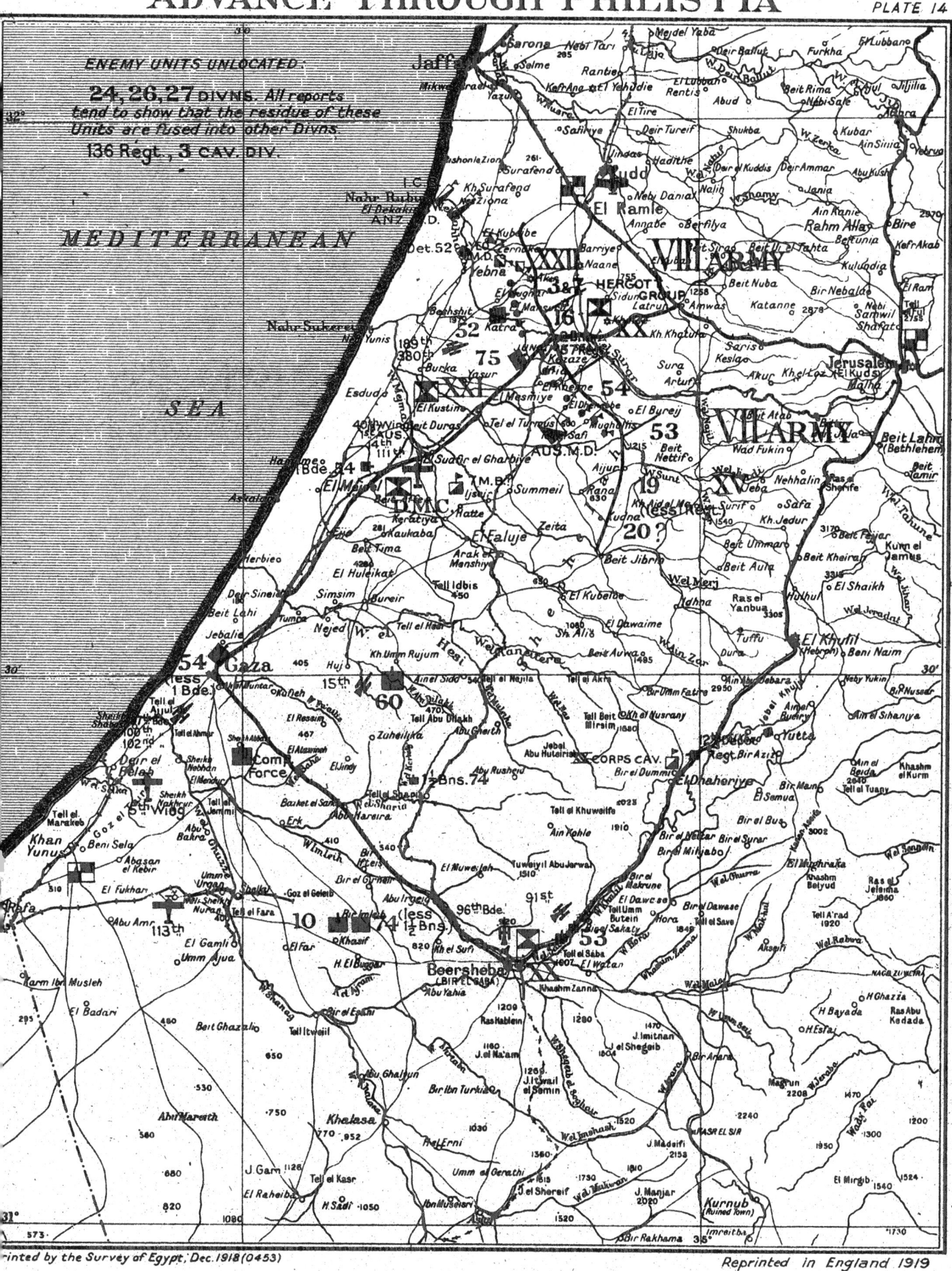

Situation at 6 p.m. on 13-11-17 as known at G.H.Q. E.E.F.

November 14.

At 0400 on Nov. 14 the 234th Brigade of the 75th Division had seized the high ground west of Junction Station, and at 0730 the station itself was captured with 100 prisoners, two guns, two undamaged locomotives, and much rolling stock. Two armoured cars of No. 12 Light Armoured Motor Battery co-operated very effectively in the capture of the station, inflicting some 200 casualties upon the enemy. At 0900 the 52nd Division captured Mansura two miles further north, and the 22nd Mounted Brigade of the Yeomanry Division drove the enemy from Akir and captured Naane, another two miles to the north, with seventy-two prisoners and one machine gun. Further north again the Australian and New Zealand Mounted Division reached the outskirts of Ramleh and the ridges north of Surafend by noon. Here the New Zealand Mounted Rifles were vigorously counter-attacked by the enemy who approached to within bombing distance and had to be discomfited with a bayonet charge. The headquarters of the Desert Mounted Corps moved up to a point near Yebna.

To face Plate 15

ADVANCE INTO JUDAEA

PLATE 15

Situation at 6 p.m. mon 14-11-17 as known at G.H.Q. E.E.F.

November 15 and 16.

On Nov. 15 the 75th Division had occupied the high ground east of Junction Station and next day advanced to the line Kezaze Khulde and Abu Shusheh where, on Nov. 15, the Yeomanry Division and part of the Imperial Camel Corps had had a very satisfactory engagement. The enemy was driven back on Amwas leaving 400 dead and 360 prisoners, in addition to another ninety captured as the yeomanry passed near Ramleh in their advance. Ramleh itself, and Ludd, were taken by the 1st Australian Light Horse Brigade on the same day with 360 prisoners. After this the section of the Imperial Camel Corps engaged at Abu Shusheh moved off to rejoin the other section which was operating among the sand dunes in the Jaffa area. The Australian Mounted Division advanced close up to Latron which was still held by the Turks after their defeat at Abu Shusheh, and on the north front the New Zealand Mounted Rifles occupied Jaffa at noon Nov. 16 without opposition, and Kefr Ana, while the rest of the division kept in touch with the yeomanry in the Ramleh–Ludd area.

During these two days the break up of the enemy forces into two widely separated bodies begins to be strongly marked. The VIIth Army was being shepherded up into the hill-country of Judæa along the dead end of a narrow gauge railway to a position of immense natural strength, but hampered by the lack of good communications with his base—all his transport being of necessity confined to the roads from Jerusalem through Nablus to the railway at Messudiyeh some forty miles away, or through the Jordan Valley to the railway at Amman, a difficult journey of about sixty miles. The other body, formed by the VIIIth Army was being driven out of Philistia into the plain of Sharon, but it was able to keep astride of its railway and had hopes of being able to take refuge behind the Nahr el Auja.

Meanwhile, the 54th Division had begun to move north from Gaza, and to make this move possible it was necessary for the transport borrowed from this division to be sent back. This greatly increased the difficulty of supplying the troops at the front, as railhead, in spite of the energetic work on the railway, was still a long way off.

Up in the hills to the north of Beersheba the Turks, under the tactical pressure of the advance along the coast, saw fit to withdraw from Dhaheriyeh to the Hebron area.

November 17 and 18.

The weather had been unusually hot and the dust and *khamsin* added greatly to the trials of the troops and animals, who were also much distressed by the shortage of water. This was accentuated by the practice of the enemy in doing his best to destroy the small and very deep wells of the area through which he had been retreating. Owing to the loss of transport caused by the return of the 54th Divisional Train to its own division, it became necessary to rearrange the transport, and this, together with the desirability of resting the troops for a few hours, made a day's halt almost necessary. The Commander-in-Chief held a conference at XXIst Corps advanced headquarters on Nov. 18, and orders were issued in obedience to which the 52nd Division moved to Ludd during the afternoon while the 54th Division, which had now come up from Gaza, moved up a Brigade from Kustineh to Beshshit and occupied Yebna. The 234th Brigade of the 75th Division covered Junction Station, while the rest of the division prepared to advance towards Latron.

Meanwhile the cavalry had advanced a little across open country occupying Sarona, Mulebbis, and Wilhelma without opposition. They came in contact with the enemy at Rantieh and held the line Nahr el Auja–Beit Nabala–El Yehudieh–Point 265–Jerisheh. On the afternoon of Nov. 18 the Australian Mounted Division executed an outflanking movement which compelled the Turks to evacuate Amwas and Latron during the night, and the Yeomanry Division forced its way into the hills to within two miles of Lower Bethhoron (Beit ur et Tahta). At 1630 the 22nd Mounted Brigade reached Shilta, but the 13-pdr. battery and all wheels had to be sent back owing to difficulties of country.

In the XXth Corps area, Advanced Corps Headquarters on Nov. 18 moved to the Red House on the Wadi Ghuzze. On the same day the 60th Division concentrated at Gaza preparatory to a further move forward, while the 10th and 74th Divisions moved to areas north of Deir el Belah.

To face Plate 17.

November 19.

When the fresh advance approached the hills, on Nov. 19, the 75th Division encountered considerable opposition east of Amwas and Latron, which had been occupied by the 232nd Brigade at noon. The main road to Jerusalem begins to rise at this point and enters narrow defiles flanked by precipitous and rock-strewn heights. On these the enemy had constructed a series of defences commanding all approaches. Our artillery had few positions from which the infantry could be assisted, but the available few were utilized to the utmost and the advance of the division was pressed forward. The experience of the Gurkhas and Indian Frontier troops in mountain warfare, was of great value during these operations. As the road had been destroyed by the Turks in several places, the problem of getting the guns up the pass was one of considerable difficulty, the more so as heavy rain had set in. This downpour, accompanied as it was by a considerable drop in temperature, was a severe trial for troops in summer clothing without greatcoats or blankets, who had, until a few hours before, been suffering from excessive heat. In spite of it the troops worked splendidly and took such rest as was possible in the rain among the rocks. Meanwhile the 52nd Division had advanced on a roughly parallel line along the Beit Likia road, where the badness of the track only permitted three sections of artillery to be brought up, and even these had to be double-horsed with the teams of the sections left at Ramleh.

In the Bethhoron area the 8th Mounted Brigade occupied Tahta at an early hour and then advanced through the Wadi Sunt where it met with opposition from some 400 Turks on the heights. The going here was extremely bad and later became impassable for horses. As advance in this direction was not possible the brigade held its position until the 6th Mounted Brigade could turn the enemy's flank by way of Beit ur el Foka. This brigade, with divisional headquarters, one battery of 13-pdrs., and the Hong-Kong and Singapore battery, reached Tahta at 1400, but the road difficulties were very great as the Roman road had deteriorated almost out of existence. Even greater difficulties were experienced by the 22nd Mounted Brigade, which, with one section of the Hong-Kong and Singapore battery struggled part of the way to Ain Arik, where but little enemy opposition was experienced.

On the plain the Australian and New Zealand Division sent patrols into Rantieh and located the enemy in occupation of redoubts at Nebi Tari and entrenched north of Hadrah on the Nahr el Auja.

On this day the 60th Division started north from the Gaza area.

To face Plate 18.

ADVANCE INTO JUDÆA

PLATE 18.

Situation at 6 p.m. on 19-11-17 as known at G.H.Q. E.E.F.

November 20 and 21.

On Nov. 20 the advance was continued against a very determined resistance on the precipitous slopes above Saris. The village itself, standing on a steep hill, was strongly held and was not stormed until 1415. The enemy left many dead among the rocks, and over fifty prisoners, including a battalion commander, were taken. The remainder of the Turkish force, estimated at a minimum of 2,000 rifles with many machine guns, covered by light guns, retired to the commanding ridge protecting Kuryet el Enab, being satisfactorily shelled by 4·5 howitzers from the road below the Makam Imam Ali during their retreat. The capture of such a position might well have cost the division dear had not a providential fog rolled up, which enveloped the Turkish lines while the attacking force was deploying. Under cover of this at 1700 the 2/3rd Gurkhas, the 1/5th Somersets and the 1/4th Wilts (232nd and 233rd Brigades) attacked with the bayonet, and listeners were able to deduce what was happening from the different timbre of the cheering which came back through the fog. By 1800 the Turks had lost Kuryet el Enab, and the division had seized the whole of the enemy's positions and bivouacked for the night in pouring rain. Next day Kustal and Soba were captured after some opposition had been overcome, by the 232nd and 234th Brigades respectively. During the advance along the crest of the ridge towards Biddu and Kubeibeh the Turkish small arm and artillery fire from Nebi Samwil (Mizpah of the *Old Testament*, Montjoye of the Crusaders) caused much annoyance. A separate attack, supported by the guns at Kuryet el Enab, was made on this position, and by 2345 Nebi Samwil was taken by the 234th Brigade, with the 3/3rd Gurkhas and the 2/4th Hants attached. The 75th Division had thus reached the furthest point of King Richard's advance in Jan., 1192. Reinforcements had been sent up by the 52nd Division and every effort was being made to make a track good enough for the guns to advance from Likia to Kubeibeh (four and a quarter miles).

Some three miles to the south, on the right of the 75th Division, the 5th Mounted Brigade of the Australian Division advanced astride of the railway up the narrow valley of Sorek (Wadi es Surar).

The 52nd Division had advanced as far as Beit Anan and Beit Dukku, three and four miles further north, while keeping a strong force at Beit Likia.

To the north of the 52nd Division the yeomanry in the Bethhoron country were being held up alike by the difficulties of the terrain and the tenacity of the Turks. The badness of the country along the left of this division's line of advance was in itself a protection, and the Turks refrained from attempting an attack from the north, but shewed great obstinacy on the ridges between Upper Bethhoron (Beit ur el Foka) and Beituna to within half a mile of which the 6th Mounted Brigade was able to advance before it was held up at 1100 by a force of over 3,000 Turks with four batteries of ·77s and some camel guns. In spite of the arrival of two regiments of the 8th Mounted Brigade at 1145 and one from the 22nd at 1400, the yeomanry found that further advance was impossible, and when the Turks were reinforced at 1600 and out-ranged our mountain guns there was nothing for it but to retreat to Beit ur el Foka, an operation which began at 1930 and was successfully covered by the 8th Mounted Brigade. The 22nd Mounted Brigade during the day was engaged near Ram Allah.

In the plain the 60th Division arrived in the Mejdel area and the 54th Division was lent to the Desert Mounted Corps for the defence of the Ludd–Jaffa line, in front of which cavalry patrols rode up to Rentis, Shukba, and Shebtin. The enemy still held the high land at Deir el Kuddis in this region as well as the northern bank of the Nahr el Auja.

By this date the moral ascendancy of the British had reached such a pitch that the following remarks occur in a letter written by a German staff officer on Nov. 21:—

"We have had a very bad time. After having had to relinquish good positions which had been held for so long, the breakdown of the army is greater than ever I could have imagined. But for this complete dissolution, we should still be able to make a good stand at Jerusalem—now the VIIth Army bolts from any cavalry patrol."

ADVANCE INTO JUDÆA

PLATE 19

Situation at 6 p.m. on 21.11.17 as known at G.H.Q. E.E.F.

November 22-24.

The Turkish VIIth Army on Nov. 22 tried to recover some of the ground which it had lost, and launched in succession three formidable but fruitless counter-attacks on Nebi Samwil. On the other hand, the enemy so strongly opposed our attack on El Jib that he was able to retain that position, although he lost Beit Izza to the 52nd Division. Next day the 75th Division made another attempt to take El Jib, supported by all available guns, but the enemy was in such strength, and his artillery and machine-gun fire so formidable, that no progress could be made. The 52nd Division relieved the 75th during the night and began a fresh attack on the morning of Nov. 24. Simultaneously, the northern end of the ridge was also attacked, the Yeomanry Division made a demonstration towards Beitunia and a brigade was pushed forward against the high land north-west of El Jib. The third assault had no better result than its predecessors and it became apparent that cold and casualties had, for the moment, enabled the Turks to bring the advance to a standstill within sight of Jerusalem. In consequence of this the 60th Division next day relieved the 75th Division from Soba northwards, while the 52nd Division was directed to discontinue the attack. The 60th Division had arrived at Junction Station on Nov. 22, where it was attached to the XXIst Corps and then proceeded to Latron.

The 5th Mounted Brigade, having the 10th Australian Light Horse regiment attached during these three days, moved up to Artuf on the 23rd and sent strong patrols as far as Ain Karim and Bittir next day. The 8th and 22nd Mounted Brigades successfully withdrew to Tahta during Nov. 22 and next day, owing to the difficulty of getting water and supplies, many horses were sent down to Ramleh. The Yeomanry Division on this day was attached to XXIst Corps and got into touch with the infantry east of Dukka on occupying Et Tire.

In the lower foothills the 7th Mounted Brigade on Nov. 22 entered Belain, Deir el Kuddis, and Shukbah without opposition, and the Turks were found to have fallen back to Abud. Next day this brigade, on being relieved along the line Sheikh el Gharbawy-Kh. Harmush by the 54th Division, withdrew to Zernukah into corps reserve. The Desert Mounted Corps was now holding the line Kh. Midieh-Kh. Harmush-Haditheh-El Yehudiyeh-Point 265-Birket el Jamus-Sheikh Abd en Neby, and the redistribution of troops shewn on the map was completed by the morning of the 24th, when the Australian and New Zealand Mounted Division, supported by two companies of infantry, crossed the Nahr el Auja and occupied a line covering Kh. Hadrah and Sheikh Muannis.

Meanwhile XXth Corps advanced headquarters had moved to Junction Station, and the 74th Division started north from Deir el Belah on 23rd, reaching Gaza on the afternoon of the next day. Patrols from Mott's detachment on the 24th established the fact that Ed Dhaheriyeh had been evacuated by the enemy.

To face Plate 20.

ADVANCE INTO JUDÆA

PLATE 20.

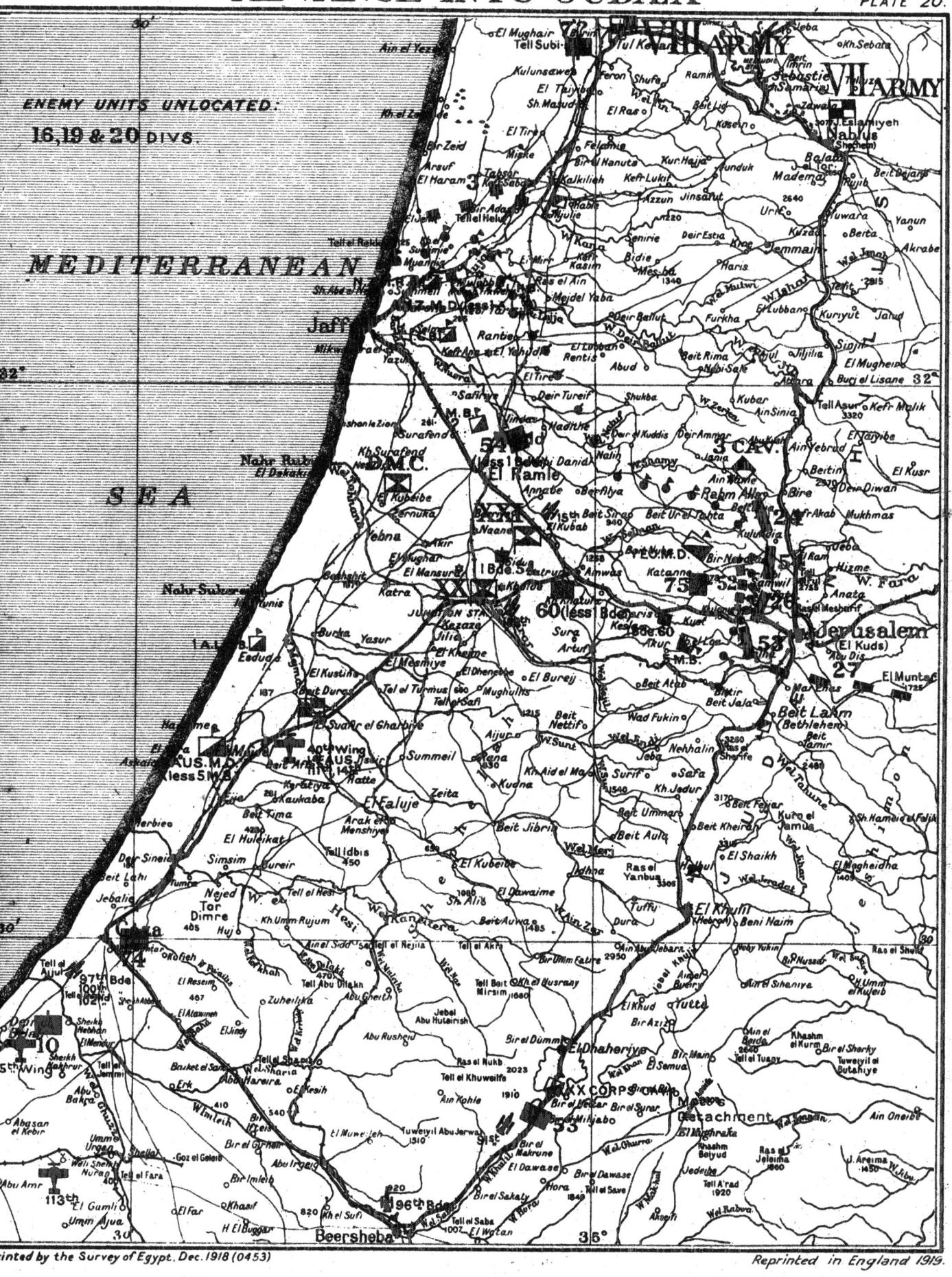

Situation at 6 p.m. on 24-11-17 as known at G.H.Q. E.E.F.

November 25.

The enemy almost at once replied to the advance across the Auja. At 0300 he attacked Kh. Hadrah and by 0800 the position could no longer be held. The infantry retired across the river and two companies of infantry in support on the south bank suffered considerably while covering the withdrawal, as they had no artillery to help them. The Auckland Mounted Rifles remained until the infantry had crossed, and then withdrew behind Sheikh Muannis, while a detachment of the N.Z.M.R. Brigade Machine Gun Squadron crossed at Kh. Hadrah bridge. During the morning the enemy, who was in some strength, also recovered Sheikh Muannis, and the rest of our people had to retire to their original line, in course of which the cavalry had to gallop the ford over the bar at the mouth of the Nahr el Auja. As a measure of precaution the 7th Mounted Brigade was brought five miles north to Rishon le Zion for a night, but the Turks were content with having recovered the line of the Auja and made no attempt to do anything more.

On the mountain front the enemy shelled Biddu and Nebi Samwil and attempted to attack Beit Izza with 300 men, but nothing came of it, and the Turks, who were quite as exhausted as the two British divisions on that front, were otherwise quiescent, except for their activity in digging-in, an operation in which they were compulsorily assisted by drafts from the local population. In the Bethhoron area at 1400 about 200 Turks with machine guns were engaged by the Leicester Battery near Foka and the Stafford Yeomanry near Kh. Meita. Their advance was checked and an attack made at 1600 was broken up. Yeomanry Divisional Headquarters was established at Beit Ur et Tahta.

The 74th Division, hurrying up from the south, reached the Mejdel area.

To face Plate 21.

ADVANCE INTO JUDÆA

Situation at 6 p.m. on 25.11.17 as known at G.H.Q. E.E.F.

November 26 and 27.

During these two days the 60th Division relieved the 75th and the 52nd Divisions on the mountain front. The 75th withdrew down the pass to Latron and the 52nd began to move over into the Beth-horon area. Apart from shelling there was no enemy activity on this part of the front. In the plain, however, on the 27th the enemy reinforced the garrison of Ferrekiyeh and the defences of the bridge across the Auja were improved. One battalion of the enemy was reported by the Australian and New Zealand Division to be advancing towards Mulebbis and another down the narrow gauge railway to Rantieh. In addition to this a number of Turks were seen digging in between Et Tireh and Rantieh and a detachment with machine guns advanced to Deir Tureif where the 54th Division was engaged as well as at Yehudiyeh. In the afternoon 4,000 Turks advanced to Mulebbis from the north.

On Nov. 27 three officers and sixty men of the 6th Mounted Brigade, held the Zeitun post against 600 Turks with machine guns who were supported by artillery from Beitunia from 1400 until dark. The garrison, by then reduced to two officers and twenty-six men was reinforced during the night by another fifty men, and successfully held until dawn in spite of enemy attacks which lasted all night, and the destruction by shell fire of the building which they had been occupying. At 1500 enemy patrols were reported to be active to the north and in the neighbourhood of Deir Ibzia, and it became apparent that the enemy was hoping to work round the left flank of the thinly held ten-mile British line to the gap of five or six miles between the left flank of the yeomanry and Shilta, the nearest post of the 54th Division. Zeitun Post was ordered to hold out as long as possible, and No. 2 Light Armoured Car Battery was posted one mile west of Tahta on the Beit Sira road to prevent the enemy from advancing by way of Suffa. A staff officer had to ride down to Berfilya, seven miles away, before he could get in touch with communications and thus secure reinforcements, and at 2130 on Nov. 27, the 7th Mounted Brigade, which had come from Rishon le Zion and Zernukah, left Deiran and reached Beit Ur et Tahta before dawn.

The stubborn defence by the Turkish forces in the hills can be explained by an appreciation of the situation written by Major von Papen on Nov. 23, 1917. In this, he states that an assault group, composed of the 19th, 20th, and 54th Infantry Divisions, will be formed by the end of the month at Tul Keram. In the meantime, every effort must be made, pending the attack of the assault group, to defend Jerusalem with the XXth Corps and the El Bire Group (IIIrd Corps). He does not, however, hold out much hope of retaining Jerusalem, as the Turkish forces had been so shattered as to reduce the comparative strength to a ratio of one to six.

On Nov. 21 the same writer had already reported to Count Bernstorff on the condition of the Turkish forces at this time:—

"We have had a very bad time.

"The breakdown of the army, after having had to relinquish the good positions in which it had remained for so long, is so complete that I could never have dreamed of such a thing. But for this complete dissolution, we should still be able to make a stand south of Jerusalem, even to-day. But now the VIIth Army bolts from every cavalry patrol.

"Many reasons have contributed to this sorrowful result, chiefly incapacity on the part of the troops and their leaders. Single men fight very pluckily, but the good officers have fallen and the remainder have bolted; in Jerusalem alone, we arrested 200 officers and 5,000–6,000 men deserters.

"Naturally Enver presses very strongly to hold on to Jerusalem with all possible means, on account of the political effect. From a military point of view, it is a mistake, for this shattered army can only be put together again, if entirely removed from contact with the enemy and fitted out with new divisions. This, however, can only take place after the lapse of months.

"Now it is just a toss-up."

That an army which had been so hammered as to break up into a condition meriting such criticism as the above should have been able to recover during the brief breathing space afforded to it by British difficulties over transport, and offer the sturdy resistance which our divisions had to overcome in the mountains of Judæa, is a further illustration of the immense recuperative power of Turks in strong defensive positions.

ADVANCE INTO JUDÆA

PLATE 22.

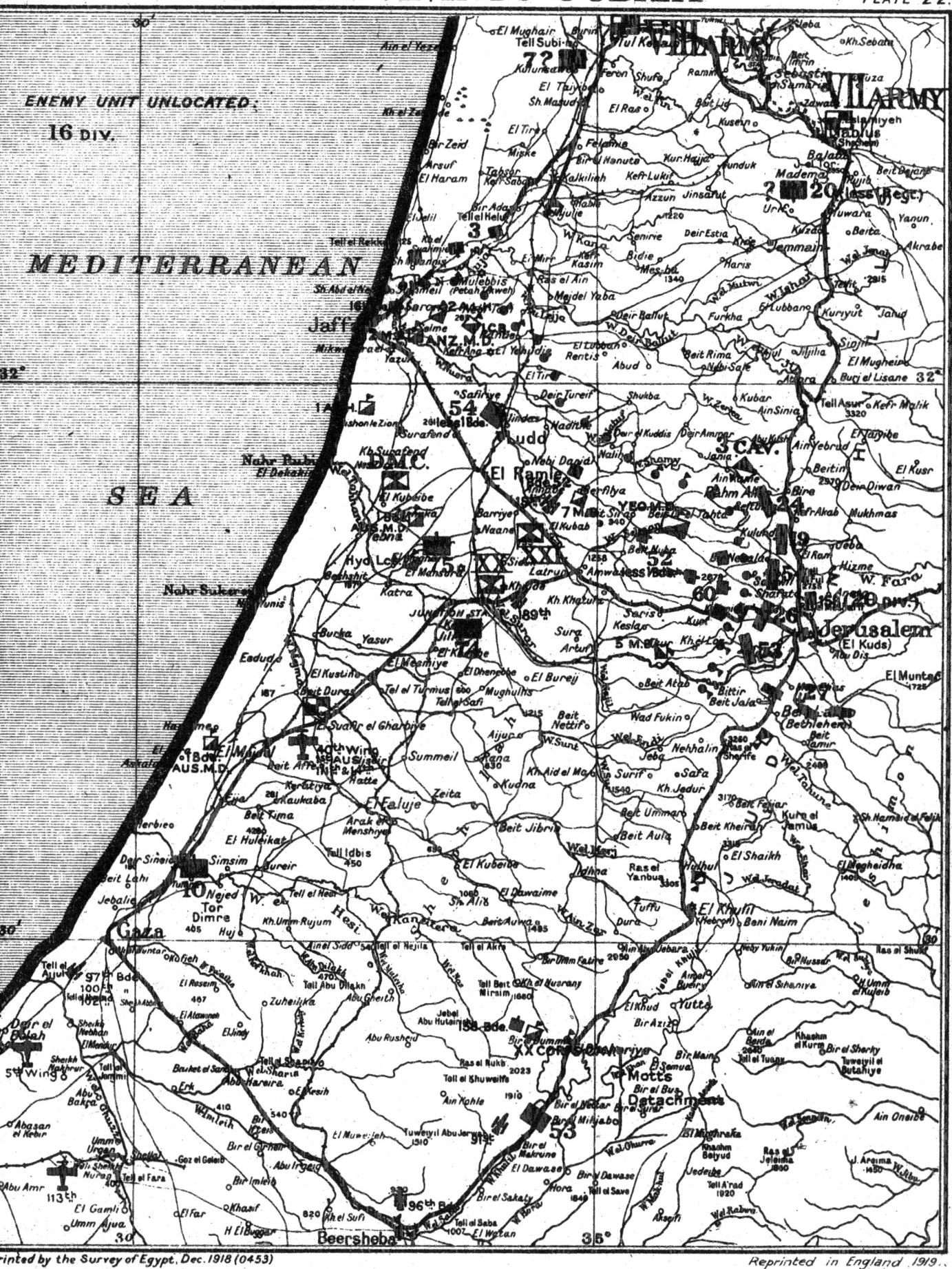

Situation at 6 p.m. on 27-11-17 as known at G.H.Q. E.E.F.

November 28, 29, and 30.

On Nov. 28, at noon, the XXth Corps took over the line from XXIst Corps, and its headquarters moved up from Junction Station to Latron. The line as then held by the 60th Division was from Sóba on the south to Kustul–Beit Surik–Nebi Samwil–Beit Izza. Near here contact was made with the Yeomanry Mounted Division which held Dukka–Beit Ur el Foka–Et Tahta, and thence to the new sector held by the 52nd Division at Suffa and Shilta after its relief by the 60th Division.

In view of the increasing stubbornness of the enemy and the consequent need to prepare a more deliberate method of attack, it was of prime importance to improve communications. New roads were begun between Latron and Beit Likia to link up with the road made by XXIst Corps between Beit Likia and Biddu, and another was started from Kuryet el Enab to Kubeibeh, while the existing roads and tracks were improved into usefulness. Even so it was found that traffic became difficult after a few hours of rain, and that during wet weather camels were of little use. Consequently the Corps transport had to be supplemented by 2,000 donkeys to assist in supplying troops in the advanced positions. At this time the rear communications of the troops on the "Mountain Front" were limited to the partly metalled road from Gaza through Mejdel and Junction Station to Latron, and the Turkish light railway, of which the maximum daily capacity was about 100 tons of Ordnance stores.

At 0500 on Nov. 28, as soon as the 7th Mounted Brigade had come into the line on the left of the 22nd Mounted Brigade at Hellabi, the Turks developed a formidable attack from Beit Ur el Foka to Suffa with some 3,000 rifles, four batteries of ·77's, and some camel guns. To meet this a composite Artillery Brigade of the 74th Division was sent up from Latron to the neighbourhood of Point 1746, and the 155th Brigade of the 52nd Division came into the line on the left of the Yeomanry Division about noon. After considerable fighting Zeitun Post was withdrawn and Foka evacuated. A new line was taken up along a wooded ridge half way to Tahta, and during the evening a battalion of the 156th Brigade and the 4th Australian Light Horse Brigade (Australian Mounted Division) came up in support.

At 1600 the 8th Mounted Brigade fell back on Dukka and the Turkish attack on Tahta was driven back by the 7th Mounted Brigade and the howitzers of the 52nd Division. At 1800 the 4th Australian Light Horse Brigade came up in support of the 6th Mounted Brigade, and half an hour later a battalion of the 156th Brigade arrived in support of the 7th Mounted Brigade.

The enemy renewed his attacks during the night, advancing south of Suffa until compelled to retire at 0800 by the fire of the 268th Brigade, Royal Field Artillery. As he was retiring he suffered satisfactory losses from the enfilade fire of the 7th Mounted Brigade's machine guns. By 1600 on Nov. 29, the Turks were tired of attacking and contented themselves with artillery work and sniping. During the afternoon and night the 8th and 6th Mounted Brigades were relieved by the 231st Brigade of the 74th Division which had now come up into the line, and the 22nd and 7th Mounted Brigades by the 157th Brigade of the 52nd Division. The reliefs were completed by 0500 on Nov. 30, and the four mounted brigades moved back to Beit Sira where they were joined in the afternoon by the 4th Australian Light Horse Brigade, on the way to Divisional Headquarters at Annabeh, where the Yeomanry Division concentrated that evening and rejoined the Desert Mounted Corps.

At a Corps conference held near Yalo, in the Valley of Ajalon, it was decided, on account of the absence of roads and shortage of water in the country to the north-west, to attack the Turkish positions covering Jerusalem from the south-west and west instead of from the north-west.

To face Plate 23.

ADVANCE INTO JUDÆA

PLATE 23

Situation at 6 p.m. on 30.11.17 as known at G.H.Q. E.E.F.

December 1 and 2.

In the morning at 0120 shock troops belonging to the 19th Turkish Division attacked the point of junction between the 3rd and 4th Australian Light Horse Brigade near El Burj. At 0150 the 8th Australian Light Horse Regiment were strengthened by some Gloucester Yeomanry and a company of the 1/4th Royal Scots Fusiliers (155th Brigade) who came up in support. The enemy was exposed to a cross-fire from rifles and machine guns as well as to that of the 268th Brigade, Royal Field Artillery, and of the Hong-Kong and Singapore Battery. At 0530 an encircling movement was made which resulted in the capture of 112 prisoners. The enemy also lost over 100 killed and twenty wounded, who were picked up. At the same time a determined attack was made on the 157th Brigade (52nd Division) holding the Tahta defences. An important position was lost for a time, but recovered after stubborn hand-to-hand fighting at 0430. After this the enemy withdrew a little, and abandoned further attempts to dislodge our troops from this sector of the front. On the same day three determined Turkish attacks were made on the Nebi Samwil positions held by the 60th Division. In these the enemy appears to have lost more than 500 killed.

On the first of the month the 10th Division, which had started north from Belah on Nov. 27, took over the line Wadi Zait–Tahta–Kh. Faaush, a mile to the north of Beit Sira, and the 52nd Division reverted to XXIst Corps.

The 5th Mounted Brigade came into Divisional Reserve at El Burj on the night of Dec. 1 and, on the 2nd, the 7th Mounted Brigade left the Australian Mounted Division and went into Corps Reserve near Akir, where the Yeomanry Division had arrived from Annabeh during the previous day.

To face Plate 24.

ADVANCE INTO JUDÆA

PLATE 24.

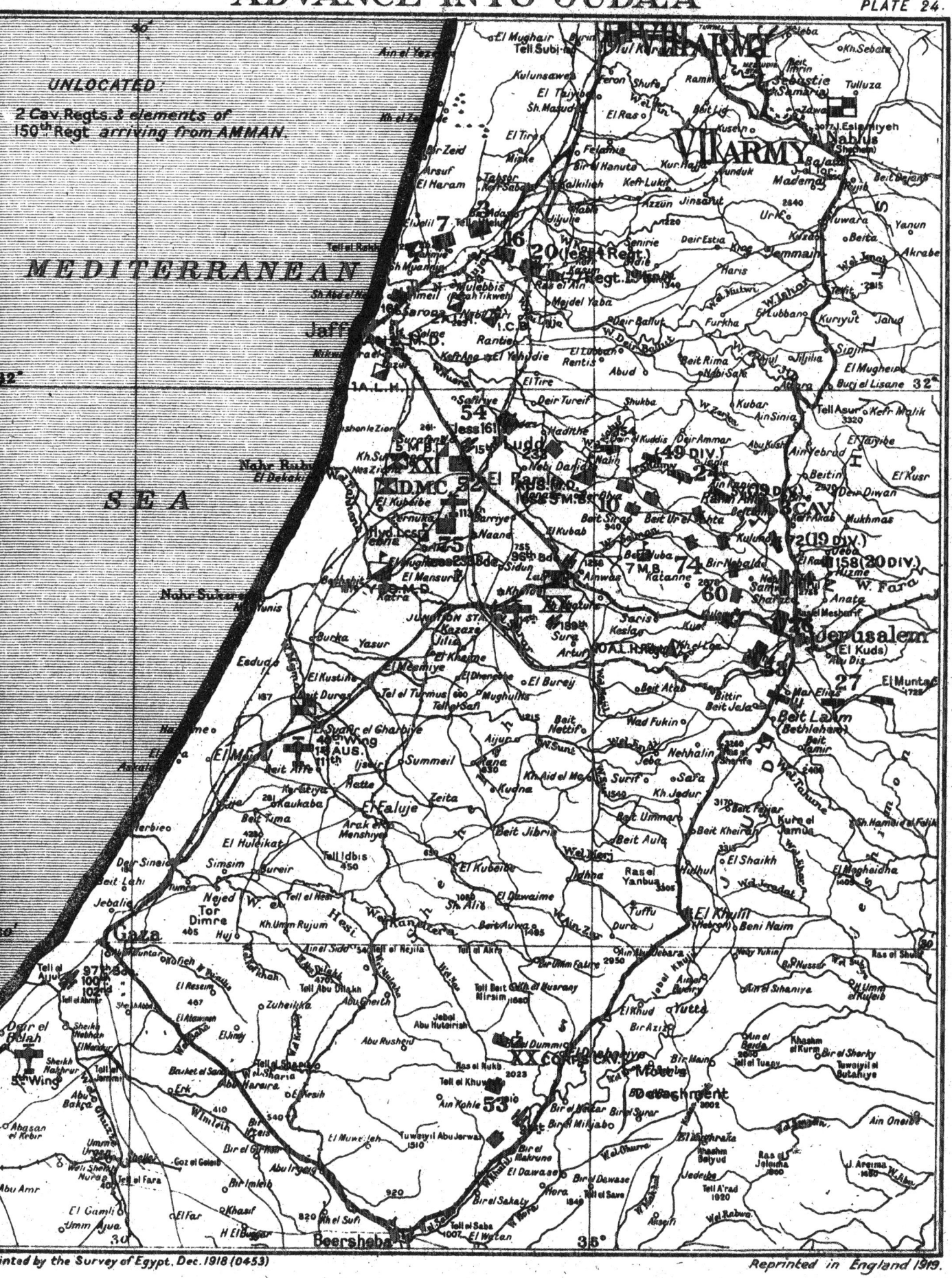

Situation at 6 p.m on 2-12-17 as known at G.H.Q. E.E.F.

December 3 and 4.

On Dec. 3 the Royal Devon Yeomanry Regiment of the 229th Brigade (74th Division) recaptured Beit Ur el Foka with seventeen prisoners and three machine guns, and repulsed a series of counter-attacks. Owing, however, to the fact that the enemy still held high ground from which the village could be dominated with machine-gun fire, the place was evacuated and our troops withdrew to their original line, leaving fifty dead Turks in the village of Foka alone.

On the night of Dec. 3–4 the Imperial Camel Corps Brigade raided Bald Hill. Further to the left the 2nd Australian Light Horse Brigade killed twenty Turks and captured five prisoners. During the next night the New Zealand Mounted Rifles Brigade relieved the Imperial Camel Corps in the line about Point 265. The latter withdrew to Yebna and thence to Shellal. During the same night the 10th Division relieved the 229th and 230th Brigades of the 74th Division and extended its line to cover Beit Dukku.

December 5, 6, 7, and 8.

In the process of concentration for the great attack which was to result in the fall of Jerusalem, a process which occupied from Dec. 4 to 7, the 53rd Division, with the exception of the 158th Brigade, and the XXth Corps Cavalry, began to move north along the Beersheba–Hebron road and reached the Bilbeh area on Dec. 6, getting into touch with the 10th Australian Light Horse Regiment which had occupied El Kudr. On Dec. 5 the enemy withdrew a little in front of the 10th Division. This enabled our troops to occupy Kh. Hellabi and Suffa, and the Australian Mounted Division also moved forward a short distance. That night the 231st Brigade of the 74th Division relieved the 60th Division in the Beit Izza and Nebi Samwil sector, and during the next night the 74th Division took over the line as far south as the Makam of Sheikh Abdul Aziz, one mile south-east of Beit Surik. At 0700 on Dec. 5 patrols reported that Kefr Rut, about one mile west from Suffa, had been evacuated by the enemy. Accordingly, an hour later, the 4th Australian Light Horse Brigade and the 5th Mounted Brigade moved forward, and at 1530 the 3rd Australian Light Horse Brigade occupied a line about 1,000 yards north-north-east of El Burj further to the west. Thus, in the evening, the Desert Mounted Corps held a line running through a point 500 yards east-north-east of Kh. ed Daty, another point 1,500 yards north of that place, Shilta, and a point 500 yards west of Shilta. This filled the gap between the 31st Brigade of the 10th Division on the right and the 233rd Brigade of the 75th Division on the left.

On Dec. 7 the XXIst Corps took over the line covering Ramleh, Ludd, and Jaffa. The 75th Division had the eastern sector on the right, the 54th Division the central sector, and the 52nd Division the coastal or western sector on the left.

On the eve of the attack the Turks were holding a line covering Bethlehem on the south and running north past Ras el Balua, Ain el Hand, Kibriyan, Kulat el Ghuleh, to the west of Ain Harim and along the formidable ridge running above the Wadi es Surar in front of Deir Yesin and Beit Iksa. It continued north to the east of Nebi Samwil, to the west of El Jib and thence in a westerly direction past Kh. ed Dreihemeh, Et Tireh, Beit Ur el Foka, Kh. Ilasa, Kh. Aberjan to a point near Suffa. As a preliminary to the main attack the 179th Brigade with the mountain batteries crossed the Wadi Surar during the night and by 0330 had captured the high ground south of Ain Karim. In spite of rain the main attack began at dawn on Dec. 8. It was supported by the Divisional Artillery, the 96th Heavy Artillery Group of three 6-inch batteries—the 383rd, 387th, and 440th—one 60-pounder battery and one section of the 195th Heavy Battery, the Hong Kong and Singapore Battery attached to the 74th Division, the 10th and 16th Mountain Batteries attached to the 60th Division and the 91st Heavy Battery attached to the 53rd Division. The 60th and 74th Divisions attacked at 0515 and by 0700 had captured the line of Turkish trenches crowning the formidable hills to the east of the Wadi Surar. Considerable difficulty was experienced before the great Heart and Liver Redoubts and the carefully prepared works at Deir Yesin could be taken by the 60th Division. The main road past Kulonieh and up the steep ascent to Lifta was exposed to Turkish artillery and machine-gun fire, which greatly interfered with the advance of this division and the movements of its guns. The country traversed was very broken and precipitous and the rain and darkness greatly increased the difficulty of the advance. The weather and strenuous Turkish resistance had delayed the 53rd Division and it was only at 0900 that it could get into position to attack the high ground west and south-west of Beit Jala, consequently this division was unable effectively to protect the right flank of the 60th. The necessity for securing this flank made it impossible for the 60th Division to advance so far as its right was concerned. On the left it encountered serious opposition at 1330 which was only overcome by a bayonet charge at 1600. Further north the 74th Division reached Beit Iksa by 1100, but was there held up by heavy artillery and machine-gun fire, and was unable to capture the El Burj ridge to the north-east owing to enfilade fire from the right. The attack was suspended and at nightfall both divisions consolidated the line to which they had advanced while the 10th Australian Light Horse Regiment at Malhah and the 1/1 Worcester Yeomanry (the Corps Cavalry Regiment) maintained communication amid the rain and mist with the 53rd Division near Beit Jala. In the morning the Worcester Yeomanry worked right across the front of the 53rd Division and cut the enemy's line of retreat by getting astride of the Jericho road where it turns east from the Valley of Jehoshaphat.

During the night the 53rd Division had pushed forward to the outskirts of Bethlehem from which the enemy withdrew, and by 0830 on Dec. 9 the division had advanced to a line two and a half miles

ADVANCE INTO JUDÆA

PLATE 25

Situation at 6 p.m. on 4-12-17 as known at G.H.Q. E.E.F.

south of Jerusalem. The enemy, having no hope of holding Jerusalem now that his positions overhanging the Wadi Surar had been forced, made no counter-attacks during the night but retired to a line north and north-east of the city which was surrendered at 0830 by the Mayor who approached the outpost of the 180th Brigade. Major-Gen. Shea commanding the 60th Division, was instructed to accept the surrender, and did so at 1300.

On the morning of Dec. 8 large numbers of the inhabitants of Jerusalem, with the remaining religious chiefs, were personally warned by the police to be ready to leave at once. The extent to which the Turks were prepared to clear the city is shown by the fact that out of the Armenian community of 1,400 souls 300 received this notice. Jemal Pasha, when warned that vehicles were unavailable for the transport of the unhappy exiles to Shechem or Jericho, telegraphed curtly that they and theirs must walk. The fate of countless Armenians and many Greeks has shown that a population of all ages suddenly turned out to walk indefinite distances under Turkish escort is exposed to outrage and hardship which prove fatal to most of them; but the delay in telegraphing had saved the population, and the sun had risen for the last time on the Ottoman domination of Jerusalem, and the Turks' power to destroy faded with the day.

Towards dusk the British troops were reported to have passed Lifta, and to be within sight of the city. On this news being received, a sudden panic fell on the Turks west and south-west of the town, and at 1700 civilians were surprised to see a Turkish transport column galloping furiously cityward along the Jaffa road. In passing they alarmed all units within sight or hearing, and the wearied infantry arose and fled, bootless and without rifles, never pausing to think or to fight. Some were flogged back by their officers and were compelled to pick up their arms; others staggered on through the mud, augmenting the confusion of the retreat.

After four centuries of conquest the Turk was ridding the land of his presence in the bitterness of defeat, and a great enthusiasm arose among the Jews. There was a running to and fro; daughters called to their fathers and brothers concealed in outhouses, cellars, and attics, from the police, who sought them for arrest and deportation. "The Turks are running," they called; "the day of deliverance is come". The nightmare was fast passing away, but the Turk still lingered. In the evening he fired his guns continuously, perhaps heartening himself with the loud noise that comforts the soul of a barbarian, perhaps to cover the sound of his own retreat. Whatever the intention was, the roar of the gunfire persuaded most citizens to remain indoors, and there were few to witness the last act of Osmanli authority.

Towards midnight the Governor, Izzet Bey, went personally to the telegraph office, discharged the staff, and himself smashed the instruments with a hammer. At 0200 on Sunday tired Turks began to troop through the Jaffa gate from the west and south-west, and anxious watchers, peering out through the windows of the Grand New Hotel to learn the meaning of the tramping, were cheered by the sullen remark of an officer, "Gitmaya mejburuz" ("We've got to go"), and from 0200 till 0700 that morning the Turks streamed through and out of the city, which echoed for the last time their shuffling tramp. On this same day 2,082 years before, another race of conquerors, equally detested, were looking their last on the city which they could not hold, and inasmuch as the liberation of Jerusalem in 1917 will probably ameliorate the lot of the Jews more than that of any other community in Palestine, it was fitting that the flight of the Turks should have coincided with the national festival of the Hanukah, which commemorates the recapture of the Temple from the heathen Seleucids by Judas Maccabæus in 165 B.C.

The Governor was the last civil official to depart. He left in a cart belonging to Mr. Vester, an American resident, from whom he had "borrowed" an hitherto unrequisitioned cart and team. Before the dawn he hastened down the Jericho road, leaving behind him a letter of surrender, which the Mayor as the sun rose set forth to deliver to the British commander, accompanied by a few frightened policemen holding two tremulous white flags. He walked towards the Lifta Hill and met the first representatives of the British Army on a spot which may be marked in the future with a white stone as the site of a historic episode.

The last Turkish soldier is said to have left Jerusalem at about 0700 by the east gate of the city, which is named after St. Stephen, but even later armed stragglers were still trickling along the road just outside the north wall, requisitioning food and water at the point of the bayonet. This is no grevious crime on the part of defeated troops, uncertain of their next meal, but is recorded as the last kick of the dying Ottoman authority in a city where it had been supreme for four centuries.

As the Turkish flood finally ebbed away into the shadowy depths of the Valley of Jehoshaphat the townsfolk roused themselves from the lethargy into which hunger and the Turkish police had plunged them and fell upon a variety of buildings, official or requisitioned for official purposes, and looted them, even stripping roofs, doors, and floors from the Ottoman barracks next to the Tower of David for firewood. It must be admitted that, as the Government had furnished and maintained itself almost entirely by uncompensated requisitions, the crowd was only trying to indemnify itself. But this disorder ceased as suddenly as it had arisen on the appearance of the British infantry.

ADVANCE INTO JUDÆA

PLATE 26

Situation at 6 p.m. on 7-12-17 as known at G.H.Q. E.E.F.

December 9 and 10.

After the surrender of Jerusalem the 74th and 60th Divisions wheeled northwards pivotting on Nebi Samwil. The 74th met with no great opposition but the 60th Division on debouching shortly after 1030 from the suburbs to the north of the Lifta road came under heavy rifle and machine-gun fire from the ridge to the west of Sir John Grey Hill's house on the Mount of Olives, which was strongly held by the enemy. At about 1600 the Turks were dislodged from this at the point of the bayonet, leaving seventy dead. Meanwhile on the left of the division the 180th Brigade which was advancing along the ridge to the east of the Wadi Beit Hannina, occupied Shafat and Tel el Ful on the Shechem (Nablus) road.

By 1100 the 53rd Division was at Mar Elias with its advanced guard on the Jericho road to the south-east of Jerusalem. The Mount of Olives was strongly defended by the Turks, and the division was not able to drive them off until nightfall.

The same day the Desert Mounted Corps extended its front to the east so as to include Suffa. This move brought the 3rd Australian Light Horse Brigade from El Burj up into the neighbourhood of Kh. ed Daty. During this period the enemy line ran westwards just in front of Khurbetha ibn Harith, Jurdeh, Deir el Kuddis, and Nalin.

On Dec. 10 the 53rd Division was engaged to the east of Jerusalem in pushing the enemy back off the ridges from which he could observe the Holy City.

Note on the Surrender of Jerusalem.

Before the arrival of the flag of truce on Dec. 9 the movement of the crowds accompanying it had been observed and reported by patrols, but definite news of the impending surrender was first actually communicated to British soldiers by civilians, who informed Pte. H. E. Church and Pte. R. W. J. Andrews of the 2/20th Battalion London Regiment. These men, who had advanced into the outskirts of Jerusalem in order to obtain water, reported what had been told to them without meeting the flag of truce. Shortly before 0800 Sergt. Hurcomb and Sergt. Sedgewick, of the 2/19th Battalion London Regiment, met the flag of truce and, shortly afterwards, Major W. Beck, R.A., and Major F. R. Barry, R.A., came up and entered into conversation with the Mayor. They turned back to report the presence of the flag of truce, and met Lieut.-Col. H. Bailey, D.S.O., and Major M. D. H. Cooke. Lieut.-Col. Bailey, as senior officer, declined to accept the surrender and reported the Mayor's wishes to Brig.-General C. F. Watson, C.M.G., D.S.O., Commanding 180th Brigade, who rode up a few minutes later and reassured the Mayor. Brig.-General Watson transmitted the offer of the surrender of Jerusalem to Major-General J. S. M. Shea, C.B., C.M.G., D.S.O., G.O.C. 60th Division, who was then at Enab. Major-General Shea communicated with Lieut.-General Sir Philip Chetwode, Bt., K.C.B., K.C.M.G., D.S.O., G.O.C. XXth Corps, and about 1100 was instructed to accept the surrender of the city. In the meantime Brig.-General Watson (with a small mounted escort, followed by the Mayor in his carriage) had ridden forward to reassure the people, and was the first British soldier to arrive at the Jaffa Gate. Guards were posted at 0930 from the 2/17th Battalion London Regiment over the Post Office, which had been occupied in the interval by Major Cooke, at some hospitals, and outside the Jaffa Gate. Shortly after Brig.-General Watson's arrival a mounted patrol from the 53rd Division appeared. Major-General Shea, on arriving in a motor car outside the Post Office, sent for the Mayor and Chief of Police. These functionaries were informed that Major-General Shea accepted the surrender of the city in the name of the Commander-in-Chief, and Brig.-General Watson was directed to make the necessary arrangements for the maintenance of order.

OCCUPATION OF JERUSALEM

PLATE 27

Situation at 6 p.m. on 9-12-17 as known at G.H.Q. E.E.F.

December 11 and 12.

On Dec. 11 the Commander-in-Chief, followed by representatives of the Allies, made his formal entry into Jerusalem. The historic Jaffa Gate was opened, after years of disuse, for the purpose, and he was thus enabled to pass into the Holy City without making use of the gap in the wall made for the Emperor William in 1898. When the time came for the great and simple act of the solemn entry of General Allenby into Jerusalem, and the Arab prophecy was fulfilled that when the Nile had flowed into Palestine, the prophet (Al Nebi) from the west should drive the Turk from Jerusalem, the inhabitants mustered courage to gather in a great crowd. They were themselves amazed, for during more than three years an assembly of more than three persons in one place was discouraged by the police by blows, fines, imprisonment, and even exile. Eye-witnesses of all three events state that the crowd gathered at the Jaffa gate to greet the General was larger than that which met the Emperor William when on his fantastic political pilgrimage, and denser than the gathering which greeted the revival of the Ottoman Constitution when it was proclaimed, ten years later, at the Damascus Gate, where there is more space. Many wept for joy, priests were seen to embrace one another, but there were no theatricalities such as the hollow reconciliations which made the triumph of the Young Turk in 1908 memorable, and sicken the memories of those who know the horrors and calamities which that triumph was doomed to bring. The General entered the city on foot, and left it on foot, and throughout the ceremony no Allied flag was flown, while naturally no enemy flags were visible.

A proclamation announcing that order would be maintained in all the hallowed sites of the three great religions, which were to be guarded and preserved for the free use of worshippers, was read in English, French, Arabic, Hebrew, Greek, Russian, and Italian, from the terrace of the entrance to the citadel below the Tower of David. When this was done the chief notables and ecclesiastics of the different communities who had remained in Jerusalem were presented to General Allenby. After this brief ceremony the Commander-in-Chief left the city by the Jaffa Gate.

In the neighbourhood of Jerusalem there was no fighting on this day apart from an attack by a small party of Turks near Tel el Ful which was repulsed by the 179th Brigade.

In the XXIst Corps area the 75th Division advanced its front to the line Midieh–Kh. Hamid–Budrus–Sheikh Obeid Rahil, meeting with slight opposition in the process. An enemy counter-attack, after preliminary bombardment of the Zeifizfiyeh Ridge, at 1000 was repulsed.

On Dec. 12 the 53rd Division improved its position by advancing several hundred yards, but there was otherwise little activity on either side.

The 3rd Australian Light Horse Brigade relieved the 4th Australian Light Horse Brigade in the Suffa–Kh. ed Daty sector of the line.

ADVANCE INTO MOUNT EPHRAIM AND SHARON   PL. 28

UNLOCATED:
3 CAV. DIV.
53 DIV. (less 136 Regt.)

Printed by the Survey of Egypt, Dec. 1918 (0453)   Reprinted in England 1919

Miles 10   5   0   10   20 Miles

Situation at 6 p.m. on 12-12-17 as known at G.H.Q. E.E.F.

December 13 to 22.

On Dec. 13 the 53rd Division further advanced its line, and the 181st Brigade of the 60th Division captured Ras el Kharrubeh (near Anata) with forty-three prisoners and two machine guns. During the fine weather which lasted until the afternoon of Dec. 14 much road work was done. Preparations were being made for the further advance which was to drive the enemy back to a respectful distance from Jerusalem, and at dawn on Dec. 17, two battalions of the 160th Brigade attacked the high ground east of Abu Dis. The ridge was captured with a loss to the enemy of forty-six killed, 126 prisoners, and two machine guns. The 53rd Division, which was taking over the line as far north as the Wadi Anata, was again engaged on Dec. 21, when the 159th Brigade stormed Ras ez Zamby (about two and a quarter miles west-north-west of Jerusalem) and White Hill. There was a good deal of fighting and the position with three machine guns was not taken until noon. The Turks made three counter-attacks which cost them a further loss of fifty killed.

The 60th Division, relieved as far as the Wadi Anata by the 53rd, took over the line east of Nebi Samwil from the 74th Division, which in its turn extended to Beit Ur et Tahta on the west. This readjustment was effected by Dec. 21.

On Dec. 14 the 10th Australian Light Horse Regiment which had been attached to the 60th Division during the operations against Jerusalem, rejoined the 3rd Australian Light Horse Brigade in the Desert Mounted Corps area.

On Dec. 15 the 75th Division again advanced their line and took in Kibbiah and Kh. Ibbaneh, while the 54th Division took Khirbet el Bornat and moved up to Et Tireh. At this place and at Kh. Ibbaneh the enemy made some resistance.

In the coastal sector preparations were being made by the XXIst Corps to remove the enemy from his positions at the mouth of the Nahr el Auja, which menaced the town and landing place of Jaffa and the main road thence to Ramleh. The River Auja, some forty yards wide and ten feet deep between abrupt banks, was in itself a formidable obstacle to an advance. The enemy had entrenched the high northern bank and also held Bald Hill with a line of trenches about a mile to the south of Mulebbis and Fejja.

Major-General Hill, Commanding the 52nd Division, on Dec. 14 submitted a plan for making a surprise passage of the river. The requisite preparations were made—portable bridges were constructed by the Engineers, under cover of the orange groves of Sarona, pontoons were assembled and canvas corracles, capable of carrying twenty men apiece, were built from local materials. A considerable concentration of artillery was also effected and, on Dec. 18 and 19, the 52nd Division was relieved in the trenches by the 161st Brigade of the 54th Division and the Auckland and Wellington Mounted Rifle Regts. At the same time the 75th Division extended its front westwards so as to enable the 54th Division to spare the 161st Brigade from near Ludd.

Three days' heavy rain followed which considerably increased the volume of water in the Auja and did much to render its south bank difficult of access by turning the plain into a mud swamp. In spite of this the surprise attack was successful. The covering parties crossed unperceived during the night of Dec. 20 amid wind and rain in their corracles, and the bridges were placed in position. Owing to the extreme lightness of their construction (they were designed to be carried nearly two miles), some of them collapsed after a time, and the 156th Brigade had to link arms and cross breast-deep at the ford.* The enemy's trenches covering the river were rushed in silence and captured. Sheikh Muannis was carried at the point of the bayonet, Kh. Hadrah was rushed and captured, and by the dawn of Dec. 21 the 52nd Division had occupied the whole line from Hadrah to Tel el Rekkeit on the sea two miles north of the river-mouth. The enemy had been completely taken by surprise and lost many killed in addition to 316 prisoners and ten machine guns.

Throughout Dec. 21 preparations were made to enable the rest of the division to cross, and during the night of Dec. 21–22, while the 52nd was establishing itself to the north of the Auja, the 54th Division stormed and captured Bald Hill, two miles south of Mulebbis, in spite of the determined resistance of the enemy, who lost fifty-two killed and forty-four prisoners. As a result of this the enemy retired from Mulebbis † and Fejja at dawn and the 54th Division was able to occupy these villages without further opposition. A little later in the day Rantieh was also occupied.

During Dec. 22 the 52nd Division advanced to the line Tel el Mukhmar at the confluence of the Wadi Ishkar and the Auja–Sheikh el Ballutah–Arsuf, on the cliffs above the sea. This operation was greatly assisted by the co-operation of a squadron composed of H.M.S. "Grafton," flying the flag of Rear-Admiral Jackson, H.M.M. 29, 31, and 32, and H.M.D. "Lapwing" and "Lizard." The ships shelled El Jelil and compelled parties of the enemy to retire rapidly northwards from El Haram and Arsuf.

As a result of this successful advance the Turks were driven back five miles and Jaffa became more secure as a landing-place for stores.

---

* This spot is now marked by an antique column with inscription.
† Mulebbis contains the important Hebrew Colony of Petach Tikvah.

ADVANCE INTO MOUNT EPHRAIM AND SHARON PL.29

Situation at 6 p.m. on 22-12-17 as known at G.H.Q. E.E.F.

December 23-31.

On the assumption that the general advance into the southern portions of Mount Ephraim would begin on the night of Dec. 24, the 180th and 181st Brigades had been instructed to advance against Kh. Adaseh and a point north of Beit Hannina respectively at dawn on Dec. 23. The 180th Brigade was unable to take its objective before the attack was abandoned owing to the postponement of the general advance on account of weather. The new advance was now fixed for dawn on Dec. 27, but at 2330 on 26th, the enemy launched an attack and drove in the outposts of the 60th Division at Kh. Ras et Tawil and the quarries to the north of it; at the same time, seven and a half miles to the west, the 24th Welsh Regiment (Pembroke and Glamorgan Yeomanry) stormed Hill 1910, close to Et Tireh, and held it in spite of a strong counter-attack, killing seventy Turks and capturing three machine guns.

At dawn on Dec. 27 the Turks made determined attacks on White Hill and Ras ez Zamby, from the former of which our troops were dislodged. The position was recovered after dark as the enemy had been unable to occupy it owing to our artillery fire. A company of the 2/10th Middlesex held Deir ibn Obeid all day and night against vigorous attacks, although surrounded and cut off for several hours. At 0130 the whole line was engaged. The enemy made eight assaults before 0800, chiefly in the neighbourhood of Tel el Ful. In one place he established himself in part of our line until ejected by the 2/15th Londons who advanced in spite of an artillery and machine-gun enfilade. Between 0230 and 0630 the 2/24th Londons repelled four energetic attacks. After a lull in the fighting the enemy delivered an assault with an unexpectedly large number of men at 1255. The Turks succeeded in reaching certain sections of the main line but a counter-attack restored our original front.

In spite of the enemy activity on the front of the 53rd and 60th Divisions the general advance began, according to plan, at 0600 on the left where the 29th and 30th Brigades pushed forward in the face of considerable opposition. The 1st Leinsters and 5th Connaught Rangers had a good deal of fighting west of Deir Ibzia but, when this was taken, there was not much trouble in reaching the line running north-westerly in front of this village through Shabuny to Sheikh Abdullah, where connexion was made with the Australian Mounted Division. This advance was supported by the 263rd Field Artillery Brigade and the 9th and 10th Mountain Batteries. The 31st Brigade (10th Division), supported by the 68th Field Artillery Brigade from near Tahta, advanced at 0700 to the line running from the right of the 29th and 30th Brigades through Kh. el Hafy to near Kh. Jeriut. The 229th Brigade (74th Division), supported by the 67th (from near Foka and Likia), the 44th and 117th Field Artillery Brigades started at 0750 and reached the west end of the Sheikh Abu ez Zeitun ridge at 0900. From now on the advance was exposed to constant artillery and machine-gun fire, and the whole ridge was only captured after dusk. At 1015 the 24th Royal Welsh Fusiliers (231st Brigade) captured Kh. ed Dreihemeh and at 1100 assaulted Hill 2450 some 600 yards to the north-east. The result of this advance was apparent by 1400 when the enemy was observed to be moving his 1st Division westwards from Bireh, thus showing that he found himself forced to conform to our movements and to abandon the initiative.

On Dec. 28 the 158th Brigade captured Anata, but the 1/7th Royal Welsh Fusiliers were held up for a long time on Ras Arkub es Suffa, one and three-quarters of a mile to the south-east, and only gained the position after dusk. The 1/1st Herefords also seized Kh. Almit, one mile north-east of Anata after dark. The right flank of the 60th Division was thus covered from an attack from the Jericho road. The 60th Division captured Kh. Adaseh at 1725 with the 180th Brigade, while the 181st was sent forward on the left and occupied El Jib, which had caused so much trouble on Nov. 23, and Bir Nebala shortly after noon. The 180th pushed on and seized the Er Ram—Rafat line at 1915.

Early in the morning of Dec. 28 the 74th Division completed the capture of Hill 2450. The main advance was resumed at 1330 and by dusk the division had reached the line from the left of the 60th Division at Rafat to the right of the 229th Brigade near Beitunia, which had been captured in face of strong opposition at 1550, when the commander of the garrison, seventy other prisoners, and seven machine guns were taken. Further west Kefr Skiyan was taken by the 31st Brigade at 1740, and the 29th and 30th Brigades had a lot of trouble from enemy machine guns cunningly hidden among the rocks in very broken country before they could take Abu el Ainein (seven furlongs north-east of Ain Arik) and Kh. Rubin. At 1430 a 6-inch howitzer of the 378th Siege Battery, which had been moved to Beit Ur el Foka during the morning, began to bombard the enemy withdrawing from Ram Allah and persevered until midnight.

On Dec. 29 enemy opposition faded away on the extreme right and the 159th Brigade pressed northwards to cover the flank of the 60th Division. Hizmeh and Jeba were thus occupied without difficulty and 271 enemy dead were buried on the 53rd Division front—the harvest of the last three days. At 0600 the 60th Division resumed its advance. The 181st Brigade was held up just short of Bireh and Ras et Tahuneh until the 303rd Field Artillery Brigade could get into action by way of the main road, as the Kulundia track was impassable for guns. At 1430 the advance was resumed, and at 1615 the 2/22nd and 2/23rd Londons were in position by the Ram Allah–Bireh road to assault the Tahuneh ridge which was captured, after a stubborn defence, at 1700. Meanwhile, on the right the 2/19th and 2/20th Londons stormed Shab Salah, a precipitous and strongly-held position. This was captured by 1530, and the 2/17th and 2/18th Londons (180th Brigade) pushed forward by 1830 and captured the ridge half a mile north-west of Burkah. At 2100 the 180th and 181st Brigades occupied the line

ADVANCE INTO MOUNT EPHRAIM AND SHARON PL.30

Situation at 6 p.m. on 31-12-17 as known at G.H.Q. E.E.F.

Beitin–Balua–Kh. el Burj without serious opposition. Ram Allah had been occupied by the 229th and 230th Brigades at 0917 and, by 2100, the latter was holding a line between the left of the 60th Division and Et Tireh, where the ridge had been occupied by the 10th Division without opposition soon after 0800.

The Royal Flying Corps by timely information during the course of the day greatly assisted the operations of the XXth Corps and, by bombing the enemy's retreating columns, caused him heavy loss and hindered his withdrawal.

By the morning of Dec. 30 enemy resistance on our right flank had died down and the XXth Corps took up the position shewn in the adjoining map. Throughout these operations the Australian Mounted Division carried out strong reconnaissances and advanced its line to the north of Deir el Kuddis and Khurbetha ibn Harith on Dec. 29. On Dec. 31 this sector as far as a point 500 yards north-west of Deir el Kuddis was taken over by the 29th Brigade and the 4th Australian Light Horse Brigade relieved the 3rd Australian Light Horse Brigade in the Deir el Kuddis–Nalin sector.

During the operations between Dec. 11 and 31, the XXth Corps took 1,301 prisoners, of whom 750 were captured during the three days Dec. 27-29. Twenty-four machine guns were also taken.

The map opposite shows the extent of territory—all Philistia and almost all Judæa—from which the Turks had been driven as a result of the successive advances of the Egyptian Expeditionary Force up to the end of 1917.

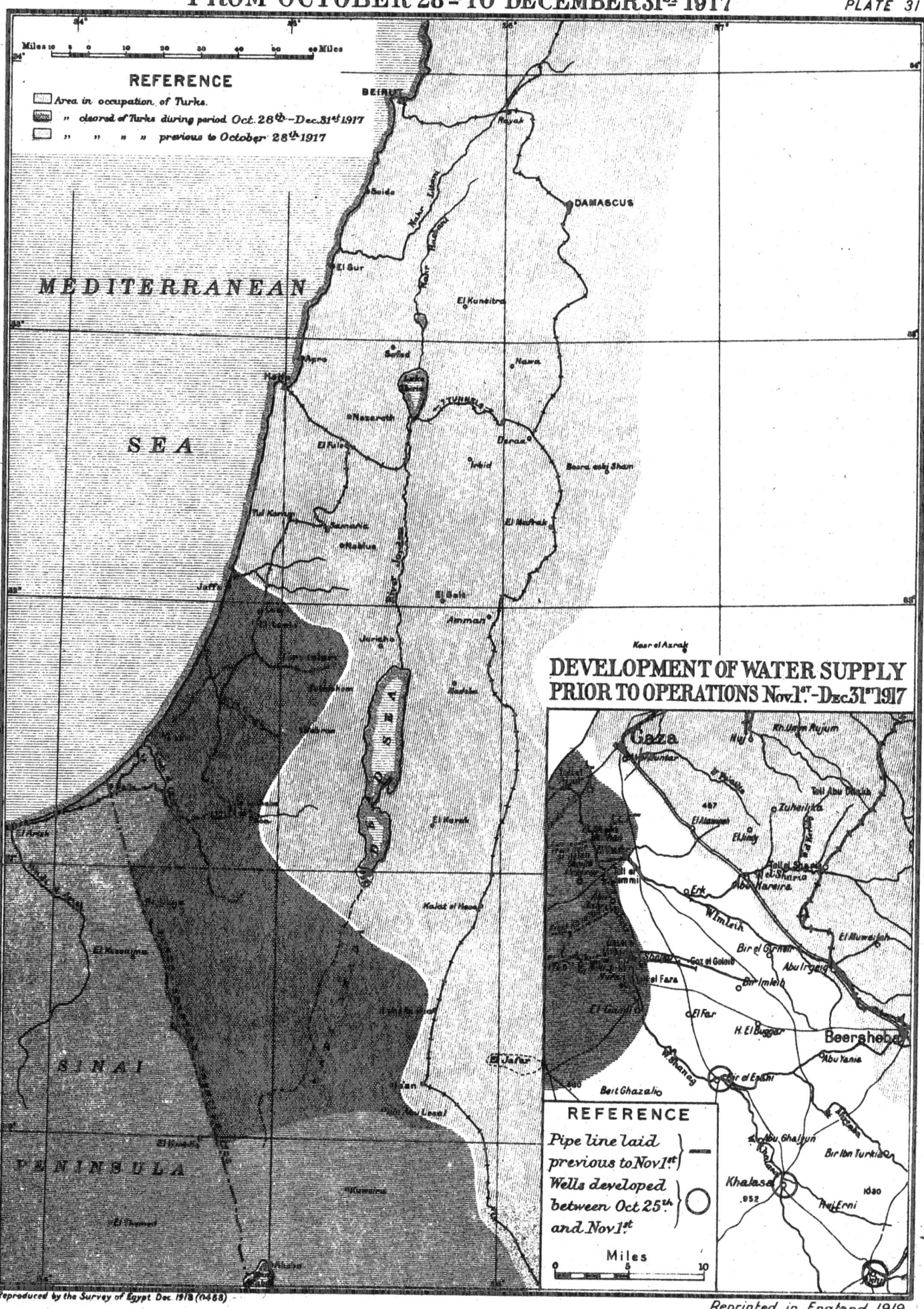

February 18.

As a preliminary to the operations for the capture of Jericho the 53rd Division relieved the 60th on the line astride of the Shechem (Nablus) road in order that the Londoners might take over the eastern front. The 74th Division detailed the 231st Brigade for service with the 60th, and the New Zealand Mounted Rifles and 1st Australian Light Horse Brigades were also attached. A week before the advance the 60th Division held a line running northward from Kh. Deir ibn Obeid to Ras Arkub es Suffa, passing about three miles to the east of Jerusalem. Thence it ran north-westerly to Hizmeh and a point three-quarters of a mile south of Burkah. Here the 53rd Division had its extreme right. At dawn on Feb. 14 the 60th Division seized Mukhmas (Michmash) and Tel es Suwan just after the 53rd had captured Kh. el Alia and Deir Diwan. By the night of the 18th the Wellington Mounted Rifles were at Kh. Deir ibn Obeid, and the rest of the New Zealand Mounted Rifles Brigade and the 1st Australian Light Horse Brigade with their Divisional Headquarters were concentrated in Jerusalem and Bethlehem.

To face Plate 32.

CAPTURE OF JERICHO

PLATE 32

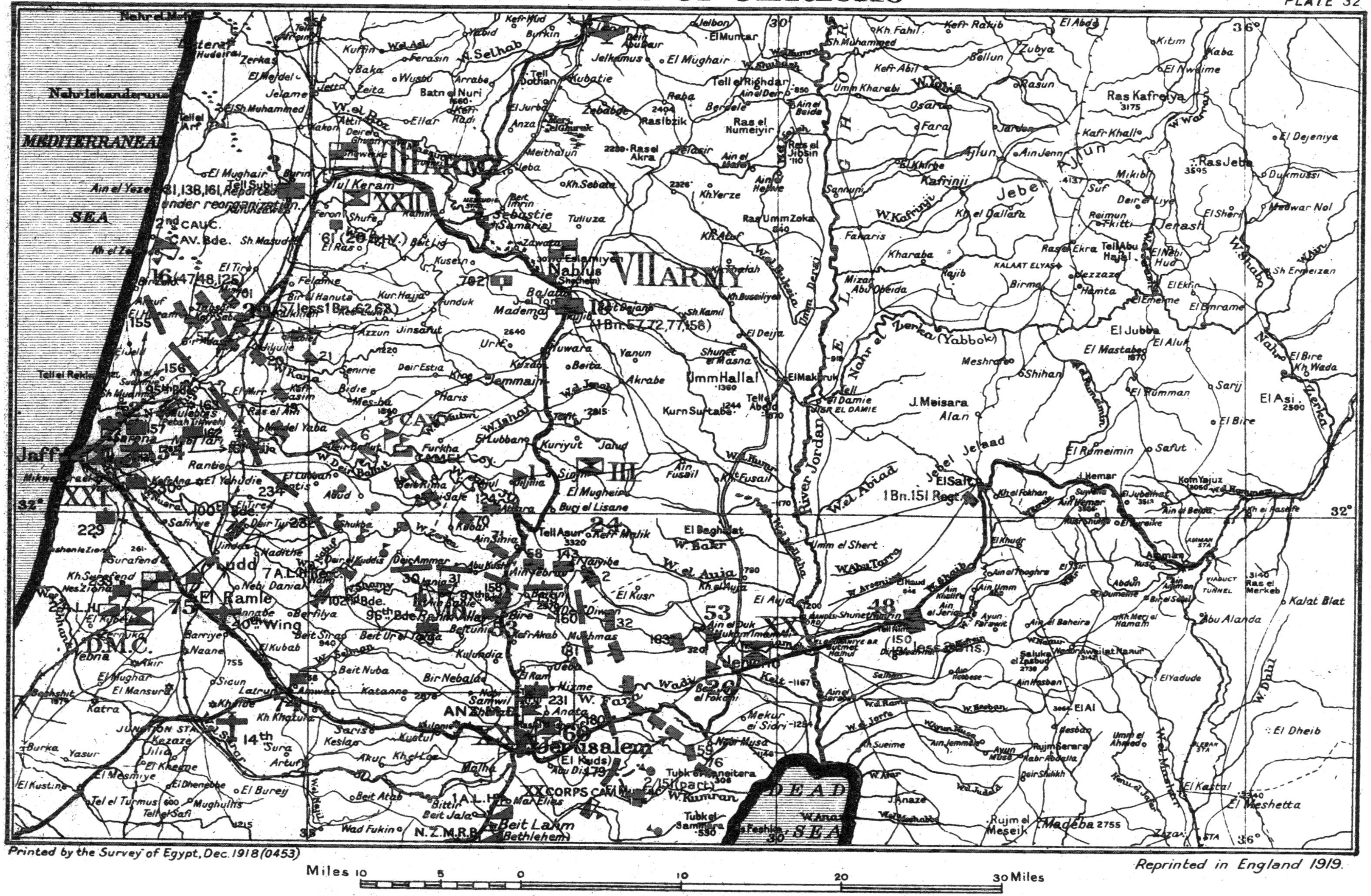

Printed by the Survey of Egypt, Dec. 1918 (0453)

Reprinted in England 1919.

Situation on 18 - 2 - 18 as known at G.H.Q.E.E.F.

February 19-21.

On the morning of Feb. 19 the 53rd and 60th Divisions attacked the Turkish positions which were held in some strength along a series of commanding heights. The 2/23rd Londons took Splash Hill, about one mile east of Tel es Suwan, with thirty-two prisoners, at 0600. Rummon was captured by the 2/10th Middlesex at 0830, and Ras et Tawil was abandoned by the enemy to the 181st Brigade at 0900, owing to our artillery fire. The Turks made a stout resistance across the Arak Ibrahim ridge to the south of the Wadi Farah, where the 2/20th Londons were held up in spite of three assaults. Finally, the position was stormed after artillery had played upon it from 1330 to 1400. While this fighting had been in progress to the north the Australian and New Zealand Mounted Division had passed through the wilderness of Jeshimon and concentrated near El Muntar, little more than six miles from the Dead Sea. By nightfall the line held by the 60th Division ran northward from this point, shewing an average advance of three miles over very bad country during the day. Armoured cars had reconnoitred the Jericho road beyond this line but were held up by a broken bridge three-quarters of a mile further on. The Turks still held a strong position to the south of, and astride, the Jericho road, and during the night the 179th Brigade moved into the Wadi Sidr to deploy for an attack on Jebel Ekteif. The 180th Brigade only reached its positions of deployment in this wadi, at dawn, as the Turks had made three counter-attacks against the sector of front held by the 2/18th Londons.

On the morning of the 20th the advance of the cavalry against Jebel el Kalimun and Tubk el Kuneitrah was necessarily slow owing to the badness of the country. In places progress was only possible in single file along tracks which were under accurate artillery and machine-gun fire from Neby Musa and the two immediate objectives. These two hills were, however, captured by a dismounted attack delivered by the New Zealand Mounted Rifles Brigade shortly after noon. Meanwhile, the 180th Brigade had successfully stormed Talaat ed Dumm, above the Good Samaritan's Inn, at 0715, in the face of considerable opposition, but the 179th had been seriously delayed in its attack upon Jebel Ekteif on account of the surpassing malignity of the terrain. On one line only was advance possible, and, after a bombardment which lasted until 0800, the 2/15th Londons stormed the first line trenches. Co-operation between the two brigades now became possible and the 2/18th Londons and a battery gave assistance on the left flank of the 179th Brigade against Turkish positions at Rujm el Kibliyeh, from which an enfilading machine-gun fire was causing annoyance. During this advance two Turkish machine guns were captured and turned upon the Turks in the Rujm el Kibliyeh positions with excellent effect. The summit of Jebel Ekteif was captured about noon.

The rest of the 180th and the 181st Brigades were also delayed further to the north by bad country, enemy resistance, and the destruction of the road which impeded the progress of the guns, but by dusk the 181st had moved forward nearly three miles and occupied a line from the ridge above the Wadi Farah, astride the Wadi Rijan up to the ridge to the south of the Wadi el Makuk. After dark two battalions of the 231st Brigade relieved the 181st on the front north of the Ras et Tawil–Kuruntul track which runs down the Wadi Rijan.

Further to the south the 1st Australian Light Horse Brigade passed through the gorge of the Wadi Kumran and reached the plain on the north-western shores of the Dead Sea. It took up a position along the Wadi Jofet Zeben at 1800 and, early next morning, started north across the slimy, marl plain and reached Jericho at 0820. At 0600 on the morning of Feb. 21 the New Zealand Mounted Rifles Brigade with the 2/14th Londons and the 10th Mountain Battery had occupied Neby Musa and it now became apparent that the Turks had retired during the night along their whole line. The 60th Division thereupon advanced to Rujm esh Shemaliyeh–Kh. Kakun and Jebel Kuruntul overlooking Jericho, the 1st Australian Light Horse Brigade pushed out patrols from Jericho towards the Wadi Aujah in the north and El Ghoraniyeh, where the enemy still held a bridgehead, on the west of the Jordan. To the south the New Zealand Mounted Rifles Brigade occupied Rujm el Bahr (Dead Sea Post) with a squadron thus seizing the Turkish base upon the Dead Sea with its workshops. The acquisition of this landing-place was afterwards of great importance in opening communications with the Northern Operations of the Sherifian Army when in the Kerak area.

During these operations one enemy aeroplane was brought down in front of the 53rd Division.

CAPTURE OF JERICHO

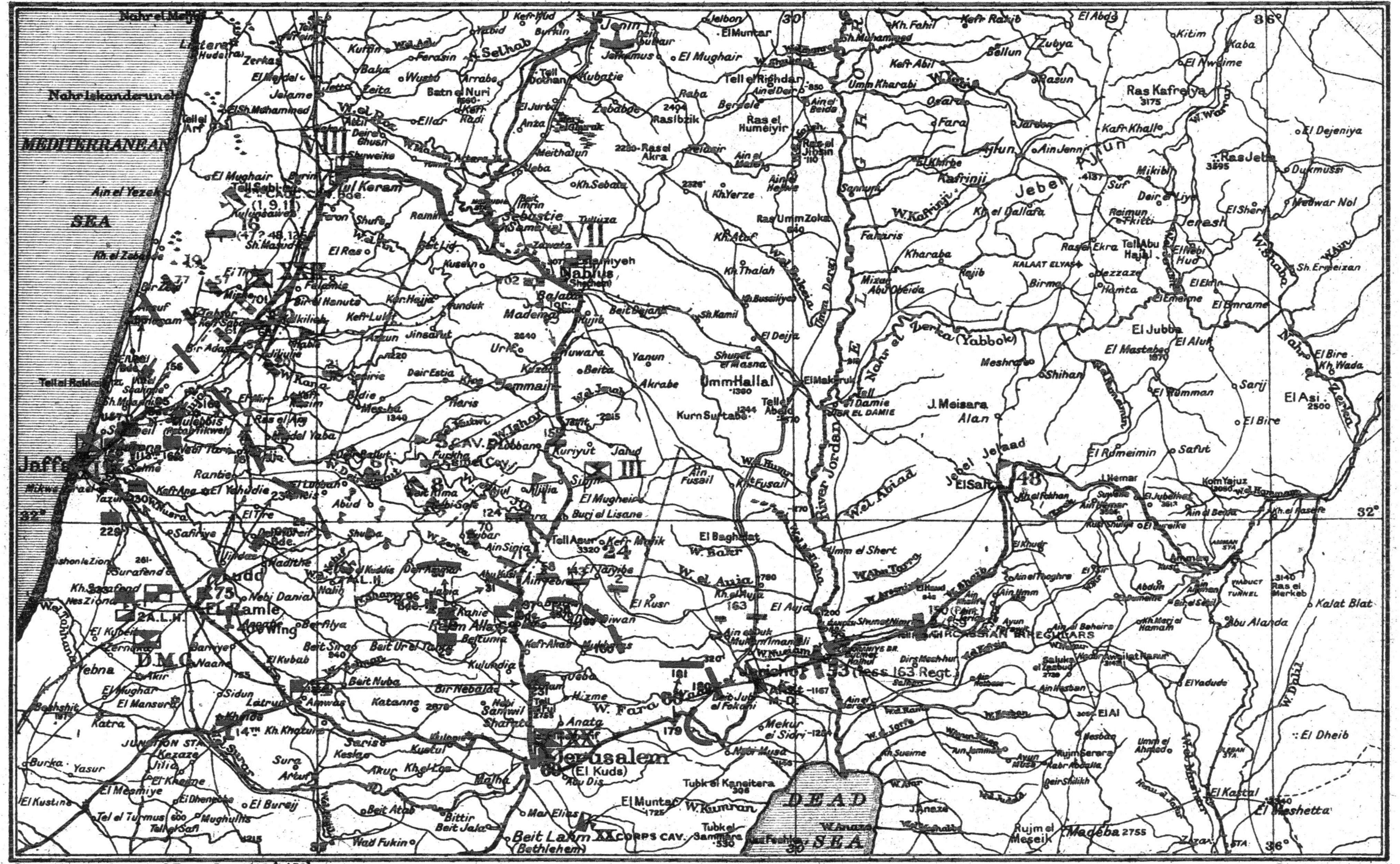

PLATE 33

Situation on 21.2.18 as known at G.H.Q.E.E.F.

Printed by the Survey of Egypt, Dec. 1918 (0453) Reprinted in England 1919

March 21.

After the advance on the northern front at the beginning of March, by the XXth and XXIst Corps, which pushed the front almost up to the line on which it remained until September, a raid upon the enemy's lines of communications in Gilead along which he was feeding his forces engaged against the Sherifian troops in the Hejaz, was decided upon. A special force was formed for this raid, known from the name of its Commander as "Shea's Group." It consisted of:—

> The Australian and New Zealand Mounted Division.
> The 60th (London) Division.
> The Imperial Camel Corps Brigade.
> 10th Heavy Battery, Royal Garrison Artillery.
> 9th British Mountain Artillery Brigade.
> Light Armoured Car Brigade.
> Army Bridging Train.
> Desert Mounted Corps Bridging Train.

On March 21, Group Headquarters, the cavalry and the camels were at Talaat ed Dumm (except a brigade at Neby Musa with the armoured cars), the 60th Division was in the Wadi Nueiameh (except a battalion of the 180th Brigade in the Wadi Kelt), the Divisional Artillery was disposed to cover the crossings at Ghoraniyeh and Hajlah, the Mountain Guns were immediately south of the Wadi Nueiameh, and the Bridging Trains were partly near Jericho and partly in the Wadi Kelt.

Reconnaissances had shewn that the Jordan at this time of year was unfordable at any available point and that the only practicable places for throwing bridges across were Makhadet, Hajlah, and Ghoraniyeh. It was decided that the cavalry and camels should cross by a steel pontoon bridge at Hajlah, while a standard pontoon bridge, a heavy barrel pier bridge, and an infantry bridge were to be built for the 60th Division at Ghoraniyeh. The 180th Brigade was instructed to force both crossings, with artillery support, and establish bridgeheads to cover the bridge builders. Feints at Aujah, Mandesi, Enkhola, Yehud, and Henu fords were to hold the enemy opposite these places while the 180th Brigade forced the passage in between.

At 1500 on March 21 the enemy reinforced his positions at Ghoraniyeh with 600 infantry and sent two squadrons of cavalry to Hajlah.

At midnight the first attempts to cross the river by swimming were made at Ghoraniyeh, but there was so much flood water in the Jordan that the swimmers of the 2/17th Londons were unable to make headway against the current. Repeated attempts were also made to cross in punts or on rafts but these were, for the same reason, unsuccessful. Our continued activities alarmed the enemy who opened fire and thus further complicated an already difficult operation. Meanwhile the 2/19th Londons and the Australian Engineers of the Desert Mounted Corps Bridging Train had been more fortunate at Hajlah. Their swimmers* had got across unobserved and at 0120 on March 22 the first raft, holding twenty-seven men, was ferried across. Ten minutes later orders were given that the attempt to cross at Ghoraniyeh was to be abandoned for the time. Accordingly the 180th Brigade Headquarters, and the 2/20th Londons moved down to Hajlah leaving the 2/17th Londons, some machine guns, and four guns of the 180th Trench Mortar Battery opposite Ghoraniyeh.

At 0500 the 179th Brigade Group moved into a concealed position west of Hajlah, and the 181st Brigade moved to Tel es Sultan at dawn.

Shortly after dawn an enfilade fire from enemy machine guns was brought to bear on our rafts from a commanding hill some 1,000 yards north-west of the crossing-place at Hajlah. Only eight men could be sent over at a time and these had to be at the bottom of the raft. One load had seven men hit. Two sections of the 180th Machine Gun Company provided covering fire and, by 0745, the whole of the 2/19th Londons were across the river. The 2/18th Battalion London Regiment, which had reached Hajlah at 0430, then began to cross and by 0810 the first pontoon bridge was finished. By noon the 2/18th Londons were also across and at 1315 efforts were made to enlarge the bridgehead, but owing to enemy machine-gun fire and the density of the jungle on the eastern bank of the river little could be effected.

The efforts of the 181st Brigade to cross at Ghoraniyeh at midnight again failed owing to the swiftness of the current, and it was not until the morning of March 23 that rafting became possible here after the swimmers had got across to the other bank from which the enemy had been driven by our concentrated machine-gun fire.

At 0400 the Auckland Mounted Rifles began to cross at Hajlah in order to clear the enemy out of the country on the east bank as far north as Ghoraniyeh, and later a regiment of the 1st Australian Light Horse Brigade was sent to Hajlah to clear the country to the east and south-east of the new bridge. The Auckland Mounted Rifles galloped down a number of Turkish detachments and secured the ground covering Ghoraniyeh by noon, capturing sixty-eight prisoners and four machine guns. At 0915 a landing party which had crossed the Dead Sea in motor boats and landed on the Turkish side of the Jordan joined up with the 180th Brigade at a point about three miles north of the Dead Sea.

The second pontoon bridge at Hajlah, 600 yards upstream from the first, was finished at 1330, and the light infantry bridge at Ghoraniyeh was ready by 1630 and was used by the 181st Brigade. The barrel pier bridge and the pontoon bridge at Ghoraniyeh were finished by 2150.

---

* The names of those Londoners who swam the Jordan on the night of March 21-22 are, 2nd Lieut. G. E. Jones, M.C.; Cpl. E. Margrave, M.M.; L/Cpl. W. H. Henderson; L/Cpl. F. Popham, Médaille Militaire; L/Cpl. W. V. Davis; L/Cpl. H. Silver; Pte. A. C. Hardwick; Pte. H. Hoxton; Pte. J. R. Powell; Pte. R. N. Williams. Of the Australians, L/Cpl. S. Dawson was awarded the Military Medal.

To face Plate 34.

AMMAN RAID

Situation on ....21-3-18.... as known at G.H.Q.E.E.F.

March 24-29.

At 0500 on the morning of March 24 the dispositions of Shea's Group were as follows: the 179th Brigade was in the Wadi Nimrin, about two miles up the gulley, the 180th was between the 179th and the Ghoraniyeh bridges, and had guards at these and at the Hajlah bridges. The 181st Brigade was on the right (south) flank of the 179th along the Shunet Nimrin road. The 1st Australian Light Horse Brigade was covering the left (north) flank of the 60th Division about one mile north of El Mandasi ford, and the rest of the Australian and New Zealand Mounted Division was to the east of Hajlah. The 303rd Brigade Royal Field Artillery which had crossed at Ghoraniyeh during the night, and two Mountain Artillery Batteries, supported the 181st Brigade in its attack on Shunet Nimrin at 0830, and one Mountain Artillery Battery supported the 179th Brigade. By 1500 Tel el Musta and El Haud had both been captured. During their attack on the former the 2/22nd Londons had taken three field guns. The presence of the 179th on El Haud enabled the left of the 181st to advance in the valley, and by turning the enemy's right flank compelled him to retire. The 181st pursued the retreating enemy as fast as possible up the Es Salt road with a squadron of Wellington Mounted Rifles in advance. The Australian Imperial Force Airline Section followed the infantry closely and erected an airline to Shunet Nimrin under fire. At midday Group Headquarters moved from the junction of the Jericho and Nebi Musa roads, about one and quarter miles below Talaat ed Dumm, to the west bank of the Jordan at Ghoraniyeh. At 1300 the 2nd Australian Light Horse Brigade was at Teleil Muslim and began following up the Wadi Kefrein, reaching Rujm el Oshir, six miles further on, at 1520. Here its advance was delayed by the bad state of the track, which was found to be impassable for wheels. All wheel transport had to be withdrawn to Shunet Nimrin and the ammunition transferred to camels. In many cases the horses and camels had to be dragged, pushed, and even lifted up the slippery track along which they could only move in single file. The New Zealand Mounted Rifles Brigade was moving north-eastwards along the Wadi Jofet el Ghazlaniye, and the head of the Imperial Camel Corps Brigade was about two miles west of Kabr Mujahid. By dusk the 181st Brigade had advanced about four miles up the Es Salt road beyond Shunet Nimrin and was in touch with the enemy who was holding positions astride of the road.

March 25 was very wet, and the cavalry and camels found great difficulty in reaching Naaur, seven miles from Rujm el Oshir, by 1030. The 181st Brigade was also much hampered by the mud and did not reach a point within a mile of Es Salt until 1615. Salt itself, which had been evacuated by the enemy, was occupied by the 3rd Australian Light Horse Regiment at 1800 and by the 179th Brigade at midnight. No opposition had been made to their advance by way of the Arseniyat track.

On March 26 the cavalry continued their march from Naaur in heavy rain, and at 0500 the 2nd Australian Light Horse Brigade joined the New Zealand Mounted Rifles Brigade at the cross-roads one mile east of Es Sir. The 2nd Australian Light Horse Brigade then pushed out north of the Amman-Es Salt road capturing 170 prisoners near Sweileh. At 1400 the Mounted Division found it necessary to rest men and horses, but sent a raiding party which blew up the Hejaz railway, seven miles south of Amman, during the night.

At 0500 on the morning of March 27 the 181st Brigade (less two battalions), which had handed over the defence of Es Salt to the 179th, advanced towards Amman with three mountain batteries. The advance was, however, interrupted by the incidence of a local feud which happened to be in progress between the Circassians of Sweileh and the Christian Arabs of El Fuheis. The column halted for the night two miles east of Sweileh. The cavalry started for Amman at 0900, and the New Zealand Mounted Rifles Brigade reached Ain Amman at 1030 with the 2nd Australian Light Horse Brigade within three miles of Amman Station on the left. The Imperial Camel Corps Brigade at 1100 advanced on Amman village but was held up by enemy fire. At 1500, after much delay in crossing the Wadi Amman the New Zealand Mounted Rifles Brigade reached the railway south of Amman, but the 2nd Australian Light Horse Brigade were unable to reach it to the north. Demolition parties were usefully employed in destroying the line and its culverts in the direction of Libben. During the night the 2nd Australian Light Horse Brigade succeeded in destroying a two-arch bridge on the railway seven miles north of Amman.

At 1100 on March 28 the two battalions of the 181st Brigade which had been left in Es Salt, started for Amman. During the day the defence of Es Salt was strengthened by the 2/14th and 2/16th Londons, who came up from El Howeij, whither they had proceeded on the 27th for supply purposes. Thus, by evening, the whole of the 179th Brigade, except the 2/13th Londons (still at El Howeij), the 3rd Australian Light Horse Regiment, and two howitzer batteries, were at Es Salt. During the morning twenty-two Turkish lorries were destroyed by the Armoured Car Brigade on the road between Salt and Swei'eh. At 1430 an enemy force was observed by the 1st Australian Light Horse Brigade advancing along the road from Jisr ed Damieh, and two batteries of Royal Field Artillery moved out in support of the cavalry. Meanwhile the attack on Amman had begun at 1300 when the 2/23rd Londons on the right, and the 2/21st Londons on the left, advanced parallel to the north of the Sweileh-Amman road against the eastern bank of the Wadi Amman. They were supported by the 9th Mountain Artillery Brigade, which also shelled Hill 3039 to assist the advance of the New Zealand Mounted Rifles Brigade. The advance over absolutely exposed ground was held up by intense enemy machine-gun and rifle fire about 1,000 yards to the north-west of Amman. Further artillery support was difficult owing to lack of observation, and co-operation on the flanks became essential for a continuance of the attack, but the 2nd Australian Light Horse Brigade on the left and the Imperial Camel Corps Brigade on the right had been unable to move, while the New Zealand Mounted Rifles Brigade was held up by machine-gun fire from Hill 3039, which dominated Amman from the south-east. During the afternoon the 2/17th and 2/18th Londons

AMMAN RAID

Situation on 24.3.18 as known at G.H.Q.E.E.F.

were ordered to proceed from Es Sir to support the 181st Brigade. On our left the 2/20th Londons and a battery of armoured cars were sent to support the 1st Australian Light Horse Brigade.

Owing to the heavy rains the Jordan bridges had been subjected to a very heavy strain by the rush of flood-water. The Jordan had risen nine feet in a very few hours, and only one bridge with its causeway had been kept open at Ghoraniyeh.

At 1730 thirteen enemy aeroplanes bombed Shunet Nimrin causing a number of casualties among the camels.

During the morning of March 29 enemy reinforcements reached Amman Station (two miles distant from Amman village), and the enemy tried to work round the left flank of the 181st Brigade through a gap which existed between it and the 2nd Australian Light Horse Brigade. There were still hopes, however, that the enemy intended to evacuated Amman, and preparations were made for a night attack and at 1530 a battery of Royal Horse Artillery started for Amman from Shunet Nimrin. At Salt the enemy began to show considerable activity and tried to work round the left flank of the 179th Brigade.

March 30 to April 3.

At 0200 on March 30 the night attack on Amman began, and at 0430 the New Zealand Mounted Rifles Brigade captured part of Hill 3039 with six machine guns, but it was unable to secure the rest of the hill. On their left the Imperial Camel Corps Brigade captured two lines of trenches with twelve prisoners, but the 181st Brigade was unable to reach the Wadi Amman "north of the Citadel" in spite of the capture of 135 prisoners and four machine guns by the 2/22nd Londons. The 2/18th Londons, between the 2/22nd Londons and the Imperial Camel Corps Brigade to the south, got within half a mile of the "Citadel," but were held up by the heavy frontal fire. Repeated counter-attacks were directed against the 2/21st Londons on the left of the 181st Brigade. Stubborn hand-to-hand fighting ensued and the enemy was constantly repulsed with satisfactory losses, but no contact could be made with the 2nd Australian Light Horse Brigade on the extreme left. Troops of the New Zealand Mounted Rifles Brigade entered Amman village at 0900 but were fired upon from the houses, and the Imperial Camel Corps Brigade was held up by enfilade machine-gun fire from both flanks. At this time the Royal Horse Artillery battery which had left Shunet Nimrin on the previous day, came into action. At 1100 a Turkish counter-attack against Hill 3039 was dispersed by artillery fire, but the Imperial Camel Corps Brigade could make no further progress, while the northern (left flank) of the 181st Brigade was hard pressed by the enemy. At 1500 after an artillery bombardment the 2/18th Londons again stormed the "Citadel" but was checked within 400 yards of its objective by machine-gun fire from the right flank. Meanwhile the New Zealand Mounted Rifles Brigade was being heavily shelled on Hill 3039, and enemy reinforcements were arriving from the north.

During the day the situation at Es Salt had become somewhat complicated owing to the arrival of enemy reinforcements in the vicinity of Kefr Huda, on the Jebel Osha, two miles north-west of the town. A battalion of the 180th Brigade was sent up from Nimrin to Howeij and the 2/13th Londons were brought back to Salt from the direction of Amman. The enemy attack from the direction of Kefr Huda was defeated at 2255, and the 3rd Australian Light Horse Regiment in a skirmish captured three prisoners, three machine guns, and killed fourteen Turks. During the night the withdrawal from Amman began.

At 0715 on March 31 the Imperial Camel Corps Brigade reached Es Sir, and the evacuation of the wounded from the advanced dressing stations was completed by 1000. The 181st Brigade withdrew from its original positions before the last attack on Amman, by way of Sweileh and Es Sir, in order to avoid the Amman-Fuhais road. The 2nd Australian Light Horse Brigade covered this withdrawal. The infantry reached Es Sir just before dusk and continued marching along the track, which was almost impassable for camels, in rain and darkness.

At 1055 the 301st Field Artillery Brigade and "B" 303rd Battery took up positions west of the Jordan to cover the crossing of divisional troops and two batteries of armoured cars, after dusk.

On April 1 the retirement continued and, during the night, the 179th Brigade withdrew from Es Salt without incident, after blowing up the whole of the captured ammunition.

By 0500 on April 2 the 2/17th and 2/19th Londons rejoined the 180th Brigade and formed a bridgehead until relieved by the 1st Australian Light Horse Brigade and one regiment of the 2nd Australian Light Horse Brigade, next day. The withdrawal of the whole force, with the exception of the bridgehead troops, was completed by the evening of April 2, without interference from the enemy.

In spite of the trouble caused by flood-water in the river, and of the feet that large numbers of civilian refugees from Es Salt, as well as 986 prisoners and 30,000 animals, had to use the bridges in addition to the troops, no delay of any kind was experienced in re-crossing the Jordan.

The medical arrangements of this raid were conducted under unusual difficulties, and as Jerusalem was the nearest base to which cases could be evacuated, the following stations and relay posts were established:—

(1) Talaat ed Dumm.
(2) Main dressing station near Jericho with special operating unit for serious cases.
(3) Main dressing station Shunet Nimrin.
(4) Advanced dressing station and motor ambulance relay, Es Salt.
(5) Motor ambulance relay, four miles east of Es Salt, on the Amman road.
(6) Advanced dressing station, two miles west of Amman.

During the raid, 1,886 sick and wounded were evacuated.

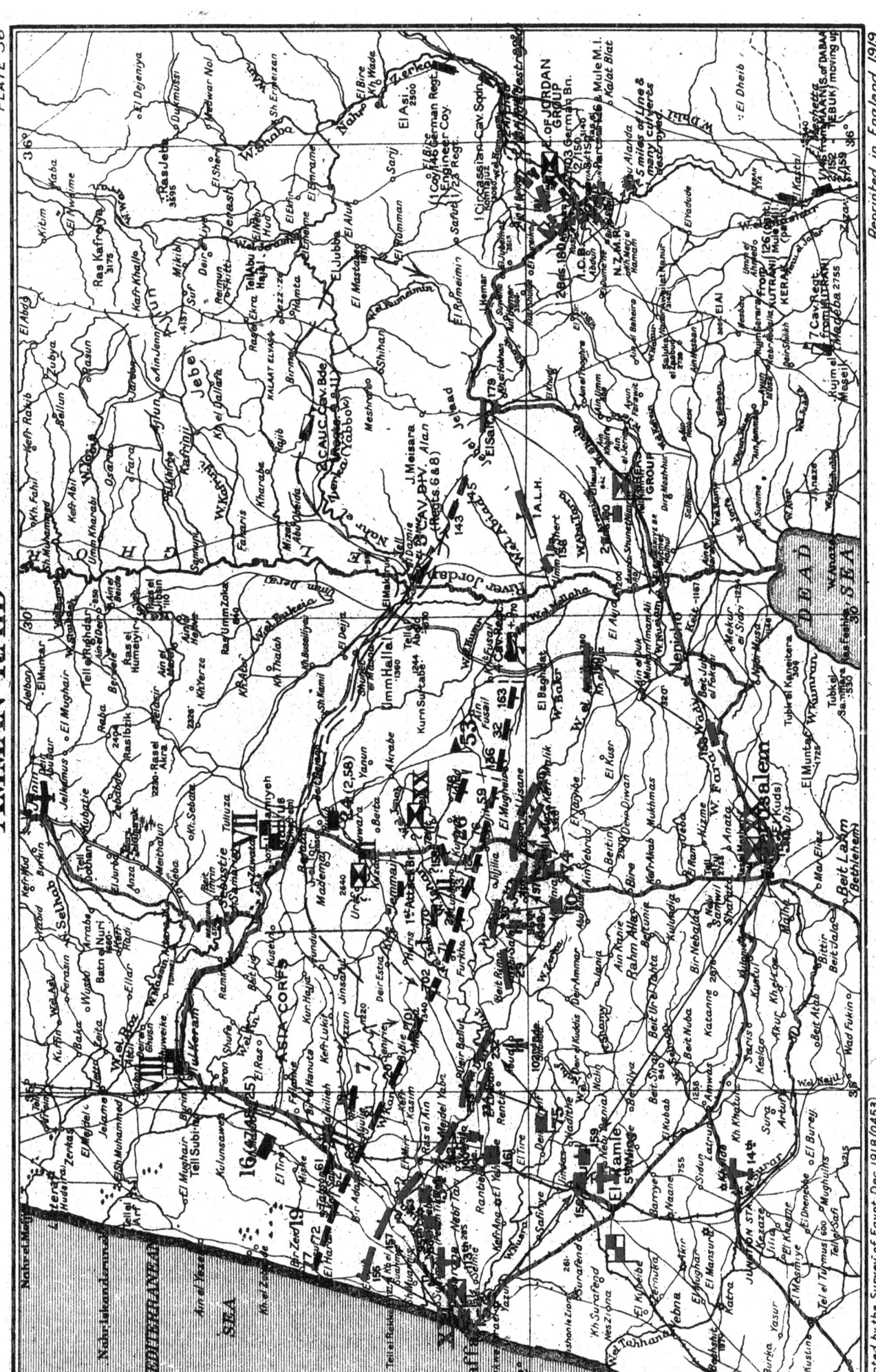

AMMAN RAID — Situation on 29-3-18 as known at G.H.Q.E.E.F.

April 29.

The second raid into Gilead, which did so much to persuade the enemy that the ultimate advance against Damascus would be made by way of Es Salt and Amman—and thereby compelled him to keep the whole of his IVth Army on the east of Jordan—was primarily intended to harass and, if possible, cut off the large concentration of Turkish troops at Shunet Nimrin, and co-operate with a Sherifian advance at Es Salt. The Desert Mounted Corps was detailed to capture Es Salt and, thereby, cut the the only metalled road serving the Shunet Nimrin position. The secondary line of communication down the Wadi es Sir ran through the territory of the Beni Sakhr tribe which had agreed to attack the Turks in co-operation with any British advance before May 4, the date on which the tribe would have to move to fresh grazing grounds. The 180th Brigade (60th Division) on the morning of April 30 attacked the Shunet Nimrin position and captured the advanced works, while the 179th Brigade attacked El Haud. The enemy, however, being in great strength offered so stubborn a resistance that no further progress was possible.

Meanwhile, the 3rd Australian Light Horse Brigade, having the Hong Kong and Singapore Battery attached instead of the Notts. Battery, detached for service with the 4th Australian Light Horse Brigade, started from Ghoraniyeh for Es Salt by way of the Jisr ed Damie track. The 5th Mounted Brigade moved on the same objective by a more direct route. The 3rd Australian Light Horse Brigade was accompanied by 360 camels, artillery, and ambulance transport. The brigade was engaged about two miles north-west of Es Salt and entered the town which was full of enemy troops and transports at 1830. A brisk action in and around the town resulted in the seizure of the junction of the Amman and Shunet Nimrin roads beyond the town, and the capture of numbers of prisoners. The General Headquarters of the IVth Turkish Army only escaped capture by the narrowest margin, given as "one minute" in a captured enemy document signed by the Chief of the General Staff of that army. The 9th Australian Light Horse Regiment then moved out to cover the town from the north-east to the north-west, and at 2200 a detachment of the 10th Australian Light Horse Regiment, with four machine guns, moved eastwards to seize the junction of the Amman–Ain es Sir roads near Ain Hemar. The Turks, however, were astride of the Amman road, 2,000 yards west of Ain Hemar, and the detachment was held up. Next day the 2nd Australian Light Horse Brigade reached Es Salt and Ain Hemar was occupied, when the detachment rejoined its regiment.

The 4th Australian Light Horse Brigade, having crossed the Jordan at Ghoraniyeh at 1900 on April 29 moved north through thick jungle at 0320, being fired upon by the enemy from Red Hill. At 0530 the main body reached the Jisr ed Damie and the 4th Australian Light Horse Regiment advanced up the Nahr ez Zerka. By 0730 the brigade held a line running from the Nahr ez Zerka to a point 500 yards south of the Jisr ed Damie–Es Salt track, about 2,000 yards west of the hills. The 11th Australian Light Horse Regiment failed to capture the Turkish bridgehead at the ford as the position was held in strength. By evening enemy reinforcements began to arrive from the north-west, and the line was shortened by a withdrawal eastwards into the foothills while Red Hill, some two miles to the south, covering the line of retreat to Ghoraniyeh was held by a detachment of the 11th Australian Light Horse Regiment with four machine guns. The 12th Australian Light Horse Regiment held the left of the line and the 4th the right of the line, with the rest of the 11th in reserve.

May 1.

At 0800 on May 1 the Turks attacked in force, bringing their guns forward. Further Turkish reinforcements were observed coming up and the "B" Battery, Honourable Artillery Company was withdrawn southwards along the track running parallel with the foothills. During its withdrawal one gun fell over a precipice and had to be abandoned. At 1000 the enemy captured Red Hill, the garrison of which withdrew to the south. At 1030 the Turks again attacked and drove in the right flank, and by 1100 had advanced to within half a mile of the main position. The enemy advance on the left flank was also pressed forward in spite of the reinforcement of the 12th Australian Light Horse Regiment by the reserves. At 1130 the Turks were only 200 yards away and afforded an admirable target for our machine guns. The batteries still in the line, the "A" Battery, Honourable Artillery Company and the Notts. continued in action, firing point blank into the massed enemy. As there was no track fit for wheels the eight guns had to be abandoned but the personnel of the batteries was withdrawn with the gun-teams, and fresh guns being issued, the batteries were again in action within forty-eight hours. At the time, however, the brigade was hard put to effect its retreat over country which was full of gullies and gorges so steep that in many cases animals fell down precipices and perished.

By noon the brigade had taken up a line running from a point immediately north of Southern Pass to a point just south of Red Hill, where a stand was made against repeated enemy attacks. This position covered the Umm esh Shert track from the Jordan to Es Salt which was now the only means of retreat for the cavalry at Es Salt.

Meanwhile, the enemy was bringing up large reinforcements, and the Beni Sakhr tribe failed to take the action which had been expected. This left the Es Sir road open to the Turks and the Shunet Nimrin force, instead of being an isolated body of troops, formed the southern claw of a formidable pair of pincers with which the enemy threatened to cut off the cavalry at Es Salt. Without the co-operation alike of the Beni Sakhr and the Desert Mounted Corps it was in vain for the 60th Division to continue a

ES SALT RAID

Situation on 29.4.18 as known at G.H.Q.E.E.F.

frontal attack in hopes of compelling a superior force to surrender. The Desert Mounted Corps was therefore ordered to withdraw from the Es Salt area, as a preliminary to a general retirement to the Ghoraniyeh bridgehead.

After having cleared their line of advance from Jisr ed Damieh towards Es Salt, the Turks made an attack at 2000, on May 2, against the 10th Australian Light Horse Regiment covering the town. In spite of constant repulses the 66th Regiment came on again at 2030, at 0200 on May 3, and at 0400. On the failure of the last attack the Turks were chased down hill with bombs, and retired nearly a mile. The 8th Regiment, attached to the 2nd Australian Light Horse Brigade, was attacked on the north-east front covering Es Salt, near Kh. el Fokan, at dawn on May 3. The Turks were vigorously counter-attacked at 0630 and lost 319 prisoners. At the same time enemy attacks were delivered on the Kefr Huda ridge, held by the 3rd Australian Light Horse Brigade. A post was driven in and, before any decision as to a reorganization could be put into effect, the withdrawal of the whole force from Es Salt was ordered. The incidence of this enemy activity interfered with the joint attack upon Shunet Nimrin by the cavalry and the 60th Division which took place on May 2. The Turks succeeded in holding the cavalry at Howeij, while the 179th and 180th Brigades were unable to make any substantial progress.

The weather during these operations was excellent, a material factor in favour of the Turks, as the Es Sir road, improved since March, was capable of carrying considerable traffic in dry weather.

The retirement was successfully accomplished under cover of the 181st Brigade which had been brought up to form an extended bridgehead at Ghoraniyeh. By the evening of May 4 all troops of the raiding force had recrossed the Jordan, and the original bridgehead was restored. The raiders had taken in all 942 prisoners and twenty-nine machine guns.

That the operations east of Jordan during April–May finally convinced the enemy that future British operations would be in this area, with the railway junction of Deraa as an objective, is shown by captured enemy documents. It was fully realized that the capture and retention of that place by the British would involve the retirement or surrender of any troops remaining to the south, and the direct line to Deraa lay east of Jordan. This belief on the part of the Enemy Command led to the dispersal of forces with a difficult obstacle—the Jordan River and Valley—between the two main groups. These two groups consisted of the VIIth and VIIIth Armies west of the Jordan and IVth Army east of that river.

The respective enemy commanders were incessant in their claims for reinforcements, multiplying their difficulties, and, in the case of the IVth and VIIth Army Commands, tendering their resignation on the grounds of neglect of their demands, and criticism of their command. The Commander of the IVth Army philosophically commences his reply to an adverse criticism by the German Commander-in-Chief—Liman von Sanders—with the remark, " In this fifth year of the war we are all accustomed to misunderstanding and friction." In this short sentence is gently expressed what had been evident to close observers of the relations between the Turkish and German Staffs and individual officers since the operations leading to the loss of Baghdad. The German's standpoint regarding his mission is well expressed in the following extract from a letter addressed to a German Staff Officer of the IVth Army on May 4, 1918 :—

" It is we, as Prussian officers, who are charged with the duty of pushing forward with the greatest energy, satisfying complaints as far as possible, but otherwise insisting with an iron-like resolution on our wishes."

and his opinion of the Turkish officer with whom he had to deal :—

" The view of the equality of right of the Turks with Europeans, originating in the abolition of the Capitulations, is, of course, just like comparing Lascars to German soldiers, and in many ways, even for enlightened senior Turkish officers it assumes quite grotesque forms."

On the part of the Turkish officer, apart from his feeling of resentment at being driven to further other aims than those which would be of advantage to his own country, there was always the—for the time being—repressed feeling against the infidel. The extent of this feeling may be judged from the following extract from a personal letter from Fevzi Pasha, G.O.C. VIIth Army, to Von Falkenhayn :—

" My departure for Amman, in order to take over the new command to which I was appointed by Your Excellency, as well as the spiritual and social circumstances of the new post, demand a succession of special measures, neglect of which will entail serious consequences. . . .

" Bearing this in mind, and I regard it as very important, it is clear that the employment of officers and men in German uniform in the neighbourhood of the Hejaz Railway, regarded by Moslems as sacred, will favour and strengthen British propaganda, and will increase the already treasonable convictions and fanaticism of the inhabitants.

" For this reason, I shall not be able therefore to take with me to Amman the officers and men in German uniform who have hitherto been on my staff, and I shall also send the German battalion now in the neighbourhood of Kerak to the XXth (Turkish) Army Corps.*

" I request you either speedily replace the German flying units and motor lorry columns now in the above-named zone with Turkish officers and men, or else equip them throughout with Turkish uniforms."

---

* The Turkish XXth Corps was at that time west of Jordan.

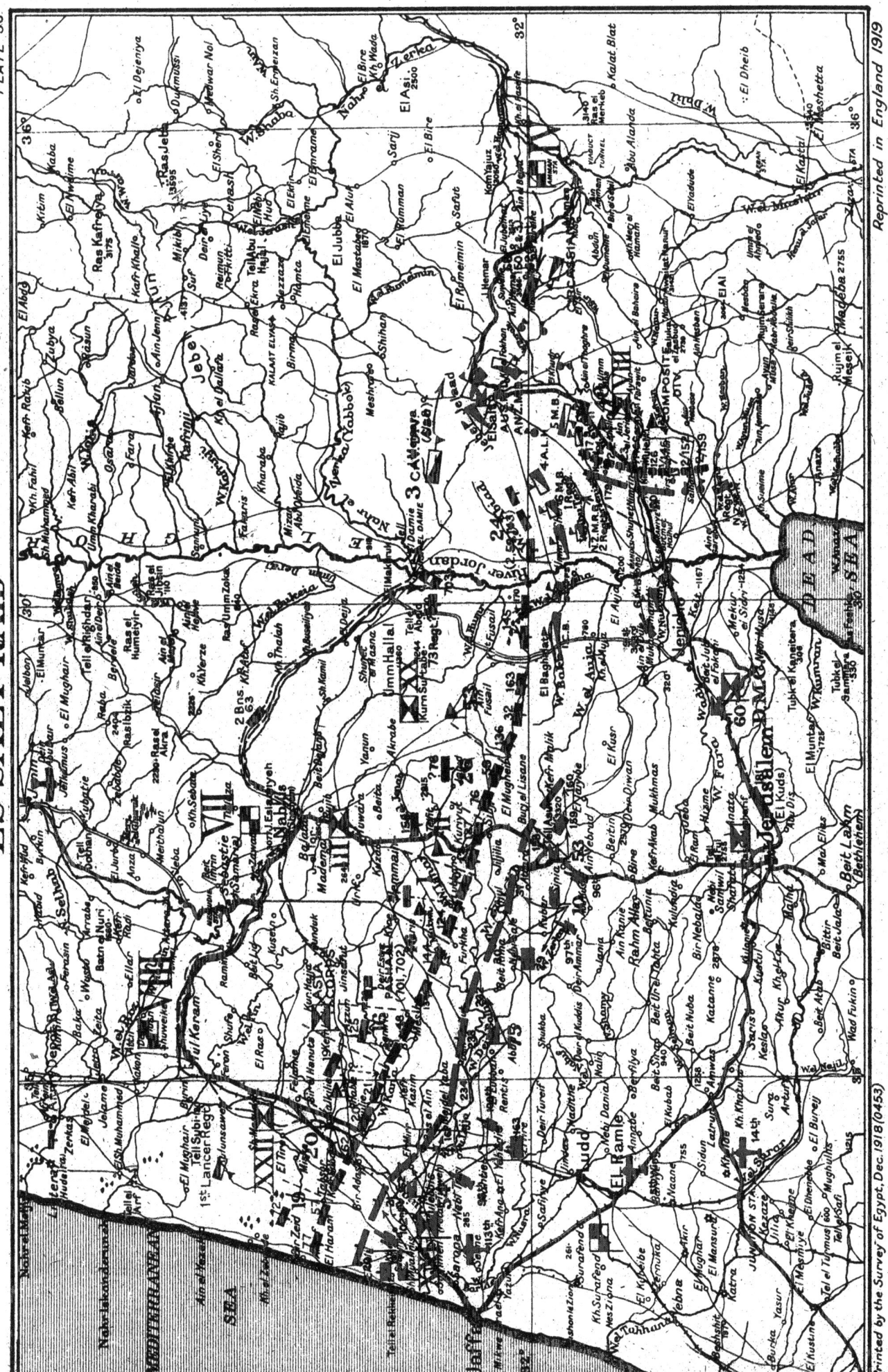

The Water Supply of Jerusalem and the XXth Corps Area.

The Engineers having completed the first part of their task, namely, the provision of a sufficient supply of water to enable General Allenby's army to march on Jerusalem, next turned their attention to roads. When the capital of Palestine had fallen, however, they were again confronted with the problem of providing water, not only for the army and its numerous appurtenances, but for the population of the Holy City itself.

When our troops entered Jerusalem the sources of water supply were :—

(1) Rain-water, stored in cisterns.

(2) Aqueduct-borne water from Solomon's Pools, a quantity of 40,000 gallons per day.

(3) The Pool of Siloam, practically liquid sewage.

Our troops perforce drew heavily upon this supply during the winter, and it was necessary, in order to avoid a dangerous shortage, to take steps that would become operative before the rainless summer was upon the city. The scheme proposed by the Engineers and successfully carried out is rich in historic and even romantic associations. It was based on a modification of the Herod-Pontius Pilate system. The ancient engineers of the Roman world had carried the water of the Wadi Arrub springs in rock-cut channels to a reservoir of 4,000,000 gallons capacity, and thence to Jerusalem by a masonry aqueduct *viâ* the Pools of Solomon. So now the rock-cut channels leading from the springs were thoroughly cleansed—they were blocked with an accumulation which can literally be described as " the dust of ages," including the remains of several individuals who may have belonged to almost any period. Next the ancient reservoir was repaired, pumps were installed, pumping water to a newly erected reservoir of 300,000 gallons capacity at a point near the springs, whence water flowed by the force of gravity to a reservoir constructed on a high point west of Jerusalem, so that now it was possible for water-pipes to carry a supply to any point in the town itself. (See PLATE 39.)

This water system in Jerusalem was laid down primarily for immediate military necessities, and partly in order to recoup the civilian population for the water stored by them and consumed by the army, but the installation will be of permanent value to the city. The work was begun on April 15, 1916, and nine weeks later, on June 18, water was delivered to the inhabitants. Twelve miles of pipe-line had been laid to ensure this result. The daily supply was 280,000 gallons, and during early summer, when supply was plentiful, storage cisterns were filled in Jerusalem for the bigger buildings. Not since the days of the Romans has running water been so plentiful in the Holy City. It is estimated, by the way, that Jerusalem contains rain-water storage cisterns to the capacity of 360,000,000 gallons, or, in other words, barely sufficient for the needs of Greater London for thirty-six hours.

The district north of Jerusalem, both immediately behind the line held by the XXth Corps, and in the reserve area near Ramallah, was extremely short of water. Beyond the cisterns in the villages, used by the local inhabitants but useless for military purposes, there were only a few good springs, and these for the most part in very deep and often almost inaccessible valleys. The positions held and the principal lines of communication, on the other hand, were, generally speaking, on the highest ground, situated 2-3,000 feet above sea-level. To get water, therefore, it was necessary to instal pumping plant in order to raise the product of the springs. In some cases a total lift of 1,000 feet had to be attained, necessitating relay pumping station and reservoirs.

The principal supplies in the hills were :—

(1) Wadi Reiya and Wadi Zerka to El Lubban.

(2) From the Wadi Darah to Umm Suffa.

(3) A gravitation supply to a point north of Ain Sinia on the Nablus Road.

(4) From Durah, Jufna, and Ain Sinia to Tel Asur and Dar Jerir.

(5) From Ain Arik and Ain Jeriut to Beitunia and Bireh.

The total number of pump houses erected was fourteen, and the total height pumped from the eleven pump houses on the above mentioned five supplies was about 3,600 feet; average height about 330 feet per pump. The total length of pipes laid was over twenty-eight miles. The masonry storage reservoirs erected in the area contained over 250,000 gallons, and the temporary storage exceeded this figure.

On the Jericho road, water was pumped from the springs in Wadi el Fara to a watering area at Talaat ed Dumm (Samaritan's Inn), a rise of 600 feet, necessitating two sets of pumping machinery, one at the bottom and one half-way up, and two additional pumping stations were installed to forward the water for distribution.

In the coastal plain, water was obtained from wells varying from 120 feet to forty feet in depth and over a wide area. Development, therefore, took the form of the installation of a large number of pumps and engines on the many wells discovered and improved in the district. Boring sections, too, were most successful in sinking for water.

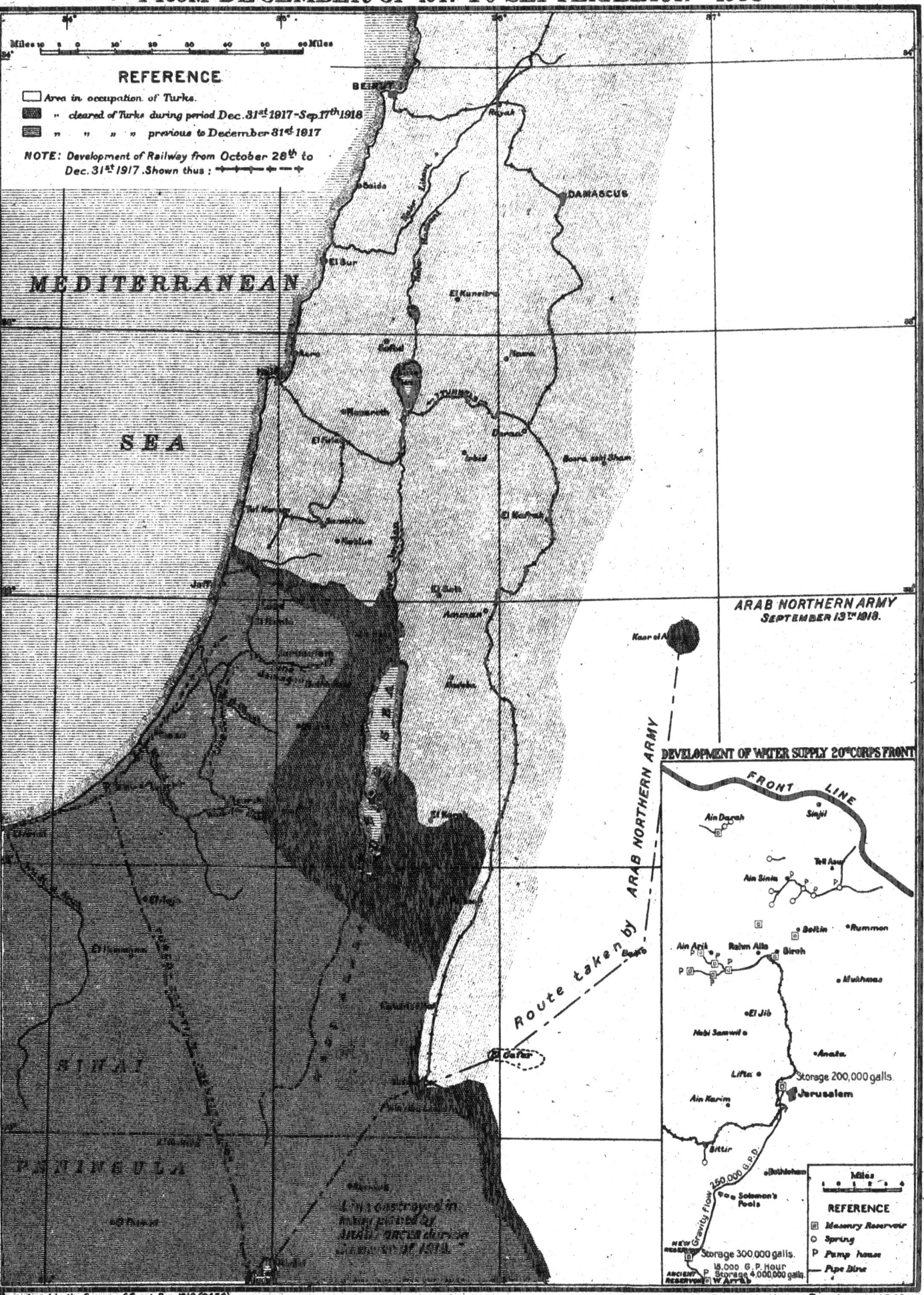

The September Advance.

The day before the September advance, the enemy Intelligence Service issued a disposition map, which was captured in the headquarters of the Yilderim Army Group at Nazareth, and is reproduced in facsimile on the opposite page. The information embodied in this map was quite in accordance with the enemy's air service reports that "no essential changes had taken place in the distribution of the British forces." No change is shown. The move of the 60th Division into the XXIst Corps area, and the concentration of the cavalry on the coast, not to mention the alteration in the front of the 10th and 53rd Divisions, are passed unnoticed. The latter was apparently considered as being in reserve to sector lately occupied by the Desert Mounted Corps. The 6th Poona Division (at the time in Mesopotamia) is shown as being within ten miles of the front line, though to be fair, its exact location is queried.

The position of General Headquarters is not shown, and that of the XXIst Corps Headquarters is placed eleven miles away from where it was actually to be found. The French troops up in the line are queried as Italians.

To face Plate 40.

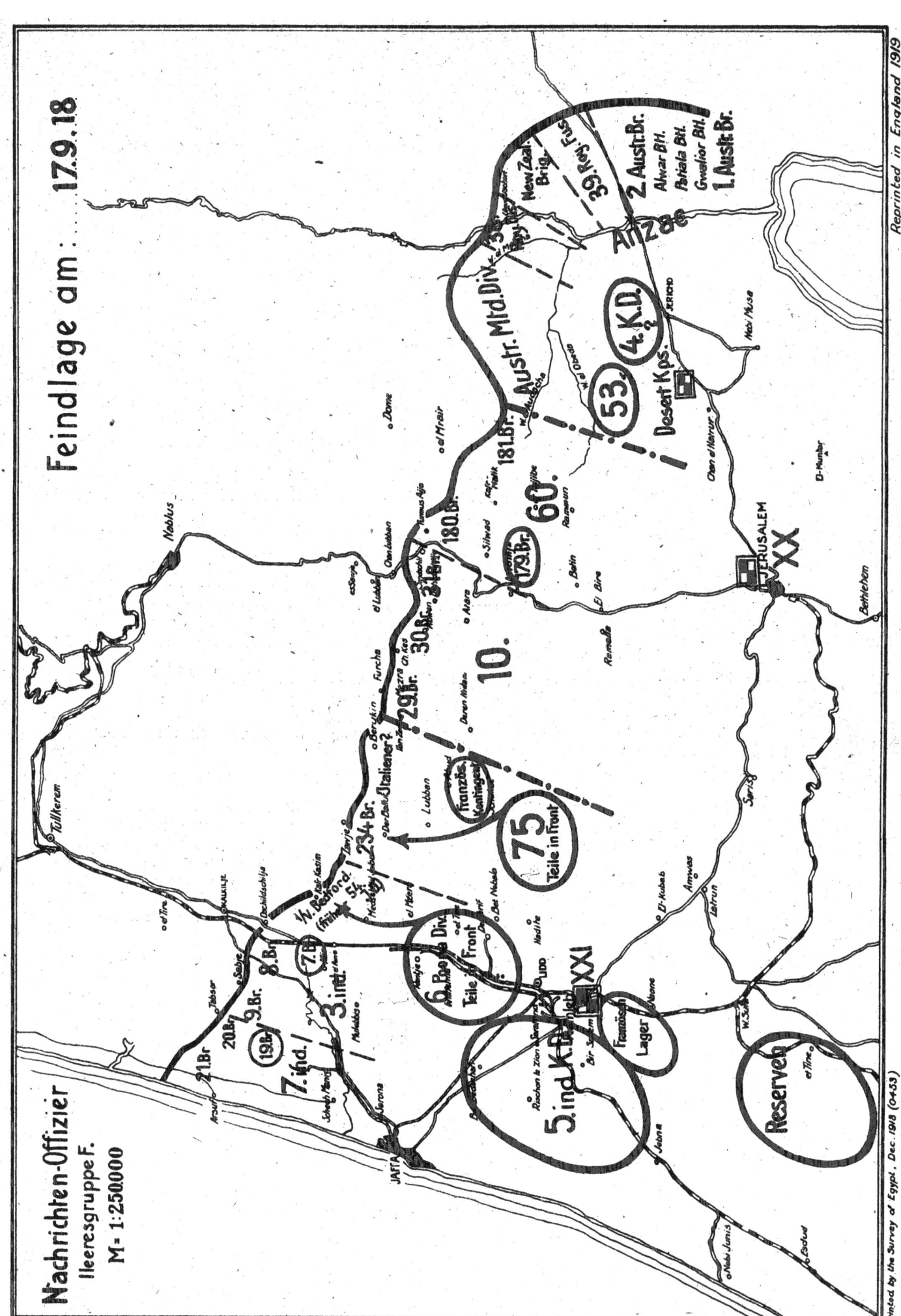

September 18.

On this day the preliminary concentration was complete. The divisions detailed for the main attack, 60th, 7th, 75th, 3rd, 54th, and the French contingent, had actually taken up their positions, the troops previously holding the coastal sector having closed up on to their own fronts of attack to make room for them.

The cavalry were concealed in the orange and olive groves, two divisions immediately north and east of Jaffa, and one (the Australian Mounted Division) near Ludd; all were within easy reach of the positions of assembly which they were to occupy during the night 18th–19th.

On the right the 10th and 53rd Divisions had closed in their outer flanks, west and east respectively, leaving their centre from Kefr Malik to Jiljulia covering the main Jerusalem–Nablus road to be occupied by "Watson's Force," a composite detachment formed from the XXth Corps cavalry regiments, two pioneer battalions, and the XXth Corps reinforcement camp. The ̅ ̅d Division were in position to launch their preliminary attack on El Mugheir as soon as darkness fell, and thus bring forward the right flank of the corps preparatory to further advance.

The way in which this preliminary concentration was carried out and concealed from the enemy, was one of the most remarkable achievements of the whole operations. A hostile aeroplane reconnaissance on the 15th reported as follows: "Some regrouping of cavalry units apparently in progress behind the enemy's left flank; otherwise nothing unusual to report"; and this at a time when three cavalry divisions, five infantry divisions, and the majority of the heavy artillery of the force were concentrated between Ramleh and the front line of the coastal sector, there being no less than 301 guns in place of the normal number of seventy.

On the same date the enemy Intelligence Staff was advised in another aeroplane report that General Allenby's headquarters at Bir Salem was "infantry camp, two battalions."

Prisoners from the coastal plain and the lower foothills of the Judæan range say that they had been told that the British would make a big attack about the 18th, but they had so often been given the same warning that no attention was paid to this one. That the Chief Command were uncertain as to which part of the front would be attacked is indicated by the fact that nowhere were troops grouped in reserve who could make an effective counter-attack. New units arriving on the front were dispersed, and the move, just previous to operations, of two German battalions from the west to east of Jordan was counter-balanced by the move of a strong Turkish regiment—the 191st—from the east to the west of the river.

To face Plate 41.

ADVANCE INTO SAMARIA

Situation at 10 p.m. on 18.9.18 as known at GHQ, E.E.F.

September 19.

The attack was launched at 0445 after only a quarter of an hour's bombardment, and broke clean through the Turkish defences on the coast with hardly a pause. On the right near Rafat the French contingent encountered determined opposition, and probably the hardest fighting of the day took place here and at Et Tireh, where the 75th Division only dislodged the reserves of the Turkish XXIInd Corps (Rafet Bey) after a sharp struggle.

But to take the main attack as a whole, the hackneyed expression that "it went entirely according to plan" is quite inadequate; the pace at which the infantry broke down the opposition and the cavalry got through and away, exceeded the most sanguine hopes. By 0730 the 5th Cavalry Division were crossing the Nahr Falik, and by midday they were across the Iskanderuneh; and the 4th Cavalry Division, though at first delayed by the wire and trenches which they had to cross, were little behind them. By evening the cavalry were in the positions shewn, and the 4th and 5th Divisions had fed and watered and were ready to continue their advance.

There is little more to be said about the infantry beyond what is shewn on the map. The 60th Division, after marching and fighting for eighteen miles, mostly over heavy sand, carried Tul Keram before dark. The 7th Division had reached the foothills about Et Taiyibeh; while the 3rd (Lahore) Division, after taking its first objective changed direction eastwards, carried the strong works round Kalkilieh, Jiljulieh, and Hableh, and established itself in the foothills to the east. A pipe-line, 7,000 yards in length, was laid in eight and a quarter hours by the Royal Engineers, while operations were in progress, from the mill-race on the Nahr el Auja, and conveyed 4,000 gallons per hour to Jiljulieh, where storage was arranged the same day for 70,000 gallons. The 54th Division and the French had secured all their objectives and were sufficiently advanced to support the northern flank of the 10th Division, which had orders to start its advance that night.

The 75th Division having disposed of all Turkish troops round Et Tireh, remained in that area and became Army Reserve.

On the front of the XXth Corps (53rd and 10th Divisions) there was no movement during the day; the 53rd Division consolidated the line of El Mugheir which it had successfully captured the night before. At 1535 telegraphic orders were sent for both these divisions to start their main advance on the night 19th–20th.

To face Plate 42.

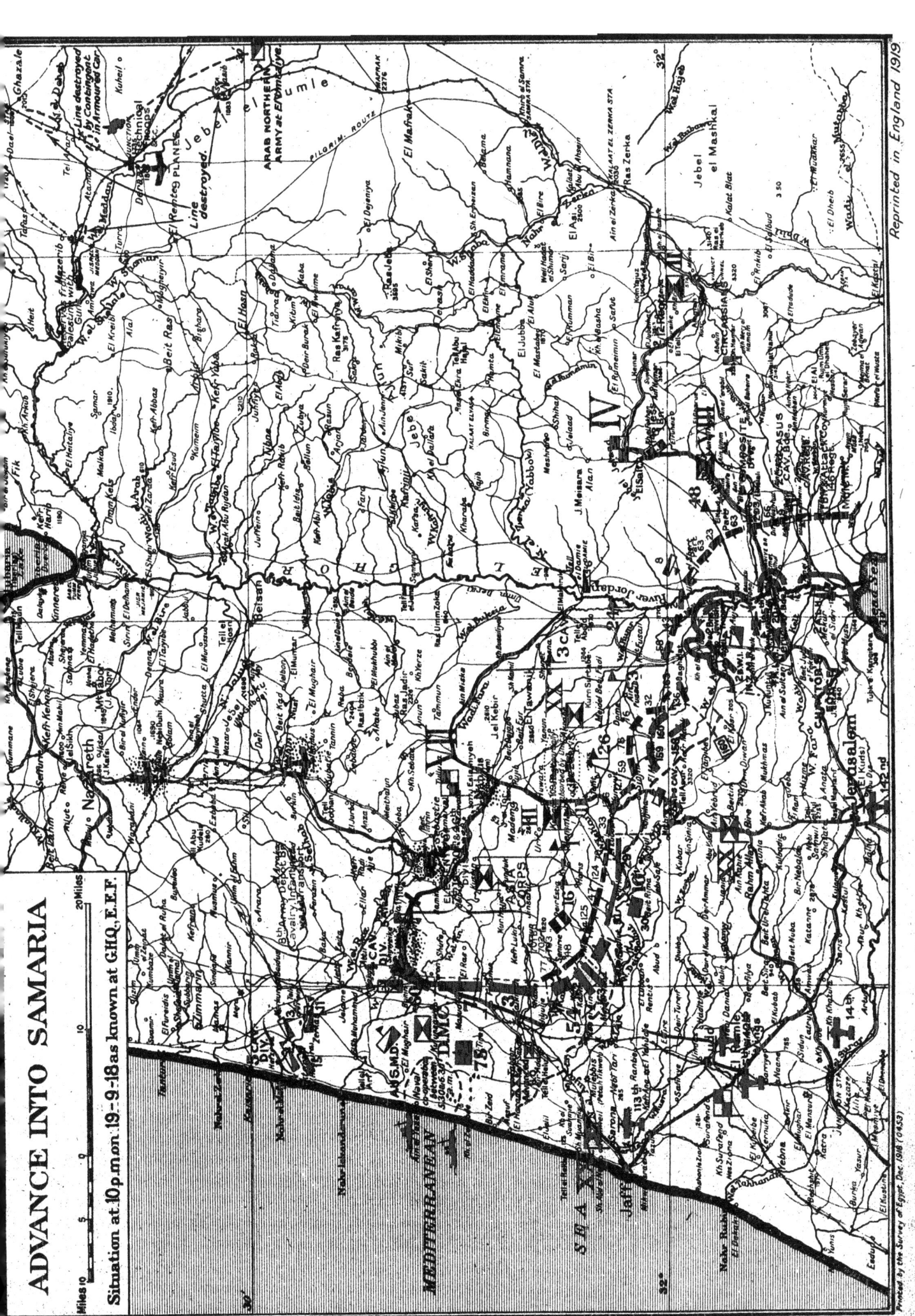

September 20.

On this day the 54th Division and French contingent ceased to be engaged, having successfully occupied Bidieh and the high ground north of the Wadi Kadah and so secured the left flank of the 10th Division attack; they were shortly afterwards withdrawn into reserve near the railway.

The 60th Division advanced up the Tul Keram–Nablus road and though engaged all day with enemy rearguards, had no very severe fighting. By evening they had occupied Anebta village and had secured the railway tunnel at Bir Asur intact, and were pushing forward towards the important railway station of Messudieh which had already been occupied by a squadron of the XXIst Corps cavalry and the 2nd L.A.C. Battery. The 5th Australian Light Horse Brigade, which was attached to the XXIst Corps for the time being, was operating north of Messudieh, and cut the railway near Ajje. The L.A.C. Battery subsequently pushed on towards Nablus.

The 7th Division pushed on all night through very difficult country, following mountain tracks over which no wheels could move; their greatest hardship was shortage of water, many men having nothing but what they carried in their water-bottles for more than twenty-four hours. Though in touch with scattered parties of the enemy all the time, they had no serious opposition until reaching the commanding village of Beit Lid, which overlooks the Nablus road, some three miles east of Anebta. Here the enemy had a strong rearguard posted supported by numerous machine guns, and the division was held up for a time, the Seaforth Highlanders suffering particularly heavily. The opposition was, however, overcome, and the division was astride the road and railway north of Messudieh by 0300 on the 21st a magnificent exhibition of marching and fighting and worthy of the best traditions of the 7th (late Meerut) Division which has seen as much hard fighting in different theatres of war as any division in the Indian Army.

The 3rd (Lahore) Division advanced steadily all day up the Azzon–Funduk track. This advance was slow in the face of strong enemy rearguards but good progress was made and all opposition overcome. Both the 7th and the 3rd Divisions had to rely for their water-supply during this day's advance on the two specially organized Camel Transport Corps water convoys each of 2,400 camels.

The 10th Division, who launched their attack early on the night of 19–20th, experienced strong opposition both from infantry and artillery, most of the German troops being engaged in this sector. However, the enemy was pressed back as far as Kefr Harris before nightfall. It must be remembered that the 10th Division, also the 53rd Division, were operating in a most difficult country, which it lends itself particularly to the defence; also, on this day they were attacking prepared, and often wired, positions.

On the right flank the Turks had concentrated comparatively large forces to oppose the 53rd Division, and in the course of the morning a counter-attack drove back our most advanced troops. The position was shortly afterwards recaptured by the 160th Infantry Brigade, the 1st Cape Corps Battalion and the 1/17th Infantry (Indian) particularly distinguishing themselves, and the advance of the whole division was continued.

While the infantry were breaking down the last organized resistance of the enemy, the action of the cavalry ensured the success of the operations and the destruction or capture of the whole Turkish force east of the Jordan. Pressing on all night in parallel columns, the 4th Cavalry Division on Megiddo (Lejjun) and the 5th Cavalry Division on Abu Shusheh (a few miles to the north), the Plain of Esdraelon was reached before dawn. Here the first opposition was met with; as the advanced guard of the 4th Cavalry Division debouched from the defile at Lejjun, a Turkish battalion with several machine guns was deploying in the plain below them. They were charged without hesitation by the leading regiment, the 2nd Lancers, and in a few minutes the division was able to continue its advance; less prompt action might have caused fatal delay. The 4th Cavalry Division continued its advance through Al Afule to Beisan which was successfully reached by evening; the 19th Lancers securing the important bridge over the Jordan at Jisr Mejamie ten miles further north. As showing the rapidity of our advance and the extent to which it surprised the enemy command, the following incident might be mentioned:—

Shortly after our cavalry had taken El Afule, a German aeroplane, arriving from the north, landed on the aerodrome, the pilot being quite unconscious of the fact that the place was in the hands of the British.

Meanwhile the 5th Cavalry Division crossed the plain, and soon after dawn the 13th Brigade rode into Nazareth. Here some hard street-fighting occurred, but the Germans and Turks were driven out of the town and only held out in a few houses covering the Tiberias road. They were not dislodged as only one brigade was available for the attack, the remainder being held ready in the plain to support the 4th Division if necessary. Yilderim Army Group Headquarters were captured in Nazareth with numbers of valuable documents, and the enemy commander, Marshal Liman von Sanders Pasha, himself only just made his escape in time; some accounts even say that he was actually in the town when the cavalry arrived, but, if so, he cannot have stayed there long.* In the evening the whole of the 5th Division were at and around Afule.

The Australian Mounted Division, which moved forward in close support of the 4th Division, reached

---

* An eyewitness asserts that at the first alarm he ran, clad only in pyjamas and armed with an electric torch, from his sleeping quarters to near Our Lady's Well, shouting for the driver of his motor car in which he made off. Subsequently the Marshal returned, dressed and superintended the removal of some of his papers.

ADVANCE INTO SAMARIA

Miles 10   5   0   10   20 Miles

Situation at 1.0 p.m. on 20.9.18., as known at GHQ, E.E.F.

Lejjun about midday and at once detached the 3rd Australian Light Horse Brigade to occupy Jenin. This was accomplished early in the afternoon, the brigade galloping over an entrenched position and speedily crushing all opposition. The only remaining brigade, the 4th Australian Light Horse (the 5th Australian Light Horse Brigade being attached to the XXIst Corps) was fully employed collecting and conveying the prisoners which had been picked up in ever increasing numbers all day.

In a word, a boldly conceived and ambitious cavalry scheme had been carried out to the letter, and all lines of retreat west of the Jordan denied to the enemy.

To face Plate 44.

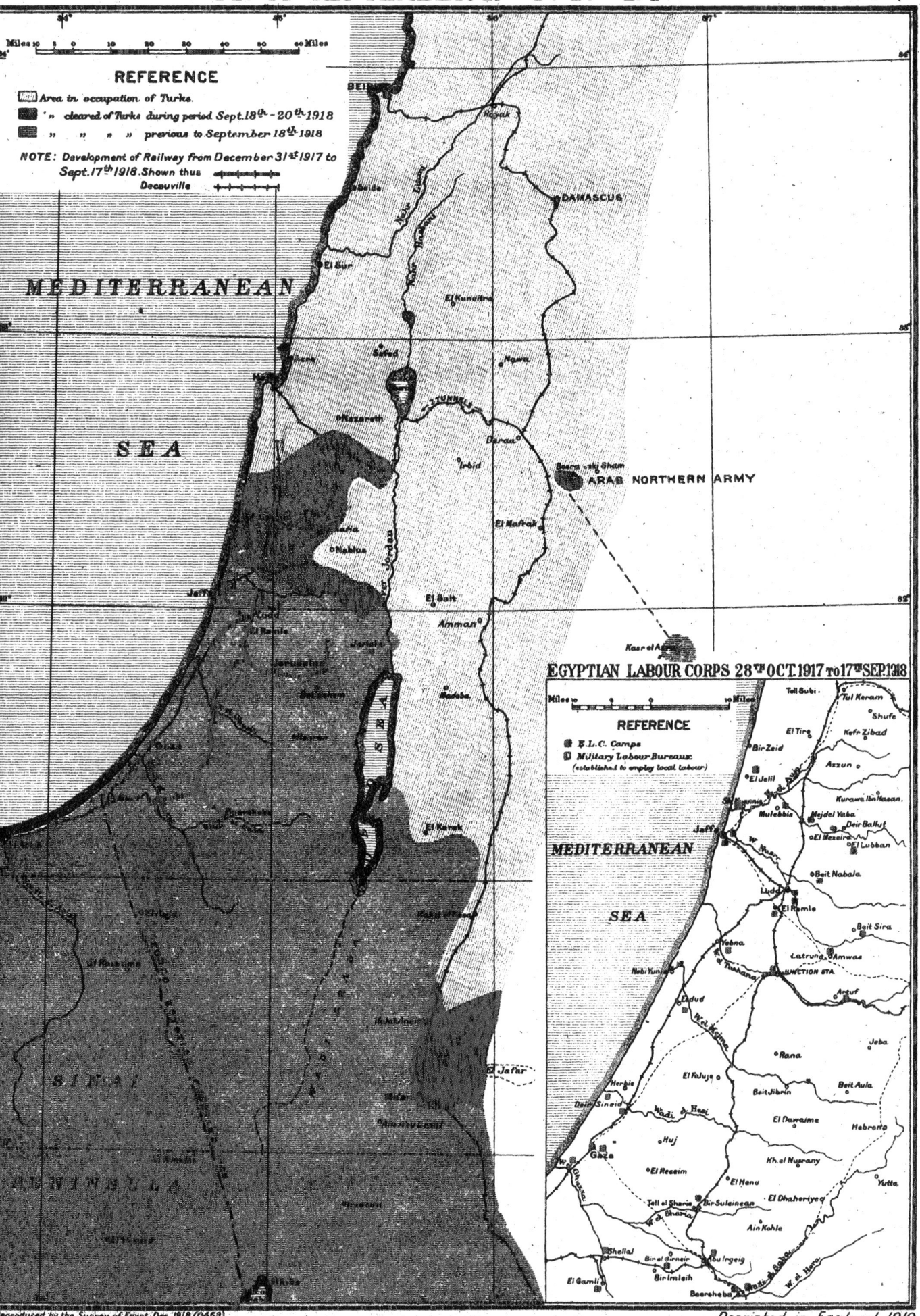

September 21.

The 60th, 7th, and 3rd Divisions had no further fighting on this day, but concentrated and moved into the positions shown covering Samaria, Messudieh, and Tul Keram, and the road and railway between those places.

The 10th Division pushed forward with little opposition and occupied positions covering Nablus from the north and east before dark. This division covered over twenty-four miles in as many hours over the roughest country; a very fine feat of marching.

The 53rd Division experienced considerable opposition during the morning, but this diminished during the day and by evening two brigades had reached the vicinity of Beit Dejan and had closed the road leading through that place to the Jordan Valley.

Chaytor's Force in the Jordan Valley had so far confined itself to vigorous patrolling to ensure that the enemy could make no move without their knowledge. The rôle of this composite force was to secure the right flank of the army and the Jordan's crossings, to keep in close touch with the enemy and take advantage of any withdrawal on their part but to run no risk of being involved with a more powerful foe too early in the battle. This difficult task was admirably carried out.

On the morning of the 21st, it was found that the enemy resistance was weakening on our northern front in the valley, and the 1st Battalion British West Indians rushed forward and seized two spurs where they were heavily shelled. Mounted patrols occupied Khirbet Fosail still further north. In the evening orders were issued for the New Zealand Mounted Rifles Brigade, and parts of the 1st and 2nd battalions British West Indians, to move forward during the night and seize the crossing over the Jordan at Jisr ed Damieh; while other troops kept up pressure on the rest of the Jordan front. The actual crossing was not secured until the following evening, as it was strongly held by infantry, but the road leading to Nablus was occupied during the night and a large number of prisoners taken, including a Turkish divisional commander. During this day the Cavalry Corps were chiefly engaged in collecting prisoners, who came in in such numbers that their evacuation became a very serious difficulty. The Australian Mounted Division patrolled the country to the east, south, and west of Jenin, and the 14th Cavalry Brigade (of the 5th Division) moved down to Jenin early in the morning to support them.

The 13th Cavalry Brigade reoccupied Nazareth and picquetted all the roads to the west, north, and east. At 0130 on the night 21st–22nd a body of about 1,000 Turks, apparently trying to escape towards Tiberias from Haifa or Acre, attacked the outposts of the brigade and were repulsed after a sharp fight, in which the 18th King George's Own Lancers made a successful charge, killing sixty and taking 100 prisoners.

The 4th Cavalry Division remained at Beisan with posts right across the Jordan Valley, and collected a large number of prisoners, who began to straggle in along the Nablus road early in the day.

To face Plate 45.

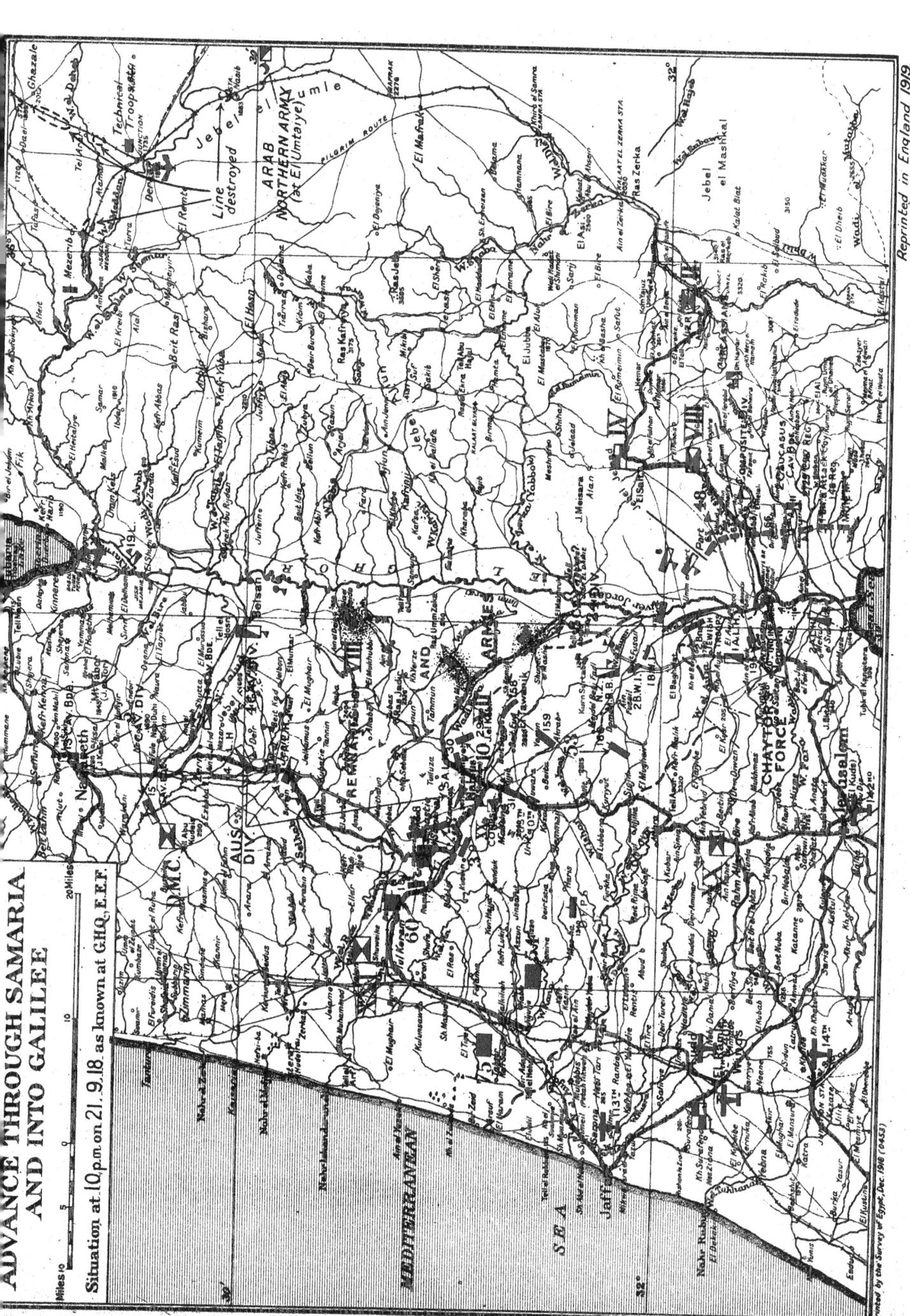

September 22.

After the 21st there was no infantry action of importance. It must not be thought, however, that the trials of the infantry were over; for some time they were busily engaged in clearing the battlefield, collecting and marching in prisoners, developing water supplies, making roads, and the innumerable other duties which remain to be done after a swift advance.

Chaytor's Force continued to press the enemy vigorously all day. Shortly after midnight the 38th Royal Fusiliers occupied the trenches overlooking the Umm esh Shert Ford and at 0300 in conjunction with two companies of the 39th Royal Fusiliers captured Umm esh Shert. Shortly afterwards these troops advanced and successfully occupied Mankattat el Mellaha. The New Zealand Mounted Rifles Brigade captured El Makhruk and Abd el Kadir with the Commander of the 53rd Turkish Division and some 500 prisoners, and by evening the important crossing at Jisr ed Damieh had been seized by that brigade in conjunction with the 1st Battalion British West Indies Regiment, though the enemy still held the crossing at Mafid Jozele further south against the 1st Australian Light Horse Brigade and the 2nd Battalion British West Indians. On the east bank their outposts were driven in, and by evening the 2nd Australian Light Horse Brigade was facing the main Turkish position in the foothills at Shunet Nimrin.

Early in the night it became clear that a general retirement of the Turkish Fourth Army had begun, and orders were issued for the force to follow them vigorously, the New Zealand Mounted Rifles Brigade by the Jisr ed Damieh crossing supported by the British West Indians, and the 2nd Australian Light Horse Brigade by the main Shunet Nimrin-Es Salt road with the 20th Indian Infantry Brigade in support. The 5th Cavalry Division concentrated towards Nazareth during the afternoon with a view to a further advance on Haifa and Acre, their place at Afule being taken by the 3rd Australian Light Horse Brigade of the Australian Mounted Division. During the day the 5th Australian Light Horse Brigade rejoined its division.

The 4th Cavalry Division remained at Beisan sending one regiment to patrol the east bank of the Jordan; and numbers of prisoners continued to come in.

At 1330 the 11th and 12th Light Armoured Car Batteries were sent to reconnoitre and, if possible, to occupy Haifa; but they met with strong opposition from artillery and machine guns a few miles east of the town and had to fall back.

To face Plate 46.

ADVANCE THROUGH SAMARIA AND INTO GALILEE

Situation at 10 p.m. on 22-9-18 as known at G.H.Q., E.E.F.

September 23.

Chaytor's Force pressed forward all day, meeting with little opposition from the enemy but being severely handicapped by the broken nature of the country. As an example of this, the pack wireless set of the 1st Australian Light Horse Brigade fell over a cliff, resulting in all touch being lost with this brigade for several hours.

By 1630 the New Zealand Mounted Rifles Brigade occupied Es Salt, and by nightfall all roads leading into the town were covered. The 4th and 5th Cavalry Divisions both had sharp fighting. Of the 5th Division, the 13th Cavalry Brigade occupied Acre at 1300 with little or no opposition, but the 15th Cavalry Brigade on approaching Haifa were met by a battery of 77 mm. guns on the slopes of Mt. Carmel and at least ten machine guns covering the entrance to the town. The space between the mountain and the Kishon left little room for cavalry to manœuvre, but the Jodhpur Lancers made a brilliant charge riding over the machine guns and pursuing the enemy right through the town. A squadron of the Mysore Lancers was sent over Mt. Carmel at the same time to turn the town from the south. They captured two Turkish naval guns mounted on the ridge of Carmel and also made a gallant charge in the face of heavy machine-gun fire. The Turks made a very stubborn defence at Haifa, and, but for the dash of the 15th (Imperial Service) Cavalry Brigade, might have held out for a considerable time.

In the Jordan Valley at 0800 the 11th Cavalry Brigade of the 4th Division intercepted a large column of the enemy trying to cross the river at Makhadet Abu Naj ford, six miles south-east of Beisan, supported by a large number of guns and machine guns. The ford was not captured until midday after sharp fighting during which the 29th Lancers captured twenty-five machine guns in a single charge on the west bank of the river, while the 35th Jacob's Horse broke up the columns on the east bank.

The hard nature of the fighting is exemplified by the fact that the Hants. battery coming into action in the open had every one of their guns hit.

Over 3,000 prisoners were captured in this action.

September 24.

Chaytor's Force pushed forward all day in touch with enemy rearguards; the New Zealand Mounted Rifles Brigade, supported by the 1st Australian Light Horse Brigade, moving on the main Es Salt–Amman road and the 2nd Australian Light Horse Brigade to the south of them through Aid Essir.

By evening the New Zealand Mounted Rifles were east of Suweileh and the 20th Imperial Infantry Brigade had occupied Es Salt.

The 11th Cavalry Brigade of the 4th Division patrolled down both banks of the Jordan to within twelve miles of Jisr ed Damieh, clearing up small parties of the enemy on the way.

The 4th Australian Light Horse Brigade marched at 1100 for Semakh at the southern end of Lake Tiberias.

Otherwise there was no movement of importance.

September 25.

Chaytor's Force captured Amman at 1510; the town and railway station were both held and hard fighting was necessary before they were captured by the 1st and 2nd Australian Light Horse Brigades and the Canterbury Mounted Rifles.

The railway was seized some miles north of Amman by the Auckland Mounted Rifles and about 600 prisoners in all captured.

Early in the morning the 4th Australian Light Horse Brigade took Semakh after some hand to hand fighting at the station, where a considerable number of Germans were killed in the defence of the "laager" which they had constructed of engines and other rolling stock.

The 5th Cavalry Division moved to Nazareth preparatory for the advance on Damascus.

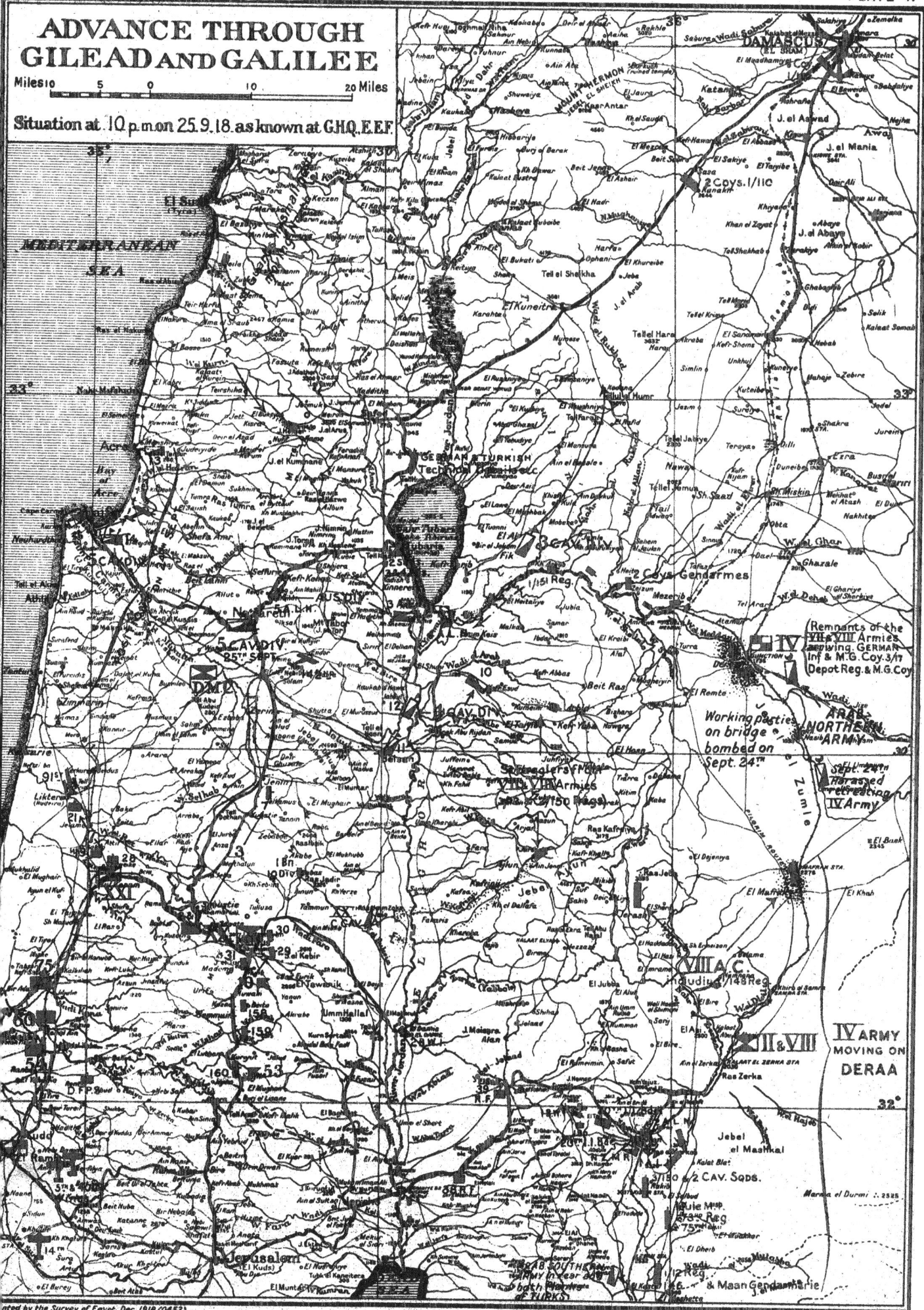

September 26 and 27.

The interest now began to shift to the crossing places of the Jordan and the country of Gilead and Bashan. In the north, the Australian Mounted Division moved up from the southern end of the Sea of Galilee to march to Damascus by way of Tiberias and Jisr Benat Yakub, followed by the 5th Cavalry Division, which had come up from its capture of Acre and Haifa by way of Nazareth and Tiberias. The two divisions were intended to capture Damascus, if possible before the Turkish IVth Army could get there. The 4th Cavalry Division left Beisan and the Jordan Valley with the intention of falling upon the left flank of the Turks, which was hurrying north along the Hejaz Railway in order to avoid the attacks of Chaytor's Force in the south. On the right flank of the retreating IVth Army, the advanced troops of the Hejaz northern operations were already active and had done much to delay the retreat by the destruction of railway and bridges. Away in the south, as far as Maan inclusive, where desultory operations had for some time past been in progress between a flying column from the IInd Corps and the Arabs who were watching the town from the Semna hills, the Turks were hurrying north in a vain hope of reaching Damascus before Chaytor's Force could effectively bar their retreat. Of the presence of Sherifian troops to the north of it, the IInd Corps was still ignorant, but it was fully alive to the danger which it ran from the energetic hostility of the country through which it was retreating and the insistent attacks of the troops of the Hejaz southern operations which preyed upon its flanks and rear. It was an interesting race and it is possible that the bulk of the IVth Army might have got through to Damascus in time to organize some sort of a defence against the cavalry, had it not been delayed for several precious hours by the destructive activities of Lieut.-Col. T. E. Lawrence, C.B., and his Arab Camel Corps and armoured cars. The part played by the Royal Air Force was also important in causing that delay in the Turkish retreat which enabled the Australian Mounted Division and the 5th Cavalry Division to get so good a start in the race.

In hopes of delaying this northern force, the enemy had blown one arch of the Jisr Benat Yakub (now generally known as "Jordan Bridge"), and had formed a laager of lorries with artillery and machine guns. Thus the Australians, at the end of their eighteen miles' advance from Mejdel on the Sea of Galilee (during which the 3rd Australian Light Horse Brigade had reconnoitred up to Safed) found themselves faced with strong opposition on attempting to cross the Jordan. The 4th Australian Light Horse Brigade, however, swam the river at El Min, a mile below the broken bridge, while the 3rd Australian Light Horse Brigade was strongly engaged in the swampy country between Jisr Benat Yakub and Lake Hule. The 4th Australian Light Horse Brigade imperilled the communications of the enemy and captured much transport, while the 5th Australian Light Horse Brigade kept the enemy busy at the bridge. At dusk the 3rd Australian Light Horse Brigade forced a passage to the north of the bridge and, pressing on through the night, captured Deir es Saras just before dawn with prisoners and guns. This operation delayed the Australian Mounted Division for some time, so that it was overtaken by the 5th Cavalry Division which had come thirty-two miles from Kefr Kenna to a point near Jisr Benat Yakub.

Meanwhile, the 4th Cavalry Division had crossed the Jordan at Jisr Mujamie, south of the Sea of Galilee and was advancing upon Deraa. The 10th Cavalry Brigade got into visual connection with the Sherifian troops on the far side of the retreating Turks at 11.30 on the morning of Sept. 26, but actual contact had still to be established. The enemy made considerable resistance west of Irbid and that town was only occupied at nightfall. The same brigade was again engaged near Er Remte, when the 1/1st Dorset Yeomanry executed a highly successful charge, which resulted in satisfactory enemy casualties as well as the capture of 200 prisoners and twenty machine guns. After this, Er Remte was taken and advanced patrols pushed on through the night towards Deraa. This the Sherifian troops occupied shortly before midnight, after an exciting race, in which Colonel Lawrence's fast camels beat the Sherif Feisal's horsemen by a neck along a course from the headquarters of the Hejaz northern operations. Troopers of the Central India Horse established contact with the Sherifian Arabs just after dawn on Sept. 28 west of Deraa, and only desisted from arresting one of the British officers serving with the Arabs under the impression that he was a German serving with the Turks, on recognising the well-known English expletive that was drawn from him by their proposal.

With Chaytor's Force, the period covered by Sept. 26 and 27, forms a gap in the operations, owing to the fact that the main body of the Turkish IInd Corps had not yet come within range to be struck at and the rest of the Turkish Fourth Army had moved away from the Amman area into the inhospitable Hauran (Bashan). The force was actively engaged in finding fresh enemies to conquer, and the 1st Australian Light Horse Brigade was fortunate in finding some Turks in the Wadi el Hammam, who fought before surrendering to the number of 105 with one gun. Other Turks were seen moving south, stragglers probably from the main body of the Fourth Army, trying to join the advancing IInd Corps for safety, in view of the hostility of the local population. The 2nd Australian Light Horse Brigade located the advancing troops of this corps near Kastal and, on the morning of Sept. 27, there was a further engagement in the Wadi el Hammam, in which the 3rd Australian Light Horse Regiment, with aeroplane assistance, captured 300 prisoners and two machine guns. Later in the day, the Australian and New Zealand Mounted Division was disposed between the water at Wadi el Hammam and Kalaat ez Zerka, and the Turks moving north, while the New Zealand Mounted Rifles had a detachment across the Darb el Haj and the 2nd Australian Light Horse Brigade held the water at Leban Station.

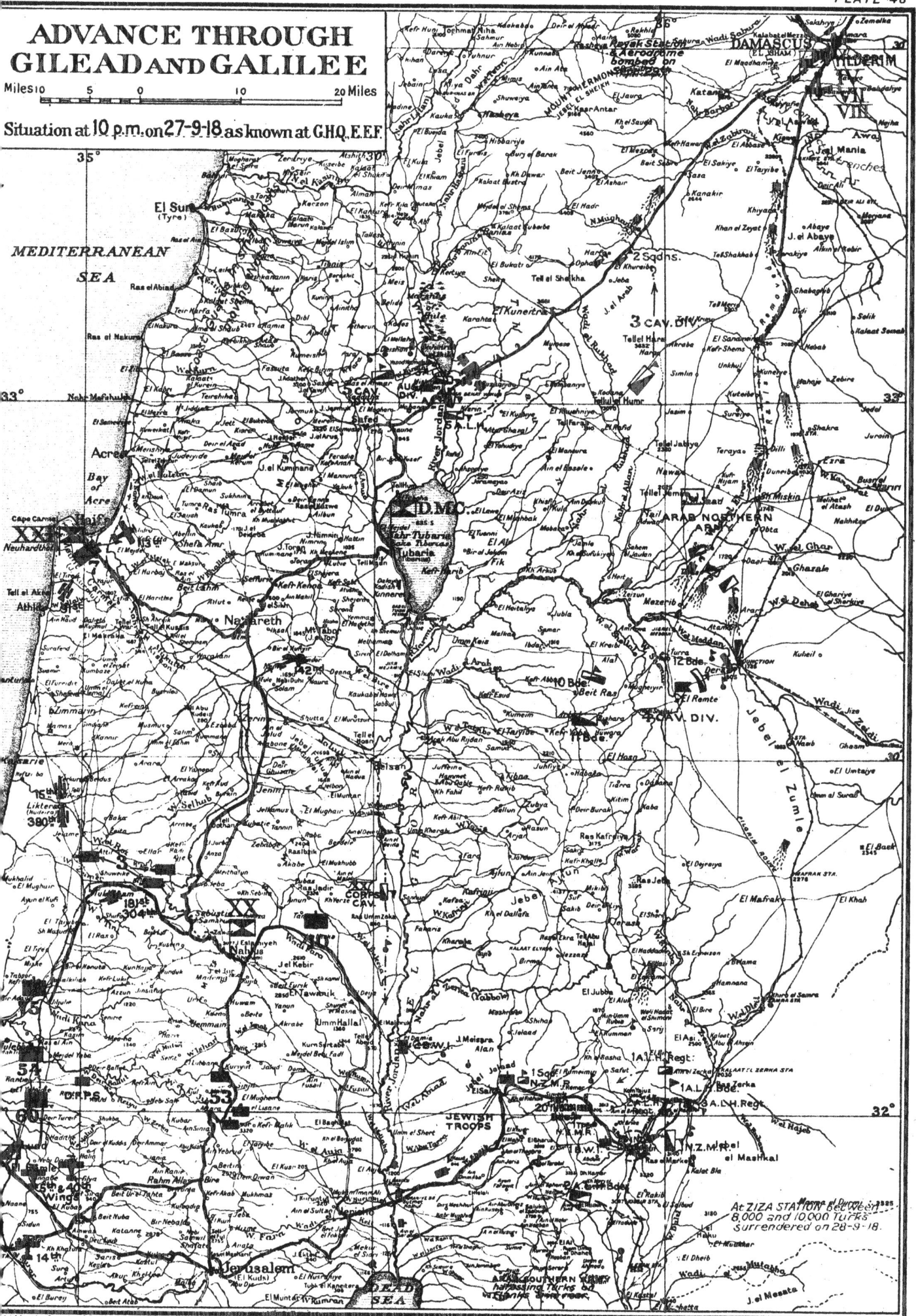

Sherifian Co-operation in September.

On Aug. 31 a detachment of the regular forces of King Husein started north from near Akaba in order to co-operate in the then forthcoming operations against the Turks. The direct route from Akaba to Damascus runs by way of Maan, Amman, and Deraa, and was, at that time, still for the most part in the occupation of the enemy. It was, therefore, necessary for a wide outflanking movement to be undertaken. That this was successfully carried through was most creditable to the troops engaged in the operation, as on one occasion they made a four days' march from water to water, followed immediately after that by a two days' march to the next supply. Nor was this water supply of the most inviting description. Leaches abounded and many of those who drank hastily found afterwards that these unpleasant creatures had got into their mouths and fastened themselves in the nasal tubes. Abu Lissa, near Maan, was reached on Sept. 2, then by way of Jafar and Bair the force reached Kasr el Azrak and continued through Umm el Jemal and Umtaiye which was reached on the afternoon of the 15th. This was made the base for the operations in the immediate future. A raid was made upon the railway between Deraa and Damascus. A point near Tel Arar was the place selected, and a bridge and 1,200 rails were blown up and destroyed during the morning of the 17th. A daylight occupation of a point only four miles from a German aerodrome invited the intervention of the enemy, and the force was attacked and bombarded by nine aeroplanes from Deraa. The work was, however, successfully carried through, and part of the force proceeded during the day to the railway station at Mezerib, which was captured in the evening of the same day. This important point on the enemy lines of communication was carefully burned, two trains were destroyed, the water tanks blown up, and a quantity of rails bent and displaced. A good day's work being thus creditably brought to a close, the Arab force passed the night peacefully astride the enemy's only railway between his front in Palestine and Gilead and his base. Next day the force retreated southwards on Umtaiye passing near Remte and reaching Nasib station on the Hejaz Railway, south of Deraa, in time to blow up a large bridge and damage a quantity of rails before bed-time. On the morning of the 19th the Arab regulars accompanied by a numerous following from the local tribes and country-side in general, arrived at Umtaiye where they were attacked by their previous acquaintances, the German aeroplanes, who were in search of vengeance. The garrison of Deraa must have felt particularly vindictive, as the Arab regulars had, in the course of forty-eight hours, completely cut their communications with Amman, the Palestine front, and Damascus alike. Bombs were freely dropped. The tribesmen and local peasantry vanished into the surrounding country, but the regular troops of the Arab Army barracked their camels, dismounted, and sat immovable, each man by the side of his beast, until the storm was passed. The Germans returned to Deraa for more bombs, whereupon the Camel Corps withdrew into a wadi and sat still among the blocks of lava which were to be found therein. By making no movement at all they concealed their presence from the questing planes, and the Germans returned disappointed, doubtless to report that the entire force had been destroyed. The picture of the Hejaz Camel Corps passing itself off as black stones recalls the story of Sherherazad in the "Arabian Nights," and, as in that story, the black stones came to life again and busily harassed the enemy. They remained among the lava until Sept. 24, issuing on one occasion by night to catch and kill a passing train, and on another occasion by day to blow up a bridge and destroy a great length of rails. On Sept. 24 the Turkish 4th Army began to surge northwards in its vain endeavour to escape disaster which had overtaken the troops to the west of Jordan. The Arab Camel Corps being immensely outnumbered by this force, which still retained a certain amount of organization, was unable to stop this retreat, and was obliged to content itself during two days with vigorous minor operations for incommoding its passage. These took the shape of a succession of raids upon selected units. A flurry of rifle fire would be followed by a charge and a swift withdrawal, leaving twenty or thirty dead Turks on the ground, and a dozen or so prisoners in the hands of the Arabs. In this way, two officers, 300 men, and twenty-five guns were captured. On Sept. 26, the Camel Corps having hurried north through the night, was able to blow up the railway and capture Ezra and Ghazale stations. Through Sheikh Miskin the force went to Sheikh Saad on one of the roads north from Mezerib to Damascus. Here thirty officers and 500 men were captured, many of the former being Germans and Austrians. The state of demoralization into which the enemy had fallen is exemplified in this force. Although provided with fifteen machine guns, as well as rifles and adequate ammunition, no resistance was made to the attacks of tribesmen and peasants, who reduced them to such a condition that only one pathetic figure had retained sufficient of his property to be able to wave portions of a white handkerchief, saying: "I am a major, we surrender." During Sept. 27, the last Turkish formations evacuated Deraa and the Es Salt force moved north by way of Mezerib and Tafas. This force was so imbued with the doctrine of frightfulness that it thought in its madness that an example of terrorism might overawe the Hauran which was bubbling in open rebellion all round it. Consequently it was decided "to make an example of" the unhappy villages of Tafas and Turaa. Eighty women and children were butchered with every revolting circumstance of atrocity, but the last hour of Turkish rule, east of Jordan, had already struck. The Arabs, so far from being overawed and terrorised into a dutiful submission to their former tyrants, were justly incensed by this thoroughly Turkish outrage. The force which was responsible for it was visited by immediate and well-earned retribution, and the units which had moved out of Deraa and Mezerib never reached Damascus. Sheikh Tallal, a fighting man of high repute and a notable of the Hauran, was with the Arab Army. On finding what atrocities

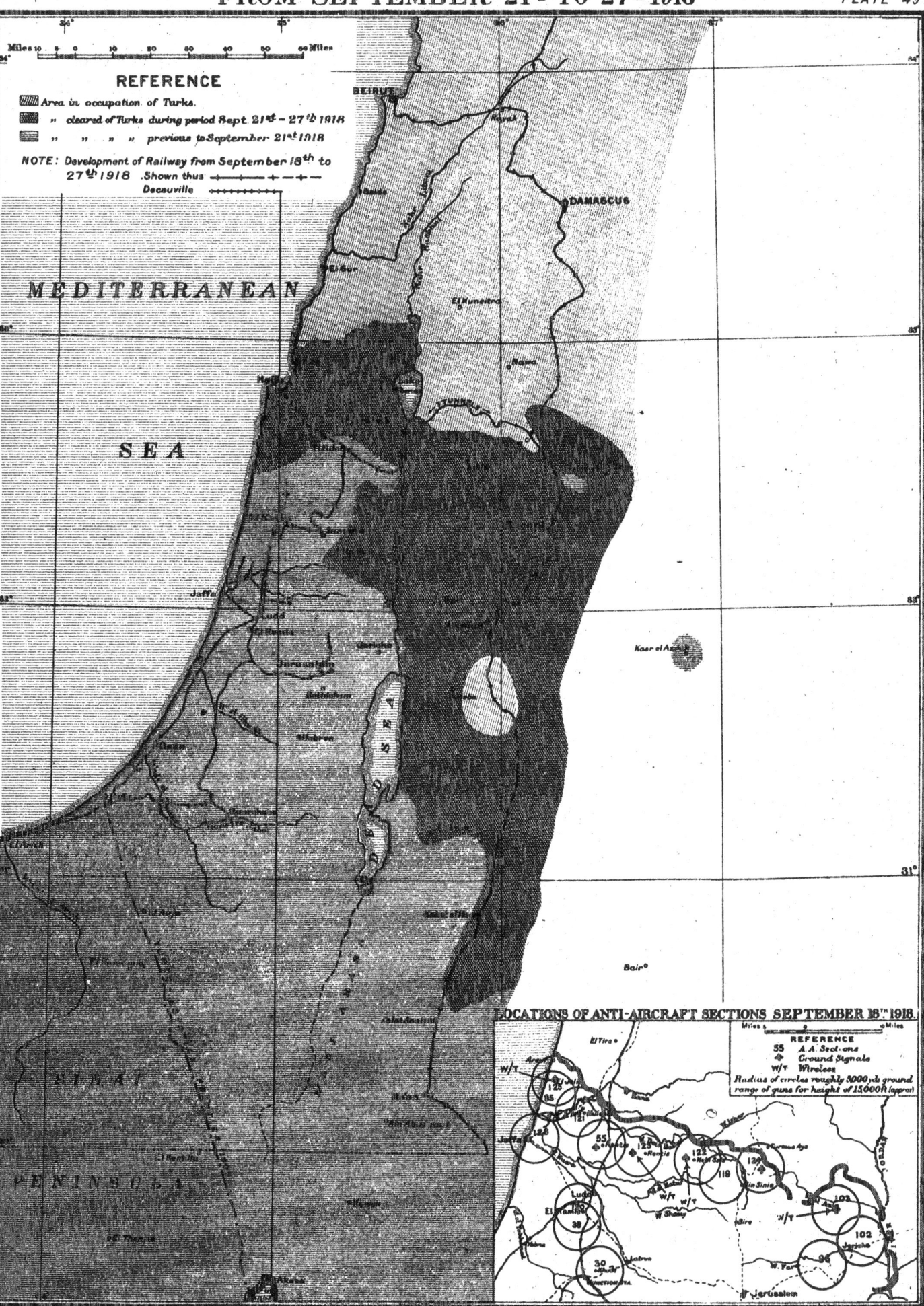

had been committed in his village he charged single-handed upon a Turkish column and furiously exacted blood for blood until he was riddled with bullets. At dawn on the 27th, the Arab Camel Corps rode into Deraa, so long a Turkish place of strength, and shortly afterwards at a point a little to the west of the railway junction, made their first contact with sowars of the 38th Central India Horse.

September 28, 29, and 30.

The 5th Cavalry Division was somewhat delayed in crossing the Jordan—a lorry broke down the temporary bridge across the arch destroyed by the enemy—and finally made use of fords. By 1800 all fighting troops and fighting wheels were across, but further delay was caused to the latter by the distressing nature of the road leading up to the plateau on the east of the river. It was not until 2030 that the division reached Kuneitra, which the Australian Mounted Division had occupied at 1300, and its rear wheels only arrived at 0600 on Sept. 29. Tired horses had been left in the Jordan Valley. The Australian Mounted Division led in the advance from Kuneitra in the evening of Sept. 29, and the 3rd Australian Light Horse Brigade was engaged with the Turks on the high ground south of Sasa at 2000. The brigade was hampered in its attack by the masses of lava deposits which made it difficult for men to move across country in the dark. The enemy's flank was protected by an impassable morass, and no attack could be made before 0300 on Sept. 30, when the enemy was disposed of by the 9th and 10th Austalian Light Horse Regiments and lost twenty-five prisoners, two guns and seven machine guns. The advance continued without check until some 2,500 Turks with machine guns were found to be holding Kaukab and the ridge east of it. A successful mounted attack was made by the 12th and 4th Australian Light Horse Regiments, supported by the Notts Battery of Royal Horse Artillery and "A" Battery Honourable Artillery Company, and the ridge was taken at the gallop. Many of the Turks fled into the woods near Daraya. Meanwhile, at 0845, an aeroplane report was received by the 5th Cavalry Division to the effect that some 2,000 Turks were retiring on Damascus by the Deraa road. The 14th Cavalry Brigade was ordered to intercept this force and then march on Damascus. This brigade cut the Turkish column in half, capturing the bulk of the leading portion including all that was left of the 3rd Turkish Cavalry Division with the Divisional Commander and his staff. The 13th and 15th Cavalry Brigades concentrated just north of Sasa in Corps reserve. At noon, after some opposition, the 13th Cavalry Brigade seized the Jebel el Aswad astride the Kiswe–Damascus road and cut off large numbers of Turks trying to withdraw to Kiswe, who tried to break away to the left and right of the brigade and up the Wadi Zabirani. Others, greatly disorganized, were streaming up the hills to the north-east and along the main road to Damascus. The former were shelled by the Essex Battery and the latter were headed off towards the 4th Cavalry Division, with the loss of about 1,000 prisoners. At 1300 the brigade advanced to Kaukab and then co-operated with the 14th and 15th Brigades (the latter being on the right, astride of the Wadi Zabirani) against the Turks who were trying to break out from Kiswe. At 1700 the 13th Brigade captured Kiswe with 675 prisoners and four guns. In the evening the 5th Mounted Division had its headquarters at Kaukab with the 13th Mounted Brigade, the 14th was astride the Kiswe–Damascus road north of the Jebel el Aswad with patrols at Kadem Station, and the 15th was round Khan esh Sheha, which had been occupied at 1000. Two troops of the 1/1st Royal Gloucester Hussars Yeomanry (13th Cavalry Brigade) had been sent forward in hopes of capturing the enemy wireless station at Kadem. This was however blown up on their approach at 1630. The yeomanry charged the destruction party, killing fifteen with the sword, but had to retire in face of considerable German reinforcements, and afterwards joined the Australian Mounted Division.

The 4th Mounted Division coming up from the south with the Sherifian forces on its right, entered Deraa unopposed on Sept. 28, and next day got into touch with the retreating Turks in the Dilli area. For two days the enemy was pressed and harassed, his columns were fired upon and broken up, and on Sept. 30 the division got into touch with the other divisions of the Desert Mounted Corps, and reached Zerakiye late at night. By dusk the 5th Australian Light Horse Brigade and the French Cavalry under Commandant Lebon, attached to the Australian Mounted Division, had worked across the Damascus–Beirut road immediately north-west of Damascus and on the hills surrounding it. Here the enemy was trapped—the defile was swept with rifle and machine-gun fire, trains were wrecked, and every form of transport destroyed. In this action the Turks lost 4,000 prisoners and very many killed.

In Gilead Chaytor's Force located the southern portion of the Turkish Fourth Army at Kastal, with three trains in the station. At 1515 the Commander was summoned to surrender by 0845 next day, in a message dropped from an aeroplane, but no reply was received. At 1145, however, on Sept. 29, the Turks opened negotiations with the 5th Australian Light Horse Regiment, on the railway south of Leban. The situation was difficult as large numbers of the local inhabitants, intent upon looting, were surrounding the Turkish position. Any sign of a white flag was likely to precipitate matters, so the 2nd Australian Light Horse Brigade advanced to Kastal and formed a cordon behind which the Turks were able to surrender. The Turkish Commander, Ali Bey Wahabi, was taken by car to Divisional Headquarters. The other prisoners to the number of over 4,000 marched into Amman under the protection of the New Zealand Mounted Rifles Brigade, while some 500 sick had to be left for a time at Kastal. The surrender also included twelve guns and thirty-five machine guns, and brought the list of captures by Chaytor's Force during its operations as a separate entity to over 10,000 prisoners, fifty-seven guns, and 132 machine guns. Large quantities of railway rolling stock, ammunition, and other material were also taken.

To face Plate 50.

CAPTURE OF DAMASCUS

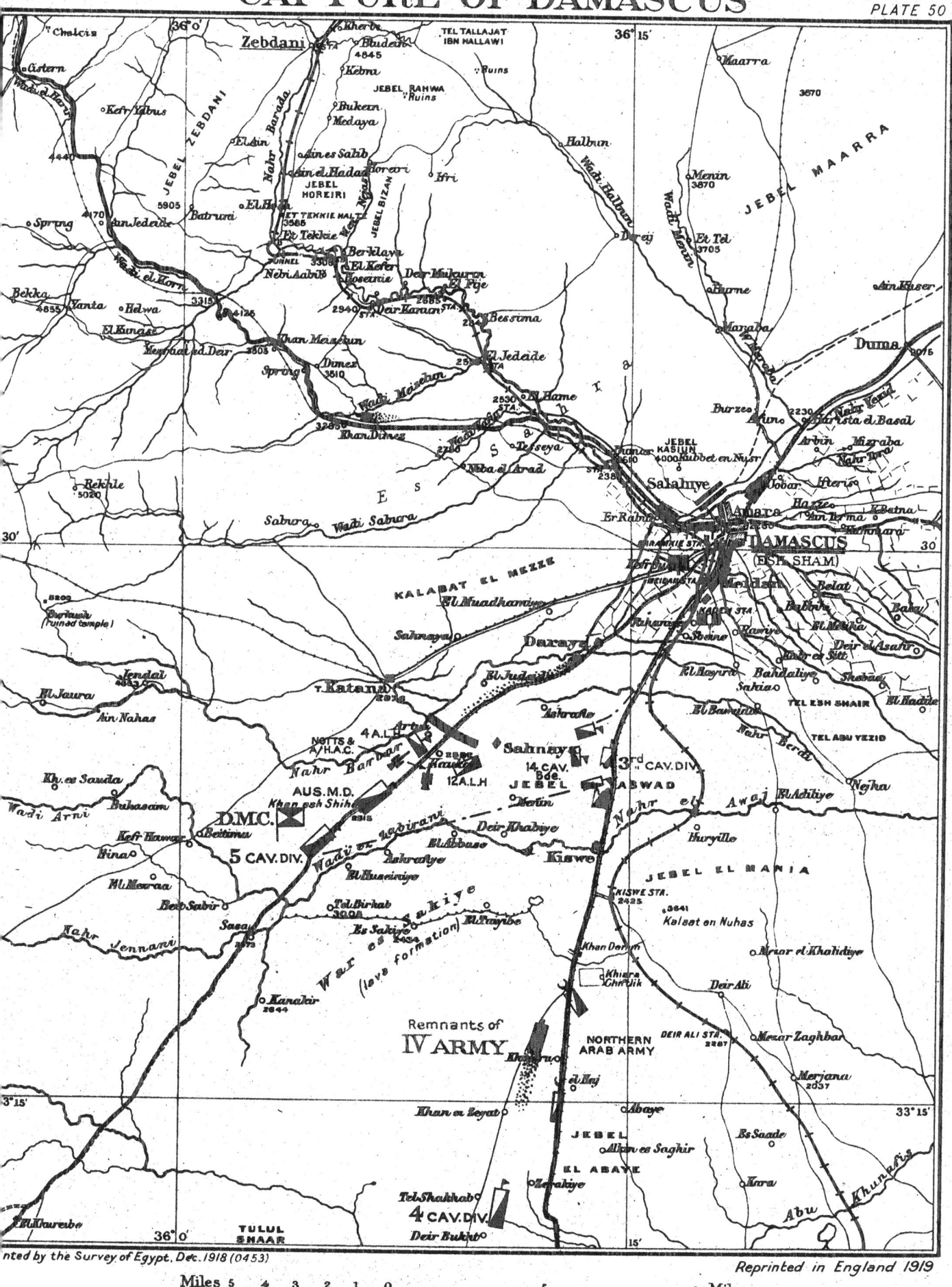

Situation at 12 a.m. on 30-9-18 as known at G.H.Q. E.E.F.

October 1.

No precise moment can be fixed for the fall of Damascus. Politically its independence from Turkish domination was proclaimed about 1400 on Sept. 30 while Jemal Pasha, Commander of the Fourth Army and numbers of armed Turks and Germans were still in the city. Yet, so reduced was the moral of these troops, that they wearily trailed out of Damascus along the north bank of the Barada and gazed apathetically at the Sherifian flags which proclaimed the jubilation of the Damascenes at their defeat and emphasized the collapse of four centuries of empire. No formal surrender took place as the municipal authorities welcomed the troops alike of the Desert Mounted Corps and of the Sherifian Army as liberators and allies, and no enemy administration survived in such a form as to be able to take upon itself the task of arranging a capitulation. The last days of Turkish rule in the famous city had indeed been full of humiliation for the defeated side. People refused to sell provisions to Turks, even for gold. It was impossible to obtain supplies for the hospitals, and the Germans forcibly seized all available transport for their own especial benefit. During the morning of the 30th the Damascenes were delighted to witness a brisk fight between Turks and Germans, provoked by the rapacity of the latter over the distribution of vehicles. Satisfactory numbers on both sides lost their lives in this encounter, which was, apparently, the most formidable of many similar skirmishes between the Turks and their Prussian patrons, evidence of which had been forthcoming in the shape of numerous German corpses all along the line of retreat. In the hospitals the Turkish sanitary department entirely collapsed during the last five days, so much so that one of the first tasks to be undertaken after the occupation of the town, was the very necessary burial of bodies which had been left three, four, and even five days, on the floor where they had died. Food was obtained for the surviving patients, and the hospital staff was forcibly induced to resume its duties. The 14th Cavalry Brigade and Sherifian troops had entered Damascus on Oct. 1, but in so large a city it is not surprising that both detachments were ignorant of the arrival of the other, and that both thought that they were first in. In point of actual time a detachment of the 10th Australian Light Horse Regiment under Major Olden reached the Serail at 0630 on Oct. 1, while Colonel Lawrence and the Sherifian Camel Corps were a little later, but it was not until 0830 that General Chauvel motored into Damascus to confer with the Civil Authorities. During the early hours of the morning of Oct. 1, the 14th Cavalry Brigade intercepted numbers of Turks who were still trying to reach Damascus, in ignorance of the fact that the city was no longer a refuge for them. The rest of the 5th Cavalry Division concentrated at Deir Khabiye at 0600 and moved up the Kiswe-Damascus road to join the 14th Brigade. The 4th Cavalry Division which had left Zerakiye at 0300 followed. At 1030 the 14th Cavalry Brigade was sent through the town to Jobar to co-operate with the 3rd Australian Light Horse Brigade in closing the Duma road to those Turks who were trying to escape that way.

Meanwhile, the Australian Mounted Division, which had been astride the Beirut road all night, at 0500 pushed forward the 3rd Australian Light Horse Brigade through the town and blocked the Aleppo road. On the way this brigade captured a train, with 483 prisoners, eight guns, and thirty machine guns, and engaged an enemy column at Duma. The 10th Australian Light Horse Regiment charged the rear of this column, killed numbers of the enemy and captured 600 prisoners and thirty-seven machine guns. The pursuit was continued and in the evening some Germans and machine guns were taken at Khan Kusseir. The brigade remained at Duma for the night. At 0825 next morning the brigade galloped for nearly six miles across country and charged an enemy column with sword. The Turks were broken and lost many dead, in addition to a captured Divisional Commander, 1,500 other prisoners, three guns, and twenty-six machine guns. This brought the operations round Damascus to a close.

Story of the Arab Movement.

A *Sherif* (Arabic plural *Ashraf*) in the Moslem world is one who claims descent in the male line from the Khalif Ali (656-661 A.D.) by his marriage with Fatima, daughter of the Prophet Mohammed (died 632). There are many of these Ashraf in Arabia, Morocco and the Sudan, but among those generally accepted as such, only the Ashraf inscribed in the Register of Mecca, which has been strictly kept for many centuries past—if not from the days of the Prophet himself, are of absolutely unquestioned authenticity. They are divided into a number of clans, living mostly in the Hejaz, and form an accepted aristocracy with peculiar privileges under a law of their own.

For the first four centuries after the death of the Prophet, the Ashraf were not very numerous and had not as yet established their position as a political power. Towards the end of the tenth century, however, one of the Ashraf of Mecca got possession of his native town and inaugurated in the Hejaz a tradition of Sherifian temporal power, the holder of which was regarded as the Emir and head of the Ashraf, or, as he has for centuries been known in Europe—" The Grand Sherif of Mecca."

In course of time a fighting Sherif of the Juheinah clan, by name Qatada, became Emir and a Prince of his dynasty during the sixteenth century, established the undoubted predominance of the Emirate of Mecca over the Hejaz, and secured for his own family an exclusive right to the throne. The reigning representative of the senior line of the dynasty founded by the Emir Qatada succeeded to the throne of Mecca as the Emir Husein in 1908, and so long as it was possible to reconcile his position as a vassal of the Sultan of Turkey with his dignity as an Arab Prince and head of the Ashraf, he remained a loyal subject of the Ottoman Empire, but at the beginning of the war the Turkish atrocities in Syria which came on the top of the violent attempts of the Constantinople Government forcibly to Ottomanize all nationalities under its authority, made a revolt of the Arab nation against its oppressors inevitable.

CAPTURE OF DAMASCUS

PLATE 51

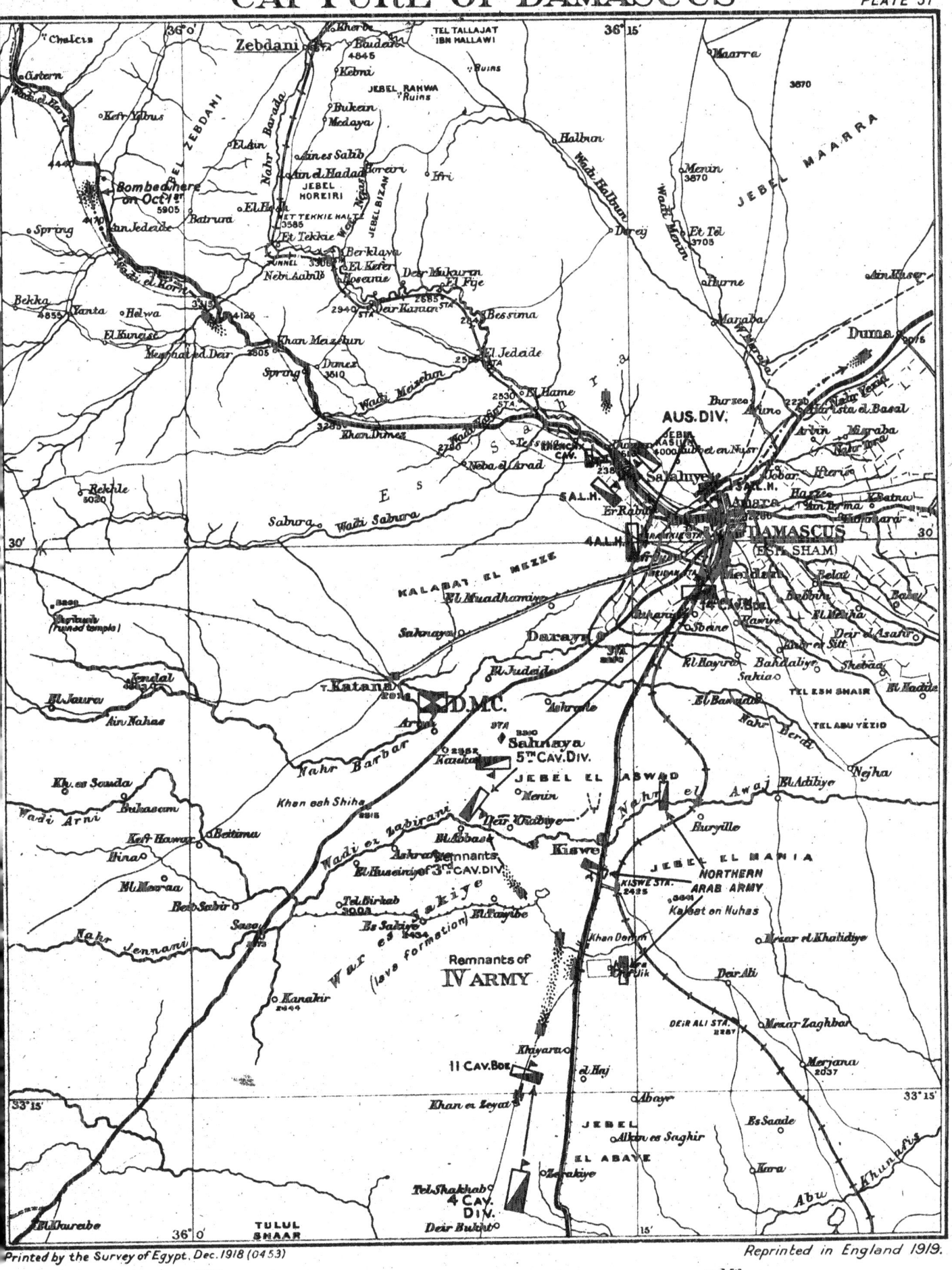

Printed by the Survey of Egypt. Dec.1918 (0453)   Reprinted in England 1919.

Situation at Dusk on 30.9.18. as known at G.H.Q.E.E.F.

In May, 1916, the position of the Emir of Mecca was threatened by the arrival of a picked force of 3,000 Turkish troops in Medina. Their plan of campaign was to march through the Hejaz consolidating the waning Ottoman authority in that principality, and then to proceed to the Yemen in order to reinforce the Turkish army operating against Aden. The foresighted policy of the Emir in preventing the prolongation of the Hejaz railway from Medina to Mecca, caused a much needed delay in the progress of the Turks, and the Emir decided that the privileged position of the Hejaz and possibly his own authority would be menaced by the arrival of so large a Turkish force. He placed himself at the head of the national cause and drew his sword in the defence of the Arab as against the Turk.

The Arab revolt began on June 5, 1916, with the formation of a thin Bedouin cordon round Medina, where Ali and Feisal, two sons of the Sherif Husein, were in command. The Hejaz railway was broken at several points between Medina and Abu Naam; but the Arabs, inexpert in demolition, did not effect enough before being driven off by relief parties with machine guns, to interrupt seriously the communication of Medina with the north, and the besieging force, short of arms and supplies, and with no guns worth mentioning, could do little but watch the city from afar. Jiddah, however, which was attacked on June 9, held out barely a week. Cut off from Mecca by the loss of the blockhouses on the road, and exposed to naval guns and 'planes, the Turkish garrison, in a weak position north of the town, yielded to the instance of the civilian population and surrendered at discretion. Mecca had passed in the meantime into the Emir's hands, with the exception of the forts and entrenched barracks, held by small garrisons, the bulk of the Turkish force being absent in summer quarters at Taif with the Governor-General. These garrisons, who had had some inkling of what was coming, opened fire on the town, putting a shell or two even into or near the Great Mosque, to the infinite scandal of all pious Moslems; and they were not reduced until artillery was brought up from Jiddah. They had all surrendered by July 16. Taif where over 2,000 men, the bulk of the Turkish force, were entrenched, with Ghalib Pasha, the G.O.C. and Governor-General, held out much longer—till Sept. 23—and then capitulated from hopelessness rather than from scarcity or fear of its assailants. It had been blockaded very effectively for three and a half months by Sherif Abdullah, the Emir's second son, with a mixed force of Ateibah Bedouins and Meccan townsfolk, but though regularly bombarded it had never been really assaulted.

Smaller places, like Lith and Yambo, surrendered as soon as they were seriously attacked, and the greater part of the Hejaz was now clear of the Turks. So far the task of the Arabs had been comparatively easy. Isolated bodies of troops, divided from all possible relief by 300 miles of hostile, ill-watered country and barred from the sea, were bound to capitulate sooner or later, however superior in fighting quality and equipment to their foes. But the Medina garrison was in a different case. It had been reinforced, re-armed, re-victualled, and reassured by successful sorties during these four months, and, late in September it was able to issue forth, driving the Arabs before it, and make Medina secure by establishing a cordon of fortified posts, thirty to forty miles out along the Mecca roads. This done, the Turks pushed farther still, realizing that their best defence was an offensive and at one time they threatened to occupy both Yambo and Rabugh, the important half-way house to Mecca. But only some 14,000 strong, they had not the forces necessary to hold such distant objectives together with the lines of communication. Considerable Arab armies moved up from south and south-west, and the Turks withdrew again behind the fortified outposts of Medina at the end of the year.

It had become clear that owing to their inexperience in modern siege warfare the Arabs could not expect to reduce Medina. The only operation likely to be fruitful would be systematic attack on the 800 miles of the single track of the Hejaz railway which connects Medina with Damascus. For such raiding however, and for ultimate extension of the revolt to Syria, more northerly bases than Jiddah, Rabugh, or even Yambo, were required. Therefore at the of Jan., 1917, Sherif Feisal, with the Northern Arab Army, installed himself at Wejh, already occupied by landing parties, and extended his hold farther north to Dhaba and Moweilah on the Midian coast. His brother, Abdullah, had arrived at Wadi Ais, north-west of Medina, leaving only his eldest brother, Ali, in the former theatre of operations.

The raiding carried out during the following six months, with British and French help, lowered the strength and spirit of the Turkish forces in Medina, provided scope for adventure which attracted many fresh Arab elements, and offered a demonstration of activity which induced many more to engage themselves on the Sherifian side in view of a move still farther north. But it did not cut off Medina. The permanent way proved harder to wreck irretrievably, and the enemy better prepared to make interruptions good, than had been expected. The alternative scheme, that of blowing up trains, was evolved, and under the direction of Lieut.-Colonel T. E. Lawrence, this form of military activity began to rank almost as a national sport. Numerous instances occurred of small parties of Arabs under Allied leadership, blowing up the engine of a train while in motion. Sometimes the disaster merely resulted in the delay and discomfiture of the enemy—sometimes the Arabs were able to inflict serious losses and capture valuable material as the result of one of these episodes. In any case such destruction invariably impaired the railway track, reduced the number of engines and the amount of rolling stock available, caused delay and laid a heavy burden upon the Turkish lines of communication.

Meanwhile, early in July, 1917, Akaba had been captured from the Turks, and Sherif Feisal moved up. Operations and propaganda could now be extended much farther northwards. Previously there had been no raiding of the railway above Tebuk. Now it was attacked, not only south of Maan but north, while Arab forces threatened both Maan itself and also the forest district on the north-west, whence the railway locomotives were drawing their fuel supply. The effect on Medina was soon evident, and had the Turks been in a position to evacuate by the railway without almost certain disaster, they would

AREA OCCUPIED AS THE RESULT OF OPERATIONS
FROM SEPTEMBER 28TH TO OCTOBER 1ST 1918

PLATE 52

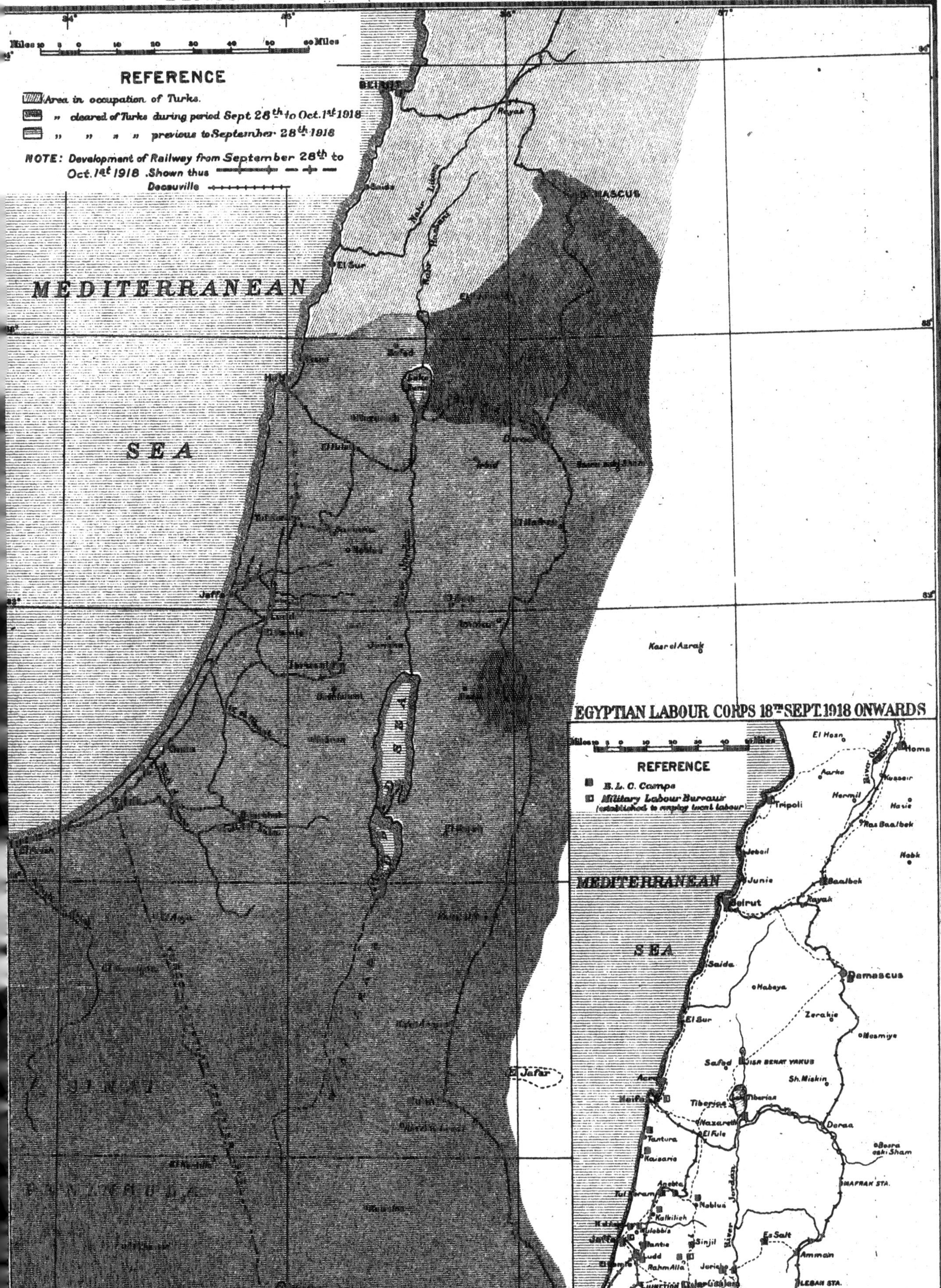

REFERENCE
- Area in occupation of Turks.
- " cleared of Turks during period Sept 28th to Oct. 1st 1918
- " " " previous to September 28th 1918

NOTE: Development of Railway from September 28th to Oct. 1st 1918. Shown thus ————
Decauville ++++++++

EGYPTIAN LABOUR CORPS 18TH SEPT. 1918 ONWARDS

REFERENCE
- E.L.C. Camps
- Military Labour Bureaux (established to employ local labour)

Reproduced by the Survey of Egypt Dec. 1918 (0458)

Reprinted in England 1919.

probably have done so early in the current year. But, for lack of sufficient rolling stock and troops to keep the line during withdrawal, they evidently decided to hold on, as the lesser evil ; for, in any case, they were secure for some months of being able to repel direct Arab attack, all reduced and scurvy-ridden though their troops had become, both at headquarters and on the line of communication. There they remained until their surrender became necessary as the result of the Armistice which the Turks were compelled to accept at the end of October. Lines of communication troops who had hoped to make good their escape northwards, when disaster overtook the Turkish armies west of the Jordan were beset by hostile tribesmen and finally surrendered to Chaytor's force at Ziza.

Having secured the adhesion or neutrality of all Arabs as far up as Maan, and made provisional arrangements with others to northward, Feisal could now contemplate an advance into the trans-Jordan country. He had collected, from one source or another, some thousands of partly-trained troops, beside contingents from Bedouin tribes of higher fighting quality than the Hejazis. Also he was much better equipped with guns, small arms, and auxiliary services than any Arab army had been heretofore. The Turks in Maan and the Hishe Forest made attempts to dislodge him from the Petra region in Oct. and Nov., 1917, but proved to weak to press home any advantage they gained. The cold of the highlands in winter, and lack of transport, militated against strong counter-offensives by the Arabs, but in Jan., 1918, they were able to begin an advance towards the eastern Dead Sea lands. There were, but few Turks to oppose them, and the local inhabitants, though jealous and suspicious of a strange force in their midst, did not obstruct. Shobak and the Hishe Forest were occupied, and towards the end of January, the Arabs had taken and passed Tafilah, raided up to Mezra on the Dead Sea, and began to threaten the Turks in Kerak and on the railway north of Jurf el Derwish.

To stay an advance, which, if not checked would bring all their Hejaz forces into an inextricable situation, the Turks renewed, in February, their efforts at offensive, from Kerak and from the railway. The first attempt by an infantry force, about 700 strong, to reach Tafilah ended in signal disaster, barely fifty men getting back to Kerak, with the loss of all guns and material. A second attempt, made from the railway early in March, with two comparatively strong columns, stiffened by German units, effected its purpose with little difficulty, the Arabs retiring from Tafilah to Shobak ; but its effect was demonstrative only, the Turks being unable to remain at Tafilah in view of the probability of an advance by the British across the Jordan. The Arabs re-occupied Tafilah on March 18, and, on the Turks withdrawing from Kerak a few days later, a detachment of Feisal's irregular troops entered this place also. They did not, however, stay long. The past month of April was marked by a great increase of Arab activity, and as a result of the capture of all the stations on the line between Maan and Mudowara and destruction of track and bridges for over seventy miles, Medina was finally isolated. Maan was vigorously attacked and the Sherifian forces, although unable at the first attempt to hold the railway station which they had entered, took up a strong position dominating both the station and the town. Further north much damage was done to stations, tracks and bridges, and the Beni Sakhr tribe gave assurances of future co-operation, which were, at the time, believed to be satisfactory. The history of the Es Salt raid (April and May, 1918) showed that this confidence had been misplaced, and the operation did not result in the wholesale destruction of Turkish troops owing to the Beni Sakhr tribe remaining quiescent at the critical moment.

The strong position taken up by the Turkish Fourth Army in the Belka during the summer made it impossible for the Arab Army to attempt an offensive owing to its lack of the resources and heavy artillery necessary for such an operation. The September advance made by General Allenby in Palestine caused the Fourth Army to retire upon Damascus and gave the Sherif Feisal the opportunity for which he had so long been waiting.

From the fall of Damascus to the Armistice.

The result of the September operations left the Turks depressed in moral, and so greatly reduced in numbers as to be almost entirely deprived of power to resist the northward sweep of the cavalry, except in the neighbourhood of Aleppo. The obstacles which still impeded the advance were chiefly those offered by long distances, by bad roads, and by disease. The troops which had passed through the Beisan area suffered severely from malaria after the period of incubation had elapsed, by which time they had advanced into the Damascus area. The widely prevalent influenza also produced many casualties.

In spite of these difficulties there were some examples of rapid advance on the part both of cavalry and infantry. The 5th Cavalry Division, which was engaged in the fighting round Damascus on the last day of September, was fighting Turks fifteen miles north of Aleppo on the last day of October. The 7th Indian Division, at Haifa on Oct. 1, marched to Beirut in a week, and occupied Tripolis on Oct. 18, after halting on the historic shores of St. George's Bay for five days. In the course of the advance to Beirut, this division found time to construct a road, over which guns were taken, across the Ladder of Tyre, a natural obstacle of imposing and picturesque magnitude. Full details of the advances of these two divisions will be found in their respective records.

During the advance of the 5th Cavalry Division on the afternoon of Oct. 22, the Armoured Car Column engaged a number of the enemy's armed lorries near Khan Sebil (thirty-five miles south of Aleppo). An enemy armoured car was captured, and the lorries, which kept up fire from machine guns, were chased for fifteen miles. One lorry was run to a standstill but some of its crew escaped in the darkness, leaving twenty-five casualties and five prisoners. Another lorry with five prisoners was captured next day but the Turkish Commander in Aleppo itself declined to surrender to the Armoured Car Column

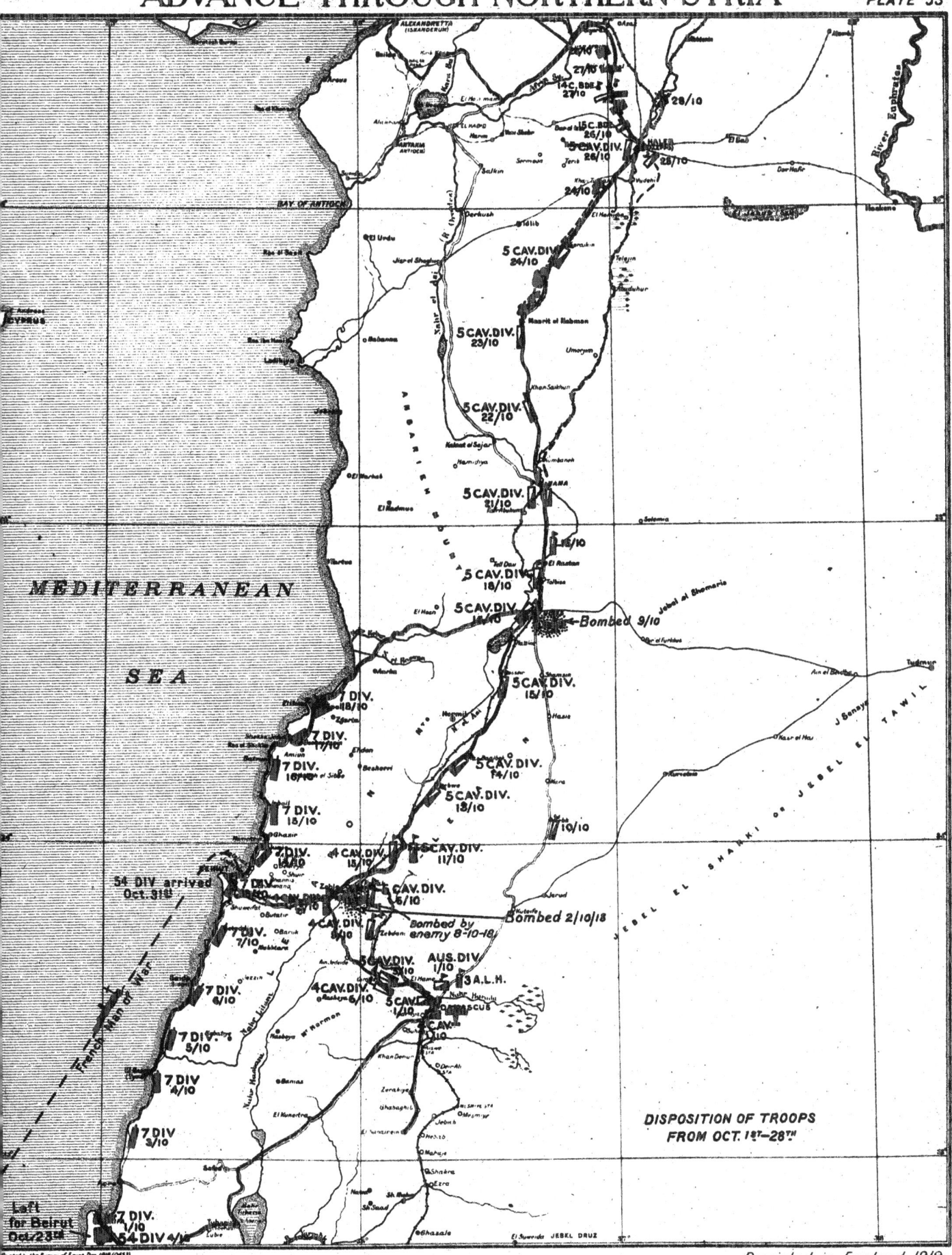

LINES OF COMMUNICATION, 1918.

British.

Early in the spring of 1918, railhead having been established at Ludd, and active operations on a large scale having ceased, preparations began to be made for the next stage of the advance.

These preparations included the doubling of the railway track from El Arish to Rafa, the relaying of the Turkish railway from Ludd to Jerusalem with a track of standard gauge (*see* PLATE 40), the formation of large hospital centres at Gaza and Deir el Belah, and the development of Jerusalem and Ludd as advanced bases; to these base camps, medical units and reserves of supplies and stores were transferred from the bases from which the November advance had been made. An immense amount of labour was expended on roads, which were rapidly put into a condition to bear the heaviest traffic; water supplies were developed; and a widespread and thorough campaign was carried on through the summer against malaria in—and immediately in rear of—the Corps areas.

The pressure of work on the Lines of Communication was greatly increased by the withdrawal of the 52nd and 74th Divisions for service in France; by the arrival of the 3rd and 7th Indian Divisions to take their places; and by the reorganization of the remaining British Divisions (except the 54th) on the Indian scale.

On July 1 the Lines of Communication were extended to include the area west of the Suez Canal known as the Suez Canal Zone, thus taking in the Canal ports of Suez and Ismailia; and on the same date the defence of Tor and Abu Zenima, together with their garrisons, came under the Lines of Communication.

In the latter part of August, advice was received that active operations would start in the near future, and on a large scale, thus involving a certain amount of preparation being made on the Lines of Communication; *e.g.* hospital accommodation was increased and medical units pushed forward close on the rear of the fighting line; arrangements were made for receiving prisoners-of-war in large numbers and for their accommodation on the journey from the front line to the base; and reinforcement camps were established from the railhead to the front line in order that reinforcements could be hurried forward during the advance. Owing to the necessity for secrecy, the final arrangements could not be made until immediately before the advance started: consequently, the night of Sept. 18 was a very busy period on the lines of communication.

The great success and rapidity of the advance involved great activity on the lines of communication, in order to keep up as far as possible with the advancing army. Reinforcement camps were pushed forward, prisoners-of-war cages were taken over, and, on Sept. 26, the area of the lines of communication was extended northwards along the whole front from the sea to the Jordan. On Oct. 4 it was again extended northwards to include Nablus and Tul Keram; on Nov. 1, Haifa, Damascus, and the railway line between these two places were taken over; and on Nov. 16, Nazareth and Tiberias were included.

Summing up, the lines of communication have grown from what they were on the arrival of General Allenby, the bases of Port Said and Kantara, with a single railway track to Deir el Belah—a distance of 220 kilometres (*see* PLATE 2)—to what they are now, with a railway line from Kantara to Damascus—approximately 650 kilometres—and branch railheads at Beersheba and Jerusalem. (*See* PLATE 54.)

The troops employed on the lines of communication at its start were entirely British, but later battalions of the Egyptian Army were substituted, who have done valuable work, including the holding of the inner cordon on the west bank of the Suez Canal, and duties with balloon sections in the rear of the front line. Battalions of the British West Indies Regiment and Jewish battalions of the Royal Fusiliers took over duties on the further extension of the line, but these were eventually withdrawn and transferred to fighting formations.

It is impossible to go fully into statistics in so small a space, but the following two points may be of interest:—

(1) The rations strength of Kantara when taken over by Palestine Lines of Communication in May, 1917, was less than 10,000, while on the day of the Armistice it reached 100,000.

(2) Up till May, 1917, no ocean-going ship had ever been berthed at Kantara, whereas, in Oct., 1918, the daily average of ocean-going ships loading and discharging in the Port of Kantara was five.

These figures alone will give some idea as to the amount of organization which was required to bring the lines of communication up to their present dimensions.

Turkish.

In the spring of 1918, Germans were substituted for the majority of the Turkish officials, and matters improved somewhat. A "Navy" was formed on the Dead Sea, and wheat from Kerak was transported up the Dead Sea by motor boats and barges. (*See* PLATE 2.)

The weak spot of the enemy lines of communication was Deraa; and the destruction of the line to the north, south, and west, by the Arab Northern Army on Sept. 17 and 18, completely cut off their supplies. During the retreat in Sept., 1918, an attempt was made to use their boats on the Sea of Tiberias, and to transport stores from the northern shore to Damascus by camels; also the motor-lorry columns, which had been extensively used from Damascus southwards, were able to remove a small portion of the stores from their advanced bases.

It was not until Oct. 9, 1918, that the first broad gauge train ran through the Taurus tunnel, and the first train to run direct from Constantinople to Aleppo arrived only a few days before the city was occupied by our troops.

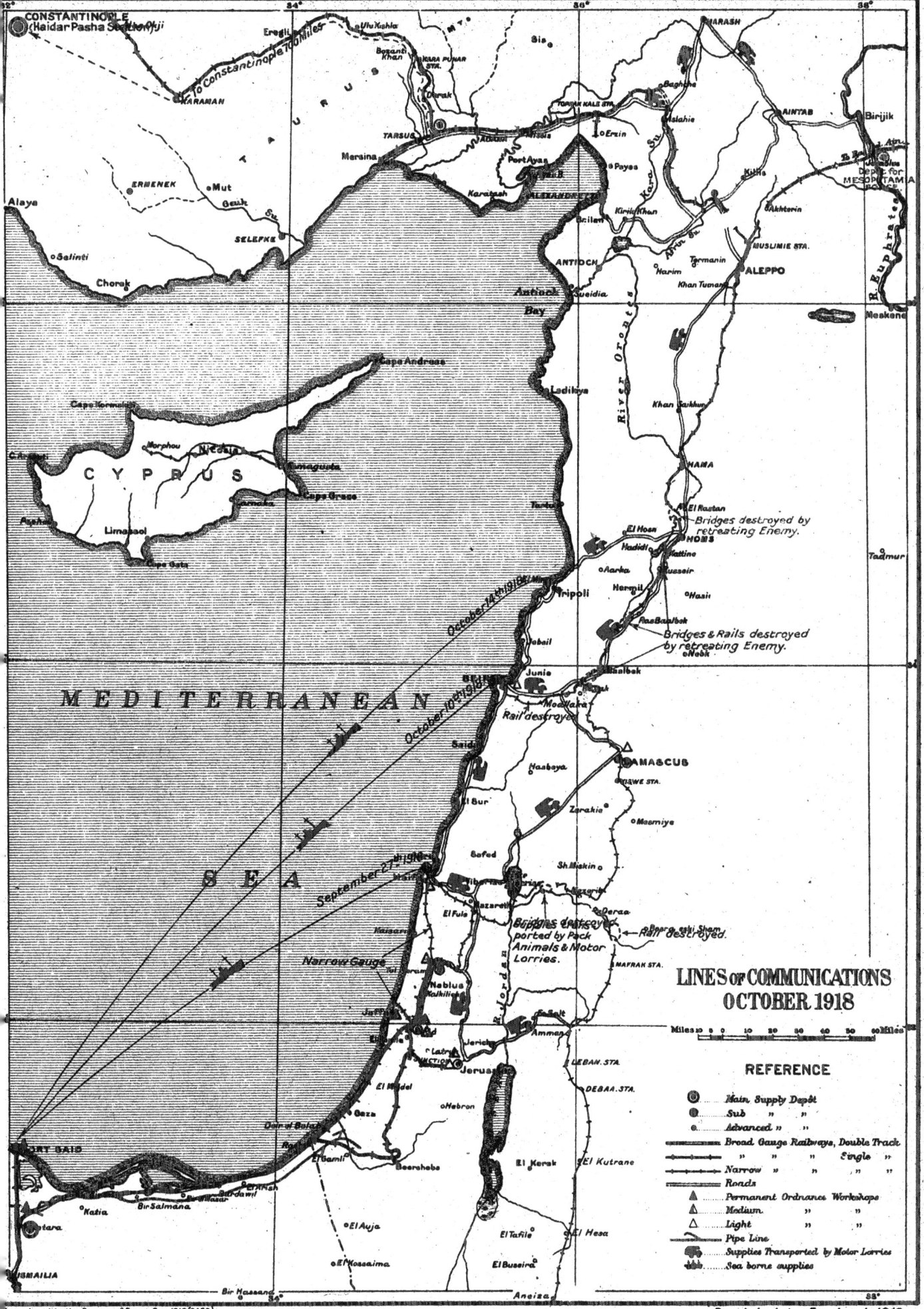

The Military Administration of the Territory released from the Turks.

As the Egyptian Expeditionary Force advanced and more and more territory was released from Turkish rule the Commander-in-Chief gradually became responsible for the administration of a large area and a considerable population. The former had suffered from centuries of neglect and the passage of contesting armies, while the latter were impoverished and ill-nourished as the result of exhaustive Turkish requisitions and the blockade to which the country, while under Turkish rule, had been subjected by the Allies. The peculiar religious status of Jerusalem and the presence of numerous privileged ecclesiastical corporations also gave rise to complicated questions of a nature seldom presented to the military administration of occupied enemy territory. General Allenby at first entrusted the administration of Southern Palestine to his Chief Political Officer, Brigadier-General G. F. Clayton, C.B., C.M.G., who built up such measures of government of the civilian populations as is provided for in "The Laws and Usages of War," laid down by the international agreements embodied in the Hague Convention. This administration, of what was technically "Occupied Enemy Territory," was entrusted locally to Military Governors, who were able greatly to improve the condition of the country and to alleviate the sufferings of a population which had welcomed General Allenby as a deliverer from the detested Turk. The work of administration developed so greatly that in April Major-General Sir Arthur Wigram Money, K.C.B., C.S.I., was appointed Chief Administrator of Occupied Enemy Territory Administration, as the control of administration could no longer be combined with that of the Political Department. Postal facilities for civilians had been restored and the introduction of the stable Egyptian currency enabled commerce to revive in spite of the necessary priority of military claims upon the transport available. Major-General Money constituted an improved system for the dispensation of justice and organized the finances of a territory which had, to all seeming, been in the last stages of economic distress in Dec., 1917. In March, 1918, taxes had again become payable, and by the summer the Military Administration was able to provide for the payment of dues appropriated to the service of the Ottoman Public Debt in accordance with international arrangements. The policing of the country was effectively undertaken, transport facilities were provided for civilian travellers, education was regulated, schools were reopened, and the administration of the property of Moslem Pious Bequests (*wakfs*) enabled the income to be appropriated to the needs of Moslem beneficiaries in Palestine instead of its being sent to Constantinople as was formerly the case. Colonel R. Storrs, C.M.G., the Military Governor of Jerusalem, was able greatly to abate the acerbity of ecclesiastical differences in the Holy City, and it was largely due to his personal efforts and influence that the Ceremony of the Holy Fire on the Orthodox Easter (May 5, 1918) passed off without disorder in spite of a long tradition of riot and violence during the Turkish period. In the new spirit of conciliation, fostered by the Military Administration, the Orthodox clergy voluntarily removed an unsightly party-wall from the nave of the Church of the Nativity at Bethlehem, and the careful handling of religious questions by the Military Administration has permitted the formation of an atmosphere contributing to the existence of a spirit of sweet reasonableness which would have struck a Turkish Mutessarif of Jerusalem as being most unusual. The deference paid on every side to Moslem susceptibilities, the guard of Indian Moslems round the Dome of the Rock and in front of the Mosque el Aska, no less than the military assistance given by the Commander-in-Chief to make the Moslem pilgrimage to Nebi Musa possible, went far to convince the Mohammedan population of the country that the interests of their religion were better safeguarded by the Allies of the Sherif of Mecca than by the Turks.

The arrival of the Egyptian Expeditionary Force was fortunately so timed as to prevent the wholesale deportation of Hebrew colonists and residents which had actually been ordered by the Turks, and these careful agriculturists were able to restore to a great extent the properties in the Kaza of Jaffa which they had been able to preserve in part from the spoliation of the enemy. Not only did the colonists benefit from the market afforded by the presence of the army, but were able to co-operate in the efforts made on behalf of the whole Hebrew community by the energetic Dr. Chaim Weiszmann and the Zionist Commission, which culminated in the ceremonial foundation of the University of Jerusalem as a symbol alike of their confidence in the future and of their recognition of the necessity of imparting higher education in their own language.

As the tide of victory rolled north and east it became necessary very largely to extend the activities of the Military Administration, and in course of time the Commander-in-Chief found it desirable to divide occupied enemy territory into three sectors, south, north, and east. The respective areas were administered under the control of the Commander-in-Chief by General Money from Jerusalem, by Colonel P. de Piepape, C.B., from Beirut, and by Ali Riza Pasha el Rikabi from Damascus. The opposite map shews the extent of these three areas and indicates the position of the kazas actually allotted to Occupied Enemy Territory Administration North but temporarily dependent, for the sake of administrative convenience, upon Occupied Enemy Territory Administration East. Throughout the whole of these extensive territories efforts are being made to enable the population to recover from the effects of four centuries of Turkish domination and to restore the ordinary amenities of civilization and commerce.

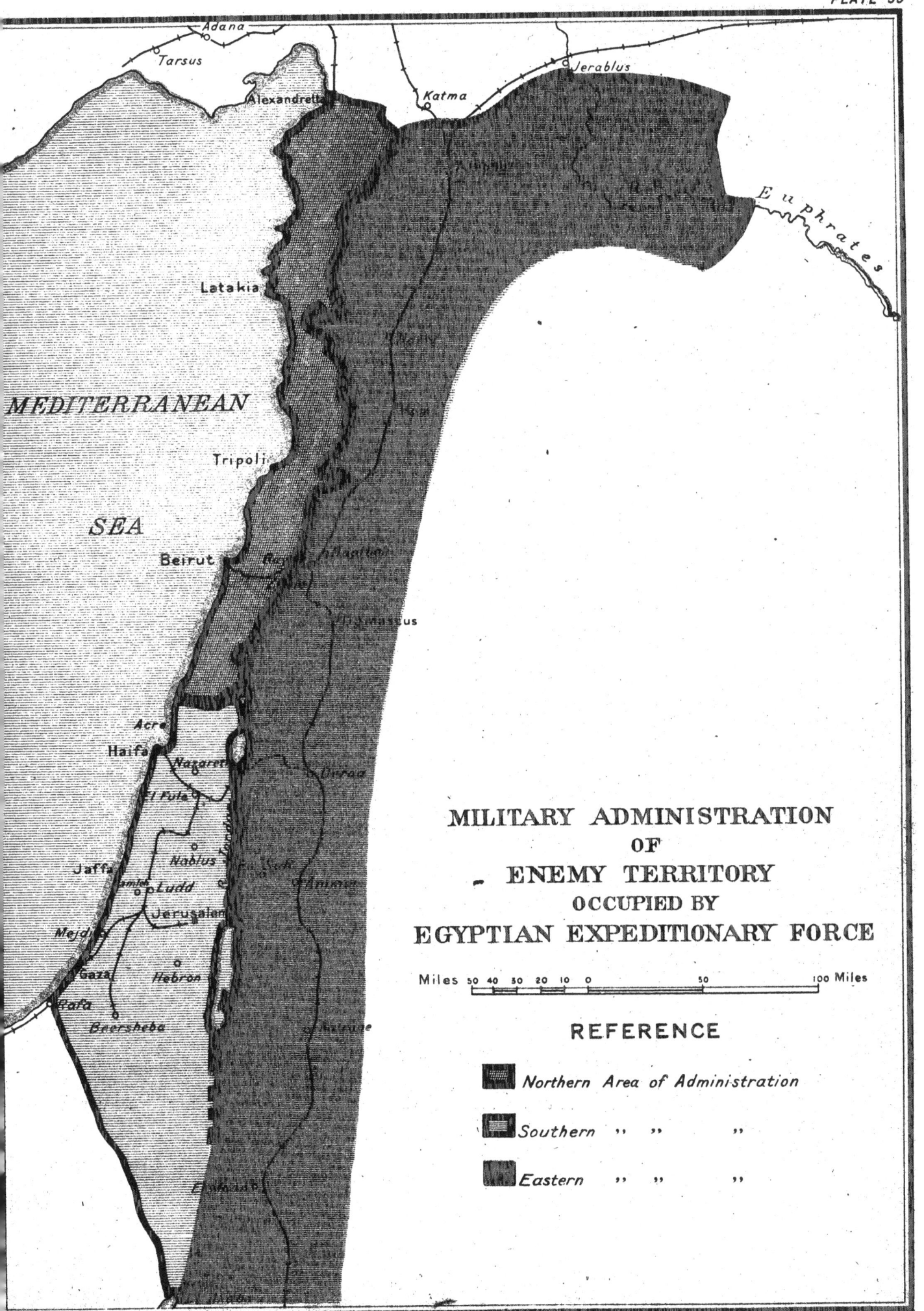

A Summary of the Terms of the Turkish Armistice (as published) which came into force on Oct. 31, 1918.

ART. 1.—Opening of the Dardanelles and Bosphorus and access to the Black Sea. The Allied occupation of the Dardanelles and Bosphorus forts.

ART. 2.—The position of all minefields, torpedo tubes, and other obstructions in Turkish waters to be indicated and assistance to be given to sweep or remove them as may be required.

ART. 3.—All available information regarding the mines in the Black Sea is to be communicated.

ART. 4.—All Allied prisoners and Armenians interned to be collected in Constantinople and handed over unconditionally to the Allies.

ART. 5.—The immediate demobilization of the army except troops required for the surveillance of the frontier and maintenance of internal order, their number and disposal to be determined later by the Allies after consultation with the Turkish Government.

ART. 6.—The surrender of all war vessels in the Turkish waters or the waters occupied by Turkey. These ships are to be interned at such Turkish port or ports, as may be directed, except such small vessels as required for the police or similar purposes in Turkish territorial waters.

ART. 7.—The Allies are to have the right to occupy any strategic points in the event of any situation arising, which threatens the security of the Allies.

ART. 8.—The free use by Allied ships of all ports and anchorages now in Turkish occupation, and the denial of their use to the enemy. Similar conditions are to apply to Turkish mercantile shipping in Turkish waters for the purposes of trade and the demobilization of the army.

ART. 9.—The use of all ship repair facilities at all Turkish ports and arsenals.

ART. 10.—Allied occupation of the Taurus tunnel system.

ART. 11.—Withdrawal of Turkish troops from north-western Persia. Part of Trans-Caucasia has already been ordered to be evacuated; the remainder to be evacuated if the Allies require after they study the situation there.

ART. 12.—Wireless and cable stations to be under Allied control; Turkish Government messages are excepted.

ART. 13.—Prohibition of the destruction of any naval, military, or commercial material by the Turks.

ART. 14.—Facilities are to be given for the purchase of coal, oil-fuel, and naval material from Turkish sources, after the requirements of the country have been met. None of the above material is to be exported.

ART. 15.—Allied control of all railways and Allied occupation of Batoum. Turkey not to object to the Allied occupation of Baku.

ART. 16.—The surrender of the garrisons of the Hejaz, Assir, Yemen, Syria, and Mesopotamia, and the withdrawal of troops from Cilicia, except those maintaining order as determined under clause 5. The surrender of all ports there.

ART. 17.—The surrender of all Turkish officers in Tripolitania and Cyrenaica to the nearest Italian garrison. Turkey guarantees to stop supplies to and communication with these officers if they do not obey the order of surrender.

ART. 18.—The surrender of all ports occupied in Tripolitania and Cyrenaica, including Misurata, to the nearest Allied garrison.

ART. 19.—All Germans and Austrians, naval, military, and civilian, to quit Turkey within a month. Those who are in remote districts to do so as soon as possible thereafter.

ART. 20.—Compliance with the Allies' orders as regards the disposal of arms and the transport of the demobilized under clause 5.

ART. 21.—An Allied representative to be attached to the Turkish Ministry of Supplies to safeguard Allied interests.

ART. 22.—Turkish prisoners to be kept at the disposal of the Allies. The release of Turkish civilian prisoners and prisoners over military age to be considered.

ART. 23.—Turkey to cease all relations with the Central Powers.

ART. 24.—In case of disorder in the six Armenian vilayets the Allies reserve the right to occupy any of them.

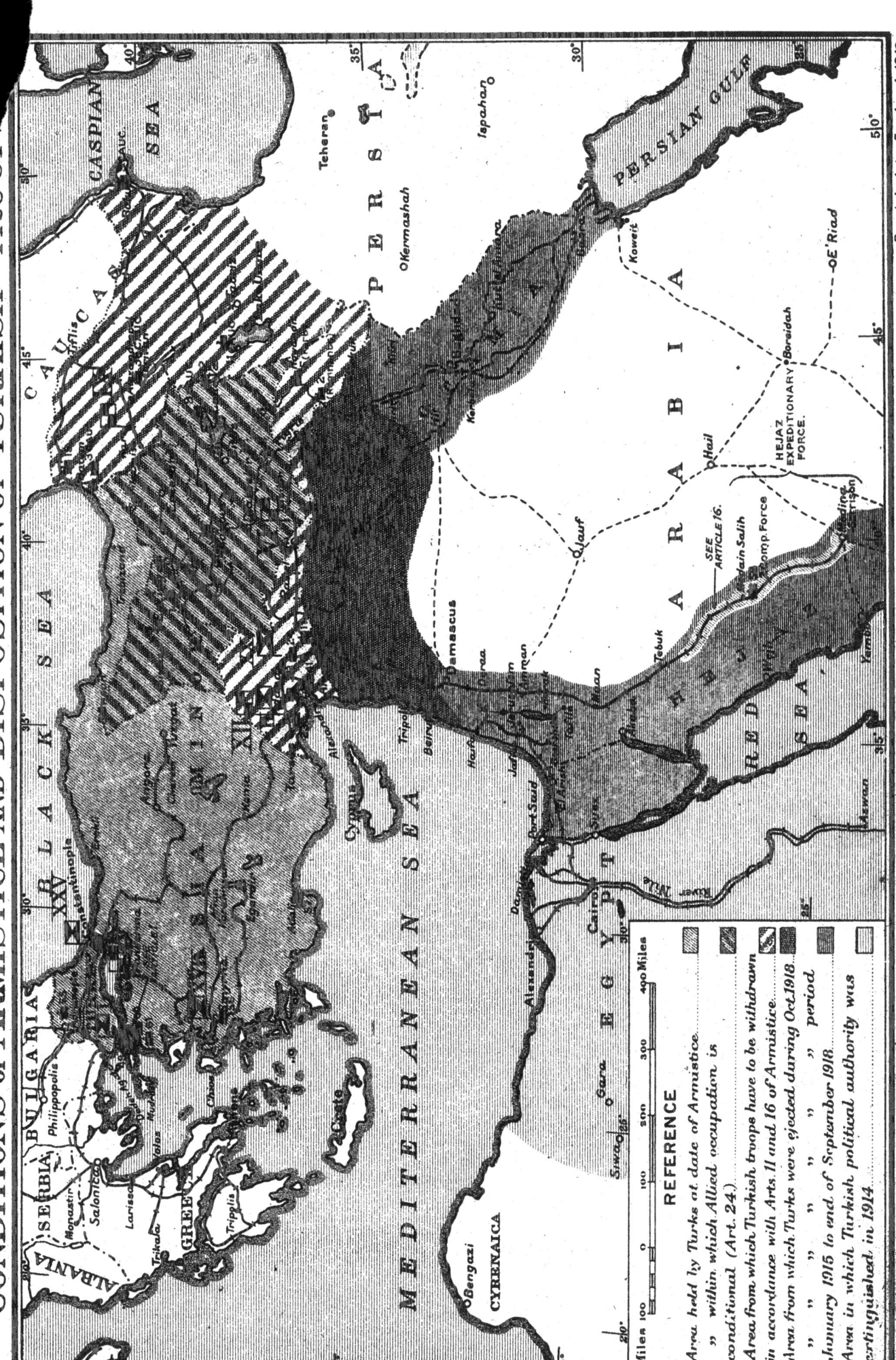
CONDITIONS OF ARMISTICE AND DISPOSITION OF TURKISH TROOPS

www.ingramcontent.com/pod-product-compliance
Lightning Source LLC
Chambersburg PA
CBHW081350160426
43197CB00015B/2718